Listening to Trauma

Listening to **Trauma**

Conversations with Leaders in the
Theory and Treatment of
Catastrophic Experience

INTERVIEWS & PHOTOGRAPHY
BY CATHY CARUTH

Johns Hopkins University Press
Baltimore

© 2014 Johns Hopkins University Press
All rights reserved. Published 2014
Printed in the United States of America on acid-free paper
9 8 7 6 5 4 3 2 1

Johns Hopkins University Press
2715 North Charles Street
Baltimore, Maryland 21218-4363
www.press.jhu.edu

Library of Congress Cataloging-in-Publication Data

Caruth, Cathy, 1955–
    Listening to trauma : conversations with leaders in the theory and treat-
ment of catastrophic experience / interviews and photography by Cathy
Caruth.
        pages cm
    Includes index.
    ISBN-13: 978-1-4214-1444-7 (hardcover : alk. paper)
    ISBN-13: 978-1-4214-1445-4 (pbk. : alk. paper)
    ISBN-13: 978-1-4214-1446-1 (electronic)
    ISBN-10: 1-4214-1444-9 (hardcover : alk. paper)
    ISBN-10: 1-4214-1445-7 (pbk. : alk paper)
    ISBN-10: 1-4214-1446-5 (electronic)
    1. Psychic trauma—Social aspects.   2. Disasters—Social aspects.
3. Crises—Social aspects.   4. Psychoanalysis and history.   I. Title.
    BF789.D5C37 2014
    155.9´35—dc23   2013044627

A catalog record for this book is available from the British Library.

*Special discounts are available for bulk purchases of this book. For more
information, please contact Special Sales at 410-516-6936 or specialsales
@press.jhu.edu.*

The Johns Hopkins University Press uses environmentally friendly book
materials, including recycled text paper that is composed of at least 30
percent post-consumer waste, whenever possible.

A percentage of the book's proceeds will go to the Grady Nia Project.

To the interviewees in this book
and to the many survivors and witnesses
who have refused to turn away from this era's most difficult truths

Contents

Foreword

This book narrates my encounters with leaders in the theory and treatment of trauma who have had a profound impact on my ways of seeing, of reading, and of thinking. The interviews in this book reflect a process of discovery that began, for me, in the 1980s, with the surprising and challenging insights of these courageous clinicians, political activists, and pathbreaking theorists who introduced into public awareness, during the last quarter of the twentieth century, the phenomenon called "post-traumatic stress disorder." The conversations in this book, extending from my first interviews in the early 1990s to more recent conversations carried on over the past several years, are meant to convey the excitement of this period of discovery (and rediscovery) of trauma in our culture, and to reflect its ongoing impact in our approaches to human suffering and our understanding of the world.

As a literary critic, and as an individual engaged in a new mode of listening across disciplines, I make no claim to clinical expertise in the area of trauma, nor does this book aim to provide an exhaustive historical or theoretical survey of the field of trauma research, treatment, and intervention. I do not attempt to cover the entire development of trauma theories from the 1990s until the present day in a field that has expanded significantly over the last two decades and now encompasses new cultural perspectives, neurobiological advances, and treatment paradigms. I have chosen, rather, to include my conversations with those whose work originally impacted and enriched my own thinking and listening and with whom I have collaborated intellectually and academically over the years. The originality and innovation of the early work of these leading thinkers and practitioners has continued to reverberate in the ongoing development of the field, and their unabated surprise at the enigma of traumatic experience has left a mark in all of their subsequent work. It is this openness to what cannot be easily or quickly grasped, and what can never be reduced to any single mode of listening or of understanding, that has defined the profundity of their work and has made possible the mirroring encounter between their various modes of approaching trauma and my own literary critical way of reading and responding. These thinkers have passed on to us the impact of an experience that continues to unsettle our expectations and our thought. In this book I am, in my turn, trying to communicate, through my own art of interviewing, the challenge of a new way of listening and the surprise of this interminable discovery.

Cathy Caruth

Acknowledgments

My undergraduate student Emily Clark transcribed five of the interviews in this volume and provided invaluable assistance in the editing of the manuscript. I am grateful for her timely, efficient, and intelligent help. My graduate student Avery Slater read the entire manuscript and provided astute responses, thoughts, and suggestions, for which I am also deeply appreciative. Hannah Wojciehowski, Michal Shaked, Elizabeth Rottenberg, and Cynthia Chase read many of the interviews and provided helpful feedback on the book as a whole. I owe a special thanks to Alian Teach, the Academic Department Administrator of Comparative Literature at Emory University, who helped coordinate the Nia group at Grady Hospital with the testimony grant that passed through the department, and who has offered, over the years, many forms of support and friendship. I would also like to thank Matt McAdam, Humanities Editor at Johns Hopkins University Press, for shepherding the book through the publication process, as well as Melissa Solarz and Katherine Curran, acquisitions assistants, for providing prompt and helpful assistance. I am grateful to Glenn Perkins for his careful and thoughtful copyediting and to Luke Donahue for an excellent index.

In addition, I would like to express my appreciation to all of my interviewees, who made themselves available to the surprises and uncertainties of the interviewing process. Usually in the position of the (clinical) interviewer, critic, or social advocate, these powerful thinkers, clinicians, artists, and activists understood that to relinquish their customary stances was to give up the claim to mastery, and their openness to this form of engagement allowed for the surprises and insights of the following conversations.

Chapter 1 first appeared in *American Imago*, special issue, edited by Cathy Caruth, vol. 48, no. 1 (March 1991). Chapter 2 first appeared in *Post-Modern Culture*, special issue, edited by Petar Ramadanovic and Linda Belau (Spring 2001). Chapter 5 first appeared in *American Imago*, special issue, edited by Cathy Caruth, vol. 48, no. 2 (December 1991). Chapter 9 first appeared in *Studies in Romanticism*, special issue, edited by Helen Elam (Winter 1997).

Introduction: *Learning to Listen*

The scholars, clinicians, and activists interviewed in this volume are all leaders in the theorization of, and response to, traumatic experience in the twentieth and twenty-first centuries. They are innovators in the theory of trauma (Part I), in the clinical, activist, or testimonial interventions in trauma in our culture (Part II), or in the creation or modification of institutions that provide a site of therapeutic, artistic, or legal response to traumatic events (Part III). Many of these thinkers have contributed in all of these areas. I have chosen them because of the impact they have had on my own thinking about the enigma of traumatic experience, which we now call "post-traumatic stress disorder" (PTSD). But they have also served the larger role of witnesses to the profound collective and cultural significance of trauma, and specifically to the ways in which this psychic experience exceeds its psychiatric definition as pathology and appears as a mode of contact with events that most people cannot bear to see or know. Indeed, events, insofar as they are traumatic, may be defined, in part, by the very ways in which they are not immediately assimilated: by the manner in which their experience is delayed, split off, or subjected to social and political denial. The survivors of traumatic experience thus provide what might be considered an *unconscious historical testimony*, to which the listeners in this volume themselves bear witness. In so doing, they have made the study of and response to trauma into a site of historical memory and have, conversely, revised our notions of what it means to remember and to act around the imperative to respond to something that consistently resists conscious assimilation and awareness.

What does it mean to bear witness to an unconscious testimony? Each of the interviewees in this volume, I would suggest, in conceptualizing and responding to the phenomenon of trauma, gives access to a new kind of historical event, the advent of a catastrophic history that requires a shift in understanding, as well as unprecedented modes of action and response. It is for this reason that the notion of trauma underlying the thinking of these innovative thinkers, activists, clinicians, and artists is less a stable object of understanding than the persistent and renewed encounter with the urgency of an event. It is the impact of this unexpected encounter that reverberates among the differing languages, in this volume, of those who respond to trauma's unavoidable demands.

UNSETTLING CONCEPTIONS

Rather than building up a unified theory or consolidating an idea, then, the interviews in this book reveal the unique way in which the notion of trauma is shaped by each individual who encounters it and attempts to provide a clinical or theoretical response. "Trauma," these interviews suggest, is not a single or systematizable concept but rather an ongoing set of clinical and conceptual discoveries. Indeed, the foundational theoretical work of Sigmund Freud on the notion of trauma was itself marked by a repeated set of encounters, first in his original work on hysteria at the end of the nineteenth century and then in his rediscovery of trauma in the twentieth century in the form of the accident neurosis and the soldiers returning from World War I. Across his career, Freud would thus formulate and reformulate the notion of traumatic neurosis in terms that captured not only the unexpectedness and shock of the event for the traumatized person but also the unexpectedness and surprise of the phenomenon of trauma for Freud's own practice and theory. The concept of trauma can be said to bear witness, in this way, to individual and collective catastrophic experience by repeating what was not yet grasped in the theory's own past formulations and passing on to the future what still remains unthought. What the interviews in this volume reveal about the thinking of trauma, I would suggest, is how the specific clinical and theoretical advances of each thinker remain bound up with what remains unconscious or unassimilable in both past and future historical experience.

Robert Jay Lifton's 'rereading of Freud, indeed, which attempts "to put the death back into the traumatic experience," takes place, as he tells me in his interview, through his own Hiroshima experience, and his surprise and horror at this momentous event of World War II. Dori Laub, as well, rereads the death drive in Freud, which is explicitly formulated in *Beyond the Pleasure Principle* as a form of repetition, in terms of the potentially absolute erasure of history that Laub, himself, encountered in the Holocaust. In my interviews with these psychoanalytically informed clinicians and theoreticians, we may thus observe the peculiar way in which Freud's later notion of trauma, formulated in response to World War I, not only points backward to an event that had already occurred but also refers forward to—and may achieve its greatest significance from—a future he could not know. This is indeed, I would suggest, one aspect of what is "incomprehensible" in the trauma, what accounts for its unlocatability in experience or thought. It is the true significance of the inherent temporal dimension of trauma that Jean Laplanche so memorably analyzed in Freud's earliest work. And it may also be, as Françoise Davoine and Jean-Max Gauldillière suggest in their interview with me, what makes the traumatized, or the mad, refuse the typical causal explanations of their symptoms and assume a sometimes prophetic quality in their visions and their words. In the ideas and formulations of the interviewees in this volume—as in the words of the traumatized to whom they respond—we may also hear a language that speaks beyond its concepts, and a vision that tells us as much about the future as it does about the past.

An Unprecedented Address

The singular unfolding of this traumatic history must also be understood, as Judith Herman persuasively argues, from a political, social, and ethical perspective. For the double constitution of traumatic historicity—as erasure and return or, in Freud's terms, as the "negative" and "positive" dimensions of trauma—is not entirely reducible to psychological, neurobiological, or epistemological determinations. What Herman calls the "dialectic of trauma," the tendency of the research in this field to appear and disappear as it is politically supported or suppressed, suggests that the struggle between knowing and not knowing in traumatic experience and its research may be inextricably bound up with collective forces of power and control. Thus the experience of trauma, one might argue, is already constituted, even on the individual level of dissociation and intrusion, as a reflection of the larger forces of erasure and witness that operate within society as a whole as they affect survivors both as individuals and as groups.

It might be argued, indeed, that the concepts of individual not-knowing that are so central to theoretical formulations of trauma—the notions of deferred experience, in Freud, for example, or of dissociation of the personality in Janet—are ultimately inextricable from the broader clinical and societal forms of denial that not only surround but also help to produce traumatic experience. Onno van der Hart thus strikingly describes, in his discussion of the treatment of people with dissociated personalities, the many difficulties in recognizing the presence of dissociation and the resulting danger of the therapist's participation in his patients' inability to grasp the import of their own life histories. Likewise, as Bessel van der Kolk argues, the physiological inscription of trauma—on the brain and in the body—occurs, paradoxically, within the context of the breakdown of the brain's integrative functions and at the expense of conscious assimilation, a form of dissociation that may repeat itself, on another level, in the controversies surrounding trauma research that have often inhibited recognition of the unconscious witness carried by traumatized in their bodies. This theme of denial, and the struggle of these scholars and clinicians with the forces of not-knowing at work in themselves, in their patients, and in the broader society, returns repeatedly throughout this volume and reveals the truly political and historical dimensions of the research, treatment, and political activism in the field of trauma. It is precisely because trauma is constituted by, and responded to with, these various forms of not-knowing—and because the experience and notion of trauma can never simply be assimilated to previous forms of understanding—that the study of this phenomenon can be said to have such high historical, social, and political stakes.

To respond effectively to trauma is not simply to reveal denied or distorted facts, therefore, but to create the conditions by which the very possibility of collective social witness and response may finally take place. In discussing his attempts at political activism during the AIDS crisis in the 1980s and 1990s, for example, Gregg Bordowitz emphasizes the need to find ways, in television interviews, to look directly into the camera as an HIV-positive person addressing an HIV-positive audience, a difficulty that shows up differently, Laura Pinsky tells us, in other modes of HIV and AIDS education. Such a form of address would presumably create a new public HIV-positive subject and a non-HIV-positive listener no longer bound to the myth of the death-free "general public." "The primary function actually has been to engender an audience with AIDS and HIV," Crimp asserts, likewise suggesting, implicitly, that the political force of AIDS activism consisted, in part, in the possibility of establishing a community around a new kind of speaking—and listening—subject and a new mode of performatively effective speech.

What would make possible such a form of precocious testimonial and political address? In his interview on Romantic poetry and the Holocaust video testimonies, Geoffrey Hartman points to the literary forms and tradition of apostrophe, which allow for a mode of speech that passes, in poetic writing and in Holocaust testimonies alike, between the living and the dead. This passage may be necessary as well for the HIV-positive and AIDS activists who also speak from the destabilization of their identities as people both living with, and dying from, the disease of AIDS, and it may serve as a challenge for any trauma survivor who feels that he or she lives somewhere between death and life. The videos also help to "return" the bodies of those from whom they were taken, which is perhaps an element of all traumatic experience and its treatment.

From the perspective of the absenting of a previous self—not only physiologically, neurobiologically, and psychologically but also socially and politically—the act of speaking out is indeed much more than a subject telling a story he or she can simply claim to possess. In the Nia Project video testimonies of abused, low-income African American suicide survivors, as the interviewer Shane Davis suggests, the women are crafting stories of themselves that first emerge at the moment the women begin to speak. In this sense the choice to speak before the camera is, in Christina Wilson's evocative words, a "revolutionary act," a claim, that is, for a right to speak—and a possibility to listen—that comes into being only with this first, unprecedented, act of address.

The Institution as Witness

In thus bringing trauma to light in the scholarly, social, and political spheres, the innovators in this volume have also frequently participated in the creation, or re-creation, of public institutions as forms of witness to the century's worst individual and collective catastrophic events. This participation has also meant, as we see in the final section of the book, a recognition of the ways in which various institutions have, themselves, participated in the perpetration or denial of catastrophic experience. In the interview with Arthur S. Blank Jr., one of the first directors of the Veterans Centers of America after the Vietnam War, the founding of this institution becomes inextricably intertwined with Blank's own personal story, which takes the form of a passage through his confrontation with, denial concerning, and re-experiencing of the war's direct effects on himself and others. The Vet Centers serve, we could say, not only as a place for vets to tell their stories and obtain treatment but also for the institution of psychiatry, as well as the US government, to acknowledge (if only implicitly) the damage that their own lack of recognition of PTSD—and the government's betrayals during the war more generally—had on veterans during the Vietnam War.

In a very different context, Mieke Bal's film of Françoise Davoine's *Mère folle* (*Crazy Mother*) also focuses on how the book ties Davoine's psychoanalytic practice of treating trauma and psychosis to an explicit meditation on her own—and psychoanalysis's—past inability to recognize the emergence of traumatic realities. Both film and book thus reflect on what disappears in their own institutional histories in order to create, anew, innovative forms of witness to the century's catastrophic events.

In the final interview in this book, Shoshana Felman analyzes the way in which the institution of law, and specifically of the trial of Adolf Eichmann in

Jerusalem, became the site of a reenactment of historical and legal acts of silencing. In passing, unconsciously, through its own reliving of the past, Felman suggests, the trial also makes possible—at the very site of its own unconsciousness—a new form of historical (and legal) testimony. In her engagement with Hannah Arendt, moreover, Felman movingly reveals how the insights of Arendt into politics and of Felman herself into psychoanalytically and literarily informed work on trauma and testimony both emerge, in part, from the writers' own unassimilated traumatic pasts. Like every interviewee in this book, Felman thus produces pathbreaking work in her discipline (and institution) insofar as she listens, and responds, from the site of trauma.

Each interview, in its own unique manner, similarly reveals the surprise and complexity of this personal entanglement of thinker or clinician with his or her subject, of theory with the catastrophe about which it speaks. In pursuing their innovative work over the last several decades, all of the scholars and clinicians I have interviewed have allowed themselves to think, to listen, to act, and to create from a locus of vulnerability, a place that is never fully outside, if it is also not fully inside, the traumatic experiences to which they respond. But the possibility of remaining in this world in between is also the great strength of these leaders in the area of trauma, each of whom attempts to create a bridge from trauma to testimony and from denial to a future possibility of witness.

PART I / Death in Theory

Robert Lifton at his home in Wellfleet, Massachusetts, October 24, 2010.

Chapter One

Giving Death Its Due
An Interview with Robert Jay Lifton

Robert Jay Lifton's work on Hiroshima, Vietnam, the Holocaust, the nuclear threat, and other catastrophic events of our age has had a tremendous impact on the consciousness of trauma in our era. On June 8, 1990, I met with him in his home in New York City to discuss his vision of a psychology of life that gives death its due, that extends and modifies psychoanalysis around a full recognition of the centrality and import of traumatic experience.

I. Trauma and Survival

CC: I would like to begin by discussing some of the implications, for trauma theory and therapy, of your notion of survival. In your essay "Survivor Experience and Traumatic Syndrome," you suggest that the experience of trauma can be approached through the psychology of the survivor.[1] And your discussion in the essay centers upon the notion of survival. Equally important in this essay is your emphasis on the view of trauma, which, as you say, "puts the death back into traumatic neurosis." This might seem to be something of a paradox: on the one hand the insistence on survival, on the other hand the insistence on death in the theory. I'd like you to comment on the significance of understanding trauma in terms of survival, and also on this apparent paradox.

RJL: Focusing on survival, rather than on trauma, puts the death back into the traumatic experience because survival suggests that there has been death, and the survivor therefore has had a death encounter, and the death encounter is central to his or her psychological experience. Very simple point, but death gets taken out of most psychological thought very readily. Lots of people are sensitive to the idea of death, beginning with Freud, but he too felt it necessary to leave death out conceptually. So that the only place you really find death, conceptually, in Freud, is in the death instinct, which tells us about Freud's awareness of the pervasive influence of death, or some representation of death for us psychologically. But putting it in that sweeping instinctual structure has confused people ever since.

CC: When you talk about Freud's introduction of the notion of the death instinct, something that interests me is the fact that you don't immediately begin by talking about what Freud says *about* trauma or about death, but rather about the relation of the movement itself, of his theory and of his own movement, to trauma and survival:

> The impact of the traumas of World War I on Freud and his movement has hardly been recorded. The war's traumas to the movement must have been perceived as a struggle for survival. This psychoanalytic survival of World War I reactivated earlier death anxieties within the movement. The problem for Freud was to assimilate these experiences into his already well-developed theoretical system. (164)

One might say, on the basis of these lines, that you are characterizing psychoanalytic theory itself as a survivor. What does it mean to say that theory is a survivor? How does the notion of theory as a survivor change the nature of the knowledge it offers us, or what it knows and the way it knows?

RJL: The survival placed certain pressures upon, and brought certain questions to, the theory. The way Freud led psychoanalysis to survive World War I was to reintegrate that death experience into his instinctual theory. That meant in some degree sexualizing the death encounter through the focus, for instance, on narcissism, which is after all a sexual theory. Narcissism means, in strict psychoanalytic theory, the flow of libido into one's own body. So he sexualized the death experience to some extent, and he evolved the death instinct, which was, in a way, a means of responding to the death-saturated world he was living in. His famous essay, written over the course of World War I, "Thoughts for the Times on War and Death," is an expression of a deepening of reflection on the part of a highly sensitive man faced with a new dimension of death saturation in his world. In that essay you can see one direction of his response, that is, to give death its due—which something in him wanted very much to do. I think that Freud was caught in a certain dilemma. He was always very sensitive to death, always aware of it, fearful of it in a personal sense. But it was never a central theme in the theoretical structure he built. And therein lay a conflict. He had to develop his theoretical structure in the way that he could. And therefore he had to bring his brilliant one-sidedness to what he created. No theory, unless it is probing and onesided, amounts to anything. The trick is to have that one-sidedness in creative tension with a certain amount of balance and fairness. But it has got to be one-sided. And his one-sidedness was in the direction of childhood sexuality, of libido theory. He therefore had to maintain his death awareness while minimally expressing it within his theory. And out came post–World War I psychoanalytic theory, the death instinct, and the key gambit that he engaged in was narcissism—really transforming death anxiety and the fear of disintegration into the idea of narcissism.

CC: It would appear from what you have just said, then, that the encounter between theory and death is a central source of insight but that it appears indirectly, through a kind of distortion. In *The Broken Connection* you describe this process as psychoanalysis itself "putting up a protective shield" like a survivor and thus warding off "the potentially transforming influence of death on theory." What is the potentially transforming influence of death on theory or, specifically, on the instinctual theory?

RJL: Let me begin with a personal anecdote. When [Jacques] Lacan[2] came to Yale in 1975, there was one small dinner I was involved in, and as he began to express his ideas, I raised the following question. I said, "Well, Professor Lacan, with your enormous stress on symbolization, which I applaud, as it is very close to my own heart, why is it that you did not come to the broadest paradigm for symbolization, that is, death and life continuity, or that of a life-death parameter, rather than remaining in the model of Freud, which is instinct and defense or, essentially, sexuality and repression?" And he looked at me as only Lacan could, he didn't know me then, and he asked his right-hand woman of the time,[3] "Who is that man?" And she said, "That's Robert Lifton." And he looked at me with those bright eyes and a smile, and he said, "Je suis Liftonian." Now he was half mocking, you know, and then he said, "Yes, you're right. The logic of the situation would *be* a life-death parameter. I agree with you. However my own formation was the other, so I stayed with it."

So what is the transformative potential of death? Well, death potentially transforms anything and everything. It's the single consistent fact of existence. Everybody's said that in one way or another. But to take in death, that is, to be open to a death encounter, always means reassessing what is ultimate, significant, or as one of the people years ago in our study put it, "what counts." One asks the question of what really matters in one's life. It has to do with what is most powerful, most life affirming, and what can survive one's own death. Freud was always asking those questions, in terms of his theory. Any really serious theorist does. And there was never a more serious theorist than Freud, or a man more concerned with the lasting or, I would say, immortalizing aspects of his theory. However, he dismissed any talk about immortality as denial of death. So the encounter with death for a theorist, and therefore for his or her theory, is a potential opening out; there are two possibilities, opening out or closing down. Freud did a little of both, as most of us do.

CC: If numbing is indeed, as you say, essential to the experience of confrontation, this seems to suggest that some of that closing down will take place in most theoretical formulations. There is a relation between that opening and that closing, that somehow they are going to occur together in a theory, when it's at its most powerful.

RJL: Yes, and that's an interesting point, to bring up the simultaneous process of closing and opening, and a key issue here is what Freud did with castration anxiety, or with death anxiety. Rather consistently, Freud said that the idea or fear of death is a displacement of castration anxiety. Once you say that, with the central role of castration anxiety in the Oedipus Complex for Freud's opus, for psychoanalysis, then you are relegating anxiety about death to a secondary phenomenon. That is, for me, a key aspect of covering over. I don't begrudge it—Freud is a great intellectual hero to me, and in a way one's capacity to step back from Freud and free oneself from Freud to a degree enables one to appreciate him more.

I really see *The Broken Connection* as a continuous dialogue with Freud, and there were so many other people, but in reworking the narrative over time, I found myself mostly cutting away the other thinkers or putting them in footnotes because I wanted to get the flavor of what Freud had originally said. And I always found things that had been neglected. And yet I couldn't say them or didn't want to say them the way Freud did because I saw myself always transmuting them into symbolizing theory, as opposed to instinctual theory. But it's very important for me that I understand myself as a child of Freud, as all of us are.

In a way, I had several encounters with Freud. I began to read him in medical school and helped to organize a psychiatry club. And of course I read him on and off during my residency training and during psychoanalytic training. But I didn't really read him in a way that had full power until I separated myself from him and really wanted to understand what I could learn from him, relearn from him, take from him for these horrendous issues I was struggling with, especially Hiroshima. Because *The Broken Connection* really stems from the Hiroshima experience. And that was the main encounter. It opened up a lot for me.

[Erik] Erikson[4] was my connection with psychoanalysis and with Freud. Erikson's identity theory was a marvelous baseline for what I was encountering with the Chinese and their identity changes [during the writing of *Thought Reform*].[5] But from Hiroshima I had to go into other spheres, and it was really death-related spheres, and that didn't exist in Erikson, really. It was more in Freud, again, but in a very different way. I still remain enormously influenced by Erikson, to this day. But that second encounter with Freud really meant reexamining what I thought about the world, and what I was seeing in Hiroshima, and what I thought about my own life, and death. It was Hiroshima and Freud together, and *The Broken Connection* is in a way the result.

CC: So you're reading Freud through Hiroshima.

RJL: That's right, I'm reading Freud through my Hiroshima experience.

CC: You mentioned just now that confronting Freud again in a creative fashion, you were forced into talking about symbolization. Elsewhere, you say that the encounter between death and Freudian psychoanalytic theory "carries Freud beyond mere libido theory toward a concept of meaning . . . what one is willing or not willing to die for" (166). And this is what you are suggesting that you carry out in your own symbolization theory. What is the significance of focusing on meaning instead of instinct, specifically in a death-oriented psychology?

RJL: Instinct is not a psychological entity. If you believe in some kind of instinct, it's a kind of driving force. And Freud himself was always inwardly divided about whether instinct could be represented psychically. Anything that is psychological experience has to do with meaning. In that sense, meaning is the broadest kind of psychological entity. When one considers a life-death model or paradigm, it has to exist in relation to meaning, or in relation to how we symbolize our life process and our vitality, on the one hand, and our prospective end or individual death, on the other. And my path to a psychology of meaning is not via Lacan but via [Ernst] Cassirer and [Susanne] Langer.[6] What they taught us is that our central motivations, our central energies, come from actual or aspired-to meaning structures. How we want to understand, how we seek to understand something, how we want to see ourselves. I came to this as I thought about the prospective element of the image. The first sentence of *The Broken Connection* is, "We live on images."

In a way, what I think happened with Freud—and I learned this partly from Erikson and very largely from Cassirer and Langer—as Freud struggled painfully to remain a scientist in the terms of his era, in the nineteenth-century terms of science, he often neglected the very thing that he had so importantly discovered, the aspect of experience, of psychological experience. He neglected it for theories of origin, which were primarily instinctual. And Erikson once called it—not so much talking about Freud as about his disciples perhaps—he called it "originology," in which you focus so much on the origin that you lose a sense of the flow of experience along the way. And one way to recover the importance of the flow of experience, as I came to see it, was to take imagery very seriously.

A very good example is in the dream. Here Erikson is wonderful. His paper on dream analysis may be the single greatest paper ever written on the dream. It's all about experience in the dream, while in no way abandoning Freud's theory of the dream. But in the quick return to childhood sexuality or the quick focus on issues of repression or ostensible sources of the dream in childhood psychopathology, the significance of the dream imagery can be underestimated. Image and meaning are inseparable. And really, in this kind of work, as in a lot of Erikson, there's a struggle to return to a focus on image, on meaning structure, and on the whole issue of form. That's why I speak of the formative process. And it's that quality of form and meaning that I think is central to human experience. Really, that's what literature tells us, as well as psychology, and when literary people embrace psychoanalytic theory, that's what they're doing—they are transmuting it into expressions of form and meaning.

CC: By talking about image and symbolization and meaning in terms of death, you seem to imply that all of that meaning at some point has a reference point in death rather than, say, in origination or in a causal model.

RJL: It's a complex matter for me. And I don't mean that death replaces instinct; I would rather say that symbolization replaces instinct. And therefore the causative principles become symbolizing principles and issues having to do with symbols, images, and meanings. And what is causative from early on is the struggle for vitality and, ultimately, for symbolic immortality, in my view. And that's why to me what I call death equivalents are crucial, because before you're about two or two and a half years old—and then it's just a glimmer of an image—you have lots of emotional experience that can relate to death equivalents: separation, fear of disintegration, or something like the experience of disintegration. And these connect with causative experience, but they're not instincts in my view; they are the precursors of imagery and symbolization. And that's where I find causation: in imagery, symbolization, and meaning. And in the end, imagery, symbolization, and meaning are in a life-death model or paradigm.

CC: I want to press you a little bit on the centrality of death in meaning, or the life-death continuum. There is a way in which your emphasis on meaning rather than on instinct—and meaning always in touch with a notion of death—helps us recognize something resistant or incomprehensible at the heart of traumatic experience. In your terms, this is what you call "numbing," "the experience of a decreased or absent feeling either during or after trauma," a "matter of feeling what should have been but was not experienced." You distinguish this numbing from repression, which excludes or forgets an idea; in numbing, rather, "the mind is severed from its own psychic forms; there's an impairment in the symbolization process itself." So it would seem in this case that a confrontation with death in trauma is a radical break with any kind of knowledge, or with what we normally think of as experience. But at the same time, you insist on the numbing experience as having potential for insight. How does one gain insight from such a radical break, or what would be the relation between numbing and insight?

RJL: The insight begins with the shattering of prior forms. Because forms have to be shattered for there to be new insight. In that sense, it is a shattering of form but it is also a new dimension of experience. One of the great difficulties in all of the extreme situations I've studied is that people subjected to them had no prior images through which to connect with them, or very few. What in one's life would enable one to connect with Hiroshima? Here the assumption is that, and this is the radical insight of symbolizing theory, we never receive anything nakedly; we must recreate it in our own minds, and that's what the cortex is for. In creating, in recreating experience, we need some prior imagery in order to do that work, in order to carry through that process. And there was precious little prior imagery that could enable people to take in the Hiroshima experience, the event of a weapon apparently destroying an entire city.

So once they struggled with it and took it in, there was the capacity to enlarge on their own inner imagery, enlarge on their life experience. So that toward the end of all of my interviews, or of almost all of my interviews with people, with Hiroshima survivors and, say, survivors of Nazi camps, as different as they are, they talk about something they've learned. Some have amazed me and troubled me by saying they would not want to have missed the experience. People have said this to me about Nazi camps. And I felt strange at hearing that because it seemed such a cold thing to say and think, cold toward themselves. But what they meant was—and they could only say it once the experience was over when in some measure it was absorbed or even mastered to a degree—was that it had enormous value for them, taught them something very important.

It was never very easy to say exactly what that was; it was rather inchoate, as much in relation to extreme trauma tends to be. But it has to do with knowledge of death. It's related to the mythology of the hero, to a degree. The traditional psychoanalytic way of looking at the mythology of the hero is the confrontation with the father in the Oedipus Complex. That's not my way; though again, there are hints in psychoanalysis, in which the ordeal of the hero is a powerful confrontation with threat and death, and, really, the threat of annihilation. And he or she undergoes that ordeal: it's a call to greatness, it's the call that the hero experiences, and the ordeal is the struggle with death. And what the hero achieves is some degree of mastery in that struggle which he—it's usually a male hero—can bring back to his people. It's a knowledge of death and therefore a knowledge of life. It's a profound new knowledge. So in that sense the survivor has lived out the mythology of the hero, but not quite. And that "not quite" is the tragic dimension of it, that you see, well, in the story of Primo Levi, who seemed to have mastered it to a degree that moved us, even thrilled us.[7] And then killed himself, as an elderly man, for reasons that we don't fully understand. But still in a way that tells us that he was still haunted by that experience.

CC: I would like to pick up on that "not quite" aspect of the survivor's experience, the sense that the survivor doesn't simply bring back a mastered knowledge of death. It seems to me to be connected with your comments elsewhere that death is "anticipatory" and from the beginning has an "absolute influence" on the human being: this would suggest that the confrontation itself might have that anticipatory quality of not being fully assimilated or known but projected into a future.

RJL: That's right. When I first began to talk about psychic numbing in relation to Hiroshima survivors, I learned that they required numbing, that is, the sudden cutting off of feeling, which couldn't be understood simply by repression. It had elements of repression, elements of isolation, denial, almost any psychoanalytic defense mechanism you could name, but was primarily a cessation of feeling. And even those Hiroshima survivors who came to emerge as leaders, and who derived from their experience the greatest amount of learning or wisdom, or energy, had to make use of a certain amount of numbing, certainly at the beginning and subsequently in various subtle combinations with confrontation. So confrontation in the sense of letting in the death encounter is never total. It's always a mixture of how much you can take in and how much you keep out. And I think that's important to understand, and I probably haven't made that sufficiently clear in my work. Because it seems to hold out some ideal of absolute confrontation, which none of us is capable of. And going back to Freud's wisdom, you know Freud spoke of the protective shield, and he really saw the organism as constantly having to keep things out, as that being as much a requirement of the psyche as taking things in.

CC: This also seems linked to your notion of death as anticipatory, that is, as something you don't confront immediately but is always there.

RJL: Yes, anticipatory in the sense that one brings to a death encounter one's own death imagery and one's own lifelong experience not only with death but with death equivalents, such as separation, and with the way in which these interact and become, in some degree, interchangeable over the course of one's life. So these feelings always enter into the self-process, which like all psychological experience, is anticipatory or prospective, moves forward.

In trauma one moves forward into a situation that one has little capacity to imagine, and that's why it shatters whatever one had that was prospective or experiential in the past, whatever prospective consolations one brought to that experience. And being shattered, one struggles to put together the pieces, so to speak, of the psyche, and to balance that need to reconstitute oneself with the capacity to take in the experience. Something tells one, or one becomes partly aware, that if one doesn't take in some of it, one is immobilized by the numbing, that the numbing is so extreme, in that kind of situation. But this is not a logical process, and it's not a conscious process primarily. So one is inwardly or unconsciously struggling with how to cohere and how to absorb and in some measure confront what one has had thrust upon one, what one has been exposed to. And that's what trauma is all about.

I also think about trauma in a new way that I've just begun to write about, in terms of a theory of the self. That is, extreme trauma creates a second self. What I mean by that is, as I came to think about role, and self, and identity: strictly speaking, in theory, there's no such thing as role. There's a lot of talk about role, but it can be misleading. Because to the extent that one is *in* anything, there's a self-involvement. But in extreme involvements, as in extreme trauma, one's sense of self is radically altered. And there is a traumatized self that is created. Of course, it's not a totally new self, it's what one brought into the trauma as affected significantly and painfully, confusedly, but in a very primal way, by that trauma. And recovery from posttraumatic effects, or from survivor conflicts, cannot really occur until that traumatized self is reintegrated. It's a form of doubling in the traumatized person. And in doubling, as I came to identify it, there have to be elements that are at odds in the two selves, including ethical contradictions. This is of course especially true in the Nazi doctors, or people who doubled in order to adapt to evil. But also in doubling in the service of survival, for life-enhancing purposes, as I think is true of people who undergo extreme trauma, as with Auschwitz survivors, who say, "I was a different person in Auschwitz."

CC: Literally.

RJL: And it's almost literally true. So the struggle in the post-traumatic experience is to reconstitute the self into the single self, reintegrate itself. And it's in that combination of feeling and not feeling that the creative aspect of the survivor experience, or the potentially illuminating aspect of the survivor experience, takes shape.

II. A Perverse Quest for Meaning

CC: That brings us to my second major area of interest. You talk a lot about the notion of witnessing in trauma and the survivor mission, the impulse to bear witness, which is presumably part of the recovery process. But at the same time you talk about the possibility of what you call "false witness." And you say specifically, referring to incidents in Vietnam (My Lai), that atrocity is a "perverse quest for meaning, the end result of a spurious sense of mission, the product of false witness."[8] What is the relation between witnessing and survival, and what are the implications for this process of the very possibility of false witnessing?

RJL: When one witnesses the death of people, that really is the process of becoming a survivor, and the witness is crucial to the entire survivor experience. The witness is crucial to start with because it's at the center of what one very quickly perceives to be one's responsibility as a survivor. And it's involved in the transformation from guilt to responsibility. There's a lot of discussion, and some of it very pained, about survivor guilt. I sometimes talk about the paradoxical guilt of survivors. I want to make clear, of course, that there can be self-condemnation in survivors or what we call guilt, but it's paradoxical in terms of ethical judgment, because the wrong person can castigate himself or herself in terms of what is ethically just. . . . But carrying through the witness is a way of transmuting pain and guilt into responsibility, and carrying through that responsibility has enormous therapeutic value. It's both profoundly valuable to society and therapeutic for the individual survivor. And it's therapeutic in the sense of expressing the responsibility but also because that responsibility becomes a very central agent for reintegration of the self. One has had this experience, it has been overwhelming, the self has been shattered in some degree; the only way one can feel right or justified in reconstituting oneself and going on living with some vitality is to carry through one's responsibility to the dead. And it's carrying through that responsibility via one's witness, that survivor mission, that enables one to be an integrated human being once more.

CC: What happens in false witness, then?

RJL: Yes, well in false witness there is a compensatory process that is very dangerous. Because one has the same need to bear witness, and to take on the survivor mission, but through various pressures or needs one can block out elements of the death encounter in a dangerous way. The example I mention at My Lai was a very painful one and a very extreme one, in which the members of the company were survivors of the deaths of other soldiers in the company, which were very painful to them, in a situation that was inherently confusing, and the life-death elements were especially confusing, as were the elements of meaning. Why was one there; why were buddies and comrades dying? Nobody really knew. Bur the only thing one could do was to try to make sense of the dying that had taken place, to witness the death of their comrades by carrying on their work of killing the enemy; by carrying it on immediately, even though no enemy was readily available. And this was also a way for the soldiers to shut out their own death anxiety. One might think of it this way: the false witness at My Lai was a suppression or numbing toward certain elements of death, and the way that that happened was by converting very quickly, almost immediately, one's own death anxiety into killing. Other factors went into that, including aspects of the counterinsurgency war; certain circumstances of a situation can encourage false witness. False witness tends to be a political and ideological process.

And really false witness is at the heart of most victimization. Groups victimize others; they create what I now call "designated victims," the Jews in Europe, the blacks in this country. They are people off whom we live not only economically, as is often the case, but psychologically. That is, we reassert our own vitality and symbolic immortality by denying them their right to live and by identifying them with the death taint, by designating them as victims. So we live off them. *That's* what false witness is. It's deriving one's solution to one's death anxiety from extreme trauma, in this case in an extreme situation, by exploiting a group of people and rendering them victims, designated victims for that psychological work.

CC: So it's attempting to witness, although in a perverse way, our own relation to death, our own traumatic relation to death—*that's* what our relation to various groups represents.

RJL: Yes. You know, I find it useful to look at the broad survivor response to World War I. You cannot understand, as many historians have said, the second world war except as a survival of World War I. So that the Hitler movement centered on undoing World War I and on witnessing World War I by reversing its outcome. It's what the Rambo movies do for the Vietnam War.[9] And to some extent, Pétain's role in World War II also had an element of survival from World War I.[10] He was the hero of Verdun because he simply stopped the slaughter. And by the time of World War II he was exhausted and also somewhat right wing. He didn't have the heart to fight or try to fight the German armies anymore; he surrendered very quickly, and ignominiously, one might say. And consistently then gave in, as head of the Vichy regime, to the Nazis. This could also be a certain kind of survivor reaction to World War I. So that these survivor reactions color all kinds of individual and collective behavior. The false witness is partly a moral judgment on my part, of course, but it also has to do with certain psychological currents one can tease out—the act of using, exploiting, certain groups violently for the sake of coping with one's own death anxiety.

CC: It is psychological specifically insofar as it is, as you say, "a perverse quest for meaning." And thus this false witnessing seems central, since your entire theory is about meaning, and this is a perversion of meaning. Can you explain, with an example such as Pétain or whatever example you choose, how meaning is created perversely in this case? What kind of meaning is created, let's say, by creating a victim, or in the My Lai incident?

RJL: What is perverse is that one must impose death on others in order to reassert one's own life as an individual and a group. And the problem is that the meaning is *experienced* as real. It's *perceived* as meaning. And it's perverse in the way that in all psychological judgment there has to be ethical judgment. There's no separation in an absolute way of ethical and psychological judgment. Nonetheless, one does one's best to get to the psychological dimension, as you're doing and I'm doing. So my view is that you cannot kill large numbers of people except with a claim to virtue. Killing on a large scale is always an attempt at affirming the life power of one's own group. Now there's some interesting work by a sociologist named Jack Katz, who wrote a book called *Seductions of Crime*.[11] And he talks about how even in individual violence, when say a man kills his wife or a woman kills her husband, there's a moment of what you might call moralism in carrying through the murder. "This woman deserved to die because she is a bad mother to her children and an unacceptable wife." Or "This man must die because he is a horrible husband and a terrible father." So the act of killing becomes a morally necessary act. It's a perverse act in the sense of having to reaffirm one's moral system or sense of self by destroying, violating, murdering another.

CC: So the perversion might be thought of as the following: instead of relating to your own death, that is, instead of making your life have meaning in relation to your own death, you make it have meaning in terms of another's death.

RJL: That's right, exactly, because full life power, or genuine life power, depends upon some degree of confrontation with the idea of death, some degree of death being part of one's life, and artists have always known this. You know my favorite quotation from Heinrich Böll; he says that "The artist carries death within him like the good priest his breviary."[12] That's a brilliant economical statement of what I'm after, and many people know this. So that death is constitutive in this sense for all of us. That's not the only thing it is, but if we're to be constitutive in our work we need death. And that goes for social theorists as well as for artists, writers, whatever. So in one sense the perversion is a literalization of our struggle with death also (just as suicide can be a literalization instead of a symbolization of the confrontation with death), which ordinarily uses its full metaphor, or uses its metaphor more fully. Instead, in some literal way, one attaches the taint of death to an other in order to reassert life's power.

CC: This suggests then that, whereas what you were talking about before was that you cannot actually confront death fully in a trauma—that it remains, let's say, somewhat partial—the illusion of meaning here, the perversion of meaning, is the belief that you can know it directly, and the way it's known here is by the other being dead, by killing off the other. So not only are you trying to substitute the other's death for your own, but you're also attempting to confront it in a way that you can't really do.

RJL: You're attempting to confront it and claim a knowledge of it that you can't have, but you're also reasserting a denial of death, or a form of numbing. You're reasserting powerfully the very issue you are struggling to deal with. You're taking on death anxiety through a reassertion of numbing, so that the Nazi movement saw itself as conquering death and never dying. The "thousand-year Reich" is a biblical phrase, and the Nazis took on all kinds of Christian imagery even while attacking Christianity. So it's a claim to have mastered death while deeply denying it, and numbing oneself to it. That's another dimension of that false knowledge, or perverse witness.

CC: That puts it at the center of every politics. It is fascinating to think of politics, of political relations, as a kind of false witness.

RJL: Yes, it's very much there, all the time.

III. Double Witness

CC: Since you also say that this issue is more generally connected with "ideology," what about therapy? Presumably, the therapeutic process would be a matter of helping some kind of true witness to take place. Is there a way in which therapy (of trauma survivors) can be itself perverted in some sense, as a form of false witness?

RJL: I think that therapy could become false witness in its own way. At any level, we could be capable of false witness because the therapist does undertake a form of witness, witness through the patient's or client's own pain and death equivalents. Especially if patients are survivors, what becomes false witness is the all-too-frequent experience in therapy of having that trauma negated as the source of psychological significance. And I've heard accounts of this again and again in which the therapist insists that the patient look only at his or her child-hood stress, or early parental conflicts, when that patient feels overwhelmed by Auschwitz or other devastating forms of trauma. Because, as I say, adult trauma is still a stepchild in psychiatry and psychoanalysis. Now less so than before, there is much more awareness of it than in the past, but really certain therapists and psychoanalysts can be so deeply entrenched in a style that quickly focuses on childhood stress or trauma that they can find it difficult to give, not just death, but the death immersion its due.

CC: So in a way what you're saying is that the ideological moment is when the therapist draws on this paradigm—it is perhaps itself a kind of "originology"—the moment at which the trauma gets assimilated into that narrative of "you must have had a stress in your childhood."

RJL: That's the false witness.

CC: That would be the moment the false witness occurs in therapy, and that's the moment of ideological collapse.

RJL: Well, you see, it's the therapist's false witness to the survivor's trauma. And it's taking the survivor on a false path, or path of false witness, to his or her survivor experience. And it has to do with the absence of death on two levels. One is the numbing or denial of death in therapists, like everybody else, and the other related idea is the absence of death conceptually, which is very important. Because with the interest in death in the United States, in American culture, you know with a lot of concern about death, beginning with Evelyn Waugh's book on Hollywood,[13] with various exposés of death denial in the United States, and then various forms of focus on consciousness of death by many people in the social sciences and psychology, there has been a greater awareness of death—it's even called the death-awareness movement, sometimes—in this society. But there has been relatively little in the way of development of theory that includes death importantly. That's been harder to do. And that can very much affect therapy. Be-cause therapy is affected by theory, even though many therapists work differently from what their theory may tell them to do, nonetheless theory is very impor-tant. So the absence of death or of a quality of knowledge about traumatic experience—its relationship to a struggle with death anxiety and what that entails—can lead to false witness in therapy.

CC: Then you're saying that it is not only the process of getting the traumatized person to witness, because also on some level the therapist has to be in a position of constantly witnessing for him or herself; in his or her encounter with a patient, the therapist is also in a process of his or her own witness.

RJL: That's right. There's a double witness there. And really what a therapist does, what any psychoanalyst or psychiatrist does in listening to a patient or client, or what I did in listening to patients when I treated patients, but over more years in listening to research subjects and people I've interviewed, is to take in their stories and to form imagery in my own mind about what they're saying. And as one forms that imagery, one is forming a narrative about their story. And the narrative involves elements of their pain, the causation of their conflicts, and also the source of their knowledge, the nature of their experience. It's all forming itself or being reconstructed, recreated in the symbolizing process of the therapist. That's why a therapist having, in the truest sense, an open mind, is crucial, but an open mind to death-related issues as well as sex-related issues. God knows we've developed open minds in relation to sex-related issues or you'd be run right out of the psychoanalytic movement. But less so in relation to death-related issues; because they're less acceptable for the reconstituted imagery of the therapist.

CC: The therapist's own participation resists that.

RJL: Yes, because it's not present in the theory of the therapist and he or she can resist it personally.

CC: So there's a gap between the theory and the experience of the survivor.

RJL: It's the problem again that the therapist faces. It's very similar to the problem Freud's followers faced after World War I. What do you do with the death imagery in relation to our theory? Freud did what I think was the wrong thing, but the understandable thing, given the fact of everything he was creating. In one sense, he took the death out of death imagery or death anxiety—yet not quite, because he did struggle with it in some ways, ways that some of us could help recover, I think. But for contemporary therapists it could be even worse, because they may take the death out of the death instinct and have even less death-related material to work from. And this has to do with the difficulty psychiatry and psychoanalysis have always had in addressing adult trauma. Believe me, it is very painful to sit in one's office and hear the description from an Auschwitz survivor or a Hiroshima survivor of what it was like, of the concrete details; you know a story has to have very concrete details. From Hiroshima survivors—the corpses, the grotesque appearance of people, I wrote some of this in my book. Or from Auschwitz survivors—what people actually did, what the Nazis actually did, what it was like when you smelled, you know, the smells of the crematoria, or when you learned that your children or your parents had been killed. It is very hard, for anybody, but all the more so as a therapist or as a researcher, to sit in your office and let the details in to reconstitute them in your own imagery. And it's such a temptation to push them away, leave them out; to take that patient or client back to childhood is much more comfortable, and we're used to that. Or anywhere but in that terrible, terrible traumatic situation.

CC: Do you feel a little bit yourself like you're going through the trauma as they talk, that you're participating in it?

RJL: More than a little bit. This is the significance of the encounter. Well, you know I didn't say it in my book *The Nazi Doctors*,[14] but there's no reason why I can't say it. It was an encounter with Elie Wiesel. Wiesel and I are old friends, and he had been very interested in my work on Nazi doctors and had supported it in various ways. And when I came back, when I first began to immerse myself in those interviews and began to read all the things I had to read, I had coffee with Elie. I said to him, rather low key but not entirely casually, "It's good that you're enthusiastic about my work, but I'm having terrible dreams. Dreams of being behind the barbed wire, and not just me, my wife and my children, and it's quite painful." And he looked at me, with a look that was neither unkind nor especially sympathetic, just looking at me, and then nodded and said, "Good. Now you can do the study."

What he was saying is that you must in some significant psychological way experience what they experience. You can never do that quite. Bur it's being a survivor by proxy, and the proxy's important. You're not doing what they did, you're not exposed to what they were exposed to, but you must take your mind through, take your feelings through, what they went through and allow that in. It's hard, it's painful, and yet you know you must do it as you come into contact with it, and the people who have done the best therapy with survivors and who have written most importantly and movingly about survivors have done that.

CC: So there's a double survivor situation, but a survivor and a proxy survivor, and it's the meeting of those two that constitutes the witness.

RJL: It's an encounter, it's an encounter and a dialogue. With me it was very openly dialogue. I was never doing therapy with survivors of Hiroshima or of Auschwitz. It was a dialogue with them, and it was very powerful. I say it very briefly and very gently in the introduction to the book on Nazi doctors, that interviewing all the Auschwitz survivors was a spiritual balance or a spiritual counterpart—no, was a way of maintaining spiritual balance while interviewing Nazi doctors. It was a way of hearing about the experience from the mouths of those who have been victimized or subjected to it, and therefore hearing a deeper truth than anything the Nazi doctors could tell me about what they had done to people. Because it's a distorted story you get, sitting in their studies. You get their stories about their lives, and you've got to supplement them with other information, as I did. But if it were the only version, it would be a very misleading one. So it was a dialogue with survivors that I had, and they were teaching me a great deal, and I think that they were learning some things from the dialogue as well, as we talked very frankly and openly. And it became extraordinarily intense for me because of what it was, and because many of the Jewish survivors, and they were the majority of the survivors I interviewed, were rather similar in their backgrounds to me. They were doctors; they were maybe ten years older than I; they or their families came from places not too far from where my grandparents came, emigrated from; and they happened to emigrate, you know, at the turn of the century, so my parents could be born in the United States, and I could be what's called a third-generation American. But just by some chance developments in history, I was the third-generation American, who had had a privileged existence interviewing them, people who had had a less than privileged existence. And that made the encounter and the dialogue so intense. They understood it immediately, and we talked about such things, as my research interviews always have a certain amount of give and take, in which the psychoanalytically oriented interview is radically modified in the direction of dialogue. And taking it in the direction of dialogue of course means you can take in more because it's an exchange among equals, as opposed to therapy, which has other purposes.

CC: Do you feel that, in the dialogues of your work over the years, you were yourself attempting, in some sense, to bear witness?

RJL: In each study, I experience something of the event and upheaval I'm exploring, and of course there must be a certain element of witnessing in that. And there is also a sense of commitment to the idea that illumination, or some kind of insight, can help serve human purposes. I don't have any simple explanation for how I came to do this kind of work and follow this particular path. But over time, doing study after study, one develops a sense of what is right for one as a scholar and a human being. And for me it's extremely important to listen to one's own voice, whatever its uncertainties. In any case, this is the path I have chosen to follow.

Robert and BJ Lifton at their home in Wellfleet, October 24, 2010.

NOTES

1. Robert Jay Lifton, *The Broken Connection: On Death and the Continuity of Life* (New York: Basic, 1979).

2. Jacques Lacan (1901–1981) was one of the most influential psychoanalysts of the twentieth century. He claimed to "return to Freud" through the advances of Saussurean linguistics and integrated mathematical theory into his rethinking of the psyche. His seminars have had a profound impact on French psychoanalysis and on philosophical and literary theoretical thought, and his innovations in clinical work are debated to this day.

3. Dr. Lifton is referring to Shoshana Felman, who was teaching at Yale University in those years; she had studied with Lacan in Paris, and it was at her invitation that Lacan agreed to visit Yale. See chap. 13 for an interview with her.

4. Erik H. Erikson (1902–1994) was trained as a psychoanalyst in Germany and left after the Nazis came to power. He eventually emigrated to the United States, where he developed a theory of the psychosocial development of human beings. He was also a co-founder, with Robert Jay Lifton, of the Wellfleet Seminar in Psychohistory, which meets yearly to this day.

5. Robert Jay Lifton, *Thought Reform and the Psychology of Totalism: A Study of "Brainwashing" in China* (Chapel Hill: U of North Carolina P, 1969).

6. Ernst Cassirer (1874–1945) was a German philosopher known for his theory of symbolism and his writings on science and culture. Susanne Langer (1895–1985) was an American philosopher of mind who also wrote on the philosophy of art and developed a theory of symbolization and human meaning-making.

7. Primo Levi (1919–1987) was a Jewish Italian author and survivor of Auschwitz. He is known for, among other writings, *Survival in Auschwitz* (*If This Is a Man*), *The Drowned and the Saved*, and *The Periodic Table*. He committed suicide in 1987.

8. Robert Lifton writes about My Lai in *Home from the War: Learning from Vietnam Veterans* (New York: Simon & Schuster, 1973), chap. 2. During the My Lai massacre, on March 16, 1968, over 400 older men, women, and children were slaughtered by members of the US army. The atrocity was eventually brought to light in 1969, when journalist Seymour Hersh broke the story. Hersh interviewed, among others, Paul Meadlo, a soldier in the unit that went into My Lai. Photos were published in 1969, famously, by *Life Magazine*. The incident is considered a crucial moment in US public opinion turning against the war. See Seymour Hersh, *My Lai 4: A Report on the Massacre and Its Aftermath* (New York: Random House, 1983).

9. The *Rambo* movies, which starred Sylvester Stallone and the first of which appeared in 1982, originally depicted Vietnam veterans returning to save prisoners of war still being held by the communist regime. The notion that there were many soldiers missing in action (MIA) had gained a political significance when Nixon helped initiate this notion, which became associated with the MIA flags, whose significance lay not only in their remembrance of the missing in action but also their implicit political positioning in relation to the war.

10. Philippe Pétain (1856–1951) was a general in World War I (the "Lion of Verdun") who became chief of state in Vichy France during World War II.

11. Jack Katz, *Seductions of Crime: Moral and Sensual Attractions in Doing Evil* (1988; reprint, New York: Basic, 1990).

12. For an English translation, see *The Clown*, trans. Leila Vennewitz (New York: Melville House, 2010). The original German version was published in 1963.

13. Evelyn Waugh, *The Loved One* (New York: Little, Brown, 1948).

14. Robert Jay Lifton, *The Nazi Doctors: Medical Killing and the Psychology of Genocide* (New York: Basic, 1986).

Jean Laplanche at his home in Paris, October 23, 1994.

Chapter Two

Traumatic Temporality
An Interview with Jean Laplanche

Jean Laplanche (1924–2012) was a leading French thinker and psychoanalyst. His pioneering work on Freud's early writing first revealed the temporal structure of trauma in Freud and its significance for Freud's notion of sexuality. In his later work, Laplanche elaborated on this understanding of what he called Freud's "special seduction theory" in a "general seduction theory," which examines the origins of the human psyche in the "implantation of the message of the other." I interviewed him in his home in Paris on October 23, 1994.

I. TRAUMA AND TIME

CC: The seduction theory in Freud's early work, which traced adult neurosis back to early childhood molestation, is generally understood today as representing a direct link between psychic life and external events. When people refer to this period of Freud's work in contemporary debates, they tend to refer to it as a time in which Freud still made a place for the reality and effects of external violence in the human psyche. In your understanding of the seduction theory, on the other hand, the theory does not provide a simple locating of external reality in relation to the psyche. As a matter of fact, your temporal reading of seduction trauma in Freud's early work would rather suggest a dislocating of any single traumatic "event." You say specifically, on the basis of your reading of the seduction theory, that there are always at least two scenes that constitute a traumatic "event,"[1] and that the trauma is never locatable in either scene alone but in "the play of 'deceit' producing a kind of seesaw effect between the two events."[2]

Would you explain what you mean when you say that in Freud, trauma is never contained in a single moment, or that the traumatic "event" is defined by a temporal structure?

JL: This question about the seduction theory is important, because the theory of seduction has been completely neglected. When people talk about seduction, they do not talk about the *theory* of seduction. I would argue that even Freud, when he abandoned the so-called seduction theory, forgot about his theory. He just dismissed the *causal fact* of seduction. When [Jeffrey] Masson, for example, goes back to the so-called seduction theory, he comes back to the factuality of seduction, but not to the theory, which he completely ignores.[3] To say that seduction is important in the child is not a theory, just an assertion. And to say that Freud neglected the reality of seduction or that Freud came back to this reality, or that Masson comes back to this reality, is not a theory.

Now the theory of seduction is very important because it's highly developed in Freud. The first step I took with [J.-B.] Pontalis a long time ago, in *The Language of Psychoanalysis*, was to unearth this theory, which has very complicated aspects: temporal aspects, economic aspects, and also topographical aspects.[4]

As to the question of external and internal reality, the theory of seduction is more complicated than simply opposing external and internal causality. When Freud said, "Now I am abandoning the idea of external causality and am turning to fantasy," he neglected this very dialectical theory he had between the external and the internal. He is neglected, that is, the complex play between the external and the internal.

His theory explained that trauma, in order to be psychic trauma, never comes simply from outside. That is, even in the first moment it must be internalized, and then afterwards relived, revivified, in order to become an internal trauma. That's the meaning of his theory that trauma consists of two moments: the trauma, in order to be psychic trauma, doesn't occur in just one moment. First, there is the implantation of something coming from the outside. And this experience, or the memory of it, must be reinvested in a second moment, and *then* it becomes traumatic. It is not the first act which is traumatic, it is the internal reviviscence of this memory that becomes traumatic. That's Freud's theory. You find it very carefully elaborated in *The Project for a Scientific Psychology*,[5] in the famous case of Emma.

Now, my job has been to show why Freud missed some very important points in this theory. But before saying that we must revise the theory, we must know it. And I think that ignorance concerning the seduction theory causes people to go back to something preanalytic. By discussing the seduction theory we are doing justice to Freud, perhaps doing Freud better justice than he did himself. He forgot the importance of his theory, and its very meaning, which was not just the importance of external events.

CC: So you are saying that, in the beginning, Freud himself never understood seduction as simply outside, or trauma as simply outside, but as a relation between an external cause and something like an internal cause. Are you suggesting, then, that when he said that he abandoned the theory, he himself forgot that complex relation? That is, when he told [Wilhelm] Fliess he was turning away from seduction by an adult to the child's fantasies,[6] that he himself misunderstood his own seduction theory as being only about external causality?

JL: Yes, something like that. I think that when he abandoned the theory, he in fact forgot the very complexity of the theory.

CC: You have just explained this complexity in terms of the relation between the first and second moments of the trauma: you say that in order to be psychic trauma the memory of the original implantation must be revivified. In your written work, you describe this relation between the original moment and its revivification in terms of *Nachträglichkeit*. This term, used by Freud, is usually translated as "belatedness" and is understood to refer to the belated effect of the traumatizing event. But you are careful to distinguish various interpretations and translations of the word. Would you explain the various meanings of *Nachträglichkeit* and your own alternative understanding of Freud's use of the term?

JL: We translate *Nachträglichkeit* in French as *après-coup*, and in English I have proposed that it be translated as "afterwardsness," which is now gaining acceptance. After all, the English language can use such words with "-ness." I read something about "white-hat-edness," so why not afterwardsness?

Now this is not only a question of finding a word. Because in the translations of Freud, the full sense of *Nachträglichkeit* was not preserved. Even in Masson's translation of the Fliess letters, he doesn't preserve the full complexity of *Nachträglichkeit*.[7] This is very important because there are two directions in afterwardness, and those two directions he translates by different words. The phrase "deferred action" describes one direction, and the phrase "after the event" describes the other direction. So even in Masson's translation the seduction theory is split.

CC: So he splits what you have called the deterministic theory, in which the first event determines the second event, from the hermeneutic theory, in which the second event projects, retroactively, what came before.[8]

JL: That's it exactly, yes. Now, this is not so easy. Because even *après-coup* in French, and "afterwards" in English, have these two meanings. For instance, I can say, "the terrorists put a bomb in the building, and it exploded *afterwards*." That's the direction of deferred action. And I can also say, "this bridge fell down, and the architect understood *afterwards* that he did not make it right." That's an after-the-event understanding; the architect understood afterwards. These are two different meanings.

But you have to understand how those two meanings have been put into one meaning in Freud. I think even Freud did not completely grasp these two directions, or the fact that he put them in one and the same theory. Let me quote a passage I have referred to before. It's a passage from *The Interpretation of Dreams*, which is very interesting because it's a long time after Freud has abandoned the seduction theory, and even the idea of afterwardsness. But afterwardsness came back again later on. This is his very amusing anecdote:

> Love and hunger, I reflected, meet at a woman's breast. A young man who was a great admirer of feminine beauty was talking once—so the story went—of the good-looking wet-nurse who had suckled him when he was a baby: "I'm sorry," he remarked, "that I didn't make a better use of my opportunity." I was in the habit of quoting this anecdote to explain the factor of deferred action [or as I would say, "afterwardsness"] in the mechanism of the psychoneurosis.[9]

It's very interesting because here you have both directions. That is, you can say on the one hand, that there was sexuality in the small child, and afterwards, this man, who was once a small child, becomes excited again when he sees himself as a small child. That is the direction of determinism; sexuality is in the small child, and afterwards, as a deferred action, it's reactivated in the adult. Or, on the other and, you can say that it's just a matter of the reinterpretation of the adult: there is no sexuality in the small child, the small child is just sucking the milk, but the older man, as a sexual being, resexualizes the spectacle.

So for Freud there were two ways of explaining afterwardsness, but I don't think he ever says that there must be some synthesis of those two directions. Now the only possible synthesis is to take into account what he doesn't take into account, that is, *the wet nurse*. If you don't take into account the wet nurse herself, and what she contributes when she gives the breast to the child—if you don't have in mind the external person, that is, the stranger, and the strangeness of the other—you cannot grasp both directions implicit in afterwardsness.

CC: So to understand the truly temporal aspect of *Nachträglichkeit*, or afterwardsness, you have to take into account what is *not* known, both at the beginning, *and* later. What is radically not known.

JL: Yes.

CC: Whereas the other two models of afterwardsness imply either knowing later, or maybe implicitly, biologically, knowing earlier.

JL: Yes.

CC: There's too much knowledge, in a way, in the first two models, but in what you describe there's something that remains uninterested or unassimilated.

JL: Well, what I mean is that if you try to understand afterwardsness only from the point of view of this man, being first a baby and then an adult, you cannot understand afterwardsness. That is, if you don't start from the other, and from the category of the message, you cannot understand afterwardsness. You are left with a dilemma that is impossible to resolve: either the past determines the future, or the future reinterprets the past.

CC: Another way in which you have talked about this position of the other in trauma is in terms of a model that is less temporal than spatial. You note, in "Traumatisme, traduction, transfert et autres trans(es),"[10] that the word "trauma," in its three uses in Freud (as physical trauma, as psychic trauma, and as the concept of the traumatic neuroses) centers around the notion of piercing or penetrating, the notion of "effraction," or wounding. This notion of wounding seems to imply a spatial model, in which the reality of the trauma originates "outside" an organism that is violently imposed upon. You have suggested that the temporal and spatial models are complementary,[11] and I am wondering what the spatial model can add to our understanding of the role of the other in trauma.

JL: One might ask, since I have emphasized a temporal model of trauma, what need is there to go back to a spatial one, to what is called the structure of the psychic apparatus? Now the spatial model is first of all a biological model. That is, an organism has an envelope, and something happens inside, which is homeostatic, and something is outside. There is no need of psychoanalysis in order to understand that. Biologists understand that. But when I speak of "outside," I am not speaking of an outside in relation to this envelope; I am speaking of something very much more "outside" than this, that extraneity, or strangeness, which, for the human being, is not a question of the outside world. As you know, many psychoanalysts have tried to produce a theory of knowledge. We don't need a theory of knowledge. Psychoanalysis is not a theory of knowledge as a whole. The problem of the other in psychoanalysis is not a problem of the outside world. We don't need psychoanalysis to understand why I lend reality to this scale, to this chair, and so on. That's not a problem. The problem is the reality of the other, and of his message.[12]

CC: The reality of the other.

JL: The reality of the other. Now this reality is absolutely bound to his strangeness. How does the human being, the baby, encounter this strangeness? It is in the fact that the messages he receives are enigmatic. His messages are enigmatic because those messages are strange to themselves. That is, if the other was not himself invaded by his own other, his internal other, that is, the unconscious, the messages wouldn't be strange and enigmatic. So the problem of the other is strictly bound to the fact that the small human being has no unconscious, and he is confronted with messages invaded by the unconscious of the other. When I speak now of the other, I speak of the concrete other, I don't speak in Lacanian terms, with a big O or a big A. I speak of the concrete other, each other person, adult person, which has to care for the baby.

CC: So the figure of wounding or "piercing," as a model of trauma, does not have so much to do with, let's say, a metaphor of the body, but rather with this invasion of the unconscious of the other?

JL: Yes. Nevertheless, the topographical model is very important because the very constitution of this topography of the psychic apparatus is bound up with the fact that the small human being has to cope with this strangeness. And his way of coping with this strangeness is to build an ego. And as I have said elsewhere, Freud's topography is from the point of view of the ego.

So it is in relation to the seduction theory that the subject builds himself as an individual. He Ptolemizes himself, being at the very beginning Copernican, that is, circulating around the other's message. He has to integrate this, and he builds an inside in order to internalize.[13]

CC: So the trauma or the seduction, in your terms, anticipates or precedes or originates that envelope.

JL: Yes, that building of the psychic structure. So I don't think the ego is something bound to psychology in general. It is bound to the very fact that we have to cope with the strangeness of the message.

CC: And thus the ego is very closely linked to this temporal structure of originary seduction, too.

JL: Yes, absolutely. It's bound, I would say, to the second moment, that is, the moment where the message is in some way already implanted, but not yet processed. And to process it, that is translate it, the ego has to build itself a structure.

CC: Is that why the ego is, after that, always open to the possibility of being traumatized again?

JL: Yes, yes. The other traumas of the adult, or later traumas, are to be understood with the ego already in place, and the first trauma, which is not trauma but seduction—the first seduction—is the way the ego builds itself.

CC: So in every subsequent trauma there is always a relation between the specific event, whether it's a real seduction or a car accident or whatever, and the originary founding of the ego.

JL: Yes.

II. Sexuality and Trauma

CC: As you point out, in *New Foundations for Psychoanalysis*, after Freud "abandons" the seduction theory in 1897 he continues to develop various aspects of it in different ways throughout his work, but it no longer appears to have the same familial (or even sexual) character.[14] When trauma reappears in *Beyond the Pleasure Principle*, for example, it is linked to "accidents" and war events, first of all, and ultimately to foundational moments of consciousness and the drive.[15] In your own work, however, you insist that it might be possible, even in the example of the train accident, to link the seduction theory of trauma to a nonsexual theory:

> With any disturbance, even if it is not specifically sexual—for example the
> train trip, or the train accident—a sexual drive can be released and, in the
> case of the train accident, it is really an unleashing of the drive, traumatiz-
> ing the ego from the inside on its internal periphery. In other words, it is not
> the drive's mechanical impact that is traumatic; it requires a relay of sexual
> excitation, and it is this flood of sexual excitation that is traumatizing for the
> psychic apparatus.[16]

Your insistence on the sexual dimension of the accident, here, seems allied to your own general interest in the language of seduction and the earlier seduction theory. In what way does *Beyond the Pleasure Principle* retain elements of the seduction theory?

JL: *Beyond the Pleasure Principle* is a very complex text, which must be completely dismantled. It is a speculative text, and it has to be interpreted from the very beginning to the end. It's a text which, I would say, follows the logic of the cauldron: the cauldron was not broken, you never gave me the cauldron in the first place, and so on. This is the logic of the text. So this text must be dismantled, it cannot be taken just as a form of reasoning; there are ruptures in the reasoning. And it's all in the ruptures.

For me, the significance of *Beyond the Pleasure Principle* lies in the fact that

Freud was beginning to forget the destructive character of sexuality. This started with the introduction of narcissism. After the introduction of narcissism, sexuality was enrolled under the banner of totality and of love: of love as a totality, of love as the object as a totality. *Beyond the Pleasure Principle* is a way of Freud's saying, "sexuality is, in the end, something more disruptive than I thought in narcissism, which is only Eros, that is, the binding aspect of sexuality. Beyond this Eros, no, not 'beyond' but before—."

CC: *Jenseits.*

JL: Yes, *jenseits* of this Eros, this is what I first discovered: the fact that sexuality is unbound, in its unconscious aspects. In my opinion, that is the meaning of *Beyond the Pleasure Principle.*

CC: Is there also something new that he discovers as a consequence of his forgetting?

JL: Well, what he discovers, which is a very important discovery, is narcissism. That's one of the most important discoveries of Freud. The discovery in 1915 of narcissism.[17] But the danger of the discovery of narcissism as love of oneself as a totality, and love of the other as a total object, was precisely his forgetting that there is something not totalizing in sexuality.

CC: Doesn't he also introduce, in *Beyond the Pleasure Principle*, the importance of death, since now trauma becomes linked to death, to accidents that threaten your life?

JL: The traumas that Freud treats there are adult traumas. And they are usually gross traumas, train accidents and so on. Now there are many interesting points in this regard, which have to be reinterpreted. First, he says, the dreams of the traumatic neurosis prove that some dreams are not the accomplishment of desire. But he did not try to analyze those dreams. He simply took them for their manifest content. That's very strange, to see Freud being fascinated by the manifest content of those dreams and not being able to see that even those dreams could be analyzed. They are repetitive, but they are not completely repetitive; there are always some points where the analytic method could be used. And this he forgets completely. That's my first point.

My second point would be more positive. It's very interesting to take seriously the fact that when the trauma is associated with a wound, a corporal wound, there is usually no psychic trauma. It's just trauma in the medical sense, as in an earthquake and so on; you also have traumas in the medical sense of the word. And the observation is very interesting that if there is some wounding the trauma does not become psychic trauma.

Now the other point which is important is that he says all traumas make sexuality active again, that is, by developing sexual excitement.[18] This question of adult trauma, I think, has to be examined through experience. One of my followers, Sylvia Bleichmar, who is Argentinian, was in Mexico at the time of the big earthquake in Mexico. She had a team of people trying to treat the post-earthquake traumas. And what was important even in that treatment was analytic work. Even in so-called physical trauma, the way to find a point of entry was in what was psychic, in how it revived something from infancy. If there weren't this revival of something personal and sexual, there would be no way of coping with those traumas. In this context she has made some important inroads concerning the resymbolization of trauma.

CC: When you say, "if there weren't a revival of something personal and sexual," what do you mean by "sexual"?

JL: I mean that, ultimately, a trauma like that may be—and this is very strange—in consonance with something like a message. After all, even an earthquake could be taken in as a message. Not just something that is factual but something that means something to you.

CC: And that message is, in some sense, linked to origins.

JL: Linked to earlier messages.

CC: Then it's a message that resists your understanding: the meaning of it is partially that you can't assimilate the message fully.

JL: Yes. But at the same time, if there is not something enigmatic in those gross traumas, something where you must ask a question—why this? why did this happen to me?—there wouldn't be a way of symbolizing them.

CC: Do you think that what is called flashback or repetition, the constant return of the message in dreams and so on, could be understood as the imposition of that question, *what does this mean*?

JL: Yes.

CC: In that case, if we go back to the dream, you said Freud forgets that the dream can be interpreted. But could you reinterpret the dream, in this context, as being not exactly literal but also not a symbol in the normal sense because it has to do with this enigmatic message? I mean, isn't there a difference still between traumatic nightmares and other kinds of nightmares?

JL: Yes. There's certainly something that resists interpretation. But we have something similar in symbolic dreams, dreams that have an overtly symbolic content: there are dreams that impose on you by the fact that there are themes in which there is nothing to interpret after all. That is a repetition too. We have this experience in the dreams of our neurotic patients; sometimes they bring you a dream which is so real, which is a repetition of what happened yesterday, and they say, "there is nothing to interpret." So I'm very skeptical about the impossibility of interpreting those traumatic dreams.

CC: Could you say perhaps, though, that traumatic nightmares are linked in a more direct way to the ordinary traumatic message?

JL: Yes, there may be a shortcut between them. But in those shortcuts you always have to find the small details, the changing details in such dreams, and it's those changing small details that can be the starting point of the analytic method, which is interpretation and free association.

CC: You mean what changes in them . . .

JL: Yes, what changes even in these dreams as well. Freud said the repetitions are the same, but they are not always the same, and that's the difference that makes all the difference.

III. The Primal Situation

CC: This brings me to your own rethinking of what you call the "special seduction theory" of Freud in terms of a "general seduction theory," or the origination of human consciousness and sexuality in the "implantation of the enigmatic message of the other." Your own theory of seduction seems to involve the larger philosophical and foundational quality of Freud's later work on trauma while insisting on the story of the "scene of seduction" from the earlier work. Would you explain what you mean by "primal seduction" and the "implantation of an enigmatic message," and why you insist on retaining, in this philosophical context, the language of seduction? What is the relation between a universal foundational structure or moment (the primal seduction trauma) and the contingency of the accidental or unprepared for that is so central to the notion of psychic trauma?

JL: For me, seduction must be understood as a primal solution. That is, it goes back to the constitution of the unconscious. And seductions—infantile seduction or adult seductions, seductions in everyday life—are derived from this original situation. This original situation, as I understand it, involves an adult who has an unconscious—I'm very realistic, I say "he *has* an unconscious," I'm not afraid to say that; I think that seems very strange to philosophers, "he *has* an unconscious," like a bag behind him . . .

CC: It's our baggage!

JL: It's our baggage, yes. So, the original situation is the confrontation of an adult, who has an unconscious, and the child or infant, who at the beginning has no unconscious—that is, he doesn't have this baggage behind him. (You must understand that I am completely against the idea that the unconscious could be something biological or inherited. I think the idea of an inherited unconscious is something that has to be forgotten.) The unconscious of the adult is very deeply moved and revived by this confrontation with the infant. And especially his perverse sexuality—in the Freudian sense of "perverse," that is, not perversity as an overt perversion, but the perverse sexuality of the human being that involves not only genitality but all the pregenital trends (I wouldn't say stages, but trends).

Now, you asked me why I keep sexuality in this. This question seems very odd to me because, at this very moment, sexuality in the United States is being put on trial, especially by the children who say that they were sexually attacked. And so sexuality is everywhere; it is in every court, in every trial. I would say that this is a way to forget the idea of generalized sexuality, which Freud has put forward. That is, sexuality cannot be identified with specific forms of perversity; it's not just something that can be isolated here and there. Perversion, rather, is in everyone, as an important component of sexuality. What Freud has shown, in the *Three Essays on the Theory of Sexuality*, is that in every adult's so-called normal sexuality there is perversion: there is perversion in the means of talking pleasure, in the forepleasure, and also in the fantasies.[19] So why sexuality? I say that there is much more sexuality than they think in those trials. More sexuality, that is, in the sense that sexuality and perverse sexuality are everywhere in the most "innocent" relation of parent and child. And there is no reason to make a trial about that!

Coming back to this story of the wet nurse, something has been forgotten, I would say, not only in the United States (and France) but by all of psychoanalysis. Let's take the Kleinians for example. They speak of the breast, the good breast, the bad breast, the breast as the first object, and how you have to internalize it and so on. But there is more to understanding sexual life. Who before me has reminded people that the breast was an erotic organ for the woman? That is, the breast is something that is a part of the sexuality of the woman. And why is this sexuality of the breast now forgotten? When one speaks of the relation of the child to this breast, why does one forget this very fact of its sexuality? Now the fact that there is no reason to make a split between the sexual breast and the nursing breast has been noted by many pediatricians, who point out that many women have sexual pleasure in nursing, although they don't dare to acknowledge it. This has been noted by many gynecologists, pediatricians, and so on. Even ancient psychiatrists noted a long time ago those sexual feelings and sexual fantasies in the person who watched over the child. So why sexuality? I say rather, why the forgetting of sexuality in the very fact of nursing?

CC: Why *do* you think there is a forgetting of sexuality?

JL: Well, the discovery of Freud was very important for generalized sexuality, but he did not go back to this point. Maybe there are some places where he touches on it, perhaps in the Leonardo essay,[20] but very few places where he deals directly with that issue. Freud talked about many erotogenic zones, but he never talked about the erotogenic zone of the breast. For me there's something missing there in the theory, including how the erotogenic zone develops in the woman (and also in men sometimes).

But what's important for me is not just the fact that the woman may have some pleasure in nursing but the fact that something passes from the nursing person to the child, as an enigma. That is, something passes of what I call a message. And the most important thing is not the breast as a shape, as a whole, as an object, but the breast as conveying a message to the child. And this message is invaded by sexuality.

CC: And that would also mean, then, that it is invaded by something that neither mother nor baby can fully know.

JL: Yes, absolutely. Something that is unconscious, mostly unconscious sexuality. Sometimes it is also partly conscious, but there is always something going back to the unconscious and to the very personal history of the person.

CC: So in this case sexuality also means that which remains enigmatic.

JL: Yes, what remains unconscious, enigmatic.

CC: In regard to this role of the other, you have suggested that by introducing the mother (or the other) into the temporal scheme of trauma, the reality of trauma—as a temporal structure—can no longer be thought of in terms of a dual model: "If one introduces a third term into this scene—that is, the nurse and her own sexuality—which is only at best vaguely sensed by the baby—then it is no longer possible to consider afterwardsness in dual terms."[21] What is the relation between the other and temporality in your model?

JL: In a paper of mine on temporality I speak of the other as immobile motor. Remember Aristotle's image of God . . . but I'm not a theologian. What I mean is that the temporality of afterwardsness develops in the child, but the message of the mother itself is not temporal. It is rather atemporal, simultaneous. That is, what is going to develop itself as temporality in the child is simultaneous in the mother. It is a simultaneity of the message, which, at the same time, and at the same moment—in the same message—is self-preservative and sexual. It is compromised by sexuality. And to go back to this model of the wet nurse, perverse sexuality is in the very atemporality of the adult. So I wouldn't say there is a passage of temporality from the adult to the child. I would say rather that there is a concentration in something that is not temporal, that is, the compromised message of the other.

CC: You say that the message in the adult is not temporal. If the message is enigmatic, which means it contains or conveys some of the unconscious of the mother, and if that unconsciousness in the mother is also formed around an originary seduction, what has happened to the temporality of that seduction?

JL: When sexuality has been repressed, let's say, in the adult, it becomes unconscious, and in the unconscious there is no temporality. So I would say there is something that is extracted from temporality.

CC: Is that why it's compromised?

JL: Yes. That's the reason why it's compromised. And I understand "compromised" as something not temporal, not bound to temporality. Except that our work, our psychoanalytic work is to retemporalize it. The very representations of signifiers that have been repressed are from then on subjected to temporality.

CC: So that's why, in order to be passed on, the message cannot be completely temporal.

JL: When it's passed on, it is passed on as something simultaneous. And from then on, the child develops a temporal dialectic, that is, a traumatic dialectic, first receiving the message and then reinterpreting it in a second moment.

CC: When you speak of the passing on of a compromised message, you are speaking of something repressed and unconscious. In *New Foundations for Psychoanalysis*, along the same lines, you suggest that the theory of seduction, or a traumatic model of sexuality, can be linked to the more general theory of repression in Freud through the distinction between primal repression and secondary repression. For most trauma psychiatrists today (in the United States, at least), the theory of trauma and the theory of repression are opposed, since repression doesn't engage the same temporal structure as trauma. How do you link the two?

JL: I'm mostly interested in the humanizing trauma. That is, the first trauma, which most people wouldn't describe as trauma: the originary seduction of the normal, average subject or future neurotic subject (not the psychotic). So I have been much more interested in that aspect of trauma that ultimately leads to repression and restructuration, as opposed to something that has not been translated. Now, I completely agree that in the framework of the two-moment theory of trauma and seduction, one has to ask the reason why, in many instances, there is no second moment, or why the second moment is hampered or paralyzed. And that is really the trauma which cannot be reinterpreted, which is implantation, what I call *intromission*.[22] And here we come back to the question of psychosis, and to the question of the superego. Because I think that in some way the messages that become superego messages are messages that are not being translated. So I would speak of the superego as some kind of psychotic enclave in everyone, something that consists in part of messages that cannot be translated.

CC: Did you say that in some instances there is no second moment?

JL: Sometimes there is no second moment. In everyone. I think that there are some things that are not repressed after all.

IV. The Other and Death

CC: We have been speaking about the role of the other in trauma and primal seduction. In *Life and Death in Psychoanalysis*, your analysis of seduction trauma takes place within a larger framework in which you analyze, on the one hand, the relation between the vital order and sexuality (in *The Project for a Scientific Psychology* and in the *Three Essays on the Theory of Sexuality*) and, on the other hand, the relation between sexuality (not including the vital order) and death (in *Beyond the Pleasure Principle*)—hence the title of your book, *Life and Death in Psychoanalysis*. In the introduction to that book, moreover, you talk about the significance of death for Freud:

> Might it be that death—human death as finitude and not the sole reduction to zero of vital tensions—find its place, in psychoanalysis, in a dimension which is more ethical than explanatory? . . . [Freud say,] If you would endure life, be prepared for death. . . . More modestly perhaps in relation to the temptations of the heroic formulation, "If you want life, prepare for death" might be translated as "If you want life, prepare for the death of the other." If a certain ethic in relation to death might be evolved from the Freudian attitude, it would be in the sense of a distrust concerning every form of enthusiasm, and of a lucidity that does not hide the irreducible meshing of my death with that of the other.[23]

Is there a relation between the role of the other in the seduction theory and the relation between the other and death in psychoanalysis?

JL: I'm afraid that the more I advance in my thinking, the more I disintricate the question of death, the enigma of death, and the so-called death drive of Freud.

CC: You take them apart?

JL: Yes. That's why I'm very critical about the term "death drive," and why I have called it a "sexual death drive," with the emphasis more on the "sexual" than on "death." For me, the sexual death drive is just sexuality, unbound sexuality, the extreme of sexuality. And more than death, I would point to primary masochism.

I see more of a sense of the sexual death drive in masochism or in sadomasochism than in death. And it was not only on the side of sadism but on the side of masochism that Freud placed the core of his death drive.

Now as to the question of death—in the sense that we are all subject to the question of death and to the enigma of death—I wouldn't say it is as primal as some people would have it. We all know that infants up to a certain point in their development don't know death and don't have any questions about death. I see the issue in a very Freudian manner, or at least from a certain perspective of Freudian thought. I would say that the question of the enigma of death is brought to the subject by the other. That is, it is the other's death that raises the question of death. Not the existentialist question, "*why should I die?*" The question "*why should I die?*" is secondary to the question, "*why would the other die?*," "*why did the other die?*," and so on.

CC: When or how does that question of the other's death get put to the subject?
JL: Well it's put at very different times in everyone's life. And it's also bound to absence. I don't think that metaphysical questioning about one's own death is primary. It doesn't mean it's not important, but I think it comes from the question, "*why should the other die?*"

CC: So would you say, then, that it is not necessarily linked to the implantation of the enigmatic message?
JL: I don't think it's bound to the very first enigmatic message. But there are enigmas that come afterwards.

CC: By suggesting that the question of death is raised through the death of the other, you seem to be returning now to the notion that death is situated in an "ethical dimension." Can you say more about what that means?
JL: I am a little surprised to hear you ask about ethics, because in my opinion the alterity of the unconscious in everyone has very little to do with ethics. I would say that it is deeply antimoral.

CC: I am not referring to ethics in the sense of everyday morality but rather in relation to your comments in the introduction to *Life and Death in Psychoanalysis*, where you say that death as a finitude might ultimately be placed in an ethical dimension, rather than an explanatory dimension in Freud. And I wanted to understand what you meant.
JL: Oh, yes, sure, sure, yes . . . I agree with you that an ethical dimension is introduced by the question of the death of the other. But I don't think there is a link to the primal seduction; I would see it a little after. Even in the Oedipal situation, which includes the question of the death of the other.

CC: Maybe when you said to me, at the very beginning of this interview, that for psychoanalysis the question is not about knowing but about the reality of the other, perhaps that's what you meant by ethics. That is, it is not about epistemology but rather about confronting the reality of the other.

JL: Yes. And especially in regard to knowing, I would repeat what I have said about knowledge as an intellectual process: when I speak of translation or interpretation by the individual, I don't mean an intellectual way of processing messages. Because they are processed in many languages, that is, also in an affective language or an image-language. I don't see the question of translating as having to do with intellectual translation.

CC: So there, too, it's not about knowing something but about being linked to the other.

JL: Yes.

V. Translation and Detranslation

CC: When you discuss the role of the other in the original seduction, you also use a specifically linguistic terminology (the implantation of the "message" of the other). Likewise, your interpretation of repression and the drive, as well as of psychoanalytic work, is tied to what seems to be a linguistic terminology of "translation" and "detranslation." Can you say more about the meaning of these terms and about their specific significance as linguistic terms?

JL: I wouldn't say my view is a linguistic point of view; it is much less so than Lacan's and some others'. And up to now my linguistic vocabulary has been very minimal. But why do I use the term "translation"? When I use this term, it is a linguistic metaphor, in the sense that Jacobson speaks of translation. Which means not only verbal, linguistic translation but also inter-semiotic translation, that is, from one type of language to another. So if I take translation as a model that is verbal, it's just a model. And for me, when Freud, in his famous Letter 52,[24] speaks of translation or the failure of translation, he doesn't mean translation into words. He means translation into what he sometimes calls "drive language," or a type of drive language. You may also have a translation into a type of code which is internal to language, for instance, the castration code or the Oedipus myth, which is a type of code into which you can translate something.

So why do I speak of translation and not of interpretation? Interpretation may mean that you interpret some factual situation. Translation means that there is no factual situation that can be translated. If something is translated, it's already a message. That means you can only translate what has already been put in communication or made as a communication. That's why I speak of translation rather than of understanding or interpretation.

CC: It also has to do with the message and its enigma.

JL: Yes. I'm very interested, now, in the debate with hermeneutics. One of my last papers is called "Psychoanalysis as Anti-Hermeneutics," which suggests that the aim of analytic work is not translation but detranslation.[25] Translation is very important, but it's not an activity of the analyst. I'm not anti-hermeneutic in general; I'm anti-hermeneutic only insofar as people try to make analytic work a specialty of hermeneutics.

But the other point is that the only translator, the only hermeneut, is the human being. That is, the human being is always a translating, interpreting being. But what is he translating? That's why I'm using the word "translate" and not "interpret." Take for instance Heidegger's hermeneutic position. He says there is a proto- or first understanding, which is the understanding of the human condition. But as I see it, there is no translation if there is not something already being put into words, not necessarily verbal words. So I would go back to the idea of a hermeneutics of the message, which was also the first meaning of hermeneutics. Because, as you know, hermeneutics in the past was a hermeneutics of the text. And especially of sacred texts, like the Bible and the Koran and so on. So I think that we have to go back to a hermeneutics of the message. Not a hermeneutics of the message of God but a hermeneutics of the message of the other.

CC: So you're saying that the modern notion of hermeneutics as a process of understanding has forgotten that hermeneutics originated as a reading and translation process.

JL: Yes, a translation process. Hermeneutics at the very beginning was a hermeneutics of something being *addressed* to you. And in Heidegger what is interesting is that it became a hermeneutics of the human situation. But he forgot that the human situation in itself cannot be translated. It's just facts, it's just factual. In the framework of the hermeneutics of the human individual, what is important is to go back to the idea that the first interpretation is an interpretation, not of one's own situation but of the situation of receiving a message.

CC: If one can make an analogy with the original message from the mother, could one say that it is an address also?

JL: Yes.

CC: Is it a matter, then, not simply of translating any message, but a message that is addressed to you?

JL: Yes.

CC: So it's specifically then—what makes it more complex—the translating of an address, which is different from, let's say, the translating of a statement. Because an address takes a specific form.

JL: Yes. It's always the translating of an address.

CC: And so something of the enigma and the resistance has to do with that structure of address?

JL: Yes.

CC: In this context, how does "translation"' help us understand what you have called "psychic reality"? You have commented that psychic reality is the "reality of the message."[26] In what way is translation a rethinking of the general problem of the relation between reality and the psyche?

JL: My problem is not the old epistemological, philosophical problem of the reality of the external world . . . On this point, I must say, I'm very much an empiricist, or, even if you want, I'm colored a bit by phenomenology—in the sense that every consciousness is consciousness of something. Even animal consciousness is consciousness of something. And there is no problem for me of rebuilding the external world, starting from something internal. I think that any living being is so open to the *Umwelt* that there is no problem of rebuilding the reality of reference starting from representations. The problem of representation and reference for me is completely wiped out by phenomenology.

Now, my problem is not that. It's not a problem of the other world, the other thing, which is taken care of by phenomenology, and it is not also an analytic problem. As I said before, it's a very big error on the part of psychoanalysts to try to make a theory of knowledge starting from so-called psychoanalysis—for instance, starting from the breast and the reality of the breast. Or even Winnicott's starting from the first not-me possession and building on the external world beginning with what he called the transitional object, and so on. The problem, on our human level, is that the other does not have to be *reconstructed*. The other is prior to the subject. The other on the sexual level is intruding on the biological world. So you don't have to construct it, it first comes to you, as an enigma.

CC: So it's the opposite problem. Too much other!

JL: Yes, the opposite problem. Too much other, exactly! And instead of saying the first not-me possession, the problem for the human sexual being is to have a first-me possession. That is, to build an ego starting from too much otherness.

CC: So your interest is in how that takes place.

JL: Yes. What I say in *The Copernican Revolution*[27] is that we are first Copernican, that is, on the sexual level, which is invaded by the other's messages, and the problem is to recover from that.

CC: Since trauma, at least later on, is connected with accidents, would you say that when the adult trauma interrupts like an accident, it is the reemergence of that too much other?

JL: Yes, absolutely. That too much other coming back. And there is a destruction of the ego. The ego cannot cope with it, or even is no longer there. So in that sense I agree with you. The otherness comes back full strength!

VI. The Practice of Psychoanalysis

CC: As a final question, I would like to ask you how you became interested in the problem of trauma in Freud, and if there is a link between your becoming interested in that and your philosophical training. Would you say your interest in trauma grew out of your philosophical training?

JL: Perhaps my questioning came from philosophy; I went to psychoanalysis as a philosopher. I would say my main question is about psychoanalytic practice, not about clinical work as such but rather the question, "what is the very invention of Freud in psychoanalytic practice?" Is it just a kind of role-playing? Or is there something else more fundamental? For me the understanding of analysis as just reconstructing some events that have not been constructed correctly, or as role-playing—that is, you play the role of the mother or father, but you must say that you are not exactly as they were—never seemed very interesting to me philosophically. Nor did it get at the true invention of Freud. I felt that the analytic situation could not be understood just as reviving a factual situation but as reviving the situation of being confronted with the enigma of the other. So at the heart of my inquiry is really the analytic situation, and the question of what we are doing in it, and whether or not it is just something that any other kind of psychotherapy would do, which I do not think to be the case.

CC: You are also now going back, in your work, to the question of time, which you appear to believe is a crucial element of Freud's discovery. Is this also linked to your clinical inquiry?

JL: I think that there are at least two aspects of time in Freud, and I think he mixed them together. On the one hand, there is the question of time as the experience of the outside world, which is linked to perception and to what he calls the system of consciousness. But this, in my opinion, is the biological aspect of time. And that aspect of time is very limited; it is immediate time, immediate temporality. But what Freud tried to discover, through *Nachträglichkeit*, is something much more connected with the whole of a life. That is another type of temporality. It is the temporality of retranslating one's own fate, of retranslating what's coming to this fate from the message of the other. That's a completely different aspect of temporality.

CC: And that's what you're exploring in your clinical practice.

JL: Yes. That's what we're exploring in the analytic situation. Freud stressed the fact that psychoanalysis was first of all a method. And I think he was right. Not a method in the sense of a scientific method—not an objective method but the method of the cure. That is, the method of free association in the frame of the address of the other, which remains enigmatic. That is something completely new in the experience of humanity, I believe. I think that's a new era in humanity.

CC: Do you think it would be important for people to continue to explore this relation to the address of the other in the psychoanalytic situation in the context of the current work being done on trauma?

JL: Yes, I think that the analytic situation, and the analytic understanding of how the human being responds to the message of the other, can also be extended to the question of why, in some instances, there is no translation. I was very interested in psychosis, although I don't have much experience with it anymore, but I think that psychosis can be understood as a negative of the seduction theory. A negative that says how the seduction theory doesn't work. In the treatment of children, as well, it's very important to understand that before a certain point, interpreting has no meaning, if there is no unconscious yet. So the problem for the treatment of children would be to help constitute an unconscious rather than interpreting the unconscious as being there from all eternity.

CC: So hopefully psychoanalysis will be renewed through a different kind of understanding of the original insights of Freud that have been somewhat forgotten.

JL: Yes, but there is some strangeness in this seduction theory. For every one of us it is difficult to give an account of this strangeness and to face it. Think of it in terms of grammar. In grammar, you say the first person is the person who speaks. The second person is the person to whom I speak. The third person is the person of whom I speak. But who is *the person who speaks to me?*

CC: And that is what . . .

JL: And that is what we have yet to cope with.

NOTES
1. Jean Lapanche, *Problématiques III: la sublimation* (Paris: Presses Universitaires de France, 1977), 202.
2. Jean Laplanche, *Life and Death in Psychoanalysis*, trans. Jeffrey Mehlman (Baltimore, MD: Johns Hopkins UP, 1976), translation of *Vie et mort en psychanalyse* (Paris: Flammarion, 1970).
3. Jeffrey Masson, *The Assault on Truth: Freud's Suppression of the Seduction Theory* (New York: Penguin, 1984).
4. Jean Laplanche and J.-B. Pontalis, *The Language of Psychoanalysis*, trans. Donald Nicholson-Smith (New York: Norton, 1973), translation of *Vocabulaire de la Psychanalyse* (Paris: Presses Universitaire de France, 1967).

5. Sigmund Freud, *Project for a Scientific Psychology*, in *The Origins of Psychoanalysis: Letters to Wilhelm Fliess* (New York: Basic, 1954), esp. 410–13.

6. Freud, *The Origins of Psychoanalysis*, Letter 69, pp. 215ff.

7. Sigmund Freud, *The Complete Letters of Sigmund Freud to Wilhelm Fliess, 1887–1904*, trans. and ed. J. M. Masson (Cambridge, MA: Belknap Press of Harvard UP, 1985).

8. Jean Laplanche, "Notes on Afterwardsness," in *Seduction, Translation, Drives: A Dossier Compiled by John Fletcher and Martin Stanton* (London: Institute of Contemporary Arts, 1992), 217–27, reprinted in Jean Laplanche, *Essays on Otherness* (New York: Routledge, 1998). See also "Interpretation between Determinism and Hermeneutics: A Restatement of the Problem," in *International Journal of Psychoanalysis* 73 (1992): 429–45.

9. Sigmund Freud, *The Interpretation of Dreams*, in *The Standard Edition of the Complete Psychological Works of Sigmund Freud*, trans. under the general editorship of James Strachey in collaboration with Anna Freud, assisted by Alix Strachey and Jan Tyson, 24 vols. (London: Hogarth, 1953–1974) [hereinafter cited as *SE*], 5:4–5.

10. Jean Laplanche, "Traumatisme, traduction, transfert et autres trans(es)," in *La révolution copernicienne inachevée: trauvaux, 1967–1992* (Paris: Aubier, 1992), esp. 257ff.

11. Ibid., 258.

12. See, for example, Jean Laplanche, "The Theory of Seduction and the Problem of the Other," in *International Journal of Psychoanalysis* 78 (1997): 655–66. See also his "Seduction, Persecution, and Revelation" in *International Journal of Psycho-Analysis* 76 (1995): 663–82.

13. Jean Laplanche, "The Unfinished Copernican Revolution," in *Essays on Otherness*.

14. Jean Laplanche, *New Foundations for Psychoanalysis*, trans. David Macey (New York: Blackwell, 1989).

15. Sigmund Freud, *Beyond the Pleasure Principle*, *SE* 18.

16. Jean Laplanche, *Problématiques I: l'angoisse* (Paris: Presses Universitaires de France, 1980), 218.

17. Sigmund Freud, "On Narcissism," *SE* 14.

18. As an extreme illustration, see the movie *Crash*, directed by David Cronenberg [Jean Laplanche's note].

19. Sigmund Freud, *Three Essays on the Theory of Sexuality*, *SE* 6.

20. Sigmund Freud, "Leonardo de Vinci and a Memory of His Childhood," *SE* 11.

21. Laplanche, *Seduction, Translation, Drives*, 221–22.

22. Jean Laplanche, "Implantation, intromission," in *La révolution copernicienne inachevée*, 355–58, reprinted in *Essays on Otherness*.

23. Laplanche, *Life and Death in Psychoanalysis*, 6.

24. Freud, *The Origins of Psychoanalysis*, Letter 52, pp. 173ff.

25. Jean Laplanche, "Psychoanalysis as Anti-Hermeneutics," *Radical Philosophy* 79 (1996): 7–12. See also "Temporality and Translation: For a Return to the Question of the Philosophy of Time," *Stanford Literature Review* 6.2 (1989): 241–59.

26. Laplanche, *Seduction, Translation, Drives*, 75.

27. Laplanche, *La révolution copernicienne inachevée*.

Dori Laub at his home in Woodbury, Connecticut, June 15, 2013.

Chapter Three

A Record That Has Yet to Be Made
An Interview with Dori Laub

Dori Laub is a psychoanalyst in private practice in New Haven, Connecticut, and a leading figure in the clinical treatment of trauma survivors, in particular survivors of the Holocaust. His foundational writing, with Shoshana Felman, on Holocaust testimony and his own important essays on the art of listening to testimony have had wide influence on the clinical and theoretical work in the field. He is, himself, a child survivor and a founder of the Fortunoff Video Archive for Holocaust Testimony at Yale, the first Holocaust video archive in the United States. I met with him in his home on June 15–16, 2013, to discuss the notions of testimony, historical erasure, and witness as they emerge in his clinical and theoretical work and as they arose from his own experience during the Holocaust.

Part One. June 15, 2013

I. The Imperative to Tell

CC: I would like to begin by discussing the implications of your notion of bearing witness for the theory and treatment of trauma. Your written and institutional work, as well as your clinical work, have focused on the specific notion of bearing witness to trauma or testimony, which you developed at length in your book with Shoshana Felman, *Testimony: Crises of Witnessing in Literature, Psychoanalysis, and*

History.[1] Here, you speak of "the imperative to tell" that is crucial to the experience of many survivors:

> Survivors did not only need to survive so that they could tell their story, they also needed to tell their story in order to survive. There is in each survivor an imperative need to tell, and thus to come to know one's story, unimpeded by ghosts from the past, against which one has to protect oneself. (78)

What do you mean by an "imperative" to witness trauma, and specifically Holocaust trauma?

DL: In a way the pressure to testify is like an instinct. There's an urgency to deal with the experience, to shape it, to make it happen, and it's like something is born. And survivors definitely have the pressure to do so. They need appropriate circumstances—a totally present listener who creates the holding space for them to do it. But once they find it, they really allow it to come. And it comes out with a force. They don't want to stop. And sometimes even when you try to let them know that you have to keep to a timetable, they disregard you until you say it several times. There is a force to have it happen.

Maybe one can use the metaphor of the wound. The wound also has a healing process. And there are things that begin to happen when the wound heals—and it wants to heal. "Trauma" is actually the word for "wound" in ancient Greek, so testimony is the healing of the wound by shaping and giving shape to an experience that's fragmented, a healing way of pulling fragments together.

But to get it out in the interpersonal space there has to be a companion. Basically I think it's also the necessity for an internal companion, because the process of symbolization and the formation of narrative only happens within an internal dialogue. And a listener temporarily takes the place of that internal other, that addressee.

CC: So the dialogue is crucial, and having an external addressee who helps the internal addressee to be created?

DL: If you allow the appropriate conditions of sterility and temperature, the wound heals. But you have to create the conditions in which it can heal.

CC: Is this problem of having the adequate conditions—the internal and external addressees—why you also say that the imperative to witness is haunted by its "impossibility"? In *Testimony* you write:

> The imperative to tell the story of the Holocaust is inhabited by the impossibility of telling, and therefore silence about the truth commonly prevails.

Many survivors interviewed by the Yale Video Archive have only begun the process of witnessing now, forty years after the event. Some have hardly spoken of it, but those who have feel that they managed to say very little that was heard. (79)

It seems, from what you have just said, that the "impossibility" of witnessing is bound up with the complex relation of internal and external listeners, and the difficulty of setting up these conditions of listening after the Holocaust.

DL: As long as the memory is inside, it is in fragments, in intense affects, and they need the proper conditions in which they can come together. Not all the way, necessarily, but the story begins to be told. It's not tell-able in vivo, without this additional circumstance of an adequate listener.

CC: So the notion of bearing witness does not simply involve telling a story that already exists, but producing a story in the process of addressing it to a listener, so that the internal addressee can come to be created and to hear it as well. Why would one need to create an internal addressee?

DL: There has to be a certain amount of ego structure, a certain amount of object relationship, a certain connectedness, and appropriate others in order to speak. In the patients we interviewed in Israel, the hospitalized patients,[2] who were designated as psychotic, there was less of an ego structure, and they were much more frightened of what was coming up. They were extraordinarily motivated, they had this urge, and they would wait in line to be able to testify and then find themselves at a great loss because they couldn't shape it. It was very clear that, as interviewers, we had to be much more present and much more active in literally forming the story for them that we intuitively grasped, putting it together, and presenting it to them. And then they would either vehemently agree or disagree. But that's how they participated in the telling of their story and the creating of their narrative. These hospitalized survivors are an extreme case of what I was describing before—the need to have a listener from outside to help create an internal audience.

CC: The story was thus literally impossible to tell, for these particular survivors, because they did not have the adequate internal conditions, and there was no one to serve as a listener who could help them produce the internal listener. Do you think this is one reason they became psychotic?

DL: Yes. They were not told by outsiders, by friends, by relatives, by society, to come forward. And they were not assisted in beginning that process of transmitting, and then they atrophied. And the ego strength and the ability to verbalize and to symbolize atrophied—when it's not in use it goes through atrophy. And so they eventually became mute.

I want to emphasize here that there are two kinds of listeners: first, internal listeners, and internal forces that give shape. And second, there's the external listener, who is a necessity because very few people are able to maintain the dialogue with themselves without an outsider.

CC: The hospitalized survivors would reveal, then, the importance of the external listener when the internal listener is lacking or not fully developed. But you suggest that even with adequate ego strength, the listener is still important in helping for the testimony to be realized. Can you explain the roles listeners have (or haven't) played in more ordinary cases of Holocaust testimony?

DL: I would like to respond with two examples, which illustrate, on the one hand, how productive an appropriate listener can be to allow the imperative to witness to be realized, and on the other hand, how destructive it is when the imperative to tell is not met by a responsive audience. The first example is of one of the survivors interviewed in 1946 by [David P.] Boder, an American Jewish psychogist from Indiana Technical Institute—Avraham Kimmelman.[3] I remember listening to his taped testimony, and already in 1946 he was able to give a full narrative. He had maintained the internal other in the dialogue, and could give details and could give reflections. He's perhaps the example par excellence of the urge to testify—giving such a complete, developed, and multilayered testimony already in 1946. Which means he kept an internal process going all the time.

On the other hand, as [Annette] Wieviorka writes, there were testimonies being written during the Holocaust itself—she calls it "the writing from beyond the grave."[4] These were the large ghetto chronicles, as in the Warsaw ghetto.[5] The Jews attempted their utmost to leave traces, not to be erased. This self-observation was a way of being, and of resisting, and of trying to survive; not to be completely erased. And those documents were found, but only many years later. So during as well as after the Holocaust there were instances—as in the case of Kimmelman—in which people talked, but no one listened. There needs to be both an inside and an outside listener for testimony to take place.

CC: Given that people were trying to prevent themselves from being erased by documenting their experiences, we would have to interpret your phrase "the impossibility of witnessing" as referring to an impossibility of hearing. That people didn't see or hear what was there. In other words, there were stories, but there was no one to give them to, and in that sense they were waiting to be heard.

DL: It's a story that fell apart because there was no one inside or outside to listen to it.[6] And you know, there is this myth that survivors didn't want to speak. Now in the years after the war, 1946, '47, '48, there were about twenty thousand testimonies that were given, mostly in writing, that can be found in Yad Vashem and the Warsaw Historical Institute, including the one that was tape-recorded by David Boder. They were given, but they remained on shelves. There was no means of transmittal. And by 1950 there were a lot fewer testimonies. They were not being heard.

CC: So then they stopped being told as well?

DL: In general, the testimonies stopped being told (with some exceptions such as the Eichmann trial, of course, and cases where survivors had to give evidence), and they stopped being whole narratives, continuous narratives.[7]

CC: So aside from some formal, institutional witness, the giving of true testimony was not occurring. Can you explain what you mean by that fragmentation of narratives?

DL: Because they were not communicated, they were not transmitted into a holding space, they remained fragmented and eventually were transformed into nightmares and into symptoms. The Germans called it *Brückesymptome*, bridge symptoms. For about a decade or so, people were asymptomatic. Only after that they became symptomatic.

CC: So what we would now call "post-traumatic" symptoms really were delayed in that case.

DL: I think the energy was put into rebuilding. And in denying what happened. The yearning was to be the *sabra*, the Israeli soldier, the one who fights back, not to accept that "other" part of one's history. And so the emphasis was on having families and bearing children. With no attention to emotions. All of the attention was given to rebuilding lives, as if when you rebuild lives, nothing else will be there. But it wasn't so.

CC: When you said that there was no holding space for the testimonies, were you suggesting that when they weren't heard, they not only disappeared from collective sight but also disappeared, or became fragmented, internally?

DL: We've had this experience repeatedly, that when survivors finish their testimony they say, "I didn't know I could say all that," or "I didn't know I remembered all that." So it's as if they didn't know that there was a story or what the story was, or how detailed or how in depth the story went. And I think that if there were research, one would see how the nature of the testimonies have changed over the decades. For example, when I compare the Boder testimonies in 1946 to our testimonies in the [Fortunoff] Video Archive, I notice that there was almost an uncertainty in the Boder testimonies. "My daughters were taken to Auschwitz in 1942"—this was 1946—"and they haven't come back. Perhaps they are dead." Although the facts were known, people didn't quite know that their children were dead.

CC: So people would know and not know—they would know the facts and yet not know the facts.

DL: That's right. And also there was a quality in the early testimonies of trying to alert people. The assumption was, and it was a correct assumption, that the interviewer doesn't know, or that the world doesn't know. It was like they were asking for intervention and rescue. So in those early phases of memory storage or testimony storage, all kinds of processes were going on.

II. The Collapse of Witness

CC: I think this sheds light on your frequently misunderstood statement from *Testimony*, that "the collapse of witnessing is precisely what is central . . . to the Holocaust experience" (80). There are those who have criticized your statement as a claim that the Holocaust was a kind of absolute mystery or was "not known" in some literal way by those who were there. Yet your ideas concerning the necessity, in testimony, for a relation between internal and external forms of witness suggest that you are attempting to communicate, in your notion of the collapse of witness, the ways in which an event that was seen and experienced may still resist psychic assimilation as a real and meaningful event.

DL: The loss of the internal other is often central to this collapse. You know that survivors often, to this day, have a disbelief of what they survived. "I can't believe I lived through that." And I see a version of this in myself as well. You mention criticism of my work, and this problem of believing in one's own experience is relevant to my responses to some of that criticism. Take, for example, the article by [Thomas] Trezise that attacked my discussion in *Testimony* about an Auschwitz survivor who witnessed the uprising and the blowing-up of the chimneys in Auschwitz. Trezise claimed that I had listened to her testimony selectively and mischaracterized it.[8] My first thought was to doubt myself and to think, "maybe he's right, maybe I omitted something, maybe I didn't pick up on something." Although I was quite certain that I had heard things right.

CC: So your doubt was like the doubt of survivors who don't believe their own experiences? Why did that happen?

DL: Because as a Jew in Romania, I had faced in my life, during the war, another tyrannical force that was fundamentalist and that believed that only it knew what it was all about. Not a dialogic force. Not a dialogic presence.

CC: Can you explain what you mean when you refer to that tyrannical force that actually makes you lose your capacity to believe in yourself?

DL: The perpetrator was a totalitarian fundamentalist; he had absolutely no doubt in the righteousness of his acts and his ideology and his feelings. And there was no shade of gray there. There was a complete absence of empathy, or of a sense of alternative experiences. That was it. And in the presence of such an absoluteness, the "normal" person begins to have doubts because we are all ambivalent to some degree. And when you meet a fundamentalist who feels so absolutely certain, and he has the power, he must be right. It's the Patty Hearst phenomenon, the Stockholm syndrome.[9]

CC: Is that what you mean when you say, in your book and other writings, that in the Holocaust there was no dialogue, no one to say "thou" to, and no one who would treat you as a "thou"?

DL: Yes. And I think that's where the Jewish resistance turned into the attempt to witness—to document. That was the resistance. There was no resistance possible with arms. So they resisted by verifying what they experienced, documenting what they experienced. To make sure that there is another story that is there and will last.

CC: In this context I'd like return to your statement in *Testimony* that the Holocaust "had no witness, either from inside or outside the event" (81). Could you elaborate on that in a concrete way?

DL: The easiest way to answer that is to approach it quantitatively. Because what was documented, even later on, in the Fortunoff Video Archive testimonies and in the testimonies of the Shoah Foundation,[10] is a small fraction of what really happened. In Belzec, for example—the place where six hundred thousand Jews were killed—two survived. One of them was murdered during a perpetrator trial in Poland in 1946.[11] The two were somehow able to flee, and then one was murdered. So who is there to describe it, to share it, or to be present to the events and transmit them? Nobody. [Jan] Karski is the only one that describes infiltrating Belzec in the uniform of an Estonian guard.[12] Deborah Lipstadt, whom I spoke to a few months ago, said that it's not even clear that this was Belzec. There are doubts now. So where's the record of 600,000 people killed?

And this brings us to the qualitative question: can you really keep the memory of getting out of a grave of corpses? Can you keep such a memory intact? Can you make it be a conscious part of your memory network? And I think that there are certain things that a human being is overwhelmed by, trying to keep them conscious, trying to integrate them. So in that sense, it's an event without a witness.

CC: You've also written, with reference to a phrase by the survivor Louis Micheels, about the Jews being the "bearers of the secret"—that there was a kind of pact of secrecy that the Nazis imposed on the Jews.[13] Which goes back, perhaps, to that tyrannical mode in which people were sometimes convinced that they deserved this fate. Can you explain more about what it means to have had this secret pact imposed on you, and to maintain the secrecy surrounding your own annihilation?

DL: I have met families in the United States who keep their Jewishness secret or covert to this day. And they keep secret that they converted to Christianity during the Nazi era because the Nazis are still around and will come back. So there is a certain reality that makes such an imprint that one never gets out of it. I think it's addressed metaphorically by the anecdote that Simon Wiesenthal or Elie Wiesel tells, in which a German SS officer says to a Jew, "Do you think you will be able to tell people after the war what happened? Nobody will believe that such a thing is possible. They will think you're crazy." So that is also, I think, taken on from inside, that this is not believable. "Maybe even I don't believe it—it must have been a nightmare, a bad dream. And if it was, then they're definitely right, because they're so certain."

I think there's a kind of psychotic quality in the way the Germans conducted the whole extermination. I remember Gardelegen—a little town near Hannover —where there were a number of prisoners from death marches encamped. And the German police, and the firefighters, exterminated them on the morning of April 15, 1944; fifteen hundred of those inmates. In the evening, they surrendered to the Americans. Who in his right mind would do that?! And what is that? It is the sense of omnipotence, part of the dictatorial mind.

CC: You know, growing up I had very little relation to my Jewish past, which was on my mother's side. But once when I was maybe about thirteen, my mother and I went together to the mall in Century City [Los Angeles] to go shopping. And an Orthodox Jew came up to me with Hanukkah candles. And because Jews don't proselytize, he first said, as they all do, "Are you Jewish?" And if you said, "Yes," they gave you the Hanukkah candles. And I said, "Yes." And he gave me some Hanukkah candles, and he left. And my mother came up to me and said, "You never, ever tell someone that." She was furious. And I said, "But he was Jewish. He was giving us Hanukkah candles, that's all. It wasn't anything else." She said, "You don't know about this person, you don't tell a stranger." I've never understood that story; I never asked her why. But I have since wondered if there was something there that perhaps reached back, beyond our personal history. That would perhaps be another version of carrying on a secret.

DL: Yes, that is what I am speaking about.

III. Testimony and History

CC: One aspect of what you are saying, which I think is very important, is that while the Holocaust is a historical event—an event that includes empirical facts like the gas chambers and the various details of annihilation—the Holocaust is also, as both a personal and a collective trauma, more than these facts. This is because the specificity of this event is, in part, constituted by these various kinds of "collapse of witnessing" that we have been talking about.

Thinking about this question, years ago, I asked you, during lunch at a trauma conference at which we were both speaking, what it means to try to bear witness to an event of this kind and, specifically, what survivor testimony can give us beyond what we receive from traditional forms of historiography. You replied,

> Imagine the selection ramp at Auschwitz. Imagine the many box cars or trains lined up there and thousands of people unloaded from them onto the ramp. Now think about the selection process taking place to divide all these thousands of people into those who would be killed and those who would be sent into the camp. How long do you think that process took?

I said I couldn't answer. You pressed me, and said, "Just take a guess." And I imagined the line of boxcars and thought about it and finally said, "Several hours?" And you said, "Twenty minutes." I was stunned. "This," you said, "is what testimony can tell us. You can't see that from looking at pictures."

I have never forgotten that moment. Can you tell me more about what you were trying to convey in this exchange?

DL: In our everyday imagination, as well as in history books, the speed and the pressure of that experience were not adequately given a voice. In still pictures, everyone looks like he or she is waiting. But the element of speed and of terror is a very major element in that experience—that within twenty minutes you never will see your father again, or your children again. And so it's eternal; there's no return. In twenty minutes it's all gone, and then you have a lifetime after that to deal with those twenty minutes of rushing.

This is one element. You may also notice that the film footage we have is in black and white. And what is more striking is that there is no sound. Everybody was screaming. So where are the screams? The technology to record on photographic film already existed at the time, but the screaming was not recorded. Neither were they written down. There is a whole quality of the experience that historical research usually doesn't inquire into and historical facts don't necessarily give.

Another thing as well: I remember when Geoffrey [Hartman][14] and a group of us went up to Canada, I think in the early '80s, to McGill University in Montreal to start a branch of the video archive there. And they had a little museum of photographs from the camp. The curator said to us, "One photograph here is taken by a Jew. Jews ordinarily didn't have cameras. Can you find it?" And I pointed to that one photograph. It was two women kissing each other through a chain-link fence. Through a chain link fence. A German would not have taken this photograph. So the record that remains are the German photographs.

CC: How do you understand that?

DL: They were not going to photograph Jews that had feelings other than either terror or misery.

CC: Because that's love and that's life and that's survival. And a bond. So the documents that we have from the Nazis actually not only show but also enact what you have described as the refusal of the Jew as an addressee: they cut the bond. They're not about a relation. Whereas this photograph was a witness because the content was about a relation, kissing, and also the act of taking the photograph was a relational act.

DL: Yes.

CC: And so that's true testimony. It also occurs to me that the example that you gave me so many years ago, about the ramp at Auschwitz, was effective because it demonstrated to me, pedagogically, how we often expect a narrative of events, like the arrival at Auschwitz, to go a certain way—in this case, you wait for hours and hours and then terrible things happen. But when you suddenly said to me, "twenty minutes," all of my expectations—narrative, conceptual, experiential— were shattered. And that is one reason why the story—or the testimony—stayed with me.

DL: We all have screen memories.[15] Through these screen memories we create narratives and images that we can live with. One of the authors I quote said that the first task of the psychoanalyst is to dismantle the screen memories, to take away the defensive, calming narrative we have created and to leave the field open so that truth can come in.[16] We are open to hearing.

For example, I think of survivors I have interviewed who have drifted into what they saw in a movie, what they read in a book—historical facts. Stories that other people told. And one of the tasks of the interviewer is to encourage them not to talk about this kind of history. Because we can all read historical books. So it's what you have seen through your own eyes; that's where the surprise comes in.

CC: So the testimony is a kind of breaking of paradigms, which may have come from historiographical texts, and don't capture what is completely surprising. It reminds me of Claude Lanzmann saying that in many years of preparing to film *Shoah* he had read all the books he could find on the Holocaust, but the first time he spoke to a survivor, he realized he knew nothing.

DL: This can happen on a quantitative level too. There is a book recently written by a Yale historian, Timothy Snyder, and it's entitled *Bloodlands*,[17] and it covers the Soviet and Nazi genocides. He comes up with many findings that we didn't know before about certain geographies playing a repeated historical role. That one decade Ukrainians were murdered there, and the next decade Jews were murdered in the same place. These kind of observations were not known.

IV. IMAGINING TESTIMONY

CC: I was struck by something you wrote about the nature of listening to testimony. You say that the listener to testimony is listening to "a record that has yet to be made."[18] And you speak about the listener having to be in the place of the survivor's trauma, "waiting for her there." Can you explain what you mean by that?

DL: The *Gestalt* [shape] of the testimony isn't simply there [prior to the listening], in the form of a record. I compare this act of listening to the work of a midwife. The listener to testimony is in a way like a midwife. He imagines the baby coming.

CC: But you don't know what's going to come out, right?

DL: You don't know; sometimes you do not know, but you imagine, you create a place in the imagination. That's what I mean by being ahead of the survivors. You create a place in the imagination for the trauma.

CC: So are you saying that, as a listener, you make possible the testimony by imagining it taking place? Does your imagination, then, make that place that isn't yet there?

DL: Yes.

CC: It sounds like what the listener is doing is, in part, an imaginative act in relation to the *possibility* of the testimony. Are there clues from early on in the interview about what you're going to pick up?

DL: It's analytic work. There are associations—now I think this is going to come up, and frequently it does come. You know, when I watched the testimonies again in order to write my response to Trezise, I saw what was happening on the tape, and I said to myself, "Oh, I have to say this and this." And then the next half minute, on the tape, I say it. It's over thirty years later. Thirty-eight years. And I wasn't remembering. I imagined it again. I imagined again what she will say or what I will say, particularly my intervention, my response, and then I hear myself on the screen saying that.

In our conversation prior to this interview, you indicated that you might ask me why I worked with a scholar in literature [Shoshana Felman].[19] You know, a historian is more attentive to the facts and to the written document, or even the written testimony by the Germans—which is valid, though it is not survivors' testimony. The psychoanalyst is more attentive to the internal reality and has a difficult time with the external reality. With the literary scholar, it's imagination. It's not limited to reality. It continues a back-and-forth flow between reality and imagination.

CC: So what you're saying is that the moment of imagining what will come is literary. It's not saying, "I know what happened," because that would be the historian, and it's not saying, "This is your internal fantasy of what happened," which would be the psychoanalyst. It's saying, "There is something we don't know, but it could have a reality, and I'm going to help you articulate it." In other words, it's the imagination of what is not known yet. Would that be the literary element of being a listener?

DL: Yes, that would be the literary element of being a listener, of imagining what is to be transmitted. What I'm saying is that in order to transmit the testimony, it needs a process with an imaginative midwife who's there ahead of time, ready to receive. And in the process of transmission, it becomes a witnessed story, and it becomes a narrative.

CC: So essentially, what you are doing is not only finding people to witness but creating the conditions for, or helping people to learn to be, witnesses, which is something that is not a given.

DL: Yes. But there still remain islands that are not quite representable. Or transmittable.

CC: What do you mean?

DL: Just think of Belzec and the 600,000 people who perished and nobody knows. Or creeping out of a pile of corpses.

CC: Or inside the gas chambers.

DL: Or inside the gas chambers.

V. The Death Drive

CC: I would like to turn now to what seems to me a somewhat newer phase of your writing, which you developed after your work in *Testimony*. It seems to me that you have pushed further the notion of the "collapse of witness" in your essay,

"Thanatos and Massive Psychic Trauma," which speaks of the "release of Death Drive derivatives in cases of extreme trauma." You write,

> Not knowing trauma or experiencing or remembering it in a dissociative way is not a passive shutdown of perception or of memory. Not knowing is rather an active, persistent, violent refusal; an erasure, a destructive of form and of representation. The fundamental essence of the death instinct, the instinct that destroys all psychic structure is apparent in this phenomenon.[20]

What does it mean to think about psychic trauma as an active erasure?

DL: Here I have to become a bit more abstract. Freud said that we never observe the death drive directly, only indirectly.[21] So when you experience or witness the presence of so much oblivion of something that cannot be easily remembered (something that for example, Avraham Kimmelman could remember), what is at play here? You said to me a moment ago, "It occurred to me later that my mother may have hidden the fact that we were Jews." What was at work until then, when it occurred to you? What force? And that force takes away, or diminishes, what is grasped and sort of hacks away a part. And it's quite forceful and can result in complete amnesia.

So I feel it is a manifestation of something psychological. And this is the formulation of the derivatives of the death instinct—you don't see the death instinct directly but the derivatives are at play. And because of the diminishing libidinal forces, the ties, the contacts, the embraces, which are weakened—including in yourself, with yourself—the death instincts are no longer neutralized, are no longer bound.

CC: So when the relation to an other that constitutes witness is broken—such as in a genocide where you are obliterated as an addressee—then the lack of witness is passed along, both internally and externally, and thus proliferates?

DL: It proliferates at the moment that the death instinct derivatives are no longer neutralized by libidinal forces. There are fewer of them, there are fewer objects, so they roam.

CC: As you know, Freud had a theory of trauma in the late-nineteenth century, but he didn't formulate the notion of the death drive until after World War I, in *Beyond the Pleasure Principle*. Would you say, then, that this psychological force is also historical?

DL: It's also a historical force, absolutely.

CC: Freud also called it a "drive" and linked it to something fundamental in the organism. How would you understand that?

DL: It's a drive released by the organism in the twentieth century, which re-moved libidinal constraints en masse on a huge scale and brought it more to the fore. Think of Rwanda.[22] Every ten seconds someone was being murdered. And nobody knew. And the US president didn't know. There were still three, four thousand soldiers with [General] Roméo Dallaire in Rwanda, and he withdrew them to the periphery of Kigali. He could have stopped everything. But nobody knew. And Kofi Anan years later goes to Rwanda where the murder took place and castigates them for their behavior. He never knew. And he was in charge of the international rescue, of the UN interventive military forces. And he gave the order to Dallaire not to raid the machete caches several months before the kill-ing started. So, how can intelligent people, knowledgeable people—how can you understand this level of oblivion?

CC: One way I came to understand this on a very personal and concrete level happened at that conference at Cornell University years ago at which we were both speaking. I had prepared a lecture from notes about the latest developments in trauma research and also about Freud, including some comments on the death drive. I gave the lecture very passionately and articulated what was not written down. And you came up to me afterward and said, "I certainly hope that was recorded." And I looked down at the tape recorder, which I was supposed to have turned on before I spoke, and realized I hadn't pressed the "record" button, and I blurted out, "I forgot to turn on the recorder." And you said to me, "That's the death drive."

It's a personal and small example, but it struck me, and I would like you to explain what you meant, and its more general application.

DL: The death drive is against knowing and against the developing of knowledge and elaborating, of capturing those free associations that are finally spelled out. And now they're lost again, and they're drawn into oblivion. What part in you, what agency in you was it a derivative of?

To speak more broadly, it's the whole Armenian genocide, which is not yet talked about, and in Turkey it never existed. And also Cambodia. A young Cam-bodian woman at Yale tried to create a Cambodian video testimony archive; all she managed to gather were a few hundred testimonies over two decades and not the 15,000 she originally planned to assemble. It didn't succeed. And Yale is a major international center for the study of the Cambodian genocide in the world.

CC: So it occurs even in institutions focused on trauma and, as in my case, in somebody who is theoretically involved with trauma.

DL: You're never just theoretically involved with trauma.

VI. Psychoanalysis and Not-Knowing

CC: Are there other ways in which you've noticed, either in the articulation of the theory or in psychiatry or in psychoanalysis, that simultaneous recording and erasing taking place?

DL: Let me give you one example. In the last ten years or so, there's increasing evidence that a number of SMI—severely mentally ill—patients over ninety years old have had a serious traumatic experience.[23] The current psychiatric literature pays no attention to that. No consequences; it's not included in any diagnostic criteria—nothing.

CC: Indeed Judith Herman, among others, has noted that so-called borderline personality disorder may in fact be a misdiagnosis of long-term or chronic traumatization.

You also note about psychoanalysts specifically, in "Traumatic Shutdown and Narrative Symbolization," that "the totality of the empathic shut-down, the absolute quality of the blindness of professionals attuned to the subtlest of hints, points, in my opinion, at forces more powerful and deeper than defensive ego operations."[24] Here you also speak about the way in which this death drive derivative can occur in analysts (including yourself) by simply not being curious, by becoming suddenly indifferent about certain issues that might lead to traumatic events if the clues were followed up. And yet psychoanalysis is also presumably one place where this testimony *can* happen, if people listen.

DL: In that essay I mentioned my first patient, who kept screaming on the couch. The patient's father had been absent for years starting in 1942, but the analysis focused on her envy of her brother born after World War II. And nobody—not I, not my supervisor—asked the question, "Where was your father between 1942 or '43 and 1945?" He disappears, is presumed dead, and he comes back from Japan with a Congressional Silver Star. And my supervisor was Hans Loewald, a very prominent psychoanalyst who was highly respected for his creativity and his originality.[25] And Hans Loewald was a refugee. A refugee from Germany first of all. Eventually, Hans Loewald would gave me his own testimony [for the Fortunoff Archive].

CC: But with this patient, he didn't know, he didn't encourage you. You were listening to this patient, and he didn't say, "Ask the question . . ."

DL: . . . where her father was. We all focused on the envy of the brother.

CC: So you were still caught up in some of the amnesia yourself.

DL: It was before the Yom Kippur War, when Egypt and Syria carried out a surprise attack on Israel in October 1973. That's where I saw children of survivors being the most severe casualties on the battlefield. And I was able to speak to, to listen to them for days, and I realized how their battlefield experiences resonated with their families not speaking about the Holocaust.

CC: I see. So after that you looked back at this early analytic situation where you didn't ask questions. You learned from it, and you became a theorist of testimony, and then you turned to the supervisor you had had, and you helped him give his testimony as well.

We will come back to your experience of war, but I would like to ask you, while we are discussing this general topic, about the institution of psychoanalysis as you have experienced it. Although your own work derives in many ways from Freud, the institution of psychoanalysis seems, over much of the twentieth century—and perhaps to a certain extent today, though with some major exceptions—to be one place where no one is thinking about trauma very much. What has been your experience?

DL: I was invited to present my work with testimony to the Western New England Institute [for Psychoanalysis] only in November 2012.

CC: That was the first time they asked you to talk about your work?

DL: Yes. I've talked in many places in the US and in Europe. Mostly universities outside the country. And in many audiences there were hardly any analysts.

CC: Would you say that the struggle Freud described in *Beyond the Pleasure Principle*, between Eros and Thanatos—the life drives and the death drive—takes place, then, in the psychoanalytic institution as well, when it comes to massive psychic trauma?

DL: Absolutely. There is a social worker analyst [at the] William Alanson White [Institute], Emily Kurrilof, who is writing now about European analysts' impact on psychoanalytic theory and the fear of being refugees.[26] She has chapters including interviews with Martin [S.] Bergmann[27] and many other people, including me. And Martin Bergmann said it had no effect on him.

This is a book on the impact that American Jewish refugees had on psychoanalytic theory, and she interviews many who say that being a refugee had absolutely no impact. The only analyst who wrote about it was Heinz Kohut. He wrote about it; he wrote about the Nazi personality.[28]

CC: So that is an example of the operation, in psychoanalysis, of a force of not-knowing.

DL: If you speak to psychoanalytic leaders, they would say absolutely not. They all insist that being refugees had absolutely no impact on them or how they built their theories.

I was invited to speak in many places, but not in many psychoanalytic institutes. Philadelphia invited me, and it was a wonderful experience. In the Stockholm psychoanalytic Institute, many in the audience walked out in the middle. Not so in Israel, in recent years. But generally you're a bit of an outsider if you do that.

Part Two: June 16, 2013

I. A Child Witness

CC: Yesterday we were speaking about your theoretical, institutional and psychoanalytic work with survivor testimony. But you are also a survivor yourself. How did the process of witnessing begin in your life?

DL: To answer that I must begin very early, as these memories continue to return to me. I continually experience something, reflect on it, and keep it as a memory—and that memory was something that was very important in my growing up. I have sometimes wondered, who was the person who experienced and remembered that from my childhood? I was a child of five, and I witnessed somebody getting a public beating.

CC: At five. And you remember that.

DL: I remember it very distinctly, and I remember that I wanted to know what the person thought. And I approached him—everybody had had to watch the beating—and I came close to him, and he was smoking a cigarette. I remember that. There were about twenty-five lashes on his back. I could see the signs of the lashes on his back, and I didn't dare to ask him, but I was very curious. Now I wonder to myself, who was this little boy who had this interest to know that man? It wasn't a child of five; it was somebody else who was present.

CC: Was that always in your mind as an adult, that memory, or did it only begin to come back at a certain moment?

DL: That was always in my mind. And there were other memories like that, memories from the deportation [to a labor camp in the Romanian-occupied Ukraine during the Nazi occupation], which I have remembered in that way very clearly. And I remember even before that: there was a photo taken, and I was in a new suit, and I had my hand in the pocket, and I knew it was in a studio, and I knew that this marked the end of an era, and it did. Because it was the beginning of wearing the yellow star. And I remember that moment of the photo being taken very clearly. It was like I was an adult already at the time.

CC: And you realized it was the end of an era because you were wearing a yellow star in the picture?

DL: The yellow star was not obligatory for children. And I insisted that I wanted to wear it (though I did not end up wearing it) because I wanted to show that I was a Jew and a proud Jew. So there were particular childhood memories that felt as if somebody else, much more grown up, experienced them. And I have wondered about it; how could I have been that grown up, that mature, to have these kinds of experiences and remember them as such? And these were not things that were later reworked, because at ten, when I was in grade school in Romania, I wrote out those memories, the memories of the persecution.

CC: At ten?

DL: At ten. And I put them up on the billboard of the school. Instead of a newspaper we put things there for everybody to read. And I wrote probably ten or fifteen pages, and I wrote it in sections. One week it was this part, and the next week it was another part. And I had quite a bit written down of my experiences.

CC: You were trying to bear witness already then.

DL: I think there were not many Jews in my class, so I doubt that the other students read it. But I had definitely already "published" it. And then when we left Romania for Israel, before we got to the border my mother tore it up because she was afraid that the Romanian controls at the border would be suspicious of such a written document. And maybe rightly so, because they did a thorough search. I had a red tie—I was a member of the "Pioneers," the communist scouts. And I remember clearly how the man who searched us took the tie away and said, "You won't need that."

CC: So your first act of public witness was literally destroyed—that record was destroyed. How did you feel?

DL: I always missed it. It was very hard because I may have written down memories that I no longer have. So I was quite upset about it, but I realized that it was a question of security.

CC: When you emigrated to Israel, did these memories and questions still remain with you?

DL: They remained, but in Israel there was no space for them. The major interest was to become a *sabra* [the new Israeli-born Jew] and to become like everybody Israeli. And I was in a school where we were the only two immigrant children in my class, also refugees, and the others were all born in Israel. So again we had no way of speaking between us. The other refugee child didn't want to speak about it—he had not been deported from Romania.

CC: So you were the only survivor in your school?

DL: I was the only real survivor in my class in grade school. And to my knowledge, I was the only survivor throughout high school, too, because there were mostly children born in Israel.

CC: What I've heard about grade school in Israel in those years was that children were taught how the Jews of the Holocaust went like lambs to the slaughter. Was that part of your education?

DL: There was a word, *sabon*, which was applied to a survivor, which meant "soap." It was a myth that the bodies of gassed Jews had been turned into soap by the Nazis, but the word was used anyway.

CC: So you were aware, then, that you couldn't speak to anybody because you were a victim. Did you talk to anybody about your experience?

DL: I don't think so. Everyone wanted to become Israeli, the new Jew. Sometimes the grown-ups would gather and sing. We were living for two years in tent huts because there were no houses. And then in the evenings there were songs from the old time.

CC: So you were in an environment where for years you were not able to speak. Did you and your mother discuss the past at all?

DL: I was very angry with my mother and hardly spoke to her for ten years. So there was literally silence there.

CC: Do you recall any period in Israel when you began to be aware of the importance of witnessing?

DL: I became aware of it when I first listened to the Eichmann trial.[29]

CC: You remember that?

DL: I was glued to the radio. There was no television in Israel at that time. And I remember the opening remarks of Gideon Hausner, who was the prosecutor. I followed it very closely. And on my way to medical school classes I passed near the courtroom, and I saw the people in line waiting to go in. And I always thought I would like to go in, but I never did.

CC: Was that the first public testimony that you recall of your kind of experience?

DL: Yes.

CC: And do you think that had an impact on your own feelings about the importance of testimony, or it was just an event that was important to you?

DL: It sort of confirmed something I already knew about my own memories from the camps. I realized that this is what people carried with them. They carried these memories, their reflections—there is something there. And I was very moved by the testimonies and experienced them as true. I realized that many people around me had a similar kind of internal residue, that they carried memories also. And if they spoke, this is what would happen—a story, a narrative would come out. Something very explicit, something intense, would come out. There were also novels that were published at the time by K-Zetnik.[30] But did I connect it to the work I would do in the future? Not necessarily.

CC: How did it feel to have others sharing openly what had just been these private memories before?

DL: You know, I think it was to some extent, but only to some extent, a turning point. I could see the whole country listening and reflecting about it and waiting for the next testimony. And also when Eichmann was convicted it was a very important moment. Everybody was really glued to it and followed it. And with the capture of Eichmann, something in history was being set right. Until then it was not, and now, something started moving. Not completely, but it was being rectified.

II. Psychoanalytic Beginnings

CC: After you completed your studies in medicine and psychology in Israel, you came to the US in 1966 and, after working in Boston, began your analytic training while doing a fellowship at Austen Riggs.[31] Was there a time when your own history, or your interest in testimony, began to emerge in your analytic work?

DL: It first emerged in my own analysis, which was required for becoming an analyst. My training analyst at Austen Riggs was Swedish. I remember a very important moment, which I have written about, when I was still, I suppose, in denial about my experience. I was telling him about sitting in the camp, on the bank of a river, looking out at the blue water and the green meadows, and arguing with a little girl who was also five. We were arguing whether or not you can eat grass. She claimed you can, and I claimed you cannot. My analyst interrupted me at that point, and said, "I interviewed women from Theresienstadt, which we liberated, and they claimed conditions were so good that they received breakfast in bed by SS officers."[32] And that was a sort of a shock. And after that I stopped talking about green meadows.

CC: So your story was a kind of illusory fantasy covering over the realities of the camp. But I wonder if there is any chance that the argument over eating grass was because you were, in fact, hungry?

DL: Hunger was an element. My parents force-fed me so that I would have calories and fat in case there was hunger. They didn't eat anything. My mother was barely walking—she was so thin, she had lost so much weight. But they didn't want me to go hungry. I remember the *kau-schluk* [*kauen und schlucken*], which meant "munch and swallow." They would put food in my mouth and say it.

CC: In your testimony for the video archive you also tell a striking story about how one day you and your parents were waiting in groups of thirty people about to be sent over to the other, German-occupied side of the River Bug, where people were exterminated. And your mother had found out about this, and she was prescient, and she followed a man who had managed to gather money to bribe the guards. And your father, who was at the head of such a group of thirty, was reluctant to leave. And she went off with you and said to him, "We're going." And finally he came after you. And your mother managed to force herself, your father, and you into a shed where people were hiding. And weren't you sick?

DL: I mentioned that I had to keep quiet in spite of having whooping cough.

CC: Do you remember trying to keep yourself quiet with the whooping cough? How did that feel?

DL: Very self-restrained, a pressure, like now when I have to persist, no matter what I have to persist. And I persist.

CC: So can you tell me more about the process of rediscovering or reconnecting with your past experience? Was it your work in your analysis that eventually brought you to the question of your own experience and of Holocaust testimony?

DL: I didn't think of that yet. With the help of my analyst's interpretations, I started thinking more about my own experience, my own life. But unfortunately my analyst left after a year. So I was in analysis with him for a year, a year and a half. When he left, I left too, for Yale, where I continued my training and found another analyst. I had five years of analysis in which absolutely nothing happened. And literally the man said nothing. I remember that in my last session with my Swedish analyst, it was springtime, and I had had a very clear memory of my father's death during the war. So essentially I was in mourning. And this "very traditional" analyst in New Haven didn't pick up that I was in mourning. Eventually I changed analysts to finish my training.

CC: It's striking that your first analysis was really another beginning of testimony for you, which again got interrupted. Once more you had an experience of your own testimony being cut off.

When did you, yourself, start to see survivors as an analyst? Were you previously just seeing ordinary neurotics?

DL: In 1969, when I was graduating and leaving Riggs, three months before the end of the year, the clinical director, Dr. Martin Cooperman, said, "I have a new patient for you." And I told him that I couldn't do much in three months. And he said, "Well, maybe he'll leave with you." And it turned out to be a man exactly my age who, during the second world war, was in flight and in hiding in southern

France, and eventually got out, in '43, to South America. This was his second hospitalization at Riggs. The first one was four or five months, and they talked about his homosexual conflicts and not much else. I read the notes of the first patient conference, and the only person who said something related to the patient's story was Erik Erikson.[33] It was Erikson who said that he thought this young boy was afraid of losing his mother. It was the only reference to what had actually been happening in his life. And I listened to this patient talking to me, and I wrote his life story in a way that he himself didn't know it.

CC: When you say "wrote it," when did you do that?

DL: I had to prepare it for the admission conference (every new patient was seen four to five times a week in order to obtain a full life history and psychological evaluations, and frequently family members were also seen; the findings were summarized and presented at a meeting of the clinical staff, where the psychodynamic diagnosis and treatment plan were discussed and decided on). You had five weeks to prepare it, and I wrote it out in detail. At the conference I presented the intake summary. I presented his evolution and experiences. And the staff—the analysts—asked me, "How do you know that much?" And I said I know it because I know it, and this is what happened. And the recommendation was divided. Otto Allan Will, who was director, and Sullivanian, said, "It is this man's second hospitalization, and this time it has to be done right, he has to stay here for a couple of years and go through a deep regression, and that will help him then come out of it"—that was the Sullivanian approach: a very deep regression.[34] And others on the staff said no, they thought the man had found an analyst who knows him, understands him, and he should leave with that analyst. And after the conference I met the patient, and I told him it was a divided opinion. And his answer was, "I can't put my life in the hands of somebody who is just a beginner, a green nut." I wished him the best. And two days later he said he was coming with me.

III. A Psychoanalyst Goes to War

CC: So this was your first survivor patient. Was this when you began to think about doing testimony?

DL: That began in 1973, when the Yom Kippur War happened. And I remember that I heard about it on Yom Kippur in the synagogue, but it was a holiday weekend—Columbus Day. I was learning to ride a bike and had a little transistor radio, and I listened and heard about what was happening in Israel. And Israel had setbacks, and things were really bad. So I decided to go.

CC: Go fight?

DL: Yes. I was at Yale, I was a full time faculty member at Yale, an assistant professor. And I bought a ticket on Monday, and a friend who was a travel agent brought the ticket to a parking garage where we met. The ticket was for Tuesday night, and Tuesday we drove down and then you couldn't get on a plane, ticket or no ticket. Too many people wanted to return.

Somehow, my then wife met somebody whom she knew as a child, so he got me on the plane. And, you know, approaching Israel there was the fear that we would be shot down, but we landed. And everything was completely empty. Everybody was on the front. I mean, nothing was happening. There were hardly any men that you could see. And people were listening to radios. It was like the end was coming.

I was still in the reserves, and I had my uniform still, my boots. I managed to get permission to enlist. I was an officer in the army, and that was it. No paperwork. And I was sent to a medical unit that received casualties from the Syrian front, which were lightly wounded. And also all the psychiatric casualties. And there was another American psychiatrist from Israel, Yehuda Nir.[35] We established a unit, and we had several psychologists, social workers, and nurses; we had a larger staff. And to everybody's surprise, there were hundreds of psychiatric casualties.

CC: Psychiatric causalities?

DL: Casualties from the front line. Because of the suddenness. People were taken from synagogues directly into tanks, and there was a complete absence of organic units. When they had five crew members, they sent a tank, or sent them to a tank in the north. It wasn't the unit these people belonged to and trained with. So they were strangers, and they are thrown into battle as complete strangers. The unit was very important for resilience, for feeling safer with each other. People decompensated, and it was a very brutal battle. Israel was losing—there were four hundred Syrian tanks; at some point there were only twenty Israeli tanks facing them. And I observed among the psychiatric casualties that children of survivors were the most severe and protracted casualties.

CC: And how did you know they were children of survivors?

DL: You know, when somebody came in with a depressive coma, didn't talk, didn't know what his name was, mumbled a few things, I would sit with him in a tent for hours to hear and piece together what he was saying. And from that I heard the battle story, and I heard the family story.

There was this young man who was a radio operator at a refueling station. The tanks drove by to get shells and supplies and go into battle. And he could listen to those tanks on the radio. And he heard messages like, "I knocked out nine tanks," "I could continue but I have no more ammunition," and then the voice went silent. So that resonated for him with how the Holocaust was talked about. People were there, then they were gone, and nothing else.

That's how he decompensated. The radio went silent, and he didn't know what happened after that. And he knew they were dead.

CC: So the man who decompensated was listening on the radio, and that triggered . . .

DL: His own awareness, or rather nonawareness, of something, not knowing what happened. And not knowing for sure that this man on the radio was dead, he was gone, it was over.

And another young man was completely disorganized; he was violent, and he was brought in because he kicked a Syrian POW, an officer, in the chin with his boot. And he started talking about being a military policeman and seeing a civilian car driving toward the front and he couldn't stop it. A few hours later he saw the car with two mangled bodies in it. And he started talking about growing up with his father, who was an Auschwitz survivor, who kept talking about the babies being thrown against the wall and smashed. So the battlefield violence resonated with a lot of other violence. And he was simply untreatable, and we had to transfer him to a closed in-patient unit.

CC: And that's also what you call intergenerational trauma. That is, they literally came together for these people . . .

DL: And that's when I made the decision that I wanted to work with survivors.

IV. The Beginning of an Archive

DL: That moment I made the decision. I came back to the US, and in 1974 I applied to a hundred foundations to interview and study Holocaust survivors.

CC: Did that also have any personal resonance for you in relation to your own past?

DL: I realized that there's a story there, there's a testimony there. There's something inside, like with the Eichmann trial: that's an experience of everyone, and it's much more widespread than I thought, and it has a very powerful impact on life. And I decided I wanted to begin studying this. And then the study didn't exist. I wrote a paper about those patients, in Israel, which I never published. About the patients I saw on the front.

CC: You weren't ready to bear witness yet.

DL: No. And then later on I sent out one hundred applications or more, and ninety-eight said no or didn't answer, one was willing to consider me, primarily because of Al Solnit's endorsement,[36] and the one positive answer that I received was from the DFG, the German equivalent of the NIMH [National Institutes of Mental Health]. They were willing to support it and told me come to Bonn to talk to them.

CC: What an irony.

DL: Yes. So in 1977 I stopped in Bonn, and I was told I should do it, but I had to have a German collaborator. So I met with a famous historian in Munich, and he looked at me, "You could be a German citizen. You speak the language. Why don't you do that?" And then I had a certain expression on my face, and he said, "I realize it's awkward."

I had read a book in 1973 by the German psychiatrist Paul Matussek called *Internment in Concentration Camps and Its Consequences*.[37] There were a lot of statistics and correlations, but the only conclusion that came out was that people who had good mothering had a better chance. But I thought he might be interested in my project, and he was willing to see me. After giving me a long lecture about why the project was unnecessary and impossible, he agreed to participate. Three months later he was invited to Yale to give a presentation at a study group in which a group of German refugees and I were invited to participate. Matussek was my house guest, and after a few glasses of wine that evening he starts telling me about his experiences in the German army on the eastern front. It was rather awkward, and I felt quite uneasy. The next morning, when a study group of seven to nine people gathered, Matussek addressed them in his broken English— even though every single one of them spoke fluent German. These were the children of refugee parents who came from Germany. And then Matussek started speaking about the Jewish incarceration. And Shmuel Erlich[38] says to him, "Herr Matussek, das ist Genozid [Mr. Matussek, this is genocide]." He said, "Ach, Ja."

CC: Even in 1977 this German was still referring to the genocide of the Jews as an incarceration.

DL: So I take him to the train station, and we made plans and everything was set, but three weeks later I receive a letter from him saying, "I'm sorry I must bow out, I cannot do this work." No other explanation.

CC: So once again, the testimony began and was cut off. How did the Fortunoff Video Archive [for Holocaust Testimony] finally get started, then?

DL: In the spring of 1979, a local video producer, Laurel Vlock, called me and wanted me to give a testimony for Yom HaShoah.[39] And I said, "Only if we take the testimony of many people, so we can make a film like *The Sorrow and the Pity*,"[40] a film that had impressed me. And she agreed. A couple of months later, I get a phone call from her, and she says, "I have a video crew for this evening, can you find survivors?" So I called Renee Hartman[41] and another friend, and I called the late Arthur Spiegel, the executive director of the Jewish Federation of Greater New Haven, and got two more names, so we had four people in the evening. And we arranged my office and brought the video crew, and we thought it would last about two, two and a half hours, there being only four people; little did we know it would continue to two in the morning. That's when I first heard what survivors can tell. And if you allow it, if you help it, an extraordinary narrative is forthcoming.

CC: So that is the first time that you personally began to see what you call the pressure to give testimony.

DL: Yes, that imperative to bear witness.

CC: When you heard them beginning to testify, what happened for you as, as a survivor? Did you begin also to want to participate in that telling process, or were you still just a listener?

DL: I was a listener. Once I tried to give my testimony, but I don't consider this a very major event, because with every testimony I heard, something in me also came up and resonated, and I knew how to ask the questions because I knew where it came from.

CC: So basically what you're saying is that over the years, the way you have truly given your testimony is by listening and by helping other people give their testimony. And perhaps that's why when you write, you tell some stories from your past, but perhaps the ones that you become most invested in—at least in your writing—are the stories of other people. And in a way, your story is coming out through their stories.

DL: Yes, my story comes out through theirs.

CC: And how did that evening become the video archive?

DL: We soon enough had a group, a lawyer joined us, and we turned to the survivor organization, the Verband, in New Haven, for our first funding, and they raised 2,500 dollars, which covered the cost of editing these four testimonies.

CC: That was the beginning, 2,500 dollars.

DL: The actual beginning was that evening; I paid six hundred dollars for that filming. And thus it began.

V. PSYCHOANALYSIS AND TESTIMONY

CC: In addition to establishing the video testimony archive, you were also beginning to do extensive work as a psychoanalyst with survivors. As far as I am aware, you are one of the first analysts to do so. I know Henry Krystal was seeing survivors, and there were others,[42] but you were undoubtedly one of the first psychoanalysts to listen to survivor stories in their own terms.

DL: In their own terms, at first face to face and eventually on the couch, once they were ready for that.

CC: I'd like to ask you a little about that. One of the things I understand from your work is that one needs to learn to listen to trauma survivors in their own terms and in their own frameworks. Presumably, psychoanalysis should do that with every patient. Yet often, at least during the period prior to the flourishing of trauma research in the 1990s (and perhaps still today), psychoanalysts have tried to translate the language of patients—especially trauma survivors—into predisposed psychoanalytic terms. In his interview with me, for example, Art Blank speaks of his difficulty finding an analyst who could recognize the importance of his Vietnam experience, and Jean-Max Gaudillière, in the interview that he and Francoise Davoine did for this book, spoke of his Lacanian analyst, who translated every association that Jean-Max had—to his patients' traumatic pasts, or to the war in Vietnam—into sexual terms.[43]

DL: This is especially the case with analysts who have difficulties with particular experiences and block them out, which was true about my second analyst—the one whom I saw for five years. Even [Hans] Loewald, as my supervisor, did not pick up, as I said above, on the significance of the absence of my patient's father for several years in Japan during the war. Analysts who have a blind spot in their own lives, in their own experience, will not necessarily ask the patient about something the patient doesn't speak about. They don't pick up on it.

CC: So that's when they turn to an assumed language or theory of psychoanalysis —when they're afraid of hearing something new that they don't want to hear? Something, then, that is and isn't new?

DL: That is and isn't new. That's different from what you're prepared for.

CC: So you were an analyst on the one hand and you began to be a video testimony interviewer on the other. Do you think those impacted each other, or did one impact the other more?

DL: I would say they impacted each other, but my being an analyst was crucial to listening to testimonies. So I could listen to layers, pick up cues, wait, be aware of timing, not ask certain questions. I could interact dynamically with a patient, knowing that there will be no opportunity to really analyze transference or countertransference, which is nonetheless present. That is not something I can do in one session. You know, being an analyst provides me with a map and with tools and *Wegweiser*, pointers, and an ability to read the map.

CC: And what did you focus on when you trained other listeners you tried to help learn some of those ways of listening?

DL: Ways of looking at things. And being a witness or an interviewer is strengthened by the belief that reality has an impact. There is a truth.

CC: This brings me to my final question. I would like to come back to the thought that as an analyst, and as a listener to the testimonies of other people, you have yourself, over all these years, finally borne witness. And I assume you continue to do so—that it's not a finished process, but that it continues. But it sounds like the process of giving testimony doesn't end with one episode. At least for you, it's not over—it's not that you give it just once. At least in your case, it sounds like it's an ongoing life project.

DL: I think that's true for others too. In 2005 I re-interviewed eight people whom I had interviewed between 1979 and 1980—twenty-five years later. This was for a slave labor project sponsored by a German foundation. And the eight survivors and I just picked up the thread where we had left off. And they felt they were very connected to me; they expected me to remember everything, though I didn't. Johanna [Bodenstaub] and I published a paper comparing these two sets of testimonies, and how they varied over time, and how our ways of listening were different from what they were in 1979.[44] The meeting was also a goodbye because we knew that we were not going do it again in our lifetime. Some have died since. But I think once testimony starts, maybe not in every situation, but generally it's a process that continues.

CC: It sounds like the testimony is also going to have to change. But it seems to me that this is part of the process of it being passed on. What you write, Dori—your testimony, as well as those to whom you listen—will continue into the future through the people who read you. The testimony's going to change, and be passed on, when I read you or other people read your work. It's a continuing process.

Is there something that, in particular, you would like to be transmitted through this particular form of testimony—this interview—about your life's work in psychoanalysis and video testimony?

DL: It's very important to emphasize that testimony is a way of doing psychoanalysis. It's not two different genres. There are differences. But there is a core that's the same.

CC: And what is that core?

DL: The core is that there is a truth and an aspiration to that truth. And an increasing approach to that truth. There are layers, there are screens, and a powerful therapeutic alliance. There is an urge to give testimony in psychoanalysis. In video testimonies it is stronger. But there is a real event, a real truth for both of them.

NOTES

1. Shoshana Felman and Dori Laub, *Testimony: Crises of Witnessing in Literature, Psychoanalysis and History* (New York: Routledge, 1991).
2. For a description of Dr. Laub's work with these patients, see "From Speechlessness to Narrative: The Cases of Holocaust Historians and of Psychiatrically Hospitalized Survivors," *Literature and Medicine* 24.2 (Fall 2005): 253–65.
3. The interview with Avraham Kimmelman may be found on the United States Holocaust Memorial Museum Web site at http://collections.ushmm.org/search/catalog/irn518056.
4. See Annette Wieviorka, *The Era of the Witness*, trans. Jared Stark (Ithaca, NY: Cornell UP, 2006).
5. Dr. Laub is referring to the "Oneg Shabbat" Archive (or "Ringelblum Archive") in Warsaw.
6. Dr. Laub expands on this notion in his two chapters in *Testimony*.
7. One exception is the trial of Adolf Eichman in Jerusalem, where many survivors bore witness (on this trial, see the interview with Shoshana Felman in chap. 13). In general, it would appear that there are more testimonies from the fighters during this period than from the victims.
8. In his essay "Between History and Psychoanalysis: A Case Study in the Reception of Holocaust Survivor Testimony," *History and Memory* 20.1 (Spring/Summer 2008): 7–47, Thomas Trezise accuses Dr. Laub—in chap. 2 of *Testimony*, "Bearing Witness, or the Vicissitudes of Listening"—of demonstrating a highly "selective" form of listening to a woman who testifies to a revolt in Auschwitz. Trezise also accuses Laub of treating what was in fact a "composite figure" as a single survivor and of misrepresenting the stance of the historians with whom Laub was taking issue in the evaluation of her testimony. Dr. Laub responds to Thomas Trezise's accusations in "On Holocaust Testimony and Its 'Reception' within Its Own Frame, as a Process in Its Own Right: A Response to 'Between History and Psychoanalysis' by Thomas Trezise" *History and Memory* 21.1 (Spring/Summer 2009): 127–50.
9. "Stockholm syndrome" refers to a condition of victims in long-term capture in which they come to identify with their captors; it is often exemplified by the case of Patty Hearst.
10. Dori Laub helped found the Fortunoff Archive for Holocaust Testimony at Yale. The film director Steven Spielberg founded the Shoah Foundation, housed at the University of Southern California.

11. See Yitzhak Arad, *Belzec, Sobibor, Treblinka: The Operation Reinhard Death Camps* (Bloomington: Indianapolis UP, 1999).

12. Jan Karski (1914–2000) was a Polish resistance fighter during World War II; he attempted to bring to the attention of the Polish government in exile, as well as other Western allied powers, the dire situation of the Jews under the Nazi regime. He gives a significant and moving interview in *Shoah*, dir. Claude Lanzmann (Historia / Les Films Aleph, 1985). Shoshana Felman writes about Karski in her chapter on the film in *Testimony*, "The Return of the Voice: Claude Lanzmann's *Shoah*."

13. See Louis Micheels, "Bearer of the Secret," *Psychoanalytic Inquiry* 5.1 (1985): 21–30.

14. Geoffrey Hartman is Sterling Professor Emeritus of English and Comparative Literature at Yale University. See the interview with Professor Hartman in chap. 9 for more on his life and work.

15. "Screen memories," as understood by Freud, are memories that hide more profound or traumatic memories.

16. See Madeleine Baranger, Willy Baranger, and Jorge Mario Mom, "The Infantile Psychic Trauma from Us to Freud: Pure Trauma, Retroactivity, and Reconstruction," *International Journal of Psychoanalysis* 69 (1988): 113–28.

17. Timothy Snyder, *Bloodlands: Europe between Hitler and Stalin* (New York: Basic Books, 2010).

18. Dori Laub, "Bearing Witness, or the Vicissitudes of Listening," chap. 3 in Laub and Felman, *Testimony*, 57.

19. See the interview with Shoshana Felman in chap. 13 for more on her life and work.

20. Dori Laub and Susanna Lee, "Thanatos and Massive Psychic Trauma: The Impact of the Death Instinct on Knowing, Remembering and Forgetting," *Journal of the American Psychoanalytic Association* 51.2 (2003): 433–64.

21. See, for example, Sigmund Freud, *Beyond the Pleasure Principle* and *The Ego and the Id*, in *The Standard Edition of the Complete Psychological Works of Sigmund Freud*, trans. under the general editorship of James Strachey in collaboration with Anna Freud, assisted by Alix Strachey and Jan Tyson, 24 vols. (London: Hogarth, 1953–1974), vols. 18–19.

22. The Rwandan genocide took place in 1994; the Tutsis were slaughtered by the Hutus. It is now remembered, among other things, for the absence of help from other countries, including the United States, in preventing a massacre that had been announced on the radio.

23. See M. Vogel, C. Spitzer, S. Barnow, H. J. Freyberger et al., "The Role of Trauma and PTSD-Related Symptoms for Dissociation and Psychopathological Distress in Patients with Schizophrenia," *Psychopathology* 29.5 (2006): 236–42, and A. M. Kilcommons and A. P. Morrison, "Relationships between Trauma and Psychosis: An Exploration of Cognitive and Dissociative Factors," *Acta Psychiatrica Scandinavica* 112 (2005): 351–59.

24. Dori Laub, "Traumatic Shutdown of Narrative and Symbolization: A Death Instinct Derivative," *Contemporary Psychoanalysis* 41.2 (2005): 307–26, reprinted in *Lost in Transmission: Studies of Trauma across Generations*, ed. Gerard Fromm (New York: Karnac, 2011), 31–53.

25. Hans Loewald (1906–1993) was a German-Jewish psychoanalyst who had studied with Martin Heidegger and practiced in the United States.

26. See Emily A. Kurrilof, *Contemporary Psychoanalysis and the Legacy of the Third Reich: History, Memory, Tradition* (New York: Routledge, 2014).

27. Martin S. Bergmann is clinical professor of psychology of the New York University. He has written books on the Holocaust, the phenomenology of love, and child sacrifice.

28. Heinz Kohut (1913–1981) was an Austrian-American psychoanalyst. He created the notion of "self psychology."

29. The trial of Adolf Eichmann, the coordinator of the extermination of the Jews who was captured by the Israelis in Latin America, took place in Jerusalem in 1961. See chap. 13 for more on this trial.

30. K-Zetnik was the name under which Yehiel Dinoor wrote literary books on the Holocaust; he was the one eyewitness of Eichmann at Auschwitz who was brought to the trial to testify. He famously lost consciousness on the stand near the beginning of his testimony. See Shoshana Felman, "A Ghost in the House of Justice," in Laub and Felman, *Testimony*, and her interview in this book.

31. Austen Riggs is a highly acclaimed psychotherapeutic treatment center founded in 1913 in Stockbridge, Massachussetts, known for its pathbreaking psychodynamic work with severely disturbed individuals.

32. Dr. Laub mentioned that the analyst could not, in fact, have participated in this event but most likely heard about it from his servants.

33. Erik H. Erikson (1902–1994) was trained as a psychoanalyst in Germany and left after the Nazis came to power. He eventually emigrated to the United States, where he developed a theory of the psychosocial development of human beings.

34. Otto Allen Will Jr. (1910–1993) was an American psychoanalyst focused on the treatment schizophrenia. Harry Stack Sullivan (1892–1949) was an American psychoanalyst who focused on the dimension of interpersonal relations as constitutive of the psyche.

35. Yehuda Nir is a psychiatrist and Holocaust survivor who was born in Poland in 1930. He wrote a memoir of his early life called *The Lost Childhood: A Memoir* (New York: Harcourt Brace Jovanovich, 1989).

36. Albert J. Solnit (1919–2002) was Sterling Professor Emeritus and Senior Research Scientist at the Child Study Center at Yale University School of Medicine and a training analyst at the Western New England Institute for Psychoanalysis.

37. Paul Matussek, *Internment in Concentration Camps and Its Consequences* (New York: Springer, 1973).

38. Schmuel Erlich was born in Germany in 1937 and emigrated to Palestine in 1939. He held the Sigmund Freud Chair in Psychoanalysis and was director of the Sigmund Freud Center for Study and Research in Psychoanalysis from 1992 to 2005 and is Clinical Associate Professor (Emeritus) in the Department of Psychology at The Hebrew University. A training and supervising analyst, he was chair of the Training Committee, Israel Psychoanalytic Institute, and president of the Israel Psychoanalytic Society.

39. Laurel Vlock (1926–2000) was a filmmaker in New Haven. Yom HaShoah is an annual day of remembrance of the Holocaust.

40. *The Sorrow and the Pity* (*Le chagrin et la pitié*) is a 1969 documentary film by Marcel Ophüls about the French Resistance and collaboration between the Vichy government and Nazi Germany during World War II.

41. Renee Hartman survived incarceration in a camp during the Holocaust, where she was placed with her sister. She is a writer and is also the wife of Geoffrey Hartman, who is interviewed in chap. 9.

42 Henry Krystal, M.D., is a Holocaust survivor who emigrated to the United States in 1946 and who has long worked with Holocaust survivors in his psychiatric practice and in relation to reparations claims made under the Restitution Program for Victims of Nazi Persecution. He is professor emeritus of psychiatry at Michigan Sate University, lecturer at the Michigan Psychoanaytic Institute, and author of *Integration and Self-Healing: Affect-Trauma-Alexithymia* (New York: Routledge, 1988) and editor of *Massive Psychic Trauma* (Madison, CT: International UP, 1969).

43. See the interviews with Arthur Blank (chap. 11) and with Françoise Davoine and Jean-Max Gaudilliere (chap. 4).

44. See Dori Laub and Johanna Bodenstaub, "Wiederbefragt. Erneute Begegnung mit Holocaust-Überlebenden nach 25 Jahren," *Bios: Zeitschrift für Biographieforschung, Oral History, und Lebensverlaufsanalysen* (2007): 303–15, reprinted in *Hitlers Sklaven: lebensgeschichtliche Analysen zur Zwangsarbeit im internationalen Vergleich*, ed. Alexander von Plato, Almut Leh, Christoph Thonfeld (Vienna: Böhlau, 2008), 389–401.

Françoise Davoine and Jean-Max Gaudillière at their cabin in Burgundy, France, November 28, 2011.

Chapter Four

Mad Witnesses

A Conversation with Françoise Davoine
and Jean-Max Gaudillière

Drs. Françoise Davoine and Jean-Max Gaudillière are practicing psychoanalysts in Paris and professors at the École des Hautes Études en Sciences Sociales (EHESS). They have produced pathbreaking work on madness and trauma, which they analyze in relation to Europe's catastrophic history. Their numerous books in these areas grow out of their clinical work with madness as well as their training in sociology, philosophy and classical literature, in which they both have advanced degrees.[1] On May 18, 2012, I met with them in their cabin in Burgundy, France, to discuss how they learned to listen to their patients and, in particular, to their messages of madness concerning our traumatic pasts.

I. People of an Arrested Time

CC: Let me begin by addressing one of the central ideas in your book *History beyond Trauma*. In this work you describe madness as "research into uninscribed histories," and you say, in this context, that "sometimes a fit of madness tells us more than all the news dispatches about the left-over facts that have no right to existence."[2] This is a clinical insight; it is not simply a speculative theory but rather, as we see in all your writing, arises directly out of your work with people. It emerges in the analysis with patients and in the transference and countertransference dynamics. So I was wondering if you could tell me how you first had this insight, or how you came to understand it in your experience of doing analysis.

What happened with you and with your patients that brought you to this realization? Did each of you have it separately? How did you come to discover this pretty remarkable notion that psychosis, which is generally considered to involve a distortion of reality, is, for you, actually communicating a historical reality of a specific kind?

JMG: I want to begin with a prefatory remark. When you work in this field of research, and in places such as asylums, where the traumatized or the mad are confined, you learn that these people are the witnesses of histories that have no right to exist. But beyond that, the patients also have—and they tell you—a theory of this witness as well. Next month, when we go to speak in a conference on history and trauma with historians of our institute of research, EHESS, I will begin with the first sentence by which a patient of mine at an asylum introduced himself to me, when he was in really bad shape, almost starving in his bed. The chief medical doctor had said that I should see him. And I introduced myself; he had been confined for more than ten years so he knew who I was. "I am Jean-Max Gaudillière," I said, "I am a psychoanalyst on the ward." And he looked at me with his eyes completely wide open from fever, and he said to me, "I am an encoded of the anti-past."[3]

CC: An encoded of the anti-past.

JMG: That's it. He was not an intellectual, he didn't have a baccalaureate, he had been confined since he was 18, and that's the way he introduced himself.

CC: So you had your theory right there. He understood on some level that he was confined because of something encoded in him.

JMG: He *was* the encoded. He said: "I *am* an encoded of the anti-past."

CC: In French, what was that?

JMG: "Je suis un codé de l'anti-passé."

CC: Is there a word *anti-passé* in French?

JMG: It doesn't exist.

CC: So he invented this word.

JMG: Yes. The anti-past. The past that does not pass. He introduced himself with that sentence. So one is struck by these things. His language was the same as when a poet or philosopher is writing something brilliant. But this is just an ordinary patient in the asylum, just saying the thing and the theory of the thing.

CC: So the language of your theory comes from your patients. It's not that you had an experience with them and then you made a theory but rather that your patients actually gave you the theory itself.

FD: I will tell you a story. I remember when we first decided to go to an asylum to work as psychoanalysts. We were sociologists; we were not trained as psychoanalysts at that time. We asked our director, the sociologist Alain Touraine,[4] for permission to go to the asylum, and he thought we would do sociological research. This is how we were able to get to the asylum. By chance, this hospital was situated in the battlefields of the First World War and the Second World War, in the middle of the cemeteries with the white crosses . . .

JMG: North of Paris.

FD: The hospital, "de Prémontré," was located in an old eighteenth-century abbey. But we didn't see the crosses, we didn't see the battlefields. We went there thinking that you couldn't study neutrally, as sociologists, people who talk to you; we wanted to be psychoanalysts. And I remember one of the first patients I met. A man with a pipe. I understood very quickly that his craziness happened when the horses on his farm had been abandoned for tractors. He used to try to heal the tractor as if it were a sick horse, driving it round and round in the yard of the farm. So they told him he was crazy. And when I spoke to him, I saw that he wanted to testify to a huge break in time that he had experienced, the break from older customs that came with the war, which was a complete change for him.

JMG: You saw something similar this morning, when Françoise's father was showing you the painting of the sheaves of wheat in the field.[5] It was the desire of Françoise's mother to have that painting made when Monsieur Davoine bought the first big machine in order to cut wheat. There would be no more nice piles of straw. And Françoise's mother knew it was the last time she would see them, and she asked an artist she knew who was teaching in the Institute of Fine Arts in Dijon to make a painting, because it was the last time.

FD: That's the normal way of doing things, to inscribe the past in art or in poetry, so nostalgia or lyricism can go on. But with the mad, there is no possibility of inscription. These people *are* the memory.

JMG: They are the event.

FD: And so after I talked to that man who was a witness—he was a monument of that time, very articulate—I dreamed, and that was how I understood what I was doing there. In my dream, with his pipe, he looked like my grandfather.

JMG: From the mother's side.

FD: My grandfather had fought in the First World War and was also a very silent man. Then I understood I was there for those people.

CC: What do you mean?

FD: For the people of an arrested time. Who cannot witness with words, but by being in another temporality than we are. That's why we call it, now, "the revenge of history," an expression of the historian of our institute, Sabina Loriga: don't forget.[6] But don't forget what? It could be the stacks of hay that my mother had memorialized in the painting—that's a nice form of nostalgia. But especially don't forget events that have been betrayed. Or events that have been wiped out. Or events that have been voluntarily forgotten.

JMG: And it's not only an ethical command in order to restore something erased from the official text of history. Even while they are witnesses, they are theoreticians, and they show you the way. And the way is the transference. "Don't forget" means: *come with me* to that field.

FD: In the book we tell the story of "Blue Flower."[7] She was in the asylum; she had been standing mute for ages in front of the radiator, saying nothing. Until one day, as Jean-Max had decided to stand regularly at her side, in front of the radiator, she started to speak and told him how her mother was a prostitute with the Germans. Blue Flower was the child witness.

And as a child, I was the witness, not only of the Second World War. I was always hand-in-hand with my grandfather and a witness of his micro-history during the First World War. Only recently did I dare to read a book, *La division Barbot* by Capitaine Humbert—imagine this, I'm almost 70 now!—which was written in 1919, about my grandfather's regiment, and dedicated to him.[8] I think it was dedicated to all the surviving soldiers of his regiment. This is where the betrayal of memory is: my betrayal. When I first started to read this book, I said, "Oh no, I won't read that, it's so ridiculous, it's so patriotic, it's so nationalistic, it's so jingoistic"; that was three years ago. And yet I had been in this psychiatric hospital in 1972, thirty years ago, forty years ago, dreaming of this grandfather. And then I started to read the book again two years ago. And when I opened it the second time—which I only did because someone had asked for it, and I felt I had to read it first—I understood that the first chapter, which had that jingoistic tone, was meant to represent the way the idealistic view of war was quickly destroyed by the confrontation with war's realities.

CC: You said that your delay in reading the book was a betrayal?

FD: A betrayal, because all of those old-timers of the First World War, when I was young, in '68—the period of the Vietnam war—were despised. They were considered stupid people, who had given their blood—for what? For nothing. And when I opened the book again, it was as if I were once again in the asylum with this patient with the pipe, the first one I met. Why? Because my grandfather, I had discovered, had been on all the fields during the First World War.

Verdun, Chemin des Dames, la Somme. Exactly where this hospital was, he had fought there. Arras, back to the Vosges, back to Alsace. He had been everywhere as a stretcher-bearer. As a military hunter he had a horn which he carried during the entire war. I have it today, full of bumps.

CC: So he saw all the wounded on all the battlefields.

FD: He carried them under fire, that's what I read. When he was dying, he asked someone to bring him his trumpet. He was a very good trumpeter. Of course everybody thought he was crazy. They didn't bring him his trumpet. So for me, he whistled. And he whistled with the art of men before the time of records, before the time of radio, people who whistled like music.

Precisely after the First World War quantum physics discovered a new paradigm in which temporality is at stake: the arrow of time may go backward, the past may be present, and the future may be as well, so people become visionary. They can see in the past, and from the past to the future. So that big turmoil in temporality is exactly what we feel with such patients.

CC: Your grandfather whistled, and this patient with the pipe, the one that tried to cure the tractors, that you encountered . . .

FD: He looked like my grandfather, but he was also from that occupied land during World War I, where the civilian population endured torture, as Annette Becker has just described in *Les cicatrices rouges*.[9] Until recently, everybody spoke about the ordeals of the combatants, but nobody spoke about the children, the women, forced to leave their villages, whose property was destroyed and who were starving, who were raped, whose babies were killed, and the men forced into slave labor and old people deported with women and children into concentration camps. And all that was in this asylum.

CC: And what did you come to understand that your patient was doing?

FD: He was from a family completely topsy-turvy from these two wars, living on the terrain where they fought as civilians.

CC: And how, at that time, did you remember your own experience with your grandfather?

FD: I thought, my grandfather has transmitted to me an arrested time, which permits me to be in a relationship with people who are, themselves, in an arrested time.

CC: So it sounds like your relationship with the patients also allowed you to come back to a relationship with the history that you had betrayed.

FD: Yes. It's a miniature research—no, not miniature, it's co-research. So one step forward and three steps back, and then together, we take one step forward again.

II. Mad Co-Researchers

JMG: In the same way, I remember that the patients were asking questions of us, who we were, what we were doing in the asylum, and one of them asked us, "What is your occupation?" And Francoise answered, "We are sociologists." And he said, "Oh, you are bachelors!"

CC: What did that mean?

FD: Purely scientific researchers, who leave the "observed object" alone (and other scientists as well!).

JMG: Meaning: there is no transference.

FD: You do it all by yourself.

CC: So it's "neutral."

JMG: I am sure he didn't know the word "sociologist." He didn't know what social sciences were, but he picked up that we were in the asylum in order to escape this position of neutrality and making interpretations. "Oh, so you are bachelors! So you need . . . "

FD: Us!

JMG: "You need another in the field." That's great.

CC: He was already beginning to teach you.

FD and JMG: Yes.

CC: What's also remarkable, of course, is that you could listen in that way. But do you think that their response to you had something to do with the reason that you were going to the asylum in the first place?

FD: Of course. We were going there with questions. We probably never go without a question. Otherwise you receive meaningless information. But we didn't know what our question was, and they made our question appear in the exchange and dialogue.

CC: So you went there, to a certain extent, unconsciously, because you had questions that you didn't yet understand. You chose to go to this asylum even though you were sociologists, and they taught you what your question was. You said that at that time you already wanted to be psychoanalysts?

FD: We had been to Lacan's school, we were following his seminar, and we had started analyses with Lacanian analysts (well, Lacanian-enough analysts!)—very good, very attentive to the signifier—and we knew it wasn't right. It was right for a certain field, but the field that interested us was beyond that.

CC: So you knew were interested in psychosis, but you didn't know that the question you had was about these kinds of uninscribed histories, these larger histories?

JMG: What we knew from our own experience of psychoanalysis, through the transference with our own analysts, was that both of us had reached some limits, and these limits were connected, in Francoise's case and in my case, with matters coming from our fathers and grandfathers in connection with what we call "la grande Histoire," quoting a patient, the "philosopher" in *Wittgenstein's Folly*, who stated that his delusion had happened at the crossroad of his family history and the big History.[10] For instance, I remember very well that I had a dream that we were in the middle of the Vietnam War and there was a massacre at My Lai. I had heard the news on the radio and maybe also in the newspaper and I had a dream about that. And in my analysis I associated the dream with things coming from my father. Now ordinarily my analyst would stay completely silent; she had intervened only ten times . . .

CC: In the entire analysis? Ten times in all those years?

JMG: She really was a classical Lacanian! But this time she intervened, making a sexual interpretation. So I didn't say anything this time. But the next time it happened was when we were working at the asylum north of Paris, and at some point in my associations were things that came from my experience at the asylum. I was telling her about what was happening in my relationship with a patient, and she intervened—it was maybe two years after the My Lai massacre—and again she made a sexual interpretation. And so this time I sat up, I laughed, and I told her, "You know it's finished now."

CC: The analysis? You ended it?

JMG: Oh yes. And she was a little astonished by that. And I remember I said, "Goodbye," and she said, "You didn't pay me." And I said, "OK. I'll pay . . . "

FD: I was trying to remember before why we went as sociologists. Now I remember. Because we were interested in the anti-psychiatry movement. Our sociology center in the Écoles des Hautes Études en Sciences Sociales was called "the Center for Research on Social Movements." So we took the anti-psychiatry movements as our pretext for going to the asylum. I remember going in previous years to London every month and meeting the group of Laing and Cooper.[11] We used to go also to Italy to compare the two movements, one more political, referring to Franco Basaglia's group, the other referring to Gregory Bateson's double bind at the core of madness, as illustrated by the film *Family Life* by Ken Loach.[12]

Comparing the two movements, the English one was more attuned to patients, while the Italian one stressed contradictions in society, and we were in between the two. At first when we went to the asylum we wanted to liberate everybody. We had the key! We could open the door!

And suddenly what they had to say was so much more interesting than opening or closing the door. It was the door of time. It was a completely other world, which we had to explore.

CC: So you went with ideological ideas about how the mad could be understood in terms of their resistance to social constraints, but what you discovered was something very different: that they were, in fact, "in another time."

JMG: We have very fresh memories about that from when we arrived. After the nurses introduced us to the different areas in the hospital, to the functioning of the ward, and so on, the patients took charge in order to introduce themselves to us.

CC: The patients were introducing each other?

FD: The patients took us by the hand. We were new; we were not medical doctors; we were not psychologists; we were zombies for them—so we were the fools of the asylum.

JMG: And thus the patients tried to introduce us to that field. And I remember one man in particular: he fit the nineteenth-century stereotype of the tall blonde schizophrenic. He was a very nice guy, very polite, and he was greeting us at the door of the ward . . .

FD: He was fifty, but he looked like he was nineteen years old.

JMG: He was showing us around, and after a while he introduced himself to us. And we knew from the files that this guy was not very well-educated; he used to live with his elderly parents, and when the parents died he had no occupation, no money—the neighbors gave him food. And this guy was so polite, so delicate; he said to us, "I'm here because I am a researcher in ideopathology."

CC: And he was!

JMG: And he was! More than we. Once, before he was in the hospital, he had taken the train by himself to the Gare du Nord in Paris, to visit the man he claimed was in charge of ideopathology—whom he called "Paolo Herzog." But when he found no place to sit down and eat, he turned right around and came back. He felt at home in the asylum: for him, he was at the place of his research.

CC: So his delusion was that he was the doctor. But what you heard in his delusion was that he really was the researcher.

FD: He was the researcher, but so really empathic.

CC: And that goes to what you said you learned from these patients when you went to the asylum. They were telling you that you believed you were neutral, scientific researchers, but in fact you needed partners in your work. So what, then, is non-neutrality? How do you understand what you had to do to relate to these patients, or to what they were telling you?

FD: I think every psychoanalyst who has contact with moments of psychosis— those moments when time stops, when speech is no longer reliable—knows that there is no neutrality there. Everyone has a story about one of those moments. "I was not a psychoanalyst with this patient," they will tell you in private. I think all of them have a story, a moment that makes them fall from their armchairs, so to speak. But the difference is, some make use of it, they investigate it, they are interested in it, they are willing to be a little daring; and others fear that moment. And you cannot reproach them. They become directors of institutes!

III. The Betrayal of History

CC: So you came to the hospital, and you learned, after meeting the patients, that you hadn't fully understood what had brought you there, which was some-thing they helped you to recognize. That reminds me of Bruno Bettelheim's little essay, "How I Learned about Psychoanalysis," in particular the second part of it.[13] He describes being in the waiting room of his analyst in Vienna, where there was, regularly, a psychotic child waiting to see Bettelheim's analyst's wife, who was also an analyst. This child was always chewing on cactus leaves, which made his mouth all bloody, and he never spoke. One day, about two years into Bettelheim's analysis, when he was very frustrated with what he felt was his lack of progress, he suddenly addressed the child as he was chewing on the cactus leaves: "I don't now how long you have been seeing Dr. X, but it must be at least two years, since I have known you for that long, and here you are still chewing these awful leaves!" And for the first time the child took the cactus leaves out of his mouth, drew himself up, and said to Bettelheim: "What are two years compared with eternity!" And Bettelheim understood that the reason the child had now spoken to him was because the question he had addressed to the child was in fact Bet-telheim's own question about his analysis. The child had understood that he was not being addressed simply as a crazy person but rather as someone who could teach Bettelheim something.

FD: That's exactly the sense we had as well. I remember a woman at another hospital we worked at, to whom I felt somehow connected, without understand-ing that my connection to her was through the war. In this woman's delusion, she had long conversations with Pétain, who was in fact an old man in the common room of the hospital.[14] One day the medical doctor asked her, "How old are you?" and she answered, "500 years old." "Oh Madame," he said, "you know that's not true." And she said, "How is it not true when every second is like eternity?"

It is the same as in the Bettelheim story. There is always a statement on time. This woman was going back to her childhood, in Normandy, where she saw all the wounded in a hospital where her mother was confined when she had tuberculosis. The girl and her siblings were in the orphanage in the hospital, and she would see all of the wounded soldiers from D-Day. The nurses would, moreover, use the children to help take care of the wounded soldiers. There are moments in time that don't proceed the same way other moments do, and that lead you to an encounter with another who has had a similar experience, and to whom you can talk.

CC: So when these patients in the hospital met the two of you they understood, somehow, that there was something "out of time" in you. And "being out of time" means more than saying that, for example, the woman who was a child in the war hospital was having experiences that most children don't have. You seem to mean something larger when you refer to something that is not in time. What, then, does this mean? What kinds of histories are linked to each other—through peoples' encounters—that are out of time? These are not only histories of wars and massacres but of . . .

FD: Denial. These histories have been expelled from time by denial. And then we go to perversion. Which is an active discourse, which is an active erasure of the social link. It's not only that you forget.

JMG: I think they are also presenting, sometimes very harshly, the limits of our everyday theories. The ones we use in order to have our landmarks. For instance, since the beginning of science fiction we have been accustomed to think about the possibility of conceiving another dimension of space. And with the theory of relativity, we have been able to understand that there could be some variations in the way we think of time. But this is still with a secure reference to the normal arrow of time, even if the rhythm is somewhat different (as in a hypothetical case in which a man could travel at nearly the speed of light to another galaxy and return two centuries later being only 30 years older). But we are not accustomed to think about a temporality that doesn't work with either the normal rhythm or the normal direction of the arrow of time. Francoise said, nicely, that these patients are opening to us the door of time, and I would add that they're opening to us another theory of time. And you need that. To think preposterously, for example, that the past is determined by the future (that's Artaud).[15]

FD: Because we are impregnated by tenses, by past, present and future, the other point these patients wipe out is the sense of causality. For us, the past causes future consequences. It is necessary for science. But when the arrow of time doesn't work, when the past and future are always present, it is very disturbing. These patients always state the present.

CC: They always state things in the present?

FD: For instance, "I am in hell!" And if you say, "Oh yes, you knew hell when you were small and you had an operation," for instance, or a traumatic event, they will say, "No, I am in hell *now*." So, what is this "now"? This now is just that you get rid of causality. This now is to tell the other, "Don't try the trick of causality. Don't try to tell me, 'Oh, you were so unhappy when you were a child . . . '"

CC: So that's the challenge to the theory.

FD: Yes, the challenge is to causality.

CC: So it's also challenging your expectations. First of all, they are saying, in effect, "To enter here you're going to have to come with me," as opposed to theorizing.

FD: Dante's inscription in hell is "Abandon all hope, ye who enter here." You who enter here abandon all causality. This causality is the hope that you will understand the consequences. That is very difficult.

JMG: For instance, when, after a while, a patient first puts on the table everything concerning the trauma. And you are very proud to say, "Oh I understood everything, you are mad because of this trauma."

FD: You say, "I knew! That's true!" But it's not the sufficient truth, it doesn't encompass the area of truth.

CC: And you were saying before that this truth is linked to denial, to betrayal; so the truth is not only that this bad thing happened, this war, for example. It is also about betrayal. The betrayal is part of the truth they're trying to tell you—a truth not so easily understood by the theories one is accustomed to use as landmarks. Can you talk about this betrayal? It seems to be a betrayal of history.

FD: It doesn't need to be psychological, as in a case in which one person betrays another. Sometimes that is the case. But it can also be an entire social link that is built on the denial of what happened. A denial needed to survive, for instance. It can be for a good cause. It's not that you forget; it's rather "cut out." That is our word.

CC: The "cut-out unconscious."[16]

FD: Yes. Lacan was limited on that point, so we went to the States, and very soon we heard about Harry Stack Sullivan, who wrote that when you question the parents of schizophrenic people you cannot get any information.[17] And it's not because the parents are nasty (though sometimes they may be), or that they don't want to help their children, but rather that it is so maddening, confusing, and chaotic that they just don't want to untangle that mess. If you speak to abused children who were made objects of pornography, what kind of reality do you expect they can tell you about? And how can they make sense?

CC: Even the parents, you said . . .

FD: The parents either don't know or they don't want to know. I knew the story of one woman who was a good mother, but she didn't see, she couldn't see, her child's abuse because she had been in a similar situation herself. It's this transmission of a perverse social link that is very active, very difficult to see because it looks like normality.

CC: And so the social link, in this case, is built around the denial. Elsewhere you talk about disruption in the social link[18]—which is the same thing, it seems, as a social link that is built around denial. So what does it mean, exactly, that people construct their relationships and their truths around a denial of certain aspects of history?

FD: Take the father who comes back from the war. War is a bad thing. Therefore you identify this guy's experience with the bad experience of the war. So you are not curious about him. That's a betrayal. Because he comes from a dirty place where it's horrible, and nobody wants to hear about it. You could say the same thing for people coming from an asylum—it's a terrible place, they say, for you are left alone, in spite of the care.

CC: So you don't ask.

FD: You don't ask. And the time required to ask questions, to enter time, questions that make time move, may be enormous. As I told you before, I said that I opened my book about my grandfather's war thirty or forty years after I had first looked at it. It's like during wars, some people are actively perverse, and they want to erase things because they love power—not only power but transforming people into things.[19] Still, the betrayal can also be passive; it can be collaboration, or it can be simply, "I'm not interested, I don't want to bother." What happens to the neighbor, I'm not curious about: the camps or the abused children next door.

CC: Indifference.

FD: Yes, indifference.

CC: And so there can be different kinds of betrayal of history. Sometimes it is perverse, like the Nazis (or the Soviets) trying to erase the history they made. But can it also happen, as you seem to imply, without one's even being aware that one is doing it? I'm thinking about families where there are questions one doesn't ask.

FD: It's a common betrayal.

CC: So you just get a message, one you don't fully understand. In their book *Testimony*, Shoshana Felman and Dori Laub talk about an "event without a witness," and there are different kinds of non-witness.[20]

JMG: There is no better word to speak of this, and to describe what the patient in the asylum said when he referred to the creation of an "anti-past."

IV. The Cut-Out Unconscious

CC: That brings me to another point I wanted to address. If it's an "anti-past," it's not just absent. But it's not repressed either.

FD: We learned everything from Lacan and Freud, and what's good in Lacan is when he says the unconscious is made with repressed signifiers, "the discourse of the Other." But what happens when this agency of the given word is destroyed?

JMG: In the symbolic "function and field of speech and language," there can be a repressed. But when there is a rupture—no words, no image, the Real defined as the unnameable—there is no possible repression. Well, it's a question of definition; you may say "repressed," but we prefer to make a distinction when the Real is at stake and call it a "cut-out unconscious."

CC: It really is "cut out." And to me that makes sense because I think about it in terms of trauma. People often ask, in the study of trauma, where the traumatizing event goes if it's not inscribed. I imagine you would say that it's "seeking an inscription."

FD: That's what Jean-Max calls the "anthropological constant."[21]

JMG: Einstein invented the "cosmological constant" to explain the stability of the universe. He needed to invent that constant with no proof, in order to complete the theory of relativity. It helps us understand, I would say, the relationships among trauma, madness, and inscription, what we might call the anthropological constant: the movement by which an erased event is already in search of inscription. As soon as it is erased, even if there is no visible witness, the event by itself is looking for inscription: people themselves become the event.

CC: So the event needs to be told; it's an imperative, and it's seeking, in some sense, to emerge.

FD: From the ashes.

JMG: In psychosis, trauma, madness, the question is: to be or not to be *born*.[22]

CC: So in this sense, psychosis—or rather this history that is attempting to be inscribed again, or is imposing itself—is about life and death, about survival, or non-survival. And this is your version of the death drive and the life drive. Because if we think of the death drive as erasure, as the erasure of history, which is how I think of it,[23] the life drive is in a sense resisting that. So the return of history, here as inscription, would also be, really, the possibility of survival.

FD: The return of history when the human mouth is closed. The return is very often through the mouth of things. Things talk. Animals talk. Cats talk, stars, and so on. Because you know the human mouth has been unequal to this task; it didn't accomplish the task of transmitting. So that's the delusion. Delusions are animistic myths.

JMG: If I am a patient and I say to a psychiatrist, "This table told me such and such," the psychiatrist will say, "Hmm, that's a projection." But the table talks. That's it. That's the fact. The table talks.

FD: Or the grass, or the leaves, or a bird, you know, sometimes a bird.

CC: Because if you say it's a projection, it's about your psyche; it's not about something real.

JMG: And whatever the explanation might be, what's interesting is not that the table talks, after all—the table could talk—but what the table said, and to whom.

FD: Mieke Bal wrote a book on a Colombian artist, Doris Salcedo, who wanted to represent the massacres in Colombia.[24] And how to represent the horrors, atrocities, and perversion that are part of the general sadistic ambiance. Mieke went to see Salcedo's exhibition in Portugal.[25] And in our seminar there's somebody who is from Colombia who went to see it as well and showed us the catalog. Tables on top of others, not like coffins, but like open coffins. This is the impression you get. And between them you have dirt.

JMG: Earth.

FD: Earth, and from this, grass. Just as the grass erased the place of the mass graves—hid it—at the same time, it says, "Look, life is stronger than all your destruction." So that's what we are talking about.

CC: So if we go back to the question of where or when this uninscribed history is, part of it is that it comes back through these people. You said before that they *are* this history, they are not only talking about it. So has a history that is trying to impose itself remained anywhere? It's not simply absent, because it is lived or somehow comes through psychosis. Would you say that the whole history of madness, as folly, in literature, in culture, is about that?

JMG: Completely. We make a strong unification of the field of *folie*-madness-psychosis in literature, in clinical work, and in theory—that's all the same thing.

CC: So if we want to study history, including the left-out history, the cut-out unconscious that is also history, or anti-history, we have to study madness as well. If you exclude the fools, you will exclude part of history.

JMG: They record history with the seismograph of their bodies and psyches.

FD: That's what the Middle Ages knew and what Shakespeare knew and also Cervantes and Laurence Sterne.

JMG: We should be really afraid of the idea of eradicating madness through pills, as if it were tuberculosis or cancer or something. Because if you eradicate madness, you eradicate all the witness of the cut-out events.

CC: For me it is the same thing in the field of trauma studies.

FD and JMG: Because they are the same field.

FD: When it's madness, the track of the trauma is lost. You just have a witness of what you don't know. Perhaps a lot of time has passed, or the trauma area has been so wiped out, as in the mass graves, where there is grass and they say, "Nothing happened. It's all fantasy." And so madness happens when the tracks are lost.

CC: So these are, in a way, non-events, and that's why they can only come as madness. Because they're really not yet events in any way.

FD: Exactly. But it is the same field.

CC: And it's really about truth. That's why I've always felt that trauma is not simply a pathology, even though it is classified as one. Of course it is also a form of suffering. But it has to do with truth.

FD: Yes. Madness is always a fight against denial, double language, manipulation, and falsification.

V. The Lives of Others

CC: The issue of truth brings me to another question. There are a lot of cases of madness, or even of post-traumatic stress disorder, which seem to concern individual lives—that there was a neglecting mother or a cruel sadistic family, for example—and that if one were going to trace it back, if one were going to follow, most simply, the laws of causality, one would say, "This person had a certain kind of neglect," and so forth. But you claim, in your writing, that madness is linked to larger histories.

JMG and FD: Always.

CC: So how is it that that happens? How do you go from what might look like individual trauma to a larger history? Can you give me an example? How can you make that leap?

FD: Our certitude about this could undoubtedly be considered crazy, just like the assertions of the mad. And of course we cannot say it's absolutely always the case. But this stubbornness can be useful. I will give you an example, a case of abuse. A child was a witness of a hellish conflict between her parents about cheating, sexual infidelities, and decides to focus on studying, although her father attacks that. She becomes a child psychoanalyst. And she comes to see me for supervision [of her work as an analyst]—not for her personal story. In discussing one of her young patients, for whom the war was at stake in his far away country, I ask her out of the blue, "Where were your parents during the war?" Why do I ask always the same question? When I ask the question, I feel so stupid! You see what I mean? It's like I had . . .

CC: Like you have a compulsion.

FD: A repetition compulsion, though I always do it with some reluctance. So she says she was on a farm in Normandy; she was six, and the farm was occupied by the Germans. As my grandmother's house was. It was common, you know. The Germans occupied France during the Second World War, and they were living in people's houses. So I saw her several times, and she told me she did not visit them as often as she should; she resented her father for attacking her studies, and now her mother has Alzheimer's. They are no longer in the country. So, this *daimon*, like Socrates' daimon, pushes me to say, "OK, I want you to find out on the Internet the story of this region during the war." And again, I say to myself, "Françoise, you are really nuts, why don't you shut up? You are no good." Still, after a month she comes back with a find, which comes from the University of Caen.

At Caen there is a D-Day memorial museum. And on the Net, researchers from the University of Caen give information about the resistance in the region. Her parents' little village was in the middle of nowhere, and because it was a nowhere village, it was the center of the resistance in the region. With a lot of massacres by the French militia, who gave the resisters' names to the Germans. There were farms that were burned, people denounced. And I said, "So, the violence between your parents was larger than they were."

So this takes time. She went this past Sunday to her parents. And for the first time in her life a true conversation takes place. She says, "Look what I have found." And her mother, who has Alzheimer's, gets out of her Alzheimer's and tells her daughter for the first time, "OK, you want to know, go back to the farm in Normandy (which had been sold). Ask this cousin, this is his name, his address. Ask this neighbor, he knows everything. This is his name, his address. Do it." And this week she's there to start her investigation. If I had not had this stubbornness . . . well, I don't hear voices like Jeanne d'Arc . . .

JMG: Again, my own analyst, as I mentioned above, came with a sexual interpretation of the past, excluding history.

CC: Dori Laub talks about what he calls the "empty circle." He says that for a

Holocaust survivor, the dream, the level of the dream that is understood as the primal scene or Oedipus complex or sexuality, is itself a screen for the empty circle.[26] So that the sexual interpretation that somebody might have of his or her own dream is screening something that is empty, in the sense of not being inscribed.

FD: Exactly. For me, Dori Laub is the clinician who describes it best. It's not a simple thing, it's diverse and complex, but the complexity is around that centrality of denial, of emptiness, where perversion is embodied in a false, cheating, murderous discourse. This is a murderous disourse that comes from the others. Because the ones who denied were the others.

VI. LISTENING AS A CHILD

CC: You just told the story of a child, and in your book the two of you say that what you sometimes hear coming from the mad person is the voice of a child. So I want you both to talk to me more about what happens to your listening, what happens to you as you listen to somebody speaking through a delusion or through madness. How do you listen?

JMG: On a good day, it opens for me the field of poetry.

CC: Poetry? How?

JMG: I used to say, "trauma speaks to trauma,"[27] and I could say, as a parallel of that, "a child speaks to a child." And when a child speaks to a child, he's not or she's not speaking only about things with words. He or she is also speaking about words with things. And so at that moment the field of creativity is opened wide, beyond ordinary limits. Sometimes the patient is speaking, and I have to listen and eventually to interpret in order to give an insight. Sometimes the patient is the analyst, I am the patient, and some butterfly is arriving on my balcony and is a part of the session, and another patient is phoning me at that moment, and the voice of the patient through the phone is a part of the session. So we are weaving things together. The result will not be an explanation, it will be a creation.

CC: It will be creative. So each session, in that sense, or each of these particular sessions, is creative and new—like literature, to some extent.

FD: It is improvisation.

CC: And it can't be translated. Literature cannot simply be translated into any other form, for example into a historical document. Poetry can't just become prose. Literature is traditionally the hardest thing to translate from one language or genre into another. So if history comes out, in your sessions, in this creative way, in this literary way, then it is also a history that you can't translate into a simple form of knowledge that we could just make into a history book. Is that correct?

FD: Still, we can give a testimony of what happened in particular sessions.

CC: And so would you say, then, that in each of these discoveries that you make—this discovery or emergence of uninscribed histories asking to be inscribed—that act of inscribing is creative, and it's also new each time? It's not that you find the same facts over and over again. And it's not even just facts, it's something very creative. So this push of life to come back is also the push of creativity.

JMG: Not to come back. To come to be witnessed for the first time.

CC: To come for the first time. That's right. So this push of history, which you say is also the push of life, is the push of creativity as well. I think that's why psychoanalysis is bound up with a specific kind of creation, which might be described as literary.

You said to me earlier that this creative moment is also the site of childhood. Can you say what that means? Because some people think of the child as innocent. But your children are not so innocent, right? They are also where war and trauma reside.

FD: They know too much.

CC: They know too much. So can you elaborate on what you said before about going to that site of childhood?

FD: First, I have to say that with patients who have been witness to the things we were speaking about, who have received the transmission of trauma in a family, it takes usually, not always, a long time to be able to get to be at their shoulder as children. To be at their level. Because it doesn't mean that we are condescending, or taking the child in our lap. It's not that we are soothing them or singing a lullaby or telling stories, although I do that often. It sometimes takes years.

I am desperate to get there, or to get somewhere, because they regularly come back to square one, they free themselves, they go further, they come back to square one, sometimes they get confined in the asylum again, hell is coming back. But at some point, always, we are exactly in the place of the traumatic events as a partner, of the same age, of the same kind of mind. With the same kind of space and time apprehension. And being there with them, then we can explore.

For instance, I knew of a patient who had huge delusions, who is much better now. There were many very traumatic events in her life. But suddenly I realized what I knew and had never explored with her. And she took me by the hand, in a neighboring country, in a village—again a village—where, finally, when she was thirty-five, she was told that a crime had been perpetrated in her family, before her birth. Her great-grandfather had killed her grandfather. She was spending holidays there when she was two, three, four, five, six, all alone because her parents were working, in that village, without knowing anything. And knowing everything. It's not just anybody who lives in such a place. All the fantastic literature talks about that: the ghosts, the specters, the haunted house, the haunted village. I knew that the parents had never been with her. How can I go as a child, seeing through her eyes and absorbing all that you can absorb of silence, of people who just stop talking when you arrive, of all those details? This has been a big subject in literature.

In the novel *Pedro Paràmo*, by the Mexican author Juan Rulfo, the main character arrives in a Mexican village. And it's all whispers in the streets. And it's the dead.[28] Children are very sensitive. They have a seismograph. The word was coined by the art historian Aby Warburg, who went mad during World War I and was healed ten years later.[29] It is not infantilization. I activated my seismograph when I was this age, full of the sounds of war.

CC: So it's a specific seismograph because both of you had war experiences like this.

FD: I always say, this is not a general experience. She had recorded, as a child, what had been silenced in an arrested time. It has to be a specific seismograph that I attune to this child. Or I lend her mine, and she lends me hers.

CC: "Lend me your ears . . . "

FD: And that time she could claim the "unclaimed experience" of those years that had been, she said, completely buried. And it took us fifteen years.

CC: So you lend your ears to each other to hear these things.

FD: It takes a long time. She told me, "It takes a long time to recover my psyche." And to recover one's psyche when it has been invaded by an unclaimed experience, to create new filters by telling it to a witness, it takes a very long time.

CC: The two of you had very specific experiences of war. But a lot of analysts are going to struggle with the fact that their experiences are not anything like yours. You both had parents in the resistance; you write something about that, Françoise.[30] Your father ran a cheese cooperative and hid Jews and worked actively in the resistance in the region, and your mother was imprisoned, pregnant with you, for a while by the Germans when she was caught in the fall of 1942 carrying letters for the resistance across the "Demarcation Line" between occupied France and the free zone. And your parents too, Jean-Max, correct?

Jean-Max Gaudillière at the cabin in Burgundy, November 27, 2011.

JMG: My father fought and was a prisoner and escaped. And he was obliged to hide himself when he arrived in Mâcon, where I was born and where the militia were completely in power. And my maternal grandmother, who used to live with my mother and father, was Jewish. As far as I am aware, when my father came back after escaping from the prisoners' camps in the north of France, he participated in some actions of the resistance. I came to that conclusion because he used to know the father of the wife of Mitterrand, [the former] Mlle. Gouze.[31] Her father was the mayor of a very well-known village, Cluny, near Mâcon. One of our neighbors, named Monsieur Dubois, was a leader of the resistance in our district, and my father was connected with him. My mother's sister used to make false IDs for Jews, and she was almost caught by the militia.

CC: So both of you had parents in the resistance in one way or another, which is pretty remarkable. You're close to lots of histories that are very complicated and are tied up with a larger trajectory of historical denial in France. What about people who, like me, grew up in West Los Angeles, in the '60s . . .

JMG and FD: Oh, Cathy, you have just now come to France, entirely unsettled, from Poland, looking like an émigré in search of a state!

JMG: So do you know the history on your shoulders?

CC: I don't know much about my parents' familial backgrounds.

FD: Both your parents were analysts, but they belonged to this generation that, at least in France, completely blocked history. Even in the Lacanian School, on that issue, it was much more interesting to find psychotic structures. History was not the primary concern, even there. So your parents had a lot of history in their background. They produced a daughter who continues the work they couldn't achieve.

JMG: You think you are working on trauma by chance?

FD: It's what they transmitted to you. "Do the job we couldn't do."

JMG: Catastrophic areas are not always related to war. Almost all the American people are coming from outside. And they are coming from outside not exactly for touristic reasons. So they thought they could leave, in Europe, in Africa, in Asia, all the dead, all the trauma, and begin a new life, with nothing behind them. There is the ocean, and beyond the ocean there are the graves, or no graves of unburied people.

CC: My mother was not a refugee, but she worked with people, like Rudolf Ekstein, who were.

FD: Her parents were.

CC: I don't know about her parents.

JMG: But she did!

CC: Well, Bettelheim and Rudolf Ekstein, with whom my mother worked, had left Europe because they had to; they were persecuted. And then my mother worked early on with autistic children who could not speak. So she and her colleagues learned to listen, and to listen to the silent children. And I remember not long before he died, Bettelheim and Ekstein were interviewed in Ekstein's house, and I was there. And Bettelheim said that Freudian psychoanalysis, unlike psychoanalysis in the American context, was really not first of all about curing; it was in the first place about understanding.[32] Now I know that's not exactly your language. But what he meant was, I think, that psychoanalysis was about a certain kind of truth. And one thing you have talked about is that psychoanalysis is not simply about the kind of empathy that involves feeling bad for other person's suffering but rather about hearing a kind of testimony. A bit like Claude Lanzmann in *Shoah*.[33] You say that you tell people to do research, that they have to go explore their pasts.

FD: Understanding one's own story through a relation to, or in an interference from another's story, is healing. And I will tell you a nice story that our son, Bryce, told us, who does research in the field of immunity. So now we are speaking about hard science, about biology. The hard sciences make statistics, they take blood, they compare, and they are really objective. They don't meddle with the story of this or that patient. Recently, in *Cell*, one of the most prestigious reviews of sciences, a geneticist from Stanford, Michael Snyder, made a discovery.[34] He said, "I decided that instead of taking thousands of samples from different people, I would work on one person, and take thousands of blood samples from just this one person, over a long period. And this person is myself." A revolution! Usually the observer doesn't experiment on himself. What is amazing is that during that time he was able to say how his genes transformed themselves, how they worked to fight two viruses that he had in the meanwhile. He could see the genetic modifications with regard to the virus. Eventually he discovered he had diabetes, though he didn't yet have symptoms. And he was able to intervene in time to cure his diabetes. He published his research, and he says that knowing oneself through history is healing. Isn't that nice?

We think the same way. Because when we work with the patient, we are in an exchange with them, and they heal us, they want to heal us, and we use that to heal them. [Sandor] Ferenczi called it "mutual." I don't know if it's mutual—I prefer to say that it's co-research.

CC: Co-research. So it's not only that they know themselves, but that . . .

FD: . . . they know you.

JMG: And they know the interference.

CC: What exactly do you mean by "interference"?

FD: They know when you are touched, *toca*.[35]

CC: *Touché*.

FD: That's exactly the word, they say, "*touché*." *Toca*, when you are touched.

CC: And that's the inscription. The touching without touching that is the inscription.

FD: Well, it can be told. It is not by itself an inscription, but you can tell a story. Like Hannah Arendt says, all sorrows can be . . .

JMG: . . . borne . . .

FD: . . . when you put them . . .

JMG: . . . into a story.[36]

FD: The interference, the *toca*, you can of course forget about it. Or you can tell a story about it. There is a story to tell about it.

CC: And that's a different social link that's formed. A new social link.

FD: And if, by laziness, you just discard the story you can tell, it just fades away again.

VII. THE ANALYST'S DREAM

CC: I'd like to return to what you said early in this discussion, that the patient had a theory of his own psychosis. And the patients were also challenging what your theory was, or what they imagined it was going to be.

FD: It's a fight, at some precise points.

CC: Is that a part of the war in therapy, which you refer to when you say in your book that the patients are literally, not metaphorically, bringing you back to the war?[37] That they may be transmitting it, but also that there's always an impasse in an analysis, in which something fails. So that no matter how attuned you are to these patients, something will fail. What does that mean?

FD: It means that you will be defeated as an omniscient, or omniscient-to-be Other.

JMG: And also that they are really clever—and that's another definition of madness —because you cannot be mad and be an idiot. And they also have a lot of previous experience with other therapists. So when they are trying to work with you, or you are trying to work with them, they are already looking for your fault. Somewhere where you are not so sure about your own landmarks.

FD: And they have been submitted to mastering powers. We spoke about perversion as an enterprise of objectification.

JMG: They are looking for that point, which they will find through this kind of interference, and eventually you will receive the proof of their finding it. For instance, if you have a dream stemming from the sessions, you had better tell it to the patient. Because it's not your own dream, but the dream of the interference.

CC: That's remarkable. I can't imagine very many analysts tell their dreams to their patients. And how does the patient respond? What is that telling the patient?

FD: It's not I who say that; it is the dream. So it is some other that is produced from our encounters, where it's due to you, too, because it's not my private property. It is something that is the common product of our research. So the patient will tell me what he or she thinks.[38] This is not welcomed by the psychoanalytic orthodoxy.

Coda: Forbidden Games

CC: I would like to close with a question about the adaptability of your work to a changing social and political realm. Because these days there are new ways of not knowing and forgetting and denying. For Hannah Arendt, the world of the modern lie in the West involves a new mode of losing history.[39] As our ways of denying history change, as our relation to history changes—if it does—does the nature of your analyses change? Do you find that there's a way you have to alter what happens in the analysis or in what you do? Or do you think that basically these principles of listening more or less remain? In other words, since your histories come from a certain period, and your patients' histories come from a particular period in time, is there any chance that with different forms of denial and different forms of erasure there would be required different kinds of interaction?

FD: So you're asking us to open a breach so that we can go forward and not say, "That's it, we are at the end of all knowledge."

CC: Yes, you're always discovering new things.

JMG: If you work with trauma and madness, your analysis never ends, in the sense that Freud talked about interminable analysis. Patients are trying to make you progress, and sometimes they succeed. And so they eventually modify your technique, your theory for other patients.

CC: So each encounter with a patient modifies your theory and practice for the next one. Then you don't have a single technique that you apply, since each one is . . .

FD: . . . to be invented.

CC: Each time.

JMG: Each time, and each time for the last time. I have emphasized this over the last year. But it was already my idea for a long time, treating every session as a possible last session.

FD: But at the same time, what strikes me is that you have psychoanalysis in Greek tragedies. Greek tragedies are about trauma; epic is about trauma; all great major works in human civilizations are about trauma. The African masks are there for the spirits to come down and settle things and intervene. And in every culture, ceremonies are meant to heal the social link. And why is it to be healed? Because it has been ruptured by a trauma. Wittgenstein said man is a ceremonial animal.[40] But of course the shapes change according to the cultures involved. For instance, the African masks don't look like the Sioux Indian dances, although there are some common traits. We don't perform with masks, although there is a sort of theater sometimes in our performance where I play the clown. Sometimes without wanting to!

There was a patient who was a little older than I am—she was born in 1937. She was Jewish, and her mother was abusive toward her. They came from Harbin, China.[41] And they lived in a little village in the north of France. This lady fled from her home to America. She came back to France and now is a grandmother. She knew the work of Frieda Fromm-Reichmann,[42] and came to see me. She was at a loss, far from her children, without connections in France. And how did she get out of this morass? Through a little theater of fools that I performed. I asked her, "Where is your little village?" You know, that's another of my questions. I never let any little village be erased. I can't.

CC: They all matter.

FD: They all matter. Because a little village is also the names of woods and of fields. It's full of names. The name of the people and the name of the places where things happen. So you can't just be the Parisian who looks at native or immigrant people and says, "How peculiar," "how exotic," or "just pitiful." So I told her that during the war when she was six, or seven, on the top of her village she had this . . .

JMG: . . . cloud . . .

FD: . . . cloud of planes, all the RAF, they were going to bombard the Ruhr in Germany, then Dresden. I said, "Don't you remember? The noise?" "No, nothing happened," she said, and could remember only her sadistic mother. And then I raised my arms and I did what we did when we were kids playing the bombardment game. I said "Don't you remember?" [FD makes loud sound of planes.]

CC: You did that in the office?

FD: Yes, we enjoyed that game in my country school, when we were children.

Françoise Davoine at her home in Paris, December 12, 2012.

CC: With the noise.

FD: With the sirens. And she raised her arms, like me, and laughed. Then she said, "I remember now. The Germans arrived in our house. They were rounding up all the villagers because of an action of the resistance and putting them in the main square. We were hiding, especially, because we were Jews, and we were hiding my grandmother and me in the place for the hens. And they saw our feet. And they opened the door; they grabbed us. Right on the spot. They took us to the middle of the village where everybody was gathered. And the priest in that village said, 'OK, I will give myself up for those people.'" We were saved. That happened, and she said it. Then all the war came back to her memory, which had been blocked by the war with her mother.

There was a very nice film that we saw when we were children, *Jeux Interdits* (*Forbidden Games*).[43] It was, in our youth, one of the most famous films; its music was in every mouth. [FD sings a tune from the film.] It's about two children, and what are they playing? They are playing "burying the dead." They are playing in the cemetery with crosses. They have lost their parents, and they have this traumatic knowledge.

I hear people speaking about trauma, and they say that traumatized people lack this, they lack that, they lack, they lack, they lack, instead of seeing the active research, the inquiry, the resource of thinking in order to survive. And people don't see because, as Benedetti says,[44] in psychosis and trauma it's only the negative which appears and the positive is cut out.

So, why children? We have to go to the children, and as children, because it's children who know. Like the forbidden games. They know forbidden games.

JMG: We are analysts of forbidden games.

NOTES

1. Françoise Davoine and Jean-Max Gaudillière, *History beyond Trauma*, trans. Susan Fairfield (New York: Other Press, 2004), reprinted as *Histoire et trauma: la folie des guerres* (Paris: Stock, 2006). Françoise Davoine has also published *La folie Wittgenstein* (1992; reprint, Bellecombe-en-Bauges: Éd. du Croquant, 2012), trans. by William J. Hurst as *Wittgenstein's Folly* (New York: YBK, 2012); *Mère folle: récit* (Strasbourg: Éditions Arcanes, 1998), trans. by Judith Miller as *Mother Folly* (Stanford, CA: Stanford University Press, forthcoming); *Don Quichotte, pour combattre la mélancolie* (Paris: Stock, 2008), trans. by Horacio Pons as *Don Quijote, para combatir la melancolía* (Buenos Aires: Fondo de Cultura Económica, 2012); and *À bon entendeur salut! Face à la perversion, le retour de Don Quichotte*, with clinical essays by Jean-Max Gaudillière (Paris: Stock, 2013).

2. Davoine and Gaudillière, *History beyond Trauma*, xxvii.

3. See below for discussion of the French phrase. While the translation, here, is awkward in English, Dr. Gaudillière points out that another translation, such as "an encoding of the anti-past" or "an encoding of the non-past," would not capture the passivity of the one who has become the encoded.

4. Alain Touraine was the director of the Center for Research on Social Movements at EHESS, École des Hautes Études en Sciences Sociales, in Paris.

5. Dr. Gaudillière is referring to my visit to Dr. Davoine's father's home in Dijon earlier that day, where he has the painting Dr. Gaudillière is speaking about.

6. The expression comes from the historian in EHESS, Sabrian Loriga.

7. Davoine and Gaudillière, *History beyond Trauma*, 211ff.

8. Capitaine Humbert, *La division Barbot* (Paris: Librairie-Hachette, 1919). Ernest Barbot was a general, much loved by his men, who died at the beginning of World War I.

9. Annette Becker, *Les cicatrices rouges 14–18: France et Belgique occupées* (Paris: Fayard, 2010).

10. Davoine, *Wittgenstein's Folly*, 56.

11. R. D. Laing and David Cooper were associated with the "anti-psychiatry" movement.

12. *Family Life*, dir. Ken Loach (EMI / Kestrel Films, 1971).

13. Bruno Bettelheim, "How I Learned about Psychoanalysis," in *Freud's Vienna and Other Essays* (New York: Knopf, 1990).

14. General Philippe Pétain commanded the Second Army in World War I and was chief of state of Vichy France from 1940 to 1944; he was later convicted of treason for collaborating with the Nazis during this period.

15. Antonin Artaud, *Le théatre et son double* (1938), trans. by Mary Caroline Richards as *The Theater and Its Double* (New York: Grove Weidenfeld, 1958).

16. See, for example, Davoine and Gaudillière, *History beyond Trauma*, 47.

17. See, for example, Harry Stack Sullivan, "Research in Schizophrenia," in *Schizophrenia as a Human Process* (New York: Norton, 1974), 187.

18. See Davoine and Gaudillière, preface, *History beyond Trauma*.

19. Davoine and Gaudillière define perversion as the turning of people into things; see *À bon entendeur salut!* See also Françoise Davoine, "The Psychotherapy of Psychosis and Trauma: A Relentless Battle against Objectification," *Psychoanalysis, Culture, and Society* 17.12 (2012): 339–47.

20. Shoshana Felman and Dori Laub, *Testimony: Crises of Witnessing in Literature, Psychoanalysis and History* (New York: Routledge, 1992).

21. This is a reference to Alfred Einstein's "cosmological constant," which Gaudillière has altered in his own notion of the "anthropological constant." See the following exchange in the interview.

22. Dr. Gaudillière is making an allusion, here, to Sophocles's *Oedipus at Colonus*, in which the chorus says, famously, "Never to be born is best" (see lines 1211ff.).

23. I am referring, here, to Dori Laub and Susanna Lee, "Thanatos and Massive Psychic Trauma: The Impact of the Death Instinct on Knowing, Remembering, and Forgetting," *Journal of the American Psychoanalytic Association* 51.2 (June 2003): 433–64.

24. Mieke Bal, *Of What One Cannot Speak: Doris Salcedo's Political Art* (Chicago: University of Chicago Press, 2010).

25. Doris Salcedo's *Plegaria Muda* (Silent Prayer), 2008–2010; Mieke Bal refers to the installation, which was about to be exhibited, at the end of her book on Salcedo.

26. Dori Laub, "The Empty Circle: Children of Survivors and the Limits of Reconstruction," *Journal of the American Psychoanaytic Association* 46.2 (June 1998): 507–29.

27. Davoine and Gaudillière, *History beyond Trauma*, 209ff.

28. See Juan Rulfo, *Pedro Páramo*, trans. Margaret Sayers Peden, intro. Susan Sontag (1955; reprint, New York: Grove, 1994).

29. Aby Warburg (1866–1929) was a German art historian and founder of a renowned private library for cultural studies.

30. See Françoise Davoine, "The Characters of Madness in the Talking Cure," *Psychoanalytic Dialogues* 17 (2007): 627–38.

31. Danielle Gouze was the name of Prime Minister François Mitterrand's wife before she married.

32. The interview with Bruno Bettelheim and Rudolf Ekstein was conducted by Dr. David May in the home of Dr. Ekstein in Los Angeles on January 10, 1989.

33. Claude Lanzmann urges the survivor, Abraham Bomba, to carry on his testimony "for history," at a famously difficult moment in Bomba's testimony. See *Shoah*, dir. Claude Lanzmann (Historia / Les Films Aleph, 1985).

34. Michael Snyder et al., "Personal Omics Profiling Reveals Dynamic Molecular and Medical Phenotypes," *Cell* 148.6 (2012): 1293–307.

35. Dr. Davoine uses the Spanish word *toca* in reference to my lecture, "Disappearing History: Scenes of Trauma in the Theater of Human Rights," now a chapter in *Literature in the Ashes of History* (Baltimore: Johns Hopkins UP, 2013). The use of the French word *touché*, as the exchange continues, is an allusion to *History beyond Trauma*, xxvii.

36. The reference here is Hannah Arendt, "Isak Dinesen: 1885–1963," in *Men in Dark Times* (New York: Harcourt Brace, 1970). See also the end of Hannah Arendt's 1967 essay, "Truth and Politics," reprinted in *Between Past and Future*, rev. ed. (New York: Penguin, 2006).

37. See, for example, Davoine and Gaudillière, *History beyond Trauma*, 153ff.

38. Ibid., 76, 175; Davoine, "Characters of Madness in the Talking Cure."

39. See Hannah Arendt, "Truth and Politics" and "Lying in Politics" (1971), reprinted in *Crises of the Republic* (New York: Harcourt Brace, 1972).

40. Ludwig Wittgenstein, "Remarks on Frazer's *Golden Bough*," *Philosophical Occasions: 1912–1951*, ed. James Klagge and Alfred Nordmann (New York: Hackett, 1990), 129. See also the last sections of Davoine and Gaudillière, *History beyond Trauma*.

41. Harbin is a city in northeast China to which many Russian Jews emigrated, and some German Jews as well, during the period of the Nazis.

42. Frieda Fromm-Reichmann was a German-born psychiatrist and psychoanalyst who emigrated to the United States, introduced the analytic psychotherapy of psychosis in Chestnut Lodge, and helped found the William Alanson White Institute in New York.

43. *Jeux Interdits* (Forbidden Games), dir. René Clément (Silver Films, 1952), later redesigned as a novel by the screenwriter, Francois Boyer.

44. See, for example, Gaetano Benedetti, *Psychothérapie de la schizophrénie: existence et transfert*, previousy published as *La mort dans l'âme* (1999; reprint, Toulouse: Érès, 2010).

PART II: A Revolutionary Act

Douglas Crimp, New York City, November 16, 2013.

The AIDS Crisis Is Not Over
A Conversation with Gregg Bordowitz,
Douglas Crimp, and Laura Pinsky

Gregg Bordowitz is an activist, videomaker, and writer who was involved in the movement to end government inaction on AIDS. Douglas Crimp is the author of several books, including *On the Museums' Ruins* and *Melancholia and Moralism: Essays on AIDS and Queer Politics*, and editor of *AIDS: Cultural Analysis / Cultural Activism*. He is also co-author (with Adam Rolston) of *AIDS Demo Graphics*. Laura Pinsky is a psychotherapist in private practice at the Columbia University Health Service, where she directs the Gay and Lesbian Health Advocacy Project. She has co-authored (with Paul Harding Douglas) *The Essential AIDS Fact Book*. The following conversation took place in New York City on September 25, 1991.

I. Engendering an Audience

CC: Trauma can be experienced in at least two ways: as a memory that one cannot integrate into one's own experience and as a catastrophic knowledge that one cannot communicate to others. In what ways can the AIDS crisis be called traumatic?

DC: One of the unstated premises of my essay "Mourning and Militancy"[1] was the incommensurability of experiences. What in this context would be something like trauma producing, I think, is that certain people are experiencing the AIDS crisis while the society as a whole doesn't appear to be experiencing it at all. Richard Goldstein[2] said that it's as if we were living through the Blitz, except that nobody else knows it's happening. Here's a personal example of what I mean by incommensurability: I once was visiting a very, very sick friend in the hospital and, later that night, coming out of the hospital, experienced a minor form of fag bashing: somebody going by in a car, screaming "Fag, AIDS." Just when you feel most vulnerable and most deserving of sympathy, you get the opposite, an attack, for precisely what you are at the moment feeling the most vulnerable about.

TK: The complexity is that it's not simply that some people are living through the Blitz and other people don't know about it, but that they *do* know it, in a different way. Because they knew something, you were addressed. After all, if there's one thing that everybody knows, or thinks they know, it's something about AIDS. Isn't one symptom of the crisis precisely the fact that there's not a clean boundary between the inside, which is experiencing it, and the outside, which isn't?

GB: People with AIDS, or people living with AIDS, and the people surrounding them are seen to have a kind of causal relation to AIDS, so that those people who've heard about AIDS *are* living with AIDS but are not directly affected by the experience of having it or knowing someone who has it. They know, and they do not want to know.

LP: People don't want to hear very much about the experiences of those who are living with AIDS, for all kinds of complicated reasons. People who are ill often want a chance to talk about it: about going to the hospital, sitting in the doctor's waiting room, about what their symptoms are, what their bodies feel like, what medications they are taking. It is often hard to find someone who is willing to listen to this.

CC: So part of the traumatic experience itself is the relation to other people, others who are actively aggressive or simply don't want to listen?

DC: Apart from the corporeal reality of the disease, we could say that if there's trauma associated with it, it's a socially produced trauma. In that sense it's not like a catastrophe that just happens; it is of course itself catastrophic, a catastrophic illness, but at the same time the negative effects—the extremities—that most of us experience are social.

CC: Kai Erikson speaks of "community trauma," in the case of a town that was flooded through the negligence of a coal company (the kind of disaster he refers to as "technological disaster").[3] Part of the traumatic experience of the community as a whole was that sense that the catastrophe wasn't just an accident of nature but that no one cared about what happened.

TK: There's a double trauma here. One the one hand, there's a cataclysmic event, which produces symptoms and calls for testimony. And then it happens again, when the value of the witness and the testimony is denied, and there's no one to hear the account, no one to attend or respond—not simply to the event but to its witness as well.

GB: That's why Kimberly Bergalis is so important, because she does not speak as a person with AIDS identifying with the community of people with AIDS.[4] She never has a "Silence = Death" pin on; she is never seen in relation to or next to other people with AIDS; she has never been pictured talking about early intervention or what it's like living with AIDS. That's why she's significant, and that's why she's being pushed forward at us, over and over again: to make up for all the time that we've managed to get on TV as people with HIV or AIDS, to talk about what it's like living with AIDS.

LP: In contrast to Belinda Mason, who became completely identified with the community and became part of the political struggle.[5]

GB: Kimberly Bergalis doesn't identify at all with the community affected by AIDS. In fact, this was "done to" her *by* that community—she identifies as its victim.

TK: There's a way in which the telling of the story, the testimony of the affected community, functions or can be received as an accusation, by those who thought they were uninvolved. The testimony is an address, which means that it's a provocation to a response. And that's what they don't want to give. They don't want to respond to the person who has called—for responsibility. When someone says, "I don't want to hear about it," or counters with a slur, they are telling the truth. They are creating themselves, as something insulated in its generality from the specificity of the address, by disavowing any involvement with the one who appeals.

GB: That's how the general public is constructed. Because if you look historically at the ways in which people with AIDS have been presented, on television for instance, we have been placed behind potted palms, given masked or scrambled faces, and pictured pretty much the same way as criminals, prostitutes, terrorists have been. Then, eventually, somewhere in the late '80s, we were allowed to speak about our experiences, but only to some mediator. Finally, the last border, which has still to be transgressed, is the person with AIDS looking out into the audience and addressing another person with AIDS or HIV, forcing the realization that there are people with AIDS or HIV in the audience. Probably the closest we've come, as I recall, was a show that hybridized two different stories, a CNN news anchor who had AIDS together with the newscaster in San Francisco who did a weekly show on his illness. The trick was a kind of superimposition: show-

Gregg Bordowitz, New York City, November 16, 2013.

ing the character with AIDS talking on his news show, but always *on television*. So it was television on television, but still it was the first time you ever saw a person with AIDS look out directly into the camera, into the audience, and address people with AIDS. And that is the only instance that I have actually seen.

Two years ago, at the international AIDS conference in Montreal, I was interviewed when [New York City Health Commissioner] Stephen Joseph announced his contact-tracing plan.[6] As an HIV-positive person who had gone through the anonymous testing procedures, I tried to talk about it on television. I kept trying to look into the camera and to say that as an HIV-positive person, as a person who needed anonymous testing, I would never have gone had there been contact-tracing. I say I am HIV positive in public at great peril: there's an enormous amount of stigma attached to it; it's only because of a certain amount of privilege that I'm allowed to do it. I know I won't lose my job, etcetera. And I kept trying to look into the camera and say, "If you need HIV-antibody testing, you should go to an anonymous clinic; don't settle for confidential testing," etcetera. Because that was the content of most of what I said, none of that ended up on CNN. The only thing that ended up on CNN was a clip in which I said nothing: the camera just pointed to me, and the caption said, "Person who went through anonymous testing." But they didn't picture me saying anything.

DC: The interviewer said, "Can't you put yourself in other people's shoes?" In other words, he wanted Gregg to identify with the HIV-*negative* "general public." They had no desire to hear from an HIV-positive person.

GB: The reporter said, essentially, "Answer the questions as through you were in my shoes"—as though I were HIV negative.

CC: We're back to the question of address: what Dori Laub calls the ability, or the inability, to say "thou." The problem of witnessing the Holocaust was that when you were inside the event, you could not address anyone outside: there was no "thou," as Laub puts it.[7] Which meant that you could only be an object, without anything like a relation of address (which is what people are trying to establish now—during a time when, as people say, "the AIDS crisis is not over").[8] The attempt to address seems limited to two possibilities: either you can only address as someone completely different or you can't address at all.

DC: Identifying oneself as HIV positive or as a person with AIDS has been the intent of a lot of people with AIDS and HIV in the arena of media—not merely to humanize or to give a face to the disease but also to acknowledge that there could be people with AIDS or HIV in the audience. The primary function actually has

Laura Pinsky, New York City, November 16, 2013.

been to engender an audience of people with AIDS and HIV and not to sway people one way or the other who didn't identify with the community in some way.

LP: This problem comes up over and over again in terms of AIDS education. It's generally assumed that the reader is not HIV infected. That's the standard and has been for a long time, including most safe sex education. For a while it was very common to see as one of the safe sex guidelines "Don't have sex with anybody who is HIV infected." It was crazy-making to think of what somebody was to do with that if they were HIV infected. In our educational work at Columbia, we've made a big effort to address our information to somebody who may be himself or herself infected. And sometimes this is seen as not addressing the general public.[9] "You're being too specific, you're not talking to everybody."

CC: This raises the question of how you do address people, for example, when you address them as an activist. Do you address them as people who are like you or who are different from you, that is, who have to recognize the specificity of people who are living with HIV or AIDS? What is the value or what are the problems of addressing a public by saying, "We all have to identify with each other?" When you're speaking into the camera directly, you say you are directly addressing people who are HIV positive. What relation are you trying to establish to those who are not?

GB: None.

DC: A relation could be established . . . I would think that it could be very shocking since it is not a habit of television—at least not for any group that is reported about but never directly spoken to (this would be true of an address to queers)— to treat those people not as an ethnographic subject but as the very subject to whom you are speaking. I think that that would be shocking; there would be a kind of shock of recognition.

GB: When it first occurred to me that you could address people with AIDS or HIV in television interviews directly and try to engender them as an audience, the secondary effect was that people who were not HIV positive would realize that there were HIV-positive people in the audience.

II. Constructing the "General Public"

DC: The biggest problem with even thinking about audiences is that one usually begins with some completely absurd fiction of generality, that is, with the notion that there could be a language that could reach everyone, or anything like a general public that could simply be addressed without exclusions. I don't think you could ever make any kind of cultural work that functioned as a general address.

But the problem, of course, is that we live in a culture in which it is assumed that you can, always. And in fact almost every cultural work is made with that fiction of a general audience in mind.

TK: Which means that it is addressed to a particular audience that masquerades as a general audience.

DC: Exactly.

GB: The general public is a market, a fictional market. Advertisements are posed to it, and the intention is to get people to identify as a group that would want to buy specific products for specific reasons. For activists, the point cannot be simply to address a general audience. That's why at GMHC we're trying to produce community-specific television, produced by members of the communities for themselves and in their own interests—because a mutually exclusive criterion has been established, either general or specific.[10] As Douglas has clearly articulated, that is a false dichotomy, an opposition which does not exist. *The general public does not exist.* Except for Kimberly Bergalis, the first example.

DC: There's a certain sense of trauma in the difference between one's own experience and a sense of something like "society's" experience, which one gets in the daily assault of reading the *New York Times*.[11] I'm thinking of those occasional feature articles about the fears and anxieties of people who have in some way possible become infected—cops who get needle sticks making arrests or, for example, a story that appeared in the *Village Voice* about a woman who was raped and insisted that the rapist be tested. In this latter case (a curious one, since she had tested negative a number of times but nevertheless was taking AZT prophylactically), a significant portion of the article was devoted to her experience of her timer going off in public places in order to remind her that she had to take her AZT and the embarrassment and anxiety attached. Now, this was something that is the daily experience of a number of gay men who are my friends. And the people that I know who are taking AZT know that they are infected. I know of no stories in the media about the anxieties of gay people or IV drug users who have AIDS or are HIV infected. Nor have I seen a story in the mainstream media during the entire ten years of this epidemic that deals with the anxieties of gay men, generally, regarding for example what this epidemic has done to our experience of our sexuality. This is how one of the worst aspects of homophobia shows itself, in the suggestion that homosexuality is a simple choice, because it's assumed that we could all now make the choice not to be homosexual. It's as if the disruption of millions of gay men's lives could simply be wished away by the assumption that we could all become celibate or heterosexual or whatever. And that can be productive of a certain kind of traumatic experience.

CC: What do you think was happening there, in this substitution of people who are not infected with the AIDS community for those who are as witnesses of the crisis, as substitute witnesses? What does it do to the people who are not speaking but who could be, and who could be heard? Is it perhaps an active way of avoiding, not listening to others by listening to those people who have been constructed as the general public?

GB: I don't know if empathy is the right word, but the substitution intervenes in a kind of empathy that I think AIDS activists hoped they might be able to generate by being able constantly to bring our stories forward, to humanize the stories, to show that we are people in the communities, that we are people you know, and so on. It's very easy for Kimberly Bergalis to appear on television saying, "I am someone you know," because she is not gay and she is not other in ways that many of the people from the various communities hardest hit by AIDS are. And she refused to identify herself. So she reaffirms, and very quickly, what was a very stable notion that people with AIDS and HIV in the communities affected by it want to give it to "us," that they will not be happy until "we" are infected by it as well.

DC: The fact is that Kimberly Bergalis is a person with AIDS who has managed to achieve a kind of empathetic reaction in someone like Jesse Helms. It makes you wonder: if that's the way empathy gets constructed, is empathy anything we would even want to strive for? Because it seems that empathy only gets constructed in relation to sameness; it can't get constructed in relation to difference.

TK: In fact, you have to become Jesse Helms in order to receive the empathy: that's the structure of empathy. No one except these simulacra of the general public will receive the empathy. But that means that this phantom—the general public—is the most traumatized of all. It's having the nightmares, suffering from the flashbacks, uncertain about what has happened to it. It knows that it has undergone some change, that its world has been altered in a potentially life-threatening way, but it can't identify the event.

DC: So the general public as Kimberly Bergalis, as it get constructed in all forms of representation . . .

TK: . . . in ways that are designed to marginalize the people who are actually undergoing it . . .

DC: . . . as a transfer of the experience of AIDS (whether or not *it's* a trauma)—

there's a kind of negation of that experience, through the construction and consolidation of a traumatized "general" subject.

TK: It's not allowed to happen to the people that it's happening to, and it's allowed to happen phantasmatically to the people that it's allegedly not happening to.

GB: I'll say it again: Kimberly Bergalis is the first member of the general public. There was a big effort to get Ryan White to play this role, but he resisted. Kimberly Bergalis does not resist: in fact, this is how she identifies herself.

CC: So empathy and a certain mode of understanding, or what you talked about, Doug, as the problematic structure of empathy, would be crucial in constructing this general public. Empathy is what the public is supposed to learn to feel, but it solidifies the structure of discrimination. In this case, empathy as a kind of understanding or of relation seems to reinforce the gesture of exclusion rather than the recognition—or what Douglas called a "shock"—that might come from some other mode of contact.

GB: It's always very complex, and the identities are constantly shifting. For example, on *Oprah* today the people who were HIV positive on the panel—other than Kimberly Bergalis, who was on a television next to the people on the panel—were gay white men. So immediately there was this opposition created, the dichotomy required for the formation of the general public: Kimberly Bergalis against the gay white men. And it's supposed to be the gay white men who want to conceal this, who want to hide this, who are dishonest. One member of the audience, speaking to a doctor on the panel, said, "You are dishonest for not informing your patients you are HIV positive." Implicitly, it was the people on the panel who had infected Kimberly Bergalis, and they were dishonest about it: people in the audience actually stood up and said they were not courageous, they were cowards.

Now, the complexity resides in the fact that a huge portion of the audience were people of color, and they had legitimate questions and fears around infection —which clearly pointed to the fact that, more than anything else, there is still an enormous lack of education around how HIV is transmitted. What was interesting was that what was being constructed there, in fact what was being erased, was the fact that an enormous number of people with AIDS in this country are people of color.[12] It was simply a matter of white gay men threatening the general public. You know that on television today it's a rare instance where people of color are pictured as members of a viewing audience, and it seems to happen today particularly in the service of a certain kind of message. The fact that there was not one person of color with AIDS on the panel, and that only people of color in the audience (in the section I saw) were asking questions antagonistically to the doctors on the panel, structured a very divisive and very reactionary moment. It suggested that AIDS is primarily a disease of gay white men, who still threaten the rest of us.

III. Changing Identities: Living and Dying with AIDS

LP: You know, I would raise one objection to the way our conversation is moving, which is that it keeps moving away from the experience of people who are HIV infected. I'm not criticizing what we're talking about, but it is easy to lose sight of the issue of the variety of actual experiences HIV-infected people have.

GB: If the distinction is between going into the realm of analysis and talking about specific needs, I would much rather do the former than the latter, because I'm really tired of identifying as HIV positive. I think that that's something to speak about, now, particularly historically. Now we're at a time when there are people who've been alive long enough, other than the very few people who are long-time survivors of AIDS, to have had the experience of having been consistently and continuously thrust into the public and defining themselves only as HIV positive. It's complex, and it's something to think about. It seems like it's no longer sufficient merely to put oneself forward as surviving and thriving and having a "chronic manageable disease"—there's actually a crisis of faith around these notions. Whereas three or four years ago a lot of us were disclosing our HIV status because we wanted to put out the message that you could live with us, that it was a chronic manageable disease, now that we've been experiencing more and more the deaths of our friends, and a lot of us have been getting increasingly ill, and there is actually nothing in the pipeline as far as treatments go, it is becoming a more and more desperate situation. It is becoming difficult to believe in the compelling notions that were once the reasons for disclosing one's status. It's like walking down the street and seeing those posters with smiling faces that say in handwriting, "I'm living with HIV." And I just detest them.

DC: The difficulty is in the relation that existed between what you told yourself in relation to hopefulness and what you told the world in relation to hopefulness. In other words, by making it public, by adopting the rhetoric of "living with AIDS," you were actually, in a certain sense, persuading yourself. Now you have a crisis of faith around it because you still recognize the necessity of the rhetoric but it's no longer persuasive to you.

GB: At one time I thought it was an identity, and I realize now that it's not. I was on a panel yesterday at GMHC, and I knew I was on the panel as the HIV-positive person. I realized, and I said, that it's important that in any group such as this someone who has HIV identify as HIV positive. But in fact, it's not an identity at all. I was of a generation of people who had to come out during the AIDS crisis, which meant pride around a sexuality that was stigmatized as a disease in a way that had never been done historically before in such a concrete sense, but nonetheless, my gay identity is not to be confused with my HIV status. Now, more and more, it seems to be important to talk, among ourselves anyway, about the sense of diminishment felt by a lot of us who have consistently and repeatedly identified ourselves as HIV-antibody positive, as though our identity is just reduced to the status of our health.

LP: There is no right place to be on this question. On the one hand, HIV-infected people sometimes need to feel that HIV disease is chronic and manageable—in some way you have to believe this. People have to keep up some kind of hope since they have to go to the doctor, take AZT, and do other tedious and frightening things. On the other hand, it may feel embittering to have to talk in an optimistic way if you feel that you are going to die or if your good friend just died. One of the things you have to remember about HIV disease is that a lot of people are being diagnosed as having this disease when they're perfectly physically fine, with absolutely no clinical symptoms. There is a long period of time before people develop symptoms; the average time between infection and the development of symptoms serious enough to be called AIDS is eleven years. People are getting tested early on and then living without symptoms but with a potentially fatal disease for more than a decade. And during that period of time there's a question for the individual about identifying as a person with AIDS. People can't always go around thinking of their identity as HIV positive, and yet they can't afford not to think about the disease.

TK: Is the problem that at a certain point the assertion of this identity constituted a political intervention—and was understood as making a certain kind of progress, even transforming the debate to a certain extent—and now the gesture doesn't have the same force? Or is it that having an identity itself is becoming a problem?

GB: No. It's that the gesture has to be rethought because the terrain has shifted. There was a reason why. I identified as HIV positive for the same reason that most identities, particularly disenfranchised identities, are formed: through negation. The notion of the "AIDS carrier" was the precursor of the self-identified HIV-antibody-positive person, and that identity emerged in defiance and in resistance to the fantasy of the "carrier." Now it's no longer as compelling and as meaningful to me to say the same things over and over again—which might be just the effect of the repetition, but I do think that other things need to be said. It's not enough merely to say, "I'm living with this disease."

My discussions with Douglas, when he was writing "Mourning and Militancy," were useful to me because we were treading on ground I hadn't been on before, because I was speaking about death. It didn't seem to me that many HIV-positive people felt as though they could speak about death, and I thought that was important. It seemed very difficult to talk about mortality, and it's still difficult to give voice to things that I think, and that other people who are HIV positive think, but that we don't necessarily think about. For example, sitting in a memorial service and fantasizing that it's yours. I don't know if everyone does that, but I certainly do that. And particularly since all the memorial services that I go to are for people with AIDS. I listen and hear what people say—and I usually think that nice things will be said about me. One of my closest friends died last year, and I've had three co-workers die over the past year at GMHC, in my department. And when I see somebody getting sick, I don't say, "That *could* be me," I say, "That *will* be me." So it's very painful and sometimes intolerable.

LP: And what people want to say is, "That can't be me." They want to find things that are different between themselves and that person. "They didn't take care of themselves, they had a bad attitude, they didn't think positively, etcetera." Blame can be a way of putting distance between yourself and someone else with whom you are afraid to identify.

TK: So the same inside-outside structure we saw in the case of the general public reproduces itself here, but within the "inside."

GB: Frankly, more than anything else, I think it's important to talk about the lack of real options, and the lack of the secular thinking around death, the lack of philosophical options for people with AIDS and HIV. I think there's a paucity of different options for thinking about one's mortality. And that needs to be developed.

LP: There are two common pictures: either the image of people tortured by the world outside them yet feeling strong and fighting back (which is a particularly useful propaganda picture) or the image of the victim alone, helpless, lying alone in bed. But neither of these pictures leaves room for understanding the complexity of the psychological issues of HIV disease, for example the way disease inevitably brings up preexisting conflicts. It's a difficult topic to discuss because, when you talk about intrapsychic issues, someone may feel blamed or that you do not understand that there is a real assault from the outside, that there are real political enemies, and that the medical care system is terrible.

TK: You both seem to be saying that now there's a therapeutic as well as a political necessity for the AIDS community to think about death. That in some way it hasn't been thought about and that there are very few resources right now for thinking about it.

GB: I think that it has been thought about on the same kind of model we produced before—at once too little knowledge and too much knowledge. In the same way that the invention and exclusion of the person with AIDS has constructed the general public, we've experienced our deaths as spectacle for the general public. Until recently, the only thing you could see on national television would be images of the quilt. An aerial image of the quilt, "two football field sizes big," the shot of reading the names, and maybe someone famous like Michel Foucault —actually they always showed Rock Hudson—would have their name read. And so we experienced the representations of our deaths only as spectacle for the general public. There was a real resistance to allowing us to picture the deaths that we experienced, our experience of mortality. Things get worse because of the lack of philosophical options for thinking about death. Options are scarce, and people are desperate for ways of thinking about this. To the point where there's this notion, which I despise, this New Age philosophy, that AIDS is a gift and challenge and it's going to make me a better person. I don't think it's a gift, and I don't think it's a challenge.

DC: It's actually a huge industry, especially on the West Coast. Louise Hay runs an enormous industry: she has meetings every week in Los Angeles, called "Hayrides," and thousands of people go to them and buy her books and tapes.[13]

GB: Then there's religion. When my friend Ray died, he became extremely religious. He was not religious, was even somewhat antireligious, before he got sick. And when he got sick, he got religious, and I found myself in a predicament: I wanted to be supportive because I loved my friend Ray, but I don't believe in God. But I would be at his bedside often, and we talked about God a lot. I was instrumental in getting him a priest when he wanted it and negotiating these things because we all had weird feelings around Ray's increasing religiosity. And it made me realize that there were no options. It has been my experience that the people who get sick and who are terminally ill have two choices: the New Age-ism of Louise Hay and the religion of their childhood. And that's it. There's no specific writing about philosophical considerations around dying when you're a person with AIDS. That's changing—for instance, with the fiction of Allen Barnett[14]—but slowly.

TK: And what about the political consequences for activism and other, say, public interventions?

Thomas Keenan, Tel Aviv, Israel, July 31, 2013.

DC: It certainly has political consequences in the sense, for instance, that divisions within ACT UP, or in the AIDS community, have entailed certain moralistic positions deriving from hierarchies of oppression. The splits in ACT UP chapters around the country have generally occurred because of a different sense of priority and urgency among members. On the one hand, those who are HIV positive tend to want to stress the short term and therefore emphasize the development and testing of treatments. On the other hand, there are those in the movement—many of them HIV negative—who are more concerned with broader struggles and the long term, for example, the need to create national health care. This has often played itself out in very destructive ways.

CC: That makes me think again of what you, Douglas, said before about empathy, that its structure is something that somehow elides thinking about death. Something is not confronted there, when you think you're understanding or empathizing in a certain way. The construction of the general public, that we discussed before, also somehow doesn't allow that, to come into that kind of knowledge or empathy for anyone. And, as you point out in "Mourning and Militancy," the problem takes on an added urgency for those who *must* identify with the dead.

DC: I think there might be some kind of psychic prohibition about identifying with the dead, because then it's really about confronting your own mortality. I think that it's terribly difficult for anyone to do that in any full way.

NOTES
1. Douglas Crimp, "Mourning and Militancy," *October* 51 (1989): 3–18.
2. Richard Goldstein, "A Plague on All Our Heroes," *Village Voice*, Sept. 16, 1987.
3 See Kai Erikson, "Notes on Trauma and Community," in *Trauma: Explorations in Memory*, ed. Cathy Caruth (Baltimore: Johns Hopkins UP, 1995), 183–99.
4. Two days after this interview took place, in a story datelined "Washington, Sept. 26," and illustrated with a front-page photograph of Kimberly Bergalis, the *New York Times* reported the following:

> Kimberly Bergalis, wearing pale flowers and the strands of short, sandy-colored hair she has remaining after her treatment for AIDS, was wheeled into the witness table in Congress to utter 15 seconds of testimony. In a weak, slurred voice, the 23-year-old woman said: "AIDS is a terrible disease that we must take seriously. I didn't do anything wrong, but I'm being made to suffer like this. My life has been taken away. Please enact legislation so other patients and health-care providers don't have to go through the hell that I have. Thank you." Though extremely frail, Mrs. Bergalis traveled by train from her home in Florida to offer brief testimony in support of a bill that would require AIDS testing of health-care professionals who perform invasive procedures . . . Mrs. Bergalis has come to

personify issues in AIDS as no one has since Ryan White, the Indiana boy who was infected through a transfusion and who died last year. She has attracted widespread news coverage, partly for the anger she has focused on the medical establishment. When Mrs. Bergalis arrived here on the train from her home in Fort Pierce, Fla., on Wednesday, local television cameras covered the event live.

See Philip Hilts, "AIDS Patient Urges Congress to Pass Testing Bill," *New York Times*, Sept. 27, 1991.

5. Belinda Mason, a member of the National Committee on AIDS, died of AIDS on Sept. 9, 1991, in Tennessee. The *New York Times* reported in its obituary for her that in August she had pleaded with the president to oppose mandatory HIV testing of health care workers. She had become infected in 1987 through a blood transfusion during the birth of her second child. See Philip Hilts, "Belinda Mason, 33, U.S. Panelist and Bush Advisor on AIDS Policy," *New York Times*, Sept. 10, 1991.

6. On Stephen Joseph, and the lengthy campaign by ACT UP against Joseph's AIDS policies, including the Montreal contact-tracing proposal, see Douglas Crimp with Adam Rolston, *AIDS Demo Graphics* (Seattle: Bay, 1990), 72–76, and Douglas Crimp, *AIDS: Cultural Analysis / Cultural Activism* (Cambridge, MA: MIT P, 1988), 16–17.

7. See Shoshana Felman and Dori Laub, *Testimony: Crises of Witnessing in Literature, Psychoanalysis and History* (New York: Routledge, 1991).

8. For a reproduction of the 1988 activist sticker that bears this slogan, see Crimp, *AIDS Demo Graphics*, 40–41.

9. See Laura Pinsky and Paul Harding Douglas, *The Essential AIDS Fact Book* (New York: Columbia UHS, 1987).

10. Jean Carlomusto and Gregg Bordowitz produced the *Living with AIDS* cable television program for over three years at GMHC (formerly the Gay Men's Health Crisis) in New York City. GMHC is the nation's oldest and largest AIDS service organization, providing services and advocacy to people with AIDS.

11. See Crimp, *AIDS Demo Graphics*, 108–14.

12. According to the Centers for Disease Control, of the 191,601 people diagnosed with AIDS in 1991, 54% were white, 28.8% were black, and 16.2% were Hispanic. See Centers for Disease Control, *HIV/AIDS Surveillance Report, September* (Atlanta: CDC, 1991).

13. See Louise Hay, *The AIDS Book: Creating a Positive Approach* (Santa Monica, CA: Hay House, 1988).

14. Allen Barnett, *The Body and Its Dangers* (New York: St. Martin's, 1990).

Judith Herman at her home in Cambridge, Massachusetts, May 16, 2013.

Chapter Six

The Politics of Trauma

A Conversation with Judith Herman

Judith Herman is a renowned psychiatrist at Harvard Medical School. Her research and clinical innovations regarding incest, trauma, and the wider response to the sexual abuse of women and girls have profoundly affected the field of trauma studies, as well as societal responses to sexual abuse. Her classic books *Father-Daughter Incest* and *Trauma and Recovery* have brought together important lessons from the women's liberation movement with psychiatric research and clinical experience to provide new models for thinking about trauma and its treatment. On May 16, 2013, I met with her at her home in Cambridge, Massachusetts, to discuss the new insights into incest that she helped to introduce in the 1980s and the impact that a feminist perspective can have on our understanding of sexual abuse and trauma more widely.

I. INCEST AND SOCIETY

CC: I would like to begin with a remark that I heard you make many years ago at a lecture in Bridgeport, Connecticut. You had been speaking about father-daughter incest, and after the lecture a man in the audience asked, "Aren't most of these cases of incest perpetrated by men who were battered or abused when they were children?" You answered,

> No; only a very small percentage of men who commit incest were abused as children. The "cycle of violence" explanation is appealing because it gives us

the illusion that we understand the perpetrators, but in fact, most victims do not become perpetrators, and most perpetrators were not victimized as children. If the "cycle of violence" theory were correct, we would see mostly female perpetrators, which we do not. Incest is a far more widespread phenomenon in our society than can be accounted for by the idea of a "cycle of violence," and thus we need a larger, social explanation for this phenomenon.

I was really struck by this comment, which suggests that we cannot understand incest in terms of a psychology of the individual but must rather turn to broader social factors.

In the 2000 afterword to your first book, *Father-Daughter Incest*, you reiterate this point from your lecture: "No one has been able to come up with a psychological profile that might identify incest offenders because they look too normal. Careful psychiatric evaluations fail to uncover signs of mental illness. Indeed the majority do not qualify for any psychiatric diagnosis."[1] As you suggest later, in *Trauma and Recovery*, "this is deeply disturbing to most people. How much more comforting it would be if the perpetrator were easily recognizable, obviously deviant or disturbed, but he is not."[2]

These are remarkable statements and must have been, at least originally, controversial. They point to the political and social framework that you use to discuss incest and to examine trauma more generally in your later work. Could you begin by explaining what you mean by saying that we can't turn to hypotheses regarding the pathology of individual fathers to explain the prevalence of incest in our society?

JH: This is not just my opinion; it's what the data show. There are actually some reasonably good studies of sex offenders in general and of incest perpetrators in particular. One that I have cited often was conducted in the 1980s at New York State Psychiatric Institute by Gene Abel, a psychiatrist who is now in private practice in Atlanta, Georgia, and Judith Becker, a psychologist who is now at the University of Arizona.[3] They studied sex offenders, whom they identified by word of mouth and through various sex ring networks and advertisements. They provided enormous confidentiality protection for the subjects, and under those circumstances the men were actually quite eager to talk about what they did because they felt so misunderstood. These men were subjected to extensive SCID [Structured Clinical Interview for DSM Disorders] interviews for diagnoses of major mental illnesses, and also for character disorders. The men were then shown pornography with what is colloquially called the "Peter Meter," which measures blood flow to the penis. After the Peter Meter, the men tended to cop to quite a bit more of what they had actually done.

One of the things the study found was that there wasn't such a clean dividing line between one kind of offender and another. Incest offenders were also rapists; pedophiles would at times expose themselves, etcetera. But the study also found that, according to the SCID diagnostic criteria, over 50 percent of the men did not qualify for *any* psychiatric diagnosis. This includes alcoholism, which is a frequent excuse for child abuse.

So for over half the men there was no alcoholism, certainly no psychosis, no character disorder even. Whatever this pathology is, we don't have good information that helps us identify it. This is similar to what happened in the aftermath of the Holocaust, when psychiatric exams were done on the Nazi criminals—the war criminals—and lo and behold, they didn't qualify for psychiatric diagnoses either, much to everyone's shock and horror.

CC: This seems to be the reason that you suggest, in *Father-Daughter Incest*, that the pathology has to be understood on the level of a larger, patriarchal structure in our society. As you say in this book, "We consider overt incest to be only the most extreme form of a traditional family pattern. Overt incest represents only the furthest point on a continuum, and exaggeration of patriarchal family norms, but not a departure from them" (109–10). And you point out that incest does not occur most often in families that are falling apart, as one might perhaps expect, but rather in families that look very respectable, with traditional family and religious values. Moreover—equally surprising—women who come out of these incest histories do not necessarily end up hating men, but rather they may overvalue men and devalue women: "Thus do the victims of incest grow up to become archetypically feminine women, sexy without enjoying sex, repeatedly victimized, yet repeatedly seeking to lose themselves to the love of an overpowering man, contemptuous of themselves and other women. In short, they were well prepared for conventional femininity" (121).

These various points support a larger, sociocultural understanding of incest. Can you comment on what you mean when you say that incest must be understood as only the most extreme form of a traditional family pattern?

JH: What you see in the family dynamics of incest you can see in both strictly conventional families and families that are falling apart. There is an enormous power imbalance between the father and mother. The mother is incapacitated, either because she is physically or mentally ill, or because she is battered and is terrified of any assertion of power in the family. Under those circumstances, the oldest daughter is often deputized to be the concubine of the father as well the caretaker for the whole family.

In terms of the devaluing of women, what you often see with survivors is that, from their point of view, it doesn't matter why their mothers were incapacitated. The mother was the person to whom the child turned for protection, and she failed to provide protection that the child needed. That neglect, that betrayal of trust, felt in some ways even worse than the incest. At least the father was paying attention, however perverse his interest was.

CC: You also say that the daughters prefer to identify with the power of the father, rather than with the powerlessness of the mother.

JH: Who wouldn't?

CC: So, in that sense, the incest is, to a certain extent, about power and about perpetuating a particular power structure. Is this why we can't describe it as a mental pathology, unless we want to say our entire culture is pathological?

JH: Yes. I think we have to look at how frequently incest occurs when you get these extremely patriarchal family patterns—whether they are of the religious fundamentalist sort or of the battering sort, or of the variant where the father takes no caretaking responsibility and the mother is left to raise the children on her own, while the father simply fathers children as a sign of manhood. In all of those variations, the woman is subordinated and rendered powerless and her protective function for the children is thereby incapacitated.

CC: That's interesting; it reminds me of the comments of Shoshana Felman and Dori Laub about the bystanders in the Holocaust, who essentially did not bear witness because they could not integrate what they saw, or else because they acted powerless—they didn't act to prevent what was happening.[4] It sounds like what you are saying is that the mother, in these family situations, is turned into a kind of non-witness. By being rendered helpless in the power relations with her husband, she becomes like a non-witnessing bystander in larger, collective events of victimization.

JH: Right. And to the extent that she is also invested in the preservation of the family—and thus keeps the family secrets—she participates in the denial of the abuse. You know there are many instances where the child at least believes that the mother knew or should have known.

CC: It's striking if we look at the recent Ohio case[5] in which three women were being held captive for ten years in a man's house in the middle of a populated neighborhood, and most of the neighbors and friends say that they had no idea that it was happening and that he seemed like such a nice guy. But he had battered his first wife . . .

JH: And he had kidnapped his kids.

CC: So the question of what was known and not known is a little murky there, too.

JH: Yes. Of course this is a very exciting case because it's a rare example of "stranger danger," and the press loves those cases. The common scenario, however, is not being kidnapped off the street by a stranger but rather being held hostage and tied up by your nearest and dearest. When I talk about this and try to name the larger pathology, I suggest that the abolition of slavery notwithstanding, the idea of a woman or a girl in chains is still quite appealing to a large subpopulation of the male persuasion, so appealing in fact that we have an enormous and highly profitable pornography industry furnishing images of women and girls in chains or otherwise tied up and enslaved. And if you doubt that, just type "girls in chains" into your computer and see what you get.

We also have the bizarre popularity of *Fifty Shades of Gray*,[6] which is basically a soft porn novella trio about enslavement, in which the male is much older, much more knowledgeable sexually, and much more powerful financially and socially, and the female is virginal and naïve.

CC: Is this the structure of power that you were describing as typical of the incest family?

JH: Yes. And this is presented as sexual liberation, and much to my surprise, many women still buy it. It's the sleeping beauty fantasy or the bodice ripper[7] fantasy: the patriarchal fantasy of rescue and initiation by an older man. It's a variant of the incest fantasy.

CC: So you're staying it's still prevalent in our society in spite of the increased awareness of these issues that resulted from your book and other feminist work in the 1970s and '80s.

JH: I think women owning their own sexuality is still pretty rare.

II. Open Secrets

CC: A moment ago you spoke about the mother keeping the secret of incest within the family. You write, in your first book, of the "incest secret." Indeed, in the studies of incest that you undertook in the 1970s, you defined an adult-child sexual encounter in the family as any physical contact that "had to be kept a secret." And you found that the child in these studies often felt that the fact that the encounters must be kept secret—along with the sexual motivation of the encounters—was often more disturbing than the acts themselves.[8] You also describe how many incest survivors don't report the incest until they are safely out of the family, and sometimes the survivors don't remember the incest until later. In this sense, incest survivors seem to be, in their own ways, "bearers of the secret," a term that the Holocaust survivor Louis Micheels used to describe Jews during the Holocaust, who had imposed upon them by the Nazis the burden of keeping the secret of their own annihilation.[9]

There are, of course, some circumstantial reasons for this secrecy surrounding incest—for example, the father doesn't want to be found out so he can continue the abuse. But I am wondering if one might also say that the secrecy is part of what the incest is actually about: forcing silence on girls.

JH: It is also about shaming. To my mind the subordination involved in these forms of victimization is itself experienced as shameful. For example, many Jews who migrated to Israel in the aftermath of the Holocaust didn't talk about the enormity of their suffering because that didn't live up to the image of the healthy, strong Jewish pioneer, a militarized image that was perhaps a defense against the humiliation of having been victims of persecution and genocide.[10]

CC: So the shame involved in trauma is one means by which the secret is kept. It seems that if one is keeping a secret because of shame, then this isn't necessarily a secret one simply chooses to keep. The victim is warned, is threatened, and is shamed so that she doesn't keep, but is rather, essentially, kept by, the secret. Or perhaps turned into one.

JH: You have a secret identity. We saw this with incest survivors and with other trauma survivors as well. You have the defiled self that is kept secret, and then you have the public face. Incest survivors learn to be very good girls; many learn to perform in school and become cheerleaders or athletes or achieve in various other ways. Compartmentalizing can be lifesaving. If you have some area of confidence and strength and social reward that you can cultivate, that's healthy. But what is not so healthy is the idea that "this is my false self," that this is the facade that I present to the world, and that if people really knew the secret of my true self, I would be abhorred.

CC: Since you understand the incest phenomenon through patriarchal societal structures, and since secrecy is so central to incest, do you think you could make a larger generalization about patriarchy and secrecy or silencing?

JH: Well, patriarchy has lots of dirty little secrets, of which incest is only one.

CC: It seems, from what you say, that incest is in part a way of teaching women that they need to be silent. It starts with this one secret, but maybe that's a training in a larger kind of silence.

JH: Well, doesn't St. Paul say that a virtuous woman who keeps quiet is much to be praised?

CC: So the survivor keeps a secret and the society keeps a secret as well. We get a society with an open secret, something perhaps like Alexandre Koyré and Hannah Arendt referred to, in the context of totalitarianism, as an open secret, a secret that everyone knows.[11]

JH: Look at what's going on in India right now, where there was a huge outcry recently, after a woman and a man who had been out in public together were kidnapped, and she was raped and left to die.[12] He was beaten up and thrown out of the bus. He survived; she died a horrible death, of internal injuries from her rape. But it turned out that this kind of thing had been going on all the time. Numerous women came forward to talk about their rapes and also about being out in public and being grabbed, groped, harassed. This was about women going out in public, in the agora, and being told, in action if not in words, that the public world was not their place. The message was, "You belong indoors in seclusion, and if you come out in the man's sphere, this is what you can expect." Eventually this case became the focus of widespread outrage, and the poor, overwhelmed rape crisis centers and women's centers that had been trying to raise awareness about this for years finally had a platform—a teachable moment. This is in the country with the second largest population in the world. So it's not just a Western phenomenon.

CC: There was an outcry, but people knew before.

JH: Including the women who had been raped but had kept quiet about it because they didn't want to be cast aside by their husbands or their families.

CC: So it was not necessarily a collusion, but participation in maintaining a secret that nonetheless was an open secret of some kind.

JH: It had to be kept secret because the punishment for the women, if it was disclosed, was even worse.

III. An Affliction of the Powerless

CC: This issue of secrecy and silencing brings me to the shift in your writing from an emphasis on familial sexual abuse in *Father-Daughter Incest* to your work with different kinds of traumatic experiences in *Trauma and Recovery*. Although the word "trauma" doesn't appear very often in your work on incest, that early work nonetheless seems to influence your perspective on trauma, insofar as you refuse simply to focus on individual pathology, or on the physiological or neuro-biological bases of trauma (though you do address these matters), but insist on looking, rather, at the broader social and political arenas. Thus you write, in the acknowledgments section of *Trauma and Recovery*, that the book owes its existence to the women's liberation movement. You also designate trauma as "an affliction of the powerless" (33), which, as I understand it, can mean both that it happens to powerless people and that that it renders people powerless. For this reason, you suggest also, in the first chapter of this book, that "the systematic study of psychological trauma depends on the support of a political movement" (9)—presumably because trauma exposes various modes of domination and is thus met with various modes of silencing and denial.

Would you talk about how the feminist analysis of incest led to your particular perspective on psychological trauma and how a feminist or sociopolitical analysis helps us understand the nature of trauma beyond an analysis of the traumatized individual?

JH: Well, first of all, this perspective is not unique. I think many of the pioneer generation in traumatic stress studies had an explicitly sociopolitical understanding. Certainly Robert Lifton and the Vietnam vets who raised awareness about what they called "Vietnam Syndrome" were coming from a political perspective.[13] It was really the testimony of the Vietnam veterans that led to the recognition of a specific post-traumatic diagnosis in the *DSM-III* [*Diagnostic and Statistical Manual of Mental Disorders*, third edition] in 1980 and the opening up of a new field in psychology and psychiatry.

And to a certain extent a feminist analysis is no more or less than a human rights perspective or a democracy perspective applied to the power structures of gender or sex. The silencing of trauma survivors is always about the disempowerment of traumatized people, and that includes veterans, because, as many warriors returning home have discovered, the myth of the warrior and the actual experience of the warrior are two very different things. One is celebrated, and the other is not spoken about.

CC: It sounds like this silencing may be one important factor that makes possible the comparison of so-called male (such as war) and female (such as wife-battering) traumas, which was such an important element of your book, and something that had not really been done before. In this sense, women's "private" traumatic experiences were seen to have the "value" of men's public ones, just as men's battlefield experiences, for Freud, resulted in something like the (primarily) women's "hysterical" symptoms he had studied in his early career.

IV. Empowering Memories

CC: You also note, in chapter 1 of *Trauma and Recovery*, that the history of the study of trauma has, itself, been beset by an oscillation of knowing and not knowing that characterizes the "dialectic of trauma" that the scholarly work in the field studies (47ff.). I wonder if there is a new form of silencing that is occurring nowadays, just when the field becomes more firmly established and the notion of PTSD is more widely recognized. In the 1997 afterword to *Trauma and Recovery*, you note that the more legitimate the field becomes, and the more often the term "post-traumatic stress disorder" is used, the more it becomes a disorder and the less it is associated with social or political protest:

> Legitimacy, however, can be a mixed blessing. The next generation of researchers may lack the passionate intellectual and social commitment that inspired many of the most creative earlier investigations. In this new, more conventional phase of scientific inquiry, there is some cause for concern that integrative concepts and contextual understanding of psychological trauma may be lost, even as more precise and specific knowledge is gained. (240)

In what ways is this new conventional phase possibly dulling the original contextual understanding of trauma?

JH: Well, for example, we now see a major effort to come up with a brand of therapy, preferably very short-term, that will affect a cure and get rid of these unpleasant symptoms. They have rolled out this whole new "evidence-based" program at the VA [Veterans Administration], and of course it's a disaster. They're not reaching a lot of people. Now part of the problem is that they just don't have enough staff. The prevalence of PTSD in soldiers returning from Iraq and Afghanistan is similar to, if not higher than what was seen in, Vietnam veterans, and there just aren't enough people to treat these guys. But the new program is also not offering a treatment that would allow the vets to become therapists for one another. It's not rocket science. What do you do for people who have been isolated and shamed into keeping secrets? You bring them into a group where they can support one another and share their secrets.

CC: As you say in your book, that helps empower them.

JH: Yes, because they see that they have compassion for the other group members. You do have to structure the group properly. This is my other beef with the VA. At one time they did a very ambitious ten-site study of group therapy, but they had no idea how to do a trauma group, as far as I could see. I saw a videotape of one of these groups that they were offering. One man was talking, weeping, and just crying his heart out about what he did and what he witnessed. And the other group members were silent and checked out. They were dissociated, and unable to be supportive, because the group leaders didn't contain and didn't model anything about feedback.

Now our program has produced a workable model for a trauma-focused group.[14] First of all, group members have to be currently safe—not heavily substance abusing, not suicidal, and they have to have some social support in their current lives. And then the group leaders have to help them both contain their feelings—this is not an exorcism—and also listen to other group members, so that they learn how to give and receive feedback. Because it's only in this way that people repair their connections, discover that other people have compassion for them, and are challenged about why they don't have compassion for themselves.

They also discover they have a lot to give. They're not just receiving treatment. They're not just "compliant" patients who are simply having some "one-size-fits-all" treatment applied to them. They are actually co-therapists, who have something to offer one other.

CC: That seems also seems to be a way in which your understanding of the power imbalance integral to traumatic experiences is important, because the treatment has to alter the sense of being powerless.

JH: The last thing you want is a compliant patient. It's like nails on a blackboard for me when I hear about "good compliance." But this is the medical language.

CC: So you're seeing, in the groups, the effect of this medicalization in the VA . . .

JH: In the VA groups, yes. You know, these are not empowerment groups. These are not the kind of groups that Robert Lifton and Chaim Shatan did way back in the beginning with the Vietnam Veterans against the War.[15]

CC: I have a general question that relates to the underlying issues of traumatic experience that are being treated in these groups, especially as these issues were perceived by the Vietnam Vets against the War, and perhaps more broadly. It seems to me—based on what I have read of writers like Robert Jay Lifton as well as the vets' own poetry, that those vets understood what they called their "Vietnam Syndrome" as a first, unwitting attempt at some kind of witness—or protest. I'm wondering if there would be a way to understand the PTSD symptoms themselves as a kind of attempted witness to trauma, understood through your particular perspective on the "dialectic of trauma" as an inextricable relation between knowing and not-knowing, not only individually but socially. In other words, the traumatic symptoms may involve a kind of self-silencing, but they are also, perhaps, attempts to break that silence since they return and insist upon being noticed.

JH: But they are not empowering. People feel as though they are at the mercy of their symptoms. We do a lot of education at the beginning. In fact, our starter group is what we called a "trauma information group." We have topics that people read and discuss every week, and the first one is post-traumatic stress disorder. We go over the symptoms, and we help people try to understand that these are normal responses, if you will, to an abnormal situation, to a situation of helplessness and terror and shame, and that in some ways you can think of both the intrusive and numbing symptoms as memory distortions—as abnormal memories. Your task in trauma treatment is to transform them into normal memories that have a narrative, that serve as witness within one's internal story and in relation to others. [Pierre] Janet says that there is a narrative that we tell ourselves about our lives and also one that we tell others.[16]

CC: Which is addressed to others—which has an addressee.

JH: Yes.

CC: What you seem to be saying in response to my question, then, is that to the extent that survivors' memories are self-defeating or self-silencing memories, they are also disempowering memories rather than empowering memories. And that what you're doing in therapy, in part, is trying to enable a transformation of memories that make people less empowered into memories that can help empower them?

JH: Yes. From disempowering memories that are traumatic to memories that are just a part of your life story. And although they're terrible memories, they're not the whole story about you.

CC: You quote Janet in a number of places, who said that ordinary memory is "the action of telling a story."[17]

JH: Right. So you are moving from passively experienced symptoms to an active understanding and retelling of what happened.

CC: Part of what is happening in therapy, then, is the transformation of memory, itself, from passive to active. And that's also about a form of empowerment—in this case on the level of memory. That is, you can now *have* the memory.

JH: Yes, and you can put it away.

CC: So in that sense would this transformation of memory have a potential political significance? Because if you're a traumatized person and you are constantly defeated by your memories, you're not able to use them to challenge others.

JH: They are just challenging you all the time.

CC: And through their transformation they can become part of political action, acts of political challenge, in ways that they were not able to before? Or perhaps the political action, alternatively, is rather part of the recovery?

JH: Not everyone does this. But early research on rape survivors indicated that the ones who went on to have what Lifton called a "survivor mission"[18]—some sort of larger social understanding of the trauma that led them into some kind of social action, regardless of the kind of action—made particularly good recoveries.

V. An Act of Solidarity

CC: This brings me to a comment you make in *Trauma and Recovery* about the stance of the [trauma] therapist: "Bearing witness is an act of solidarity." You continue, "Moral neutrality in the conflict between victim and perpetrator is not an option. Like all other bystanders, therapists are sometimes forced to take sides" (247). This statement has interesting resonances with some of the comments made by Françoise Davoine and Jean-Max Gaudillière in their interview with me, where they emphasize the need to challenge the stance of traditional psychoanalysis in the case of extreme trauma and psychosis. In your case, the connotations of the word "solidarity" seem to suggest that the moral significance of the therapist's stance may also have a political dimension. How would you respond to therapists who argue that you are only supposed to help people get better?

JH: I do support what I would call technical neutrality, in which you don't have an agenda for this person, and you don't take sides in the person's inner conflicts. So if the person comes to a place of wanting to be politically active, that's all well and good, but you can't impose that agenda on a patient because that's just another form of imposition and disempowerment.

CC: What does it mean, then, when you say that you're not morally neutral?

JH: For example, when you hear what happened to a person, you say, "I feel terrible about what happened to you; that's a horrible thing that was done to you." Or, "I feel very sad; I feel very angry for you. I feel horrified." You share the fact that this is an outrage and that no one deserves to be treated, in your view, the way that this person was treated. But that's not the same as saying you should go out and do X, Y, and Z about it.

CC: Interestingly, it seems like that moral affirmation is what some groups—say, the False Memory Syndrome Foundation[19]—wrongly describe as a form of non-neutrality in the technical sense of attempting to persuade a person how to act in relation to certain memories of abuse.

JH: They were much more specific about it; they said we were going in and planting memories in gullible patients. To which I kept answering, "Don't I wish! If I could implant memories, I would implant happy ones . . . " [Laughter]

CC: It's not so easy.

JH: Supposedly we are so lacking in work that we try to drum up business that way!

I think the usefulness of a stance of solidarity becomes really clear with the political asylum work that we do. People seeking asylum are often referred to our program by their attorneys, in order to receive a psychological evaluation in support of their asylum application. And of course we cannot testify to the facts of their petitions because we weren't there, and we don't know the facts. But we can testify to whether or not, in our professional opinion, the patient has post-traumatic stress disorder and whether the symptoms are consistent with the story that the patient tells. For example, we can explain that the fact that the patient did not immediately tell a uniformed immigration officer on arrival that she had been raped would be consistent with the common phenomenon of delayed discovery—the delayed reporting that one sees with many rape victims, and that refugees might be particularly unlikely to disclose to a uniformed officer if they have been raped by members of the military or police in their home countries.

And so what happens is that these people come in to the therapist's office, and they're doing this only because the lawyer said it would be a good idea to do it, and they are terrified of the interview. It's just another authority figure to them—this time, a doctor—and they're often practically mute, looking at the floor, frozen. Then, bit by bit the story comes out, and the therapist expresses compassion and righteous indignation on behalf of the abused person. And the fact that the therapist is willing to sign an affidavit and, if necessary, appear in court and testify on behalf of the asylum application is experienced as an unexpected act of solidarity by a stranger. We work with a bunch of good lawyers who also know how to do an asylum application, but I think that, in addition, having a professional willing to testify, whether or not the professional comes to court in person, really influences the judges, and we have a very good track record. Nationally, fewer than 20 percent of asylum applications are approved, but we've been very fortunate, and most of our patients have eventually received approval.

CC: So the therapist serving as a witness to the patient seems not only to help the victim but also to affect the legal system. In the therapist's affidavit there is a larger form of witness taking place.

JH: Yes. We are using our professional credentials and power to try to influence other powerful people. So somebody who was driven from his or her country is welcomed in a way that is unexpected. And that's pretty powerful. People sometimes come back for a course of therapy after they've received asylum, but often they don't, because the cure has already been provided by the court. When their asylum petition is granted, their PTSD symptoms go way, way down. I mean, talk about "evidence-based" treatment . . . They're no longer in fear of being deported back to the same horrors, and for the first time they can sleep at night.

VI. The Dialectic of Trauma

CC: We have been talking a lot about secrecy and testimony in treating trauma and advocating for victims. One of the things that interests me most in your writing is something that has already come up, what you refer to as the "dialectic of trauma": the simultaneous presence of knowing and not knowing, of intrusive and constrictive symptoms, in traumatic experience, as well as in the social context surrounding trauma and the study of trauma. In this context you often focus on the function of denial, both on the individual and societal levels. Thus in "Crime and Memory," you write, "This conflict is manifest in individual disturbances of memory, the amnesias and hypermnesias of traumatized people. It is also manifest also on a social level, in persisting debates of historical reality of atrocities that have been documented beyond any reasonable doubt."[20] You also refer to different national sites of denial, such as Chile under dictatorship, the Soviet Union, and so on. Could you talk a little bit about how you understand the relation between the individual dialectic of trauma and the social, political, and collective ones? And how does this affect your understanding of the treatment of trauma?

JH: In order to have an ecosystem that fosters recovery, you need one that supports the truth-telling function, both on the individual and the social levels. On the individual level this is confined to the therapy room, where one of the basic ground rules is that this is a safe place to tell the truth. The effectiveness of the therapy rests on the ability to tell the truth. Similarly, in any kind of social recovery or survivor mission, or in creating a society where traumatizing events don't keep happening to people, you need to have truth-telling on a larger scale. So you go from the consulting rooms of Vienna, where the secret is privately acknowledged, to the consciousness-raising groups of the New York Redstockings and other radical feminist organizations.[21] Often when I give my talks now I show photos of two big paintings from the Salpetrière in Paris. Both are heroic patriarchal tableaux from the nineteenth century. In both paintings the courageous (male) doctor, he who dares to investigate the mysteries of the mind, is shown rescuing the mad (female) patient. One painting portrays [Jean-Martin] Charcot as he displays a (female) patient with hysteria to an auditorium filled with learned (male) doctors, and the other shows [Philippe] Pinel striking the chains off the (female) insane.[22] The women's bodices are undone, and their faces are blank empty stares. One is on her knees, and another is kissing Pinel's hand.

And then for contrast I show a picture of a consciousness-raising group from the late 1960s. (This term was created by my friend Kathie Sarachild, who became an organizer, first in the civil rights movement, and then in the women's liberation movement, and I owe the picture to her.) The photo, from the New York Redstockings, shows a bunch of alert women with their clothes on, actively engaged in speaking with one another, and there's a little sign on the wall saying, "Bitch sisters, Bitch!"

CC: That's good!

JH: And so you go from the consciousness-raising group, which had therapeutic functions but was not a therapy group, to public speak-outs, public testimony, and then to worldwide public testimonies, things like V-Day or Take Back the Night or the Clothesline Project,[23] just to name a few that have gone worldwide.

CC: Do you understand this as a progression that starts individually and then becomes larger?

JH: It always starts relationally, with people telling their secrets to someone who listens, who acknowledges and validates. Otherwise, the silencing is very powerful. The shame is very powerful. The terror is very powerful.

There's a saying in the battered women's movement that "a good beating is good for a year." And you'll hear women say things like, "I saw the expression in his face, and I saw that he could really kill me, or he could kill the kids, and he could track down my parents." Or, "He said that if you ever leave, if you ever tell anybody, I will track you down wherever you are and kill you." And after that the woman keeps her mouth shut. She obeys, and she doesn't take risks. God forbid she should actually go and get a restraining order and try to leave—that's the time of greatest risk. So you need to have little notices in hospital bathrooms and doctors' offices bathrooms that say, "Are you afraid of someone you love? Here's a number to call, and here's a tiny little card that you can hide in your shoe so he won't find this number, and someday when the time is right, you can call this number." So you have to have that kind of context.

CC: That evokes the image of people in totalitarian societies who can't risk speaking.

JH: Some families can be a microcosm of a totalitarian society.

CC: It also sounds like it is not only individual families that operate like larger totalitarian systems but also that, in a patriarchal society, there may be a whole class of people living under something like totalitarian rule. It's not just something that occurs in in this or that family, in other words, but operates, rather, as a collective phenomenon.

JH: Like any other dictatorship, a patriarchal system is ultimately maintained by force and terror. And it's also maintained by custom and shaming, and it's maintained by economic power. I don't know if you've ever seen the violence wheel; it is a graphic that originated in battered women's programs. In the middle of the wheel is power and control, and the spokes of the wheel are things like intimidation and terror, economic power, isolation, using the children, and so on. Because in order to understand what traumatized people have been subjected to, you have to understand what they mean when they say that "it's not just the violence." It's a whole system of coercive control, the purpose of which is to maintain power and control. It's a system of dominance and subordination.

CC: And in the context of the "dialectic of trauma," this system appears to be inextricably bound up with not knowing, with silencing, and with bystanders not witnessing, both inside the family and in society as a whole.

JH: In the same way, dictatorships are usually maintained by coercion and making sure that nobody says boo, and ultimately by torture. By the way, the methods of coercive control that were defined by the battered women's movement are no different from the methods practiced by torturers. We know that one clandestine police force teaches another how to do it, with political violence. But with gender-based violence, how do these guys know? How come they are so proficient in these techniques? My personal theory is that the missing link is the worldwide prostitution industry. The pimps teach men how to do it, either directly via the sale of women and children or indirectly via pornography.

CC: So it's really like an education process; it's a training process.

JH: A colleague of mine, Rick Kluft, interviewed a pimp and asked him how he recruited his women. He answered that the main thing you're looking for is obedience. You can teach the sexual techniques and all that, but what you want is somebody who has already had (forced) sex with her father or uncle or brother, someone she loves and dares not defy. And that's borne out by the research. First of all, most women are recruited into prostitution well below the age of consent, in the early teens. Thirteen seems to be the average age. Pimps look out for teenage runaways who are trying to escape abusive homes, and the pimps promise the girls love and protection. Or the girls are pimped by their parents or grandparents or other family members. So I think there is a direct connection between child abuse and the sex industry.

CC: So the sex industry and the child abuse that it helps foster maintains itself, like the dictatorships you mentioned above, through a kind of coercive silencing, or rather, it supports a society of silencing.

VII. The Passionate Discourse of Survivors

CC: I would like to turn, now, from the question of societal knowing and not knowing in the context of of traumatic experience to the problem of scholarly knowledge as it arises in the study of trauma—the nature of its theoretical knowing or witness.

My question concerns the relation between the theory and the experience of trauma: the binding together of the person who writes about trauma with the experience she or he is writing about. I believe this comes out in a striking manner in your two books through your use of survivor testimony. In *Trauma and Recovery* you say that "the testimony of survivors is at the heart of the book" (3), and you go on to talk about your own attempt to write in a language "that is faithful both to the dispassionate, reasoned traditions of my profession and to the passionate claims of people who have been violated and outraged" (4). Your work is very striking in the way it brings together quantitative research with survivor testimony. What, in your perspective, is the reason for bringing into a scholarly book on trauma—through quotation, rather than through summary—the language of survivors?

JH: Well, if people actually are going to know anything about trauma, they do need to witness it as directly as possible. I did a lot of interviews, and I tried to select from them quotations that would, in a concise way, illustrate whatever the clinical points or political points were that I was trying to make. And to my mind I'm doing enough mediating and interpreting by creating this framework for understanding trauma, especially complex trauma. It seems to me that if the vignettes or quotes are carefully chosen, they illustrate, better than anything I could say, the points I'm trying to make.

CC: In one essay you suggest that clinical work is more of a craft than a science.[24] And you talk about how struck you were at the contrast between what people do in the office and when they try to write about it. From this perspective, could we understand your quotation of the words of the patients as also conveying a little bit more of the surprise you face as a clinician when these words come at you?

JH: Yes. I try to choose language that I find moving and powerful. And I try to do the same in my own writing. I've always felt that technical jargon in psychology and psychiatry tends to be very unhelpful.

CC: Because?

JH: It tends to be hard to understand and imprecise. [George Orwell's] "Politics and the English Language"—which is my writer's touchstone—explains my preference for simple sentences, simple words, words that are clear and that any literate person can understand.

CC: This must be what you mean when you write, in *Trauma and Recovery*, that you want a language that can "withstand the imperatives of double-think" (4). Does that mean, then, that you are trying to find a language that is clear enough that we can't obfuscate around it? Is that what you mean by clarity?

JH: Exactly.

VIII. Trauma and Shame

CC: In our discussion of incest at the beginning of this conversation, you mentioned that incest was in part about shaming. Recently, you have been working on shame in relation to trauma—drawing, among other things, on your mother's pioneering work on shame.[25] When I first encountered shame in your writing I was surprised because I had been used to the models of fear and anxiety associated with trauma. In one lecture, you emphasize the importance of the shame element to the relational aspects of trauma; while symptoms of trauma such as flashbacks and nightmares may arise from the fear response, you say, people don't generally come to therapy because of those symptoms but rather because of issues having to do with their relations to other people.[26] Would you say more about how our understanding of PTSD is affected by linking it to processes associated with shame?

JH: Shame sheds more light on the interpersonal component of PTSD, and specifically on interpersonal harm. There's a very reductionist conceptualization of PTSD, now, as an anxiety disorder that can be extinguished basically by exposure, much in the same way that you would extinguish a phobia. For example, in the treatment of agoraphobia, during which you gradually expose a person to more and more frightening stimuli—as when a person with fear of flying eventually goes on an airplane at the end of treatment. And many people think that's what you do with PTSD. You just make them rub their nose in the story, and then they have to listen to it over and over until they finally get so fed up that they leave therapy.

But what people come into therapy for is not only the fear and the horror but also the shame. For example, think of the guy who sees his buddy killed in the war and feels guilt: "I should have done more, but I was afraid; at the last minute I didn't stick with him to rescue his body—I ran away." And there is shame associated with that. He doesn't just think "I should have rescued his body and I didn't"—that's guilt. He also thinks "I'm a coward"—that's shame. Vets are very secretive about what they have done, especially if they have perpetrated violence, but also what they haven't done. So whether you're talking about combat or gender-based violence, you are talking about things that people feel very ashamed of. And shame is, if you will, a signal, just the way fear is a signal. Only it's a signal not of danger but rather of something gone wrong in a social connection, something that threatens a relationship that matters.

CC: It's interesting that this interpersonal dimension of traumatic experience also perpetuates itself—as in an anxiety response—but with a different mechanism from anxiety or fear. Because you suggest that one does not discuss the shame in part because one is ashamed of being ashamed, so the affect is self-silencing.

JH: Yes, and my mother used to talk about the vicious cycles of shame and shame rage. That people are ashamed of being ashamed, or ashamed of being enraged, and around and around it goes.

CC: It seems that this new work on shame brings you back to some of your earliest work on incest. And from this perspective, the rethinking of trauma in relation to shame may offer new ways to undo the silencing that always seems to be at the heart of trauma and that makes it an effect (and tool) of power differentials and of the many ongoing and continually renewed forms of political abuse.

NOTES

1   Judith Herman, *Father-Daughter Incest* (1981; reprint, Cambridge, MA: Harvard UP, 2000), 229.

2. Judith Herman, *Trauma and Recovery: The Aftermath of Violence—From Domestic Abuse to Political Terror* (1992; reprint, New York: Basic, 1997), 75.

3. See G. G. Abel, M. S. Mittelman, and J. Becker, "Sex Offenders: Results of Assessment and Recommendations for Treatment," in *Clinical Criminology: The Assessment and Treatment of Criminal Behavior*, ed. M. H. Ben-Aron, S. J. Hucker, and C. D. Webster (Toronto: M & M Graphics, 1985), 207–22; cited in Herman, *Father-Daughter Incest*.

4. See Shoshana Felman and Dori Laub, *Testimony: Crises of Witnessing in Literature, Psychoanalysis, and History* (New York: Routledge, 1991). See also Felman's and Laub's interviews in this volume.

5. Ariel Castro was convicted in 2013 of kidnapping three women and holding them captive in his home from nine to eleven years.

6. E. L. James, *Fifty Shades of Grey* (New York: Vintage, 2012). This book immediately became a worldwide bestseller.

7. Otherwise known as romance novels. The covers of the novels often have women in dresses with bodices being grabbed by a man, which led to their description as "bodice rippers."

8. Herman, *Father-Daughter Incest*, 70.

9. See Louis Micheels, "Bearer of the Secret," *Psychoanalytic Inquiry* 5.1 (1985): 21–30.

10. See the interview with Dori Laub in chap. 3.

11. See Hannah Arendt, *The Origins of Totalitarianism*, new ed. (New York: Harcourt, 1951), 376, and Alendre Koyré, 'The Political Function of the Modern Lie," in *Contemporary Jewish Record*, June 1945; a fuller version of the Koyré's text is available in the original French as "La function politique du mensonge moderne," *Renaissance: revue de l'École Libre des Hautes Études* (1943): 95–111.

12. The 2012 Delhi gang rape case involved a rape and murder that occurred when a twenty-three-year-old female physiotherapy intern was gang-raped on a bus in southern New Delhi; she died two weeks later. The case sparked outrage in India and across the world.

13 See Robert Jay Lifton, *Home from the War* (New York: Simon & Schuster, 1973).

14. See Michaela Mendelsohn, Judith Lewis Herman, Emily Schatzow, Melissa Coco, Diya Kallivayalil, and Jocelyn Levitan, *The Trauma Recovery Group: A Guide for Practitioners* (New York: Guilford, 2011).

15. See Lifton, *Home from the War*, and Chaim Shatan, "The Grief of Soldiers," *American Journal of Orthopsychiatry* 43.4 (1973). Lifton and Shatan were asked by the Vietnam Vets against the War to lead "rap groups" in which the vets discussed their feelings concerning their war experiences and frequently integrated these discussions with their political activism.

16. For more on Pierre Janet (and his notions of narrative and traumatic memory) see the interview with Onno van der Hart in chap. 8.

17. Pierre Janet, *Les médications psychologiques*, 3 vols. (1919–25; reprint, Paris: Société Pierre Janet, 1984), 2:272. See also Bessel A. van der Kolk and Onno van der Hart, "The Intrusive Past: The Flexibility of Memory and the Engraving of Trauma," in *Trauma: Explorations in Memory*, ed. Cathy Caruth (Baltimore: Johns Hopkins UP, 1995), 175, as well as the interview by Onno van der Hart in chap. 8.

18. See, for example, Robert Jay Lifton, *Death in Life: Survivors of Hiroshima* (Chapel Hill: U of North Carolina P, 1961), as well as the interview in chap. 1.

19. The False Memory Syndrome Foundation (FMSF) was founded in the early 1990s by Pamela and Peter Freyd after their daughter made accusations of child sexual abuse against her many years after the fact. The foundation focuses on what they call "false memory syndrome" and the recovered memory therapies they blame for much of it, insisting that patient suggestibility results in the creation of recovered memories.

20. Judith Herman, "Crime and Memory," in *The Trauma Controversy: Philosophical and Interdisciplinary Dialogues*, ed. Kristen Brown Golden and Bettina G. Bergo (New York: SUNY P, 2009), 127.

21. The Redstockings was a women's liberation movement group founded in 1969.

22. "Un leçon clinique à la Salpêtrière" (1887) by André Brouillet and "Pinel à la Salpêtrière" (1795) by Tony Robert-Fleury.

23. V-Day is a global movement to end violence against women and girls. Take Back the Night is a global organization dedicated to ending violence against women; some of their events involve marches at night. The Clothesline Project started in Cape Cod in 1990. Women draw or paint on t-shirts about violence against women and then hang the shirts on a clothesline to display them to others.

24. Judith L. Herman, "Craft and Science in the Treatment of Traumatized People," *Journal of Trauma and Dissociation* 9.3 (2008): 293–300.

25. Dr. Helen B. Lewis wrote many pieces on shame; for an early essay, see "Shame and Guilt in Neurosis," *Psychoanalytic Review* 58.3 (1971): 419–38.

26. See, for example, Judith Lewis Herman, "Shattered Shame States and Their Repair," in *Shattered States: Disorganized Attachment and Its Repair*, John Bowlby Memorial Conference Monograph (2007), ed. Judy Yelin and Kate White (London: Karnac, 2007).

Bessel van der Kolk at his home in Boston, Massachusetts,
January 3, 2013.

Chapter Seven

The Body Keeps the Score

An Interview with Bessel van der Kolk

Bessel A. van der Kolk is a prominent psychiatrist who, for many decades, has been a leader in the research and treatment of post-traumatic stress disorder, with special emphasis on the role of the brain and body in the etiology and treatment of trauma. He has also been President of the International Society for Traumatic Stress Studies. I sat down with him in his home in Boston on June 17, 2013, to discuss some of the surprising elements of the neurophysiology of trauma, the problems of dissociation and denial, and his latest explorations in creative new methods of healing.

I. The Indelibility of Trauma

CC: I would like to begin with the title of your forthcoming book, *The Body Keeps the Score: Mind, Brain, and Body in the Transformation of Trauma.*[1] The phrase "the body keeps the score" is adopted from one of your patients, whose story was at the center of the first lecture I heard you give, in the early '90s, and it has stayed with me all these years. As you narrate the story, this woman, who came to you as an adult, had been abused by her stepfather for a number of years when she was a child:

> During one session me she drew a picture of her childhood experience; in
> the picture there were three stick figures with their heads separated from
> their bodies by clouds. The title of the painting was "See no evil, hear no evil,
> speak no evil." When I asked her what it meant, she said, "my mind goes up

to the ceiling and I look down and I feel very sorry for that little girl down there. My mind forgets, but my body keeps the score."

Your patient seems to describe a dissociative experience, which many people have previously described in terms of a splitting of the mind, but which she describes as a split between mind and body. I'd like you to talk about how you understand this quotation, what it means to you, and why it stayed with you for so long.

BvdK: What this woman's words capture, for me, is a central aspect of trauma. Trauma does not simply result from the fact that something bad happens, because bad stuff happens all the time. Instead, in trauma you get overwhelmed by the experience—you cannot put it together. So trauma is all about disassociation; how the experience gets registered somewhere but doesn't get integrated as "Oh, a long time ago some really bad thing happened to me." It isn't integrated. Because the integrative functions of the brain fall apart—the imprints stay on different levels—so it doesn't get put together. You see images, you have sensations, you have emotions, but it doesn't get put together as something that happened a long time ago. That's not any different from what Breuer and Freud said 120 years ago in *Studies on Hysteria*. Trauma happens on the level of the brain and body, by the way it registers sensations that nonetheless remain fragmented.

CC: When you use the word "registered," it sounds like it actually doesn't refer just to one thing. It refers to a whole variety of phenomena happening during the fragmentation. Can you describe that fragmentation a little more?

BvdK: Stuff impinges on our minds all the time. Right now, for example, we are talking, we hear the sounds of our voices, we see images, and the thalamus [an organ between the midbrain and cerebellum that takes in sensory information and motor signals and sends them to the cerebral cortex] puts it all together. I am talking to Cathy Caruth, and the experience goes on, and you flow with time. So the function of the thalamus—the integrating function of the brain—breaks down. And what is emerging in my thinking is the function of the thalamus, the integrative function of the brain.

CC: When I originally heard and read your work on trauma many years ago, I understood that there were problems with communication among different parts of the brain during a traumatic experience, but I thought that the breakdown occurred at each point for different reasons. Thus, for example, you spoke about a breakdown in communication between the amygdala [the part of the brain that assigns emotions, part of the limbic system] and the hippocampus [the part of the brain that puts sensations in place and time], which occurred in part because of chemicals released that damaged the hippocampus. Are you saying that these breakdowns in communication between or among parts of the brain result from problems with the thalamus?

BvdK: Yes, we now understand that the breakdown occurs at the core level of integration. As a result, you continue to have emotions without context, to have visual images without context; you continue to have sound that is associated with terror, but no context in which this terror relates to the past, or to the present. So the big issue is that you lose your symbolic capacity. You may be able to say, "I feel this way because I was molested as a kid," but that doesn't make a difference: when triggered you still keep reacting as if you were being molested right now.

CC: So this fragmentation produces a two-sided experience, which we see in your patient's words: on the one hand, her sense of going up to the ceiling during the molestation and the fact that later "her mind forgets" and, on the other hand, her experience that, nonetheless, her body "keeps the score." This brings me to a central (and sometimes controversial) aspect of the notion of trauma, the way in which traumatic recall—or aspects of traumatic recall—unlike ordinary memory, seems to have an indelible quality. In "The Black Hole of Trauma," the introductory chapter to *Traumatic Stress: The Effects of Overwhelming Experience on Mind, Body, and Society*, you and Alexander McFarlane, your co-editor and co-author, speak of the way in which the repeated experience of trauma, when it comes back in a person's life, "etches [trauma-related memories] more and more powerfully into the brain."[2] This etching is not like ordinary memory and is part of what you refer to as a paradox. You speak about this as follows:

> Ordinarily, memories of particular events are remembered as stories that change over time and that do not invoke intense emotions and sensations. In contrast, in PTSD, the past is relived with an immediate sensory and emotional intensity that makes victims feel as if the event were occurring all over again. Thus paradoxically, the ability to transform memory is the norm, whereas in PTSD the full brunt of an experience does not fade with time. (9)

You seem to refer, here, to the paradoxical fact that sensations and feelings seem to be more "etched" in trauma, whereas in ordinary memory they are more flexible. What does that mean?

BvdK: The paradox is that it's normal to lie and distort. And the weird thing about trauma is that you take pictures of what happens. And you cannot let go of those images. Our minds are meant to live from moment to moment in the present, and to distort the past, so we can function in the present and accurately prepare ourselves for the future. This process breaks down in traumatic stress—it keeps you back there—and you are the victim of an incomplete experience. I can best illustrate this etching with an example: My partner was in a number of car accidents while someone else was driving. We drove up to Vermont this weekend, and for a while she does fine. But then another car comes by, and suddenly she goes into a panic. It's just a car coming within ten feet of our car. When a car comes within ten feet, the memory of that old trauma rushes back and is amplified. The sad thing is that every time you overreact, that new experience itself becomes a determinant of further trouble, and the kernel of desperate attempts to shut oneself down.

CC: So it's as if you were having a series of traumas instead of just the original one.

BvdK: At the end, the original trauma barely matters. What matters is that you keep having overwhelming emotional reactions to relatively innocuous things that happen right now. And that can happen at any time. You can be in your apartment, you can listen to something on the radio, and suddenly you have a flashback. You can be sitting in a movie theater with your lover, and he puts his hand on your arm and you have a flashback. The nature of trauma is that it just happens. And it's totally meaningless. You're somewhere and suddenly it hits you. And so—people have really moved big time on this in the last forty years—it's not the original trauma. The original trauma is over. It is these sensations every time that trigger you. And every time you get triggered you feel ashamed, you feel horrible, you feel out of control, and you are enraged at yourself and the people around you.

CC: This idea which, as you say, has been emerging more recently in the psychiatric study of trauma, seems to me to be a reiteration of something that was central in Freud's thought, which is the fact that the trauma is belated: it consists, essentially in its repetition.[3] What you have said just now is a different version of this notion, but to me it is an interesting revival of that idea on the neurobiological level.

BvdK: Yes, the repetition is at the core. I'd have to think about whether or not there are exceptions, but for argument's sake, we can say: the traumatic reaction is the repetition.

CC: So one way to think about the bodily "scoring" or "etching" of the trauma that accompanies the "forgetting" of it by the mind is in terms of its repetitive aspect. Indeed, you say in *Traumatic Stress*: "This new organization of experience is thought to be the result of iterative learning patterns, in which trauma-related memories become kindled; that is, repetitive exposure etches them more and more powerfully into the brain" (8). In this context, I would like to refer you to an essay from 1994 in which you write about the experiments done by Joseph

Ledoux that show how, during traumatic experiences, the ordinary processes of extinction of stimuli are hindered. Summarizing the research of Ledoux [1991] and Lawrence Kolb [1987], you write,

> In a series of experiments, Ledoux and coworkers used repeated electri-
> cal stimulation of the amygdala to produce conditioned fear responses.
> They found that cortical lesions prevent their extinction. This led them to
> conclude that, once formed, the subcortical traces of the conditioned fear
> response are indelible, and that "emotional memory may be forever." In 1987
> Kolb postulated that patients with PTSD suffer from impaired cortical control
> over the subcortical areas responsible for learning, habituation, and stimulus
> discrimination. The concept of indelible subcortical emotional responses,
> held in check to varying degrees by cortical and septohippocampal activity,
> has led to the speculation that delayed-onset PTSD may be the expression of
> subcortically mediated emotional responses that escape cortical, and possibly
> hippocampal, inhibitory control.[4]

Here, you suggest that the repetitive dimension of trauma is linked to the damage to areas of the brain that govern the extinction of emotional responses. "Indel-ibility," from this perspective, may be less about literal "etching" than about lack of extinction.[5]

BvdK: I think that's pretty much correct. Except we have learned something more—we can change the subcortical imprints.

CC: So one explanation, then, of what seem like indelible imprints (and we will come back to the question of change in a bit) would be, for example, that during a traumatizing experience we have sensations flagged by the amygdala as "extra scary," while other parts of the brain such as the hippocampus are damaged, thus inhibiting the extinction processes. I recall sitting in on some PET scan studies on the hippocampus conducted by Douglas Bremner that also support this view.[6]

BvdK: Yes. And there's damage to the anterior cingulate and the dorsal medial prefrontal cortex, the whole self-referential part of the frontal lobe that helps you to organize what comes from your survival brain.

CC: So on the one hand, we have things that are not being extinguished and, on the other hand, we have damage to areas that would allow for integration—putting the sensations in place and time, making them capable of becoming objects of reflection, etc. Thus we have both hypermnesia and amnesia, the combination of which seems to produce what we would call the "etching" of trauma. Could we say, then, that the strange imprint of the trauma isn't as much about a permanent mental representation, or even an "etching" on the brain in some literal sense, as the disruption or breaking-down of a system that would ordinarily produce representation, memory, etcetera?

BvdK: Yes, but the story has expanded. The big expansion is the thalamus and the brain stem. Because now we understand the circuits better, and what we left out is a piece of research we had done earlier—actually it was my first piece of research, and then we forgot it. And that is that people with PTSD suffer from REM [rapid eye movement] sleep interruption.

CC: This was your very first research in a lab, right?

BvdK: Yes, in 1985. We didn't know what to make of it, so we forgot about it. I thought insomnia was a dead end until we learned about EMDR [eye movement desensitization and reprocessing], which, if you read the current treatment outcomes, looks like the most effective treatment for PTSD. I actually did a study on that funded by the NIMH [National Institutes of Mental Health].[7] In EMDR, you wiggle your fingers in front of people's eyes and you don't ask people to talk. You do this with discrete, circumscribed non-attachment traumas (because the big bad wolf is attachment traumas). This helps set up a new associative network, the very thing that, I believe, Freud was looking for and didn't find. We discovered that about 80 percent of the people with non-attachment traumas are cured. Up till now no other treatment has come close to an 80–percent cure rate.

So how does EMDR do this? Because you don't really talk with people; you don't ask people to tell you stories or to remember. You ask people to evoke an image, the sensations, the thoughts at the time of the trauma. And they set up an associative network and afterward most people say, "it's gone." I showed this to Bob Stickgold—when I first met him he was a Fellow at Al Hobson's lab—and he said, "This is interesting. This is just like REM sleep."[8]

CC: So this brought back the work you were already doing when you were quite young, with [Ernest] Hartmann.[9]

BvdK: My REM sleep paper came out in 1985, almost thirty years ago; and then colleagues of mine found other things about disruptions in REM sleep and insomnia, and from time to time other people found things.[10] But then we dismissed its importance. Later Bob Stickgold made the connection, and everything came together.

You see, bad stuff happens all the time. We come home at night, somebody has bugged us, something bad has happened during the day, and we may feel enraged, upset and miserable. Then we go to sleep, and when we wake up, the next morning we often have found a solution. Sleep has an astounding way of integrating stuff. The next morning you are calm and take care of business. And so there is a natural system in the brain that allows you to integrate unpleasant things that happen to us.

CC: Is it also related to the thalamus?

BvdK: Yes, the thalamus is central. How do dreams and sleep process stuff? You're in deep sleep, stage 3 or 4, at which time you move information from the secondary sensory areas of your brain into your thalamus. And then during REM sleep, it moves into your prefrontal cortex and gets associated with all the other memories that are already stored.

CC: What happens in trauma?

BvdK: In trauma, that process is interrupted. Your emotions wake you up. The imprints are sitting there, ready to be integrated, but as the integrative-process brain starts—whatever happens during REM sleep that makes it possible—you wake yourself up. This interferes with your natural healing processes.

CC: Has the material made it to the thalamus?

BvdK: It has made it there, but then the thalamus doesn't do its thing.

CC: So the moment of waking is also the moment of dis-integration! An interesting way in which a traumatic awakening does not necessarily or immediately bring us into full consciousness.[11] And this brings me back to my question about the "etching" of trauma. It sounds like this term is being used as a metaphor—we are not talking about something that is literally "carved" in a substance, the way letters are carved into stone, or referring to changes in the brain that might operate in ordinary memory processes—since what is actually happening in trauma is the breaking down of a set of relations. The "imprinting" of the trauma doesn't simply take place in this location or that location but occurs as the disruption of an associative process at the moment of the experience.

BvdK: Right. It's a dis-integration. And integration is the critical issue. Your brain is an integrative organ. From the thalamus up, it's all about integration. The integrative process breaks down, and all these fragments take on a life of their own.

CC: Very interesting. So the "imprinting" of trauma can be understood in terms of the breakdown of a system. Which might give us a different perspective on the indelibility of trauma and move the debates away from whether or not trauma is a matter of a straightforward imprinting mechanism or a kind of "indelibility" than a process of disruptions along the pathways of integration. At the end of your discussion of emotional memory in your 1994 essay, you say that "conceivably, traumatic memories then could emerge, not in the distorted fashion of ordinary recall, but as affects, states, somatic sensations or visual images, for example nightmares or flashbacks that are timeless and unmodified by further experience."[12] If we think of this "unmodified" quality of traumatic recall in terms of the dis-integrative process you have just described, then the "etching" of trauma into the brain would be a figure for a process of disruption of this pathway, perhaps a different way of making a traumatic "path."[13]

BvdK: Actually the biggest mystery is not the fact that things are imprinted on the brain. The mystery is how on earth we forget everything that happened yesterday except some person who smiled at you, or insulted you—emotionally relevant experiences.

CC: Do you remember chapter 4 of *Beyond the Pleasure Principle*? Freud says there that the purpose of consciousness is, essentially, not to know too much—to lessen the input of stimulus. "Consciousness arises," he says, "*instead* of a memory trace."[14] Which sounds somewhat similar to what you're saying.

BvdK: This is really important. There is nothing controversial about the fact that people remember general schemes, rather than specific events—except when you are traumatized, when that system breaks down. But in order to study traumatic memories, you have to study traumatized people. You can't put people in a lab and shoot a videotape about a car going through a stop sign or a red light, and then say, "People don't remember this very well." Because sitting in a lab has nothing to do with getting raped or assaulted.

CC: You are speaking about the work on eyewitness distortion by Elizabeth Loftus.[15]

BvdK: Yes. If you want to study trauma, you have to do it in a field hospital in Afghanistan, or an emergency room, or with people who suffer from flashbacks.

II. Speak No Evil

CC: What you're saying reminds me of something that Dori Laub said to me in our interview when I asked him about some of the attacks on his work, suggesting he has distorted some of the Holocaust testimony on which he writes.[16] As you know, he is a child survivor of the Holocaust and listens to survivors all the time in analysis and in his interviews for the Fortunoff Video Archive for Holocaust Testimony at Yale. His interpretation of some of the attacks was that people don't actually want to know about trauma.

BvdK: That's right. It's a theme that runs through my book. I thought I knew the history of the First World War pretty well. And then I find out, in the process of working on this book, that on June 16, 1917, the British general's staff issues an edict saying that the word "shell shocked" can no longer be used; no more scientific papers are allowed to be published about shell shock. And when the United

States decided to invade Iraq, all the knowledge of what happens to soldiers was forgotten, and afterwards there is an outcry about how many soldiers become addicted to drugs, and how many engage in domestic violence, and how there are so many suicides after the war. Just like after the Korean War and the Vietnam War. Society wants to forget. I wrote an editorial for the *New York Times* prior to the invasion of Iraq (which I never sent in—and I am still angry with myself for not doing that)—in which I proposed that going to war is a choice you can make, but it's important to anticipate that half of the guys who come back will become drug addicts. And we can cut food stamps to poor kids and then blame them for not becoming upstanding citizens when they grow up.

CC: So you see that kind of thing happening now, even after the field has become much more established than it was in the '80s and '90s, when the (contemporary) study of PTSD was just beginning to take off? It seems that the field of trauma studies has been beset by the same kind of shut-down that happens when traumatic sensations themselves break in on consciousness. The field breaks through, but society tries to isolate that knowledge.

BvdK: One reason the traumatic stress field has changed so much over the past few decades is there's money in them thar hills.

CC: What do you mean?

BvdK: Well, here's a great example. Last year, the Department of Defense allocated 130 million (unbid) dollars to institute a positive psychology program in the US Army, a program to be offered to 1.3 or 1.7 million soldiers to help them think positive thoughts. With the idea that if you're grateful, you won't get PTSD. It's essentially a program that advocates "Let's just forget about it. If you're just grateful . . ."

CC: What are you grateful for? That you're alive?

BvdK: You're grateful that you're alive and you have kids, and the sun is shining, and just be grateful. And think positive thoughts, and your trauma will go away. That is the largest funded study or project in PTSD treatment right now with the taxpayer's money.

CC: And that is funded by whom and done where?

BvdK: The Department of Defense. PBS called me up, the summer before last, and they told me that they're doing a show about a positive psychology program. Did I know anything about positive psychology? I said no, not really; but, as far as I know positive psychology has nothing to do with the prevention of traumatic stress. So you're calling the wrong guy. They didn't let go: would you be interested in finding out about this positive psychology program to prevent PTSD? I told them to go ahead and send me your stuff. I read through it, and I was horrified by what I read. I had promised to call them back a week later, and to tell them what I thought of it. When we came to the end of the interview the reporter summarized what I had said: "So you're telling us that it's a crock of shit?" I responded that that was a nonscientific translation of what I had said, hoping that would get me off the hook. It didn't and he asked me if I would you like to say that on national television? So they interviewed both Marty Seligman[17] and me. It's on YouTube. What struck me most was that I looked a lot happier than the person who is pushing positive psychology!

CC: It sounds like you are responding to a kind of denial—not only as a method of treatment but as a method of research. Which brings me back to the original story of your woman patient who had been abused as a child and painted a picture of her experience when she was in therapy. She said the painting had a title, which was "See No Evil, Hear No Evil, Speak No Evil." And that suggests that silence, or silencing—and they are slightly different things—seemed to be part of the process of her trauma, and indeed may be an aspect of trauma more generally.

BvdK: That's where the shame comes in. Somebody molests you, somebody rapes you, and you can't tell anybody what has happened. Kids have no choice but to see themselves in the center of the universe, and anything that happens to them is necessarily the result of something they think, do, or feel. Simple magical thinking. Kids don't disclose their abuse in part because they believe they must have been bad to make this happen to them.

CC: When there are relational issues or attachment issues in which there's an interpretation, like "I'm the center of the universe; I must have made it happen"—whether it's conscious or not—how does that link up with what you said before about the thalamus not integrating things?

BvdK: It doesn't. It's just another part of the process. But even as an adult, if something terrible happens to you, you tend not to talk about it. Whistle-blowers tend to be unpopular; family members and co-workers tend to exclude people who speak up against authority, even though they may secretly agree with you.

CC: Look at the Jews who were survivors and were diagnosed as psychotic and stuck in Israeli psychiatric hospitals and essentially ignored for years.[18] They were "victims," right?

BvdK: The only thing you're allowed to be is a hero. Another example is how the Japanese don't want to talk about Hiroshima survivors. Last year I was in Fukushima—and inhabitants of that city felt they were treated as pariahs in Japanese society.

CC: So it's very similar in different cultures. I think that when you are victimized, the very fact of being victimized turns you into "a victim." And then to speak about it, to say, "I was victimized," just says again, "I am a victim, therefore I am a helpless person," and it feels like it doesn't improve matters; it just repeats the victimization again. And people don't want to hear because they don't want to be contaminated by it. That might be another way of understanding silencing.

BvdK: That is where the relational aspect of language comes in. Not because language resolves the trauma, but because language at least gives you a voice and provides the possibility of being in touch with the rest of the human race. Language at least offers the possibility that people will acknowledge what has happened to you, and believe you. But talking won't make it go away—it makes a connection, and it overcomes a terrible godforsaken loneliness that's part of the trauma story.

III. The Black Hole of Trauma

CC: I would like to turn to another way you speak of the problem of silencing in trauma. I will never forget the time, many years ago, right after you had discovered the results of your PET [positron emission tomography] scan studies on people undergoing flashbacks,[19] when we were speaking on the phone and you told me about the results of the scans. In this experiment with victims of trauma, the voluntarily re-traumatized subjects were read a detailed sensory script of their catastrophic experiences and were then scanned as they entered into flashback states.

BvdK: Well, "voluntarily," not necessarily—there's always the question of whether that's true informed consent, of course. We didn't raise the ethical issue in part because at that point I did not know how traumatizing it was to induce a flashback. I would not do that again.

CC: OK, that's important to know. To return to the story, you said to me, with great amazement, "The right side of the brain lights up—and Broca's area goes dark!" This discovery is retold in your chapter "Trauma and Memory" in *Traumatic Stress*:

> These subjects demonstrated heightened activity only in the areas that are most involved in emotional arousal . . . This was accompanied by heightened activity in the right visual cortex, reflecting the flashbacks reported by these patients. Perhaps most significantly, Broca's area—the part of the left hemisphere responsible for translating personal experiences into communicable language—"turned off." We believe this to reflect the speechless terror experienced by these patients, and their tendency to experience emotions as physical states rather than as verbally encoded experiences. (293)

What I want to ask you concerns the surprise of this moment. It seems to me to be a different version of the paradoxes you talk about in the neurobiological studies. Can you tell me what was unexpected for you? Why did this surprise you?

BvdK: Well the big surprise was that we could demonstrate that people actually become speechless. So you are just having an experience, but you become like a Tourette's patient. You can only say four-letter words and say "mamma." And your symbolic brain shuts down. To see this so concretely on a brain scan makes you realize how central this is to the trauma experience: the difficulty of expressing what you experience in words.

CC: You presumably knew from your patients that this could happen. Why was this so surprising, then?

BvdK: You know, your patients show you a lot of things, and you need to sort out what's important and relevant on the basis of what you know. So I'd seen this speechless terror in my office all the time, but what keeps surprising me is how many things are right in front of our faces that we don't see. But when you see a piece of scientific work that makes certain issues concrete and "real," it allows you to open your eyes and you may suddenly see the relevance of something that you have ignored up until then. Another example is the way that traumatized people hold their bodies and have distorted relationships with their physical selves. How could I have missed it for so long? But once we started to study heart rate variability (HRV) and you look at the chests of people with PTSD and see that they barely move, you can no longer deny its reality or its relevance. And you realize that they are condemned to continue to lose control over their emotional reactions until they learn to restore mastery over that system.

CC: And it also seems like what you're seeing is a certain kind of paradox in the body. To me what was so telling about your reaction to the PET scans was a kind of implicit acknowledgment that the brain was itself the site of an enigma. If something's lighting up in this particular area of the brain, it ought to be speakable. One ought to be able to say, "Yes, this is important." But instead the motor speech area was shutting down. Is that what was so surprising to you?

BvdK: Well, that was surprising, and it also makes you pay attention to the right brain. Your right brain is not analytical or verbal; it's spatial and emotional. But once you realize that trauma is most of all imprinted in the spatial/emotional part of the brain, then therapy should involve moving in space, which, of course, traditional psychotherapy completely ignores. But when you start doing psychodrama, theater, or sandplay you actually can make use of what we know happens in trauma, and you can start resolving it by making spatial rearrangements, and not only verbal reorganizations. Once you know how the brain responds to trauma, you realize that you have to work with the parts of the brain that are online, and not with the parts that are deactivated. In other words: we need to have right-brain therapies for right-brain problems.

CC: I am wondering, in this context, how you would understand the nature of the language that sometimes does emerge during traumatic reenactments. In a piece you wrote with Onno van der Hart, "The Intrusive Past: The Flexibility of Memory and the Engraving of Trauma," you refer to [Pierre] Janet's patient Irène, who spoke during her traumatic hypnotic trances. Reflecting on her behavior, you note that traumatic memory, unlike narrative memory, "has no social component; it is not addressed to anybody."[20] Is it possible, then, not only to have a literal silencing but also a form of speech that is, itself, noncommunicative, i.e., traumatic?

BvdK: Irene was just replaying the words that she used during the traumatic incident. Like a flashback. Communicative speech returns *after* the treatment is successful. The narrative is the result of good treatment. It is the eventual product of allowing yourself to know what you know.

CC: Dori Laub might say that you can't do that unless someone's listening. Do you disagree?

BvdK: I would not agree with that. I am all for nuances here, but when you do hypnosis as Janet did, and [Milton] Erickson,[21] or if you practice internal family systems therapy,[22] which a lot of us do, you really go deep inside yourself and you allow yourself to know what happened to you. That work is primarily about having an internal dialogue with yourself, or rather your selves, in which you allow yourself to know what happened and how you dealt with it. Yes, an observer needs to help you make space, but the bottom line is that this is about rearranging your relationship with your self.

CC: As a literary critic and theorist, I would want to include in the word "language" or "speech" the language that is traumatic, the language "that is not addressed to anyone," that doesn't really communicate. For example, when I repeat over and over the same story and the same words in real time. It seems to me that the capacities of literature and poetry to be so effective in communicating trauma derive from the fact that they can maintain or can echo those parts of traumatic language that are not just circumscribed by rationality. Would you agree with that as a possibility?

BvdK: There are those who can talk about what has happened and give voice to things that are extraordinarily difficult to wrap our brains around. Language is unbelievably important, particularly when it comes to talking about otherwise unspeakable horrors.

But one can speak and write quite self-consciously about things and still remain traumatized. I am thinking of a very well-known writer who had written a best-selling book about a personal traumatic experience and came to speak at a conference on trauma. The first speaker at this conference, Jamie Pennebaker, an expert on language and trauma discussed his research that demonstrated convincingly that if you write about your trauma, your overall functioning improves dramatically. The next speaker was the writer who had written movingly about his own trauma and who spoke about his work in a completely dissociated state. The writing had not cured him, no matter how articulate his writing was. He is still in talk therapy discussing the trauma, but the trauma clearly has not been resolved, and I am skeptical that expanding the narrative will allow him to lay it to rest. The trauma is not primarily encoded in language, and insight and understanding have only tenous pathways into the areas of the brain that hold fear and internal dissolution.

CC: And yet he has written these amazing books.

BvdK: And yet, he remained a very traumatized person.

CC: Does being cured mean, for you, being cured forever?

BvdK: Yes. When it's over, it's over. Freud raised the question, "If you can talk about it with all the associative affects, will the trauma can go away?" And the answer turned out to be unfortunately not.

CC: Does healing mean to you that you become a person who now no longer needs to bear witness?

BvdK: Healing is like, "Yeah, it happened. Yeah, it was awful. It happened. But today I can calmly talk about what happened back then." Some people then devote their lives to trying to make sure that it doesn't happen to others, and other survivors go on to do other things.

CC: What about Holocaust survivors? I don't see how that could be the case for them.

BvdK: That's a big empirical question. And now in the EMDR study 80 percent of people were totally physiologically normally reactive. It's just done. It's a story. Even people who have been enslaved, or exposed to other horrendous experiences can sometimes go on with their lives, fully knowing the horrors that people can inflict on each other. It all depends on how well mind and brain can reorient themselves to be alive in the present moment.

CC: I guess one of the questions that arises here is if we are just healing the self, or healing the culture.

BvdK: We're healing the disintegrated mind, brain, body. The culture has a life of its own. That is the realm of politics, and I wish anybody who tries to change the political landscape all the best.

CC: What if you healed all of your patients, and no one ever came in society to find out about their trauma?

BvdK: Sadly, you don't have to worry about that. We are a messed-up species. Just read the newspaper and listen to the news. Yes, bearing witness is important, but the question is how to do that most effectively: by instituting early childhood education programs, preventing wars, setting up daycare centers for overwhelmed parents, opening domestic violence shelters?

CC: And one might also say, on your side of the argument, that if one doesn't heal to a certain extent, if one doesn't come into the present to a certain extent, one may continue not to speak, or even to commit suicide, and then there may be no testimony at all.

BvdK: Before I was president of ISTSS [the International Society for Traumatic Stress Studies], we invited Primo Levi to give the keynote speech. He said, yes, and a month after that he killed himself. A year later I asked Jerzy Kosiński to give the keynote speech, and he sends me a publicity photograph, signed "to my good friend Bessel"—I've never met the guy—"I'll see you in November." And he also killed himself.[23]

CC: So that's where I think you see what Freud calls the death drive, and the self-silencing dimension of the return of trauma. When it returns, it often comes back in a way that silences itself. In other words, flashbacks and nightmares aren't in themselves bearing witness—even if they can be understood as demanding that witness take place—because they can cause you not to speak or, sometimes, to kill yourself.

BvdK: We think about these things differently. I would say, "OK, so your frontal lobe finds a way of telling other people that you feel terrible." But your survival brain lives in a different world. People's social interactions are very different from their internal experience. You can accomplish things and still be haunted by shame and self-hatred, or you can be a lazy bum and feel perfectly content.

CC: Some people believe they have to bear witness publicly in order to be okay.

BvdK: I think they're in different dimensions. Many holocaust survivors led satisfying lives without turning back. Trauma is stored as physical sensations, in the body. You can talk all you want, and testify all you want, but until the internal wounds inside you have healed, that testimony may just tear you up. Take, for example Dori Laub's and Nanette Auerhahn's paper on knowing and not knowing.[24] That was a beautiful paper, and as far as I am concerned, it tells the truth. It's as good of a summary of memory from a sort of literary point of view as anything. It spells out that some people can't remember or tell anything, while others can tell the whole story, and everything in between. When we studied this issue in 1995 we found that there was no correlation between how much of the story people could tell and how severe their flashbacks were. There was no relationship between being able to talk and laying your nightmares to rest.[25]

CC: So, given your increasing sense of the importance of focusing on the body, as opposed to speaking therapies, in treating trauma, what does your research add to your previous work?

BvdK: Some of my current research is on neurofeedback. Rewiring brain activity to help traumatized people pay attention to their current lives, and helping them to become less disorganized when triggered. It is difficult to establish satisfying relationships as long as the brain is easily overwhelmed and goes into dissolution or panic mode.

I am, of course, as a psychiatrist, a talking-cure person; I have had a practice for many years. Because being able to communicate what's going on inside of you is an opening to getting to know yourself and doing the work of settling things down. If you can tell somebody else, you can begin to tell it to yourself. You need to have courage to go deep inside yourself, and that comes from someone believing you and taking you seriously. But ultimately the transformation happens with going into hypnotic trances or neurofeedback [the control of brain-waves by means of devices that allow an individual to see and modulate brain activity] or EMDR.

IV. Theaters of Healing

CC: With regard to these other modes of treatment, you said before that working with the body in a spatial context would address the right-brain activation in trauma. You have also said there is no treatment of choice when it comes to these calming methods. Some of them you seem to have discovered in the Eastern tradition. Actually it looks like you discovered some of them when we were on the trip to China together back in 1992.[26]

BvdK: Do you remember going to Wuxi and seeing the ballroom dancing between the psychiatrists and patients? That blew my socks off. At the hospital at Wuxi, the doctors and patients had ballroom dancing together once a week. And I was so moved by that. And, of course, people tend to respond as if it were dumb, primitive people dancing with their patients. But actually in Wuxi there were a lot of things that in retrospect I think they got. They had a lot of music therapy, a lot of rhythm therapies. But our people [on the visiting team] were totally disavowing it because Wuxi seemed primitive and Shanghai was sophisticated. But Wuxi really got it.

CC: When did you start doing these new methods for treating trauma that are focused on the body?

BvdK: Well actually our neuroimaging study [the PET scans] was the most important change agent for me. Because it showed that the analyzing part of the brain is really not involved in trauma and that the emotional brain leads a life of its own. The year that we did the study I was invited to do the keynote to the founding meeting of the US body psychotherapy conference. I met all of these body workers, and I saw their work, and I was impressed with how much they could accomplish that we couldn't. And then my involvement with the Truth Commission in South Africa was also a very big influence. Seeing Bishop Tutu at work. He was a great trauma therapist who would dance and sing with people.

CC: With whom did he dance and sing?

BvdK: With the torture victims, as part of their testimony. He knew how to calm them down by engaging in rhythmical, attuned interactions, so they could begin to integrate their trauma stories.

CC: Did he do the dancing before they got on the stand?

BvdK: He "pendulated," as my friend Peter Levine calls it—he moved in and out of the trauma story; it was all about rhythms, and moving in unison. Singing as a community, which allowed people to feel safe again, and in the context of being safely held by the community, being able to narrate what had happened to them.

CC: A couple of the new therapies that you have been talking about: yoga, but also the neurofeedback, which also has to do with brain rhythms, and then I suppose in a different way this theater that you do . . .

BvdK: None of which, of course, are new. Both yoga and theater are five thousand years old. Neurofeedback is new: it's applied neuroscience—we could not do that until we had the technical knowledge about being able to change the wiring of the central nervous system.

CC: Where did you learn the theater work?

BvdK: I first learned it from Al Pesso, who was a former principal dancer for Martha Graham, and then from theater groups in Boston who work with inner-city kids, and then from Shakespeare in the Courts, a program here in Berkshire County where judges give juvenile delinquents a choice between going to jail or taking a course in becoming a Shakespearean actor.

CC: And what do you do with the theater?

BvdK: We managed to get the Centers for Disease Control to give us a grant for violence prevention. It's about taking on a role that is different from your habitual role. Embodying a different person gives your body, mind, brain, a chance to experience what it's like to be other than your habitual frozen self. Because we all get frozen and lost for periods.

CC: So you alter your experience by positioning yourself in theater, actually positioning your body?

BvdK: Not positioning, it's actually making your whole body resonate, and it becomes, gives voice to the truth of, that person. That's where words really matter. The last chapter of my new book is about a combat veteran who had twenty-seven detoxifications in the past year, who played Brutus as he is speaking to Cassius in *Julius Caesar*. He says something about baying at the moon and being like a dog, and about being betrayed. You go over every line of Shakespeare.

The first time I was part of this I was Macbeth, and Lady Macbeth says, "If he had not so resembled my father, I would have done the deed myself." And so the theater director says: "'If he had not so resembled my father'—Who resembles your father? What was your father like? Did you love your father? Did your father really adore you? Did your father ignore you?" In that role, you really feel what it's like to have somebody resemble your father, and why you would not have been able to kill him. Every word takes on flesh. They are not just words. They are the embodiment of bodily truth. So the last chapter of my book is about embodying the truth of the words that you speak.

CC: So words, in this case, are a little more than just left brain entities, because they are actually linked to the right brain as well.

BvdK: It's the total organism that tells the truth.

CC: So the healed language, which is an integrated body-mind language . . .

BvdK: Total engagement. And so the final story of the book is of an actor we know, a Shakespearean actor, who goes to a workshop, and when he speaks the lines of the King as he transfers his crown to Bolingbroke—"Alack, why am I sent for to a king / Before I have shook off the regal thoughts / Wherewith I reign'd? I hardly yet have learn'd / To insinuate, flatter, bow, and bend my limbs"—he stops and says, "I always feel constricted when I speak these lines, as if I couldn't breathe." And so his teacher says, "What does breathing mean to you? What comes up when you think about breathing? What happens to your body when you breathe? Take a breath and see what it feels like." And the guy says, "I was a preemie, and I spent the first few months of my life in a nursery." And his teacher says, "So what was it like for people to stick all these needles into you when you're a newborn baby," and he goes crazy. And he becomes that little baby that has all these needles in him. And these full-grown men have to hold him down as he processes the traumatic memory of being stuck with needles as a preemie in a nursery. After that, he owns the experience and becomes a very well-known Shakespearean actor. That's trauma treatment.

CC: That's also literature, by the way. That is literature. It's not an accident.

BvdK: Of course the Greeks and Shakespeare are still read every day all over the globe because they articulate immortal issues.

CC: But it's also literature as the body . . .

BvdK: And so language is terribly important. Without language, we are just a bunch of traumatized animals who act and react without any choice.

CC: What you're saying, then, is that language is the vehicle by which the body comes into the present. You know, you said the body is spatial, but you also say that in order to be healed, we have to be living in the present. And it sounds like what happens in the language of the theater is that as the experience of the body, which is spatial, is integrated and spoken in the speech, that present-ness happens.

BvdK: You feel it in your gut, and you feel it in your chest. You feel it in the pneumo-gastric nerve. Charles Darwin said it's the root of all emotions. And you cannot know anything about trauma or humans if you don't read Charles Darwin's *Expression of the Emotions in Man and Animals*.

V. Oracular Speech

CC: I would like to end with a question about your own language, Bessel, because I have always found that it speaks beyond its concepts. This happens in your work, in part, because you frequently quote the somewhat enigmatic language of your patients, as in the case we started with. In *Traumatic Stress* you frame the entire book, likewise, with two suggestive lines from a poem, Auden's "New Year Letter":

> Truth, like love and sleep, resents
> Approaches that are too intense.[27]

Presumably, you're alluding through this quotation to the way in which traumatic experience is precisely "too intense" a relation to truth. The poem also insists here on the importance of language, and I'm going to read you the other lines from that section of the poem:

> Though language may be useless, for
> No words men write can stop the war

Or measure up to the relief
Of its immeasurable grief,
Yet truth, like love and sleep, resents
Approaches that are too intense . . .
And often when the searcher stood
Before the Oracle, it would
Ignore his grown-up earnestness
But not the child of his distress,
For through the Janus of a joke
The candid psychopompos spoke.
May such heart and intelligence
As huddle now in conference
Whenever an impasse occurs
Use the Good Offices of verse.

Your use of verse as an epigraph—and your quotation of patients throughout your work and of poets for many of your titles and epigraphs—suggests a way in which you refuse the simple rationality of technical terms. So how do you understand this use of language by your patients and in your own work?

BvdK: Auden says, "ignore his grown-up earnestness, but not the child of his distress." I think of possibly the greatest therapist in our lifetime, Milton Erickson. He was always talking in oracular language, because we get trapped by our language.

CC: Yes.

BvdK: And so he would just say what sounded like nonsensical things in order to mix up our preconceptions. But what we do when we treat traumatized people is that they and we always get misguided by the conclusions that we come to prematurely. So we need continuously to stir the pot so that we form new associations. Because in trauma you make the same associations over and over again; being a flexible person means that you are open to new associations. And so treatment, science, discovery are all about the creation of new associations, whether verbally or otherwise. When people say, "It's the hippocampus," you say, "Eh, well, that's part of it." Is it the amygdala? That gives some new insights. Is it witnessing? Well, having someone acknowledge who you are is really important. They're all pieces of the larger puzzle. So that getting out of trauma means that you have to get out of that rainspout that collects all the raindrops into one narrow channel.

CC: Your use of literary quotations and of your patients' quasi-literary language is thus conveying, first, how there are aspects to trauma that remain resistant to our knowledge, and second, that just as this figurative language cannot be pinned down and is open to association, so should the text you are writing be read in part through the richness of its associations, and not only as a set of final explanations.

BvdK: Of course, there are no "final explanations." Every generation discovers new frameworks. Every new discovery in human development and brain organization offers new perspectives. Culture is not static—our understanding continuously changes. When people say, "I have found the treatment of choice because my patients got 20 percent better," they always overstate the case.

CC: I have an association to the story you told about a child—the son of a friend of yours who lived near the World Trade Center in New York—who made a drawing after 9/11 of the twin towers. The child had drawn the twin towers at the time of the attacks and there was a little black spot at the base of the towers. And you noticed the black spot, and you said to the child, "What is that?" And he said, "A trampoline. So the next time when they jump they won't die." For me the trampoline is also, I think, a link also between past and future.

BvdK: Yes, absolutely.

CC: And when I think about it in the context of the research on trauma, and the importance that you emphasize in remaining conceptually flexible in this arena, that flexible link, which is sometimes hard to see—that black spot in the painting—would include the past and future of trauma theory.

BvdK: Yes, flexibility is all about being able to imagine a trampoline at the foot of the World Trade Center towers. Seeing some horrendous event and being able to imagine how things can be done differently. Another good example of that is what happened in South Africa after apartheid. Mandela and Tutu were able to envision a new society that was not based on racial divisions or revenge. And the little boy who painted the picture of the World Trade Center thought about a solution to that horrendous spectacle he witnessed, people jumping out of the towers.

CC: It seems that you have derived a lot of your own creativity in thinking about, and responding to trauma, from the creativity of your patients.

BvdK: Well, traumatized people who survive become the experts. If I were running the Department of Defense I would ask Karl Marlantes, who wrote a terrific book about how he survived being a combat Marine in Vietnam,[28] to serve as my adviser, and I'd ask kids who have been molested and abused to help run Child Protective Services.

VI. A Child's Legacy

CC: I would like to close by asking about the expertise you have derived from your experiences in your own life. I return, here, to the words of the patient with which we opened and how they show up in a brief autobiographical piece you wrote called, "The Body Keeps the Score: A Brief Autobiography of Bessel van der Kolk."[29] I read this title as "an autobiography of a keeping of the score"—that is, "my work and life are keeping the score," they themselves have testified to something. Would you like to reflect at all on that possibility?

BvdK: Well, it is really impossible to explain how we come to do the things we do, and how we become fascinated with particular issues. I am in the middle of five kids, and none of my siblings are trauma experts, preoccupied with trauma, or do anything remotely similar, even though we had very similar backgrounds. So, it probably has a lot to do with accidents, with whom you meet, who approves of the littlest statements that you make. Life guides you in particular directions, accidental meetings and chance encounters. One association with "the body keeps the score" I only started to make well after I wrote that article, back in 1994. Because a patient of mine was studying the relationship between the famine in the Netherlands in the winter of '44–45 and its relationship to an increased incidence of schizophrenia, I wondered what life was like for me during that time. I was born in 1943. Holland was also a bad place to be born during that year. About 100,000 kids of my birth cohort died. And I barely survived the war. And I was a very, very sickly kid for many years, but grew up into a very robust adult.

CC: You were sick in what way?

BvdK: I had asthma; I had eczema; typhoid fever—I was a wreck of a kid.

CC: What do you attribute your eczema and asthma to?

BvdK: There was horrible malnutrition and the circumstances probably were similar to what kids in Syria grow up with right now. It still happens—in Afghanistan and Iraq. I imagine I must have been like one of those Rwandan babies whom you see with the vultures picking on their bodies. So maybe this issue of the body keeping the score resonated unconsciously within me, because I was a kid who at some time held a lot of trauma in his body. It is interesting that I believe that the most useful treatment I've ever had was Rolfing.

CC: Rolfing.

BvdK: Rolfing. Years of psychoanalysis, years of this, years of that, I've done it all. But when somebody worked with my body and opened me up from the subtle ways in which it was frozen, my mind opened to new ways of looking at the world.

CC: And when your mind is opened and you're working on your research and you're writing your book or when you're with your patients, does that do something for your body?

BvdK: Doing yoga in the morning does something to my body.

CC: So your work is about survival . . . Your own and others, it sounds like.

BvdK: Well, not really about my own anymore—that issue feels settled. I'm alive, now. But another important thing for me was that my father was in a concentration camp. He was a very vocal Christian, who was detained because of his principled beliefs against totalitarian oppression of individual religious freedom. But after he came back from the war he often behaved like a Nazi himself. And from very early on I would say to my dad, "Hey Dad, you're saying the same sort of things that the Nazis used to say." I must have been two and a half years old when I first told my dad that he was talking like a Nazi."

CC: At two and a half?

BvdK: Oh, the mythology, you never know. What I do know is that one of the first things I ever realized was that people say one thing and do another. My father was a complete pacifist, a very religious person, and his behavior often expressed the opposite of what he professed. From very early on I confronted him with "You say one thing, and do another." From very early on I have been very skeptical of anyone who claims to have found the answer. I feel bad that many of my most esteemed colleagues who have discovered new and very effective ways of treating trauma tend to fall into that religious position of having found "the" answer, rather than one really effective way of helping people cope.

CC: Because watching your father's religious rigidity, at two and a half, you had already implicitly recognized repetition compulsion.

BvdK: I must have seen it very early in life.

NOTES

1. Bessel A. van der Kolk, *The Body Keeps the Score: Mind, Brain and Body in the Transformation of Trauma* (New York: Viking, 2014).
2. Bessel A. van der Kolk, Alexander C. McFarlane, and Lars Weisaeth, eds., *Traumatic Stress: The Effects of Overwhelming Experience on Mind, Body, and Society* (New York: Guilford, 1996), 8.
3. See the case of Emma in *The Project for a Scientific Psychology* and Jean Laplanche's analysis of this case in *Life and Death in Psychoanalysis* (Baltimore: Johns Hopkins UP, 1985), and the later reiteration of the belated structure in Freud's *Beyond the Pleasure Principle* and in *Moses and Monotheism*, in *The Standard Edition of the Complete Psychological Works of Sigmund Freud*, trans. under the general editorship of James Strachey

in collaboration with Anna Freud, assisted by Alix Strachey and Jan Tyson, 24 vols. (London: Hogarth, 1953–1974) [hereinafter cited as *SE*], vols. 18 and 23.

4. Bessel A. van der Kolk, "The Body Keeps the Score: Memory and the Evolving Psychobiology of Post-Traumatic Stress," *Harvard Review of Psychiatry* 1 (1994): 253–65, reprinted in *Essential Papers on Posttraumatic Stress Disorder*, ed. Mardi J. Horowitz (New York: NYU P, 1999), 317.

5. A thorough review of this question would also have to cover, of course, other neurochemical responses, including various encoding mechanisms, such as experiments by Stephen Southwick that have shown that norepinephrine releases during traumatic experiences can cause super-consolidation of memories. See, for example, Stephen M. Southwick et al., "Role of Norepinephrine in the Pathophysiology and Treatment of Posttraumatic Stress Disorder," *Biological Psychiatry* 1.46 (1999): 1192–204.

6. See, for example, Douglas J. Bremner et al., "Magnetic Resonance Imaging–Based Measurement of Hippocampal Volume in Posttraumatic Stress Disorder Related to Childhood Physical and Sexual Abuse: A Preliminary Report," *Biological Psychiatry* 41.1 (Jan. 1997): 23–32.

7. See, for example, Bessel A. van der Kolk, "EMDR: Beyond the Talking Cure: Trauma and the Subcortical Nature of Traumatic Memories," in *EMDR and the New Paradigm*, ed. Francine Shapiro (New York: Basic, 2001).

8. Robert Stickgold is an American psychiatrist at Harvard Medical School focusing on sleep research, with an emphasis on sleep and learning. John Allan Hobson is an American psychiatrist and professor emeritus at Harvard Medical School, whose focus has been on dreams and rapid eye movement sleep.

9. Ernest Hartmann (1934–2013) was an Austrian-American psychiatrist and psychoanalyst and a pathbreaking researcher on dreams.

10. See Bessel A. van der Kolk, Mark Greenberg, Helene Boyd, and John Krystal, "Inescapable Shock, Neurotransmitters, and Addiction to Trauma: Toward a Psychobiology of Post-Traumatic Stress," *Biological Psychiatry* 20.3 (1985): 314–25.

11. See Cathy Caruth, "Traumatic Awakenings," in *Unclaimed Experience: Trauma, Narrative, and History* (Baltimore: Johns Hopkins UP, 1996).

12. Van der Kolk, "Body Keeps the Score," 318.

13. On a possibly related—though not simply analogous—problem of "pathbreaking" in Freud and the metaphor of the neuronal pathway, see Jacques Derrida, "Freud and the Scene of Writing," in *Writing and Difference* (Chicago: U of Chicago P, 1978).

14. Sigmund Freud, *Beyond the Pleasure Principle*, in *SE*, vol. 18, chap. 4.

15. Elizabeth F. Loftus is an American cognitive psychologist who is known for her research on the malleability of human memory and in particular on eyewitness distortion.

16. See the interview with Dori Laub in chap. 3 for some of this criticism. Dr. Laub's response that I refer to in the interview with Dr. van der Kolk comes from a private communication.

17. Martin E. P. Seligman is an American psychologist who is best known for his theory of "learned helplessness."

18. Dori Laub dicusses his work with these survivors in his interview in chap. 3.

19. See S. Rauch, B. A. van der Kolk, et al., "A Symptom Provocation Study Using Positron

Emission Tomography and Script Driven Imagery," *Archives of General Psychiatry* 53 (1996): 380–87.

20. Bessel A. van der Kolk and Onno van der Hart, "The Flexibility of Memory and the Engraving of Trauma," in *Trauma: Explorations in Memory*, ed. Cathy Caruth (Baltimore: Johns Hopkins UP, 1995), 163.

21. Milton H. Erickson (1901–1980) was an American psychiatrist who specialized in hypnosis and family therapy. I recall during the 1990s that his work was being discussed at the International Society for Traumatic Stress Studies for clinicians interested in trauma. Onno van der Hart mentions Erickson's importance for van der Hart's work in his interview for this volume.

22. The internal family systems model (IFS) is an approach to individual psychotherapy developed by Richard C. Schwartz. This approach suggests that the mind is made up of relatively discrete subpersonalities that are organized in systems.

23. Primo Levi (1919–1987) was a Jewish Italian author and survivor of Auschwitz. He is known for, among other writings, *Survival in Auschwitz* (*If This Is a Man*), *The Drowned and the Saved*, and *The Periodic Table*. He committed suicide in 1987. Jerzy Kosiński (1933–1991), a Jewish Polish writer who survived World War II under a false identity and then emigrated to the United States after the war, is best known for his novel *The Painted Bird*. He committed suicide in 1991.

24. Dori Laub and Nanette C. Auerhahn, "Knowing and Not Knowing Massive Psychic Trauma: Forms of Traumatic Memory," *International Journal of Psychoanalysis* 74.2 (1993): 287–302.

25. B. A. van der Kolk and R. Fisler, "Dissociation and the Fragmentary Nature of Traumatic Memories: Background and Experimental Evidence," *Journal of Traumatic Stress* 8 (1995): 505–25.

26. Dr. van der Kolk led a delegation of scholars and clinicians working on PTSD to China through the "People-to-People" program.

27. W. H. Auden, "New Year Letter (January 1st, 1940)", in *Collected Poems* (New York: Vintage, 1991).

28. Karl Marlantes, *What It Is Like to Go to War* (New York: Atlantic Monthly, 2011).

29. Bessel van der Kolk, "The Body Keeps the Score: Brief Autobiography of Bessel van der Kolk," in *Mapping Trauma and Its Wake: Autobiographic Essays by Pioneer Trauma Scholars*, ed. Charles Figley (New York: Routledge, 2006).

Onno van der Hart at his home in Amstelveen (Amsterdam), The Netherlands, July 16, 2013.

Chapter Eight

The Haunted Self
An Interview with Onno van der Hart

Onno van der Hart has been a major force in the study and treatment of dissociative disorders over the past thirty years and is one of the major figures responsible for its increasing acceptance as a fundamental factor in traumatic experience. I met with him on July 16, 2013, in his home in Amstelveen (Amsterdam), the Netherlands, to discuss the implications of conceiving trauma in terms of what he refers to as the "structural dissociation of the personality."

I. Encounters with the Divided Self

CC: You were a pioneer in the study of dissociation in the last part of the twentieth century and have continued to be a leader in this area over the past several decades. I would like to begin by asking how you became interested in the problem of dissociation and trauma-related disorders.

OvdH: My therapeutic training and practice included family therapy, as taught by Nathan Epstein (as well as by the members of the Milan school of family therapy), and strategic or directive therapy, which uses the therapeutic methods advocated by Milton Erickson, Jay Haley, and Paul Watzlawick.[1] These involved training in hypnosis, and to understand hypnosis you must think in terms of multiple streams of consciousness. I focused, in particular, on grief therapy, in which the bereaved person often appears to be behaving normally in daily life, as if the loss hadn't occurred, but at other times becomes overwhelmed, as if the loss were occurring in the present. So the notion of different streams of consciousness was present very early in my training and therapy.

In order to learn more about these multiple streams of consciousness, I studied Fritz Perls's Gestalt therapy and the work of [John G.] Watkins on ego-state therapy, which I also used, and subsequently I was fascinated by what Henri F. Ellenberger, in *The Discovery of the Unconscious*, wrote about Pierre Janet. There I found a master in describing, observing, and doing experimental clinical research on divided consciousness.[2]

I became a therapist in 1971. And it was only in 1980 that I realized that I was encountering patients with complex dissociative disorders. I would say that since then my understanding of dissociation in people with complex dissociative disorders—trauma-related disorders—became much more developed. I also learned that the treatment principles that I applied in family therapy and ego state therapy were highly applicable in therapy with these patients.

CC: You said you had worked, early on, with people experiencing intense grief and seemed to have encountered, in them, symptoms that you would now understand as dissociative. Before you grasped what was going on, how did you understand those symptoms? Or did you see that there was something that you didn't quite grasp?

OvdH: It was more an intuitive way of approaching things. Because I had training in hypnosis, I already was familiar with the notion that somebody may have symptoms, or problems in daily life, that relate to adverse experiences from the past that he or she is not directly, or consciously, in contact with. And I found that hypnosis is a way of getting at them—for example, using the "affect bridge" method that Helen H. Watkins helped to develop.[3] And at the time I also adopted Milton Erickson's language of the unconscious. But I was already uneasy with that notion because in a dissociative state of being, there is somebody who is consciously speaking up, although with a different voice from the one that the person has in daily life. So I wondered if it is right to label this as *the* unconscious —it's already a reification. It was rather for me more like the existence of other streams of consciousness, of which one may not be conscious in daily life. Thus the idea that when we are traumatized, we have different selves—each with its own voice—made a lot of sense. And, indeed, in some patients whom I saw in the 1970s and whom I would now diagnose as having dissociative disorder not otherwise specified (DDNOS),[4] I worked with these selves or parts, helping them to accept each other, resolve their inner conflicts, and integrate with each other.

CC: And do you recall the experience of first encountering—and being aware of—more complex PTSD in the 1980s?

OvdH: When you speak of more complex PTSD, I have in mind multiple personality disorder, as dissociative identity disorder (DID) was called at the time, which is, in my understanding, indeed the most complex form of PTSD. I remember very precisely the first time I encountered it. It was on a specific day of the week that I will never forget.[5] I am very bad about dates and days of the week, but this one has stayed with me forever. I had a first session with a patient who needed some additional sessions. It was a nice intake, and I don't remember a thing of it. On Friday evening I was called on my unlisted number by a woman who gave me the most horrendous verbal abuse that I have ever received. It was this patient. The next week it was as if nothing had happened; when questioned, she seemed to have amnesia for the call. So then I started to wonder, and it became clear that she had dissociative parts that together accounted for her DID.

The second incident involved a very difficult patient being treated by one of my colleagues who said he couldn't stand it anymore and asked for another team member at the mental health center to take over, which I did. The patient was about fifty-five, with a history of severe childhood maltreatment and subsequent trauma, including, for instance, the suicide of her daughter at the age of eighteen. She told me stories that made me think she should go to the police. One I will mention in particular: she said that when she was at home, somebody had burned six hundred Dutch guilders in the toilet. I believed that it was a true story, but how did it happen? I said, "Were your husband and your [remaining] daughter still at home?" She said, "No, they left." "Did you close and lock the door?" "Yes." "Is it possible that somehow you, or perhaps some part of yourself that you don't know about, may have done this?" "Maybe." "Would you like us to find out?" "Yes, I will go through everything to find this out." So I said to her, "Okay, Ria, allow yourself to enter into a state of concentration that gives you some mental space. And if there's another part of yourself that burned those six hundred guilders, let that part of yourself come forward." She was sitting like this [hunches over], and then this happens [leans forward aggressively with hands on his knees]. "Now you're dealing with me!" And she explained, as a different part of her personality, that she had burned this money in order to get even, to get revenge on Ria for certain things.

But this was very clear and dramatic, and this was also a person with a bit of a dramatic flare. Most people with a complex dissociative disorder do everything to dissimulate their multiplicity. The point is, when she made this movement—when she was sitting like this [leans forward with hands on his knees], I recognized that she had been in my office in this attitude several times before, but I had never made the connection that there might be another dissociative part involved.

CC: The voice had changed before?

OvdH: Yes.

CC: But you hadn't realized that it was actually a different personality part?

OvdH: In hindsight, there must have been some confusion in myself with these switches. It is as if the patient hypnotizes the therapist, who in this confusion follows the direct leads that the patient gives.

CC: So you're saying that one of the issues with recognizing dissociation is that the therapist him- or herself can be drawn into it.

OvdH: That's correct. And if the therapist doesn't have a frame of reference regarding dissociation, then he or she is just lost.

CC: And would you say that this is a way in which the element of avoidance, which at least one of the personality parts desires—it says in effect, "I don't want to know"—is perpetuated?

OvdH: Yes. That is really the knowing and not knowing that Dori Laub and Nanette Auerhahn have written so beautifully about.[6] It's the characteristic, I think, of traumatized people. And something that characterizes DID patients, who are severely traumatized, to a high degree. Janet thus labeled the problems of these patients as "disorders of non-realization." And he found that at the roots of this nonrealization, there is a phobia of the traumatic memory. My colleagues and I much later reformulated this as the phobia that the dissociative part functioning in daily life has for the traumatic memory and, inherently, for the part or parts keeping this memory.[7]

CC: I understand from what you said a moment ago that your training in hypnosis and ego-state therapy and your reading of Janet helped you begin to recognize the dissociative symptoms—and thus move past this participation in the not-knowing. Did you have other people to speak to about this, or were you alone at this point in the process?

OvdH: I spoke to my colleagues—not only colleagues in my office but also colleagues in the Amsterdam area. And the reaction generally was—they didn't say it to me directly, but I heard it afterward—"He was a good, respected therapist, but now something strange is happening with him." It met with resistance and denial. But the reality that I participated in and witnessed, which was not something that I created, was of importance to me.

CC: So in a way the not-knowing got passed on through your colleagues, or they actively participated in keeping you and your patients dissociated from their own knowledge.

OvdH: Yes. Exactly. Well, you could say that they tried—but unsuccessfully so.

CC: Was ISSD—the International Society for the Study of Dissociation[8]—active at this point? Or was Janet your only witness?

OvdH: The first years I was working on my own, with this frame of reference concerning dissociation becoming more and more significant. Because once you witness something, you can't deny it. And my tendency to go after what I see and hear and to try to understand it is much stronger, for me, than conformity.

CC: You said your first patient taught you something. And it sounds like it was your capacity to listen to your patients that gave you the authority—your patients' authority—to believe what other people didn't believe.

OvdH: Or I just couldn't come up with a different hypothesis. Of course there are some people, as we learned later, who simulate the disorder. So we shouldn't say that once you see it you always see it correctly. It always involves careful checking and taking alternate hypotheses into consideration.

CC: Is there some feeling that indicates, for you, the authenticity of a true dissociative switch to another part of the personality? Freud said he was always surprised by the transference. In your case, is there something like that surprise that, aside from florid changes in personality, speaks to you as a clinician?

OvdH: I think what gives me a sense that it might be authentic seeing and witnessing—because it's not only seeing, it's also hearing—is observing the struggle between knowing and not knowing, of not wanting to know and knowing. The uncertainty, the shame, of "This is happening to me, but I have to deny it, as I want to be in control and responsible." Instead of an eagerness to impress me that the person has DID.

CC: So the struggle between knowing and not knowing is partly what gives you a clue that something is happening that you should pay attention to.

OvdH: Yes. And of course subsequently, developments in the United States and then also in the Netherlands have produced very good diagnostic instruments. And my close colleagues were also involved in that.

CC: Did the interest in dissociation emerge more in the Netherlands and Europe than in the United States?

OvdH: I should say that before the growth of this specific interest in the Netherlands, quite a few clinicians in this country were already very much focused on trauma-related disorders, in particular those related to the Holocaust. With regard to dissociation, I do think that the Netherlands was a pioneering country in Europe. There were other pioneers in the Netherlands, but we didn't know each other. In any case, knowledge in the United States was much more developed than in Europe. I thought that if we want to provide good therapy, we need to have more knowledge coming from the States. So I organized workshops to which I invited first Bennett Braun and then Richard Kluft.[9] And there was the International Society for the Study of Multiple Personality and Dissociation, which changed its name a number of times, with its annual meetings, which I began to attend in the mid-1980s.[10] I need to mention that I also learned much from Bessel van der Kolk with regard to the wider field of psychotraumatology.

CC: Who were the other people in the Netherlands doing this work, whom you didn't know but eventually got to know?

OvdH: Well I know about one; that's Ellert Nijenhuis. And subsequently Suzette Boon also became very much involved.[11] She was in my office and was a family therapist, and when I left for a yearlong sabbatical in Israel, she took over my patients. And the interesting thing is that she was very skeptical about what I was seeing, while now she's one of the real experts in Europe and has done marvelous research with regard to the diagnosis of the dissociative disorders!

CC: And was the Netherlands central in Europe specifically—in part because of your work?

OvdH: In terms of the dissemination of insights developed in the United States regarding diagnosis and treatment, the Netherlands and Germany independently started first. In Germany especially among feminist therapists, who were open to the effects of sexual abuse, including incest.

CC: And then as the 1980s went on, as I understand it, the ISSD grew. And you eventually became vice-president of ISSD—which is now the International Society for the Study of Trauma and Dissociation—and then you also became involved in the International Society for Traumatic Stress Studies (ISTSS), where you became president in 2003. So by 2003 dissociation had become more prominent in the general study of trauma.

OvdH: Yes, although you still saw the split—or the dissociation—within the field: ISTSS was focused on traumatic stress and PTSD and didn't have much of a mission concerning dissociation. And the other people were more into dissociation —and also into more complex trauma-related disorders. Many DID patients also have PTSD. But ISTSS was, and still is, mainly focused on PTSD.

CC: At that time, as I recall, there was a struggle about whether PTSD is an anxiety disorder—based on a stress model—or a dissociative disorder. It's interesting to note that the latest *DSM* (*Diagnostic and Statistical Manual of Mental Disorders*) has brought PTSD closer to dissociation; they are placed right next to each other in the list.[12]

OvdH: I am impressed that PTSD is becoming more and more linked to dissociation. I also have criticisms of the way the literature, including the *DSM-V*, deals with it. The concept of dissociation is used in many ways. The first question I would ask is, "What do you mean by dissociation?" In the literature leading up to the *DSM-V* formulation of PTSD, a distinction was made between a nondissociative subtype and a dissociative subtype. And the *DSM-V* distinguishes a subtype of PTSD "with dissociative symptoms," that is, the negative symptoms of depersonalization and derealization. And then my hair goes like that [points straight up]. Because this is, even logically, incoherent for thinking about PTSD. After all, the *DSM-V*, like its predecessor, also recognizes that certain, positive symptoms are dissociative in nature: "dissociative reactions (e.g., flashbacks) in which the individual feels or acts as if the traumatic event(s) were recurring." It doesn't make sense, then, to speak of a PTSD subtype with dissociative symptoms, when the diagnostic category PTSD as a whole includes positive dissociative symptoms.

CC: This clearly raises a larger question concerning the relation between trauma and dissociation. Would you say that dissociation is always linked to trauma? Or is dissociation something broader in which trauma is just a subset?

OvdH: First of all, dissociation is, for me, a division of the personality into different subsystems. All with their own first-person perspectives, or pseudo-first-person perspectives, since they are not real persons. And each part has its own sense of self.

In the context of this understanding, some authorities claim to know people who have no history of trauma but still have different parts, or different "personalities." So it has not been proven beyond doubt that dissociation is always related to trauma. There might also be biological factors, constitutional factors. There may be a severe physical illness that contributes to it. Janet also paid attention to this.

But it may also be that some people who do not seem to be traumatized but have a dissociative disorder, in fact had very early attachment trauma, which is unrecognized. And I think that is very often the case.

CC: So your general sense is that, with some exceptions—maybe physiological exceptions and the like—the dissociative disorders that you see in the office tend to have a traumatic basis.

OvdH: That I see in the office? Yes, absolutely. And I'd like to add one thing. You spoke about PTSD as having been at one point an anxiety disorder. In my opinion, PTSD is the simplest dissociative disorder. But, on the other hand, I regard dissociative identity disorder as the most complex kind of PTSD. I think, in all those cases, that the dissociation of the personality is the main feature. Thus, in simple PTSD there is one dissociative part functioning in daily life and phobic of the traumatic memory and one other part, which when reactivated, is engaged in the reenactment of the trauma.

II. The Structural Dissociation of the Personality

CC: That brings me to your 2006 book, *The Haunted Self: Structural Dissociation and the Treatment of Chronic Traumatization*, where you and your colleagues Ellert Nijenhuis and Kathy Steele suggest that "dissociation is the key concept to understanding traumatization" (2). And you go on to say, "Our basic premise is that all trauma-related disorders involve some degree of structural dissociation, with acute stress disorder and simple PTSD being the most basic, and dissociative identity disorder the most complex" (7). How does the understanding of trauma as a dissociative disorder differ from understanding it as an anxiety disorder or on the fear-stress model? What is the significance of thinking of trauma in terms of dissociation instead of, let's say, fear, anxiety, or stress?

OvdH: What tends to be overlooked is that when trauma occurs, people are, metaphorically speaking, mentally broken. The American military psychiatrist Thomas A. Ross published, in 1941, a book on the war neuroses based on his clinical experiences during the First World War.[13] He wrote, "All of us have our breaking-point. To some it comes sooner than to others" (66). And that scatteredness means that the fear and anxiety is, to an overwhelming degree, somewhere in the system, in some of what has fallen apart, but it is not available in other parts of this shattered or divided personality. When the part of the personality that usually functions in daily life is confronted with a reactivated traumatic memory, it is confronted with the fear, the terror, etc., of the original traumatic experience. The essence is that when this happens, another part of the personality is reenacting the trauma in which it is stuck.

CC: So by placing dissociation at the core of traumatic experience, one of the things you're doing is making more central, or acknowledging more centrally, the not-knowing aspect of it. That is, there can be terror, but it's not present to the person in the ordinary way.

OvdH: Yes, exactly. The persona as the part functioning in daily life knows *too little* of the trauma, and the part involved in its reenactment knows *too much*, so to speak. And when it becomes present, in the form of intrusions and flashbacks, to the part functioning in daily life, it is overwhelming for this part as well, and then one becomes dysfunctional.

CC: You also have very specific ways of formulating this dissociative experience, and you have rethought some of the classic traumatic symptoms through your particular theory of the "structural dissociation of the personality." Your model of dissociation, as you propose it in the *The Haunted Self*, involves a splitting of the self along prior established "fault lines." Can you talk more about that?

OvdH: I would personally not use the term "splitting" because it's too absolute. I speak about "division." This is also an approximation because different parts may share some of the same characteristics. And some parts are also a reorganization of different qualities of the person as a whole. As Bernard Hart says, "Dissociation does not separate the mind into pieces, it only produces more or less independently acting functional units, each such unit comprising material which may be peculiar to itself, but which may just as well form a part of any number of other functional units."[14] This is in 1926, and our own models reach back into the nineteenth century. Thus, in the language of Pierre Janet, I would say that each such "unit" or subsystem of the personality, that is, each dissociative part, has at its disposal types of mental and behavioral actions that may also characterize other such subsystems.

CC: OK, so in your model, the personality or self doesn't exactly split but rather divides along the lines of prior "action systems" that make up the human individual or personality as a whole. And you describe these as primarily two systems: one that involves attraction toward stimuli and another aimed at escaping or defending against aversive stimuli. You write,

> The lack of cohesion and integration of the personality manifests itself most clearly in the alternation between and coexistence of the re-experiencing of traumatizing events (e.g., a night child) and avoidance of reminders of the traumatic experience with a focus on functioning in daily life (e.g., a day child).[15] This biphasic pattern is a hallmark of PTSD. It involves a division between actions systems for defense and for functioning in daily life. This division is the basic form of structural dissociation of the personality. Trauma-related structural dissociation, then, is a deficiency in the cohesiveness and flexibility of the personality structure. (*HS* 4)

I would like you to talk a little more about the relation between these two action systems, the one that is attracted to helpful things and the one that defends against threatening things. How are they linked to what happens when the personality divides?

OvdH: The action system of attraction actually involves a whole set of action systems, like exploration, caring, play, and energy regulation; and attachment, of course, may be number one. The defensive action system has various subsystems like fight or flight, freeze, total submission, and playing dead. We propose that during trauma, during extreme threat, the defense system is highly activated. And the essence of trauma is that we cannot cope with the situation satisfactorily, we mentally fall apart, and we are doomed to repeat the experience—until eventually, with or without the help of a therapist, a closure takes place.

So if we are confronted with overwhelming danger—for instance, looking death in the eye—we go like this [cringes] and that's what's stuck in the trauma, that subsystem of defense, which becomes the main characteristic of a dissociative part that is stuck in the trauma; it is, as it were, living in trauma-time. And that separates us from when we wake up out of this state and somehow reorient ourselves and try to get on with life. And during our attempts, as part or parts functioning in daily life, to maintain ourselves in daily life and reach our various goals, these action systems that help us function in daily life become more dominant. But eventually there will be a trigger of this death threat, and then the action system in which we got stuck—represented by what we call the "emotional part of the personality"—is reactivated. So there are now two parts of the personality that have divided along its basic fault lines: the apparently normal part of the personality (ANP), which is associated with action systems related to teaching, positive stimuli, and the emotional part of the personality (EP), which is the part that experienced the trauma and remains stuck there, which is associated with the action system for defense. And in extreme or chronic trauma there may be, first, more than one EP, and eventually more than one ANP.

That's what I think happens with regard to the division between action systems for daily life and for defense, and the dissociation between them in trauma. It is not just action systems that are falling apart. Rather, we function with a sense of self, with our perceptions, with our pseudo-first-person perspective much differently in those different situations. In essence, the different dissociative parts of the traumatized individual's personality are mediated by different (constellations of) action systems. So there is a different emerging sense of self during the trauma. And when there is trauma that occurs in the midst of an activated daily life system—I think the clearest example is sexuality—then this daily life function becomes mixed together with an unsuccessful activation of a subsystem of defense. And that means that whenever we want to engage in sexuality, certain aspects of it act as a major trigger of the EP mediated by this particular subsystem of defense in reenacting the trauma.

CC: So is that one reason why sexual abuse, incest, and so on produce more complex versions of dissociation and trauma? Because unlike, say, a soldier who goes off to war and is in a situation where he would expect the defense action systems to be dominant, in the case of sexual abuse, the daily life system itself becomes the site of the defensive system?

OvdH: In other words, this daily life system and the defensive system become confounded or mixed up. I think there are also other factors at play. If we speak about child abuse, it very often happens repeatedly, and I think the number of times one is traumatized affects how complexly the mind is divided. But sexual abuse also very often happens at an early age. And it is in attachment relationships in which the parent—who should be there for safety and comfort—is the threat. How to cope with that is already mind-blowing. Furthermore, there is frequently nobody else to whom to attach in a safe way, to help the child who needs to be protected from the abuse. The perpetrator himself—say the father, for instance—is also the person needed for safety and comfort, and his child and victim can only relate to him.

So one part turns toward the father for attachment, while another part holds the experience of the father as the abuser, as the threat, and thus perceives him as such. Of course this does not always happen simultaneously. But in the ongoing relationship, this is a very strong dynamic. If, in addition, the family constellation is involved in this dynamic, with the mother not providing safety or care and being in her own world, this dynamic becomes very problematic. The father then becomes the object of the active attachment system of the child. While he also has this other, perverse side that evokes defensive subsystems, he is the one on whom the child utterly depends.[16]

CC: I would like to emphasize something that's hard to grasp here but is central to what you talk about, which is that each of these subsystems "has a sense of self." And one of those you call the emotional part of the personality, or EP.

OvdH: We start from the assumption—it's just a point of view—that all of us, however divided, have one personality. And thus we think the language of "parts" is essential. And it is very consumer-friendly, so to speak. I should mention that Bessel van der Kolk objects to the word "part." He doesn't want to use our language.

CC: Why not?

OvdH: He thinks it's not scientific and that we need to talk about states. "States" is a very nice word. I like the sound of it. But if you see a complex part of the personality that was previously called a "personality" and we reduce that to a "state," it's too reductive. Such a part has many states. And it seems to me that there's something about this dissociation model that refuses that reduction, although it's linked to physiological states.

CC: Could you say more about that?

OvdH: On all parameters—cognitive, emotional, physiological, and neuroimaging—there are huge differences between the ANP and the EP. Especially when there are reminders of trauma. And that is documented in a number of studies done by Ellert Nijenhuis and Simone Reinders [in Groningen, the Netherlands],[17] and subsequently elaborated by Yolanda Schlumpf and Ellert Nijenhuis [in Zurich, Switzerland],[18] in which they confronted the ANPs and EPs of dissociative identity disorder patients with their own trauma scripts and with a neutral memory. When the neutral story was presented, there were hardly any differences between ANP and EP. But in the face of the trauma story, the differences were very significant—on brain functions as measured by neuroimaging, on emotional parameters, on physiological parameters.

CC: So the researchers would recite a memory to a person in one part of the personality, and that part of the personality would respond a certain way. And then how would they get to the other part of the personality?

OvdH: It was just requested—the patient had to be able to switch upon request.

CC: So the simplest division you have is between an EP and an ANP, each of which has at least an emergent sense of self?

OvdH: Well the ANP, functioning in daily life, has a complex sense of self and all of its functions. But the EP might not encompass much more than the traumatic memory. (Other EPs might have some more experiences later on in daily life and become more complex.) And its own sense of self and perception of the environment are related to the traumatic experience.

CC: So the EP is somebody who is defined by that memory much more so than the ANP.

OvdH: That's right. I would say that when EPs have a new experience they fit it in the mold of their traumatic past, while ANPs have more capacity to differentiate between the past and the present.

CC: And you say that the ANP also has a kind of amnesia for, or a not knowing of, the EP?

OvdH: That is a matter of degree. Indeed, I would say that in some severe cases, characterized by a lot of dissociative amnesia, there is clear amnesia in the ANP for the EP. And indeed in DID patients we often find ANPs who may be aware of some trauma but not of others. But very often adult trauma survivors, as ANP,[19] know that they have been in a car accident and have been traumatized by it and have developed PTSD. And when they speak about it as ANP, it's often like it happened to someone else. In the language of our theory, we would say that they have not completely personified the trauma and do not realize that the EP is part of themselves.

CC: So you can "know" as an ANP, but you don't have any emotional relation to the trauma or a diminished one?

OvdH: This is a very important point. And again, this is where Janet's understanding comes in. He speaks about trauma-related disorders as *syndromes de non-réalisation*: of "non-realization."[20] Syndromes in which the process of integration does not take place, or only insufficiently takes place—that is, the process that allows me to make my own autobiography. This process of realization is the highest level of integration: "It was I in that situation; it was my father who did such and such to me"—we call this dimension of realization "personification." The other dimension being "presentification": "I realize it happened in the past and that the danger is over." All trauma-related disorders are, in Janet's language, disorders of non-realization. And that is a type of experience on a continuum. For Janet, amnesia constitutes the highest degree of non-realization.[21] And this may characterize an ANP of a survivor of severe childhood maltreatment who believes that he or she had a perfect childhood.

CC: It's interesting because in my field of literary theory we talk about the simplest (and perhaps mystified) concept of an ordinary autobiographical narrative as a story having a referent in the world—as in, say, a story about the events in one's life. This notion of structural dissociation of the personality suggests that not all referents are the same. In other words, as an ANP you can tell a story that has a referent in the world and it can be confirmed. But in some sense there's a part of you that still doesn't know—if you're not emotionally linked to it—if you are divided from an EP.

But to return to our discussion, does the idea of dissociative parts of the personality, in trauma-related disorders, mean that in all trauma—which is characterized by biphasic alterations between amnesia or numbing, on the one hand, and intrusions, on the other—that you have divided parts of the personality with separate senses of self?

OvdH: Yes, I think so. I would say that if there's an intrusion like a dissociative flashback, then the ANP is intruded on by the re-experiencing of the EP. And it can get to such a point that suddenly the ANP withdraws inside itself, and the EP takes over executive control. The EP is then completely there and has no good reference with regard to the present because it lives in the traumatic past. The ANP may be unable to relate these intrusions to a particular experience in the past, and the EP has no good reference to the present.

CC: So one part of the personality (the ANP) has no referent in the past, and one part of the personality (the EP) has no referent in the present. What's interesting is that we could then say that neither of them contains the whole truth. Because although it seems like the EP tells the truth of the past, it doesn't know the truth of the present. And the ANP may know the truth of the present but not of the past. So that's the division.

OvdH: Yes, exactly. Well, apart from the fact that the ANP is not completely oblivious of the past. And I would add that the EP also does not know the full truth of the past because it does not realize that the trauma is over, that the danger is over. And it might have experienced just a part of the whole traumatizing event, of which there are different parts involved.

CC: So in understanding the truth of trauma through dissociation, we have to understand that in the dissociative mode, no part contains the whole truth.

OvdH: That is correct. And one addition—it might also be that in some parts, EPs may have a vision or fantasy during the traumatic experience about what they think is happening or will happen, and that becomes part of the traumatic memory. So already, for this reason also, you cannot say that what they are re-experiencing by definition is the objective truth or is what really happened.

CC: Very interesting. So if we wanted to talk about truth—this is my word, of course, not yours—we could say that the truth *is*, in part, the dissociation. That is, it is the dividing itself that somehow contains that truth.

OvdH: Yes, that's right. We are in agreement there.

CC: Does this mean, then, that whenever, or almost whenever, there is a symptom of PTSD like a flashback, we are at least at the beginning of, or in some sense already in the mode of, dissociation?

OvdH: Yes. I will speak here about my own experience of a childhood medical trauma. For a long time I did not make the connection between the trigger in daily life and this original trauma. Instead, as an adult I became anxious in certain situations and when I had to encounter this trigger. And indeed, a child EP was reactivated, and that means that a latent dissociation of my personality was becoming activated.

CC: So you also learned from yourself about the division of the personality. Was it later on that you realized that about yourself, after you had studied trauma and dissociation?

OvdH: Yes. What I do recall is that I had had some early medical experiences with my throat and tonsils, and when I was five it happened again, and I thought I would die. I fought like a lion against the doctors and nurses—thirteen in total as my mother told me later. Then they got me down, tied me up, and came to put me out by placing a mask on my face, which was extremely threatening for me. Later, when I was in the air force on compulsory military duty, I had to guide fighter planes to their target through the microphone. So this was already a stressful situation. But the microphone—that was, for me, the trigger of the traumatic experience of having been overpowered and getting that mask on my face. Even though I was very good at my work, I would become highly anxious, upset. By talking in this microphone, this child part of myself came back as panic attacks. However, only years later did I make the connection—indeed, when I was already a trauma therapist.

CC: May I ask why, at five, you thought you would die?

OvdH: Because there was no preparation. Because at age three, I was going to a doctor and I was told he would be "helping" me. And he tied me down. He did something that I cannot remember, but I do know that afterward I was highly upset: it may have been the fear of death. And I think that in the second round in the hospital, this was reactivated.

CC: Ah, I see. So there you have an example of what in Freudian terms is called "repetition," where you actually don't have the original referent of the trauma.

OvdH: Yes. The actual situation is so overwhelming, and especially as a child, that you cannot think that this is linked to an earlier situation. This example is characterized by what Janet called "double emotion": the vehement emotions pertaining to the current, highly stressful event reactivate those of the previous trauma, and the two sets of emotions become merged in a completely overwhelming experience.[22]

CC: So could an EP either be carrying or holding or repeating a "vehement emotion" from another time, an earlier time that it doesn't remember? In other words, in this case the EP from the later event in your life actually was reactivating an earlier EP. So even there, too, we can't necessarily make a direct link from one emotion to one event, because it could be a previous event?

OvdH: This may often be the case. But the same EP could have also experienced the earlier trauma. It very often happens that in trauma therapies the patient or client thinks that this one thing is the original event, but it's just the beginning of a series of events that are connected to one another through an emotion. And phenomenologically speaking, in therapy I can encounter EPs that have for a long time felt themselves to be at age nine and then at another time might start to experience themselves as age five and in the therapy might even develop some sense of adulthood. But still, as long as all these traumas are not integrated, they continue to have these different layers.

III. Divided Time

CC: One of my major questions about dissociation is how it can be brought together with what has been my own interest and focus in the study of trauma, that is, the Freudian model of trauma as a delayed experience, or a repetition of something that was never assimilated. Now at one point in your book you say that EPs may be, or perhaps they always are, in another time. That is, they are in the time of the trauma . . .

OvdH: "Trauma time," we started to call it.[23]

CC: Trauma time. Whereas the ANP is more, at least seemingly, in the present. That's what you call a horizontal division, in which the temporal gap between now and then is associated with, or played out between, these two parts of the personality.

OvdH: Yes, in its basic form.

CC: So the dissociative division of the personality, which looks more like a spatial model, is actually a temporal one, too, because the EP tends to be not only in another time but in a sense there is, for it, no time. Would that mean, then, that dissociation implicitly has a temporal gap in it? And, on the other hand, that the temporal model of "deferred action" in Freud implies, or can be seen as also involving, a dissociative dimension?[24]

OvdH: Yes, I think so. I would only add that most situations are more complex. First, living in trauma time, as EPs do, means that they mix the present and the traumatic past; that is, they perceive present situations as traumatizing, or, otherwise put, they *predict* that the trauma will happen again. After all, memory is strongly related to predicting the future.[25] Second, it can also be that there is one traumatizing event and two different EPs are present at the same time. And later, as the person develops, they also may develop different ages. Or, if the trauma continues, they may switch, within the trauma frame, with each other. For example, a victim part undergoes the horror—abuse, for instance—and a part identifies with, or copies, the perpetrator. They can be there simultaneously or alternate.

CC: And when do we get more than one ANP?

OvdH: Here I should first mention that "apparently normal" does not say anything about their level of functioning in everyday life. [Charles] Myers[26] developed the term "apparently normal personality," and we couldn't find a better alternative except for modifying it into "part of the personality," as we believe that every person has only one personality, however divided it may be. It simply means that these parts of the personality, whatever their level of functioning, are not fully integrated. Indeed, ANPs can have different levels of functioning or adaptiveness in daily life. They might be a manager of a big company or a psychotherapist or a lawyer or a mother, or whatever you call high-level functioning. That is all possible with some ANPs. Or they are characterized by low-level functioning, often accompanied by frequent intrusions of reactivated EPs. In the population that Judith Herman described, of women who were highly functional in their work as professionals—when they were at home, it was often a mess. Because being at home triggers the EPs—home being associated with the abuse—and at work they could take sufficient distance from it.[27]

But to answer your question: daily life can offer challenges that the existing ANP of the developing child, adolescent, or adult cannot cope with. Then the solution may be the creation of another ANP better able to cope.

CC: And so can you describe a situation in which you get more than one ANP, as in chronic abuse and more complex trauma?

OvdH: For me, the primordial example is a young girl who, early in the morning on weekdays, is abused by her father. He goes off and prepares the breakfast. She has to go to the bathroom, but to do that she must pass the kitchen. And then she has to sit at the family table in front of him. How can she, as ANP, function at all—eat, for example—when she has to look her father in the face, with the EPs that underwent the abuse psychologically still so close? In order to cope with that situation and not be completely overwhelmed and dysfunctional, she needs to create another ANP who is there just for the function of eating.[28]

CC: I see. So to bring your example back to the question of how a temporal model of trauma is a dissociation model as well, we would have to say that in trauma it's not that we have an event over here and a later triggering of it over there—or even an event not experienced as such until later. Saying it that way still implies a continuous temporal frame in which the experience operates. But what you're describing in these divided personalities is that the not-knowing of dissociation is actually between moments in time as well. There is a division between this moment and that moment.

OvdH: Yes, there are discontinuities.

CC: So the temporality is discontinuous. It's not just that you have a personality that's discontinuous but that you have a radically discontinuous temporality. Or history. I think that is really helpful for thinking about the larger theoretical and philosophical implications of dissociation and trauma.[29]

OvdH: I would say that the episodes of intrusion and avoidance already imply this discontinuity. And another aspect is something I have become aware of that [Jean-Martin] Charcot also pointed out: that in some traumatized individuals there was a delay in symptoms regarding the trauma. And Janet too. It was already a common understanding at the time.

On a different level of complexity, in dissociative identity disorder, the discontinuity is also related to daily life and to these amnesias. "I find myself in the university library, and my last memory is having breakfast. Apparently I was looking for a book. I try to make sense of it," as a young DID patient related.

CC: Think about what that would mean if we expanded it to an entire people or collectivity, saying, "How did we get here?" "How did we get from there to here?" And that seems actually quite relevant, especially for some of our collective historical experience and political experiences right now.

OvdH: Yes, indeed. Thinking in terms of Janet's hierarchy of degrees of reality[30] in this context, one might consider, for instance, how for the Serbs the battle with the Turks at the end of the fifteenth century is, as I have heard, something that seems to have happened very recently and gets reactivated in current conflicts.

IV. Between Sleep and Awakening

CC: This brings me to a question concerning memory. You suggest that memory is a central problem in dissociation and trauma. And you distinguish between narrative or autobiographical memory, on the one hand, and traumatic memory, on the other. And narrative memory, you say, quoting Janet, is "the action of telling a story."[31] And traumatic recall is different. So what, then, is the importance of speaking about "action" in memory? Why think of memory as a form of action, as opposed to the consolidation of a representation, for example, as some people do?

OvdH: Well, one can use terms that describe mechanisms, but I prefer a more personalized language that focuses on the fact that, as human beings, we have to perform mental and/or behavioral actions—behavioral actions also have their mental component—and that's a challenge. It's a task we have. I am also facing a task if I tell you a story about a patient or about myself. I am engaged in mental actions, which include, for instance, how elaborate I will be to you as compared to somebody else. You can put those disembodied labels on it. But it is I who am doing the action in our relationship, in the world.

CC: So when we refer to trauma, at times, as an experience of forced passivity or helplessness, we could think of its return in PTSD also in terms of the memory itself: the memory is not an effective action?

OvdH: I would say that the EP is reenacting. So it's acting without the action of telling a story. Janet described this beautifully: "Such patients [that is, their EPs] are continuing the action, or rather the attempt at action, which began when the [trauma] happened; and they exhaust themselves in these everlasting recommencements."[32] But an ordinary narrative memory exists of a combination of the story and of the event. And the EP can only re-experience, even though this re-experience is also a kind of reconstruction. Even without being able to tell its own story. It's just like it is happening again. And indeed, it cannot realize that it *has* happened. Here I am referring again to Janet's notion of "realization," which he subdivides into "personification" and *présentification*—"presentification."[33] Presentification is involved when I am aware that we are talking now, that I have come from a morning of doing therapy with patients, that I will be doing something else in the evening, that you have come here by taxi, and that soon you will go to Schiphol [Airport], and so on. So I am focusing on the present moment with the corona of all these other moments in time.[34] And an EP is unable to do that.

Now the ANP may have some knowledge of the traumatizing event and can say something like, "It happened then and there. I know the incest happened." But the ANP is not strong in the other component of *personification*. It cannot say, "It happened to *me*." And it cannot engage fully in those actions—those mental, verbal, and social actions—in order to say, "It happened to me then and there, and it had such and such effects on me, and it happened *to me*, and it was my father." These are a whole lot of very difficult integrative challenges in terms of mental and behavioral actions. An example is a DID patient of mine who, as ANP, was writing reviews of books on incest for a newspaper without realizing it had also happened to her.

CC: So EPs and ANPs have different kinds of senses of self. Because for an EP, there is an event that happened to me, but it's not *my* event. I don't possess it. In other words, you said, the EP can't necessarily state, "I had this experience."

OvdH: Right. It's reenacting.

CC: So it's a sense of self, but not as self-possession. It is, rather, *being* possessed. It's a different kind of self. So when you say there are two senses of selves, or, let's say, two "I"s, at least one "I" (and perhaps both, in different ways) doesn't own its experience.

In your book you give an interesting and powerful quotation from Charlotte Delbo in order to speak of this. I will quote the entire paragraph in which you and your co-authors turn to Delbo:

> Charlotte Delbo, a survivor of Auschwitz, recounted the differences between the depersonalized memory of ANP and the traumatic memories of EP. She had recurrent intrusive nightmares in which EP relived the traumatizing events:
>
>> [I]n these dreams, there I see myself again, *me*, yes *me*, just as I know I was: scarcely able to stand . . . pierced with cold, filthy, gaunt, and the pain is so unbearable, so exactly the pain I suffered there, that I feel it again physically, I feel it again through my whole body, which becomes a block of pain, and I feel death seizing me, I feel myself die.
>
> Upon her awakening, her ANP would struggle to regain emotional distance from the EP:
>
>> Fortunately, in my anguish, I cry out. The cry awakens me, and I [ANP] emerge from the nightmare, exhausted. It takes days for everything to return to normal, for memory to be "refilled" and for the skin of memory to mend itself. I become myself again, the one you know [ANP], who can speak to you of Auschwitz without showing any sign of distress or emotion . . . I feel that the one who was in the camp [EP] is not me, is not the person who is here, facing you [ANP] . . . And everything that happened to that other, the Auschwitz one [EP], now has no bearing upon me, does not concern me, so separate from one another are this deep-lying [traumatic] and ordinary memory.[35]

Delbo has different "I"s here. "In my anguish I cry out." Now the "I" in the dream is the EP, right? The "I" in the dream is the EP, and the "I" of the ANP cries out. So in the movement from sleep to awakening, the "I" of sleep and the "I" of awakening is also a split between an EP and and ANP.

OvdH: When Charlotte Delbo goes to sleep, she is an ANP. But in the sleep the EP awakens, and she's re-experiencing, cries out, and that awakens the ANP, who still is in touch with the crying of the EP. So there is a moment of connection, but then the ANP makes avoidant actions to try to get out and leaves the EP behind, stuck in the cry.

CC: So could you say that, metaphorically—or perhaps not metaphorically—speaking, the therapy office is, in a way, the site of that transition from sleep to awakening, that cry that wakes one up?

OvdH: Yes, metaphorically.

CC: Because, metaphorically, there is a moment where they might touch. And is that where you're trying to lead?

OvdH: That is what I'm trying to create in my work with patients with trauma-related dissociative disorders. To create, let's say, the conditions in which the EP comes with its re-experiences, its reenactment, and the ANP stays present, in a state of compassion. And apart from the necessary structure, the therapist needs to provide the outside compassion and safety—that's the essence of trauma work.

CC: So in that contact, they have, metaphorically speaking, crossed that divide in therapy—they begin to touch each other.

OvdH: Yes.

CC: And then you no longer have either an EP or an ANP. You have something else. When you talk about that moment, which is the beginning of the moment of what you call integration . . .

OvdH: Actually, two different levels of experience are combined here. When an EP and an ANP start to share their respective experiences—for instance, the EP's traumatic experience is shared with the ANP—then, metaphorically speaking, their boundaries become more permeable. This integrative action of sharing takes place, initially, at the level of synthesis. And in many cases it does not immediately lead to a compete integration ("fusion") of the EP and the ANP, which might be the case in simple PTSD, in which the sharing can take place, say, in one session, and then would also include the fusion of the EP and ANP into a unified personality (in which case the dissociation has been overcome). But in many cases of complex trauma, in particular the complex dissociative disorders, often much more is needed in terms of sharing between the EP and the ANP before they are ready for a complete fusion.

CC: So what, then, do you get? You don't get an ANP anymore, right? Because the ANP was a little amnestic, or was not remembering everything about the EP. Do you have a name for when you begin to integrate?

OvdH: This is a very good point that you raise, and I might not have a complete answer. But it might be that the EP and the ANP are sharing something with each other. This sharing, in itself, already involves integrative actions. (I generally use the word "shared" with my patients.) If what is shared in this contact, for instance a traumatic memory, is what was keeping an EP apart from an ANP and all of it is shared, then I would say that what is taking place is an integration, a fusion between the ANP and the EP. That is, the EP stops being separate, and the ANP has become more of an encompassing part of the personality.

However, in the complexity of trauma, it is very often the case that this EP has many more traumatic experiences. So this part of the trauma is shared, and the ANP has taken that in, and it becomes part of her or his life history. But there is still much more to share from this EP or, as is usually the case, from other EPs.

CC: Or from the EP behind the EP. So the touch of ANP and EP may carry with it another experience that is not quite present.

OvdH: Yes.

V. Language without an Address

CC: I would like to turn to another way of thinking about this difference between traumatic or non-narrative memory and narrative memory that you discuss in the essay you wrote with Bessel van der Kolk, "The Intrusive Past: The Flexibility of Memory and the Engraving of Trauma,"[36] as well as in *The Haunted Self*. This is Janet's case of "Irène." As you recount her story: Irène was a young woman who had nursed her mother for sixty days and nights when her mother was dying. And when her mother did die, Irène was unable to acknowledge it. And she kept trying to talk to the corpse, to lift it up when it fell from the bed, and to feed it. And when she was brought to the funeral, she still didn't accept that her mother was dead and laughed inappropriately.

She was brought to the Salpêtrière,[37] and there two things would happen. On the one hand, as you tell us, citing Janet, she would say: "I love my mother, I adore her, I have never left her. If she were dead, I would despair, I would feel very sad, I would feel abandoned and alone. Well, I don't feel anything; I am not sad at all, I don't cry; thus, she is not dead."[38] On the other hand, she periodically goes into trances, in which she appears to relive, at least partially, the events of the night of her mother's death. In Janet's recounting of one of these trances, she says (and I quote here from the larger context of the passages you discuss, not all of which is included in your article):

> Oh, it's finished. If one had known how one suffers when one no longer has a mother. Isn't it so, my little mother? It would be better that I die. You told me we should die together. Ah, you see, you come to find me and her eyes which

were open, and this mouth which was open, I had closed it ten times. Oh, she falls on the floor.[39]

Now while this speech at times seems to narrate some events, it's not really a narrative memory. You and van der Kolk summarize some of the points about memory that this case illustrates: "In contrast to narrative memory, which is a social act, traumatic memory is inflexible and invariable. Traumatic memory has no social component; it is not addressed to anybody. The patient does not respond to anybody. It is a solitary activity" (IP 163). Can you talk more about the way in which this speech "is not addressed"?

OvdH: Well, hearing this again after many years brings to mind her complexity. I would say that this part, who has some narrative quality in what she is relaying to Janet, is a different part—an ANP—from the part who is reenacting. Or, at the very least, the address to the mother may also be an implicit communication to the therapist, to let him know what she is experiencing. The true reenactment occurs at another time, which we discuss in the book—when Irène happens to see a bed on the ward in a certain position and starts going through the motions of trying to feed her mother, and addressing her and so on. That's complete traumatic memory. Truly traumatic memory is a reenactment.

CC: So would you say that although as an EP she is suffering through her mother's illness and dying, as an ANP she is not grieving?

OvdH: Indeed, as an ANP she is not grieving, not realizing that her mother had died: "I don't believe it." This is an example of the syndrome of non-realization. And in Janet's efforts to have Irène recount the tragic event, he is helping her to realize it, that is, to personify and presentify it. And this can be accompanied by the unification of the ANP and the EP.

CC: And to return to your comment in the article I quoted above, you say that her speech, in the trance, is "not addressed to anyone." Now at one moment, she's saying, "Isn't it so, my little mother? It would be better if you die. You told me we should die together." So she is addressing the mother, but she's not addressing whoever is in front of her when she's in the trance. Is that something you feel in the office when an EP is emerging? Can you feel that in your sense of whether or not you are present as an addressee? In other words, do you begin to disappear as an addressee?

OvdH: The issue is perhaps not whether or not an EP emerges but whether an emerging EP is not in touch with present reality, in particular the reality of the therapy room, with me being the patient's therapist. During a traumatic reenactment, an EP may be almost completely out of touch with the present, not responding to me and my communications. It is also possible that at the same time, some other part, in particular an ANP, may stay oriented to the present to some degree and thus in some contact with me. Then I have the impression that someone wants me to bear witness to her suffering in the traumatic reenactment. So whether or not I am present as an addressee is a matter of degree.

What I try to do is to help the ANP to become aware of the other parts, the EPs, and to develop a caring, accepting attitude toward them. And to tell the EP that the trauma is over, even though it has not yet been shared. To have a little bit of time orientation, which I now speak of as if it were simple, but is in fact a lot of work, which means the EP comes to have some new experiences aside from the traumatic reenactment.

CC: So in a way you're asking that the ANP become the addressee for the EP. In other words, the ANP becomes the one who can make the EP begin to address its speech.

OvdH: Yes, but I think that the therapist, who should bear witness, also needs to be addressed.

CC: So the person learns to address him or herself, and at that point it may be possible to address another person as well?

OvdH: That's true. But sometimes a part may emerge spontaneously, and you sometimes have to deal with it, and sometimes I have to explain to the new parts where they are, whose office they are in, who I am; and then I ask them to check in with the other parts to confirm that what I am saying is correct.

CC: I'm wondering if there's a way in which you could understand that original lack of address, at least in some cases, as a result of the fact that there was no one to listen during the event, as Felman and Laub say that there was no "thou" in the Holocaust, and hence no one to speak to.[40]

OvdH: This is what I think is the essence of trauma: the lack of support, of help, of comfort; being utterly left alone with the experience and having no one listening. And in cases of child abuse and neglect, having it denied by someone who should be there for providing safety, care, and compassion—the betrayal trauma, as Jennifer Freyd calls it.[41]

CC: So it seems like there is a relation between the individual experience of dissociation as the absence of internal address and the lack of the possibility of an external address. And is there, then, also a relation to a world—which can be a political world or a social world—in which you cannot be an addressee or address others?

OvdH: Absolutely. I would say that the inner division is also a mirror of the outer division.

As Jean Goodwin says, "We observe, in interactions with patients with [DID] and abused children and their families, a shared negative hallucination . . . The [DID] patient and the physician cling to the series of false symptoms and false diagnoses in proportion to their mutual need to blot out the reality of multiplicity, and to blot out the unbearable experiences of real pain that triggered it."[42]

CC: So dissociation, for you at least, is frequently tied up with a power struggle and a silencing that is also potentially political.

OvdH: Yes. The surrounding in which a trauma occurred is replicated inside the victim's personality system, between the parts you could label for the time being as "victim parts"—actually all parts are victims, whether or not they perceive themselves as such—and the parts whom I call the "perpetrator-imitating parts." There is a huge struggle inside. And then there are the parts who are the bystanders, merely observing this struggle or internal replication of the abuse, as well as those who try to protect the "victim parts" and those who go into hiding.

And this affects the way I do therapy. I was trained as a family therapist or family systems therapist, and I use the same approach with the inner world of dissociative parts that I do in treating relationships among family members. This also means that the relationships both in the therapy and around the therapy are essential. And it's not just that I treat separate parts; I treat the way they relate to each other. Those divisions can only be treated and healed if the relationship between the therapist and the patient is beneficial, is providing safety. If the therapist is threatened in dealing with issues that he or she is not able to relate to—or there are time limitations, like you need to do this in ten easy sessions—then the conditions for doing this inner healing among these inner relationships cannot adequately take place.

CC: Has that been a problem for you?

OvdH: Not so much for me. Here in the Netherlands, I have been in a fortunate position most of the time. But this is becoming more problematic in our country, and it is a major problem in America and, I would say, all over the world. Here, the trend is to offer patients with complex problems treatment programs in which, in short modules, you have to treat this problem and then that problem, quickly, otherwise you lose money. And these people I work with not only have complex dissociation but often have character pathology that is related to it, which is very understandable given where they come from. And there's cutting, self-harm, crises, suicide attempts, and so on, which all basically involve attempts at solving profound problems. This is what mental health organizations generally don't want to deal with; they do not recognize that these problem behaviors are desperate attempts at problem-solving. It disrupts the rigid ways of functioning in these organizations.

CC: It seems to me what you're saying is that ideally you're not only operating as a therapist for the patient but as a vehicle of synthesis for a larger context, and that larger context may not want to know. So it is maintaining the dissociation on a social or cultural or institutional level.

OvdH: Yes, indeed. In other words, a group, culture or society can also be characterized by a syndrome of nonrealization. Society may claim—pay lip service to—the fact that child abuse is something terrible yet not be willing to provide the necessary treatment for its sequelae. Realization involves taking responsibility for what is realized. Furthermore, at these various levels, incredulity may be used as a weapon to maintain the dissociation and nonrealization. As Jean Goodwin wrote, "[L]ike the dissociative defenses, incredulity is an effective way to gain distance from terrifying realities. Thus, physicians can be counted on to routinely disbelieve child abuse accounts that are simply too horrible to be accepted without threatening their emotional homeostasis . . . By placing limits on what we believe, we maintain for ourselves a more sane and manageable world . . . Disbelief is a way of . . . freeing the physician from worries about his or her own (or his or her parents') lack of impulse control, inability to care or to protect, and memories of painful, secret experience."[43]

To put this differently, at all these levels the testimony that something is terribly wrong and in desperate need of corrective measures is usually met with neutralizing countermeasures.

VI. Addressing the Dead and the Living

CC: I would like to return for a moment to the story of Irène. As we recall, she speaks to her mother when she is in a trance, whom she doesn't realize has died: "Isn't it so, my little mother? It would be better that I die." Here, although Irène isn't necessarily addressing the person who is with her in the hospital while she is in a trance, she is addressing someone—her dead mother. So I'm wondering if the issue may be that for integration, you need not only to create the possibility of address, but the possibility of address to a living person. That, as a therapist, you are life—as opposed to the dead one.

OvdH: Yes, this is essential. And the therapist or other person bearing witness needs to be responsive, exhibiting emotional resonance. And that's why sometimes classical psychoanalysis is so contra-indicated. Because with the patient on the couch, he or she doesn't see the therapist and misses the resonance in the eyes. This may be very disruptive to many traumatized people because it reactivates their attachment trauma, the unavailability of their parents, who might have responded with blank faces to them as children or turned away.

CC: So what's important is that the person learns not only to address another but also to be addressed by another.

OvdH: Exactly. And that is a therapeutic skill in the assessment of a patient. Because the patient needs resonance, and so as a therapist you need to be expressive, that is, in an empathic, compassion-based way. Otherwise you might be seen as the unresponsive parent. But, of course, if you are too expressive, you might be perceived as the intrusive parent. So it's a dance, so to speak, which is different with each patient.

CC: Because neither of those—the unresponsive parent or the intrusive parent—are true addressees, since they're in the past. And you are trying to talk about an address that is in the present. So in a way, what you're doing in creating this address between the EP and the ANP, and between the patient and the therapist, is also about bridging two time periods. It's a bridge across a time gap.

OvdH: And there is the important concept of time reorientation, which actually involves bridging two time periods, that is, trauma time—or the experience that the trauma is still happening—and the shared present in the therapist's office. With some emerging, disoriented EPs, the therapist might ask if the patient knows which year it is, what place he or she is in, or how old the body is. The therapist might also invite the ANP, if its phobia of such a part is not too strong, to gently contact the EP and eventually begin to share with this part those experiences that pertain to the safe present. In this way, even without having shared their traumatic memories yet, EPs may develop a—still fragile—sense of the present reality. However, when triggers occur, then this new layer of experiences is quickly disrupted; it needs to be strengthened all the time.

VII. Grieving Time

CC: This brings me to my final question. In "The Intrusive Past," you spoke of Janet's use of hypnosis with a traumatized grieving mother:

> His case example concerns a thirty-one-year-old woman who had lost her two infants in close succession. She was in constant despair and suffered gastroin-

testinal cramps and vomiting. She was admitted to the Salpêtrière, emaci-
ated, preoccupied with reminders of her children, and regularly hallucinating
realistic scenes of their deaths. Janet began treatment by having her give him
the reminders for safekeeping. Using hypnotic suggestion, he substituted her
traumatic death images with those of flowers. He then made them fade away
altogether. (179)

This therapy was considered successful, and indeed has a moving, even beautiful
quality to it. But you and van der Kolk also say, "The question arises whether it
is not a sacrilege of the traumatic experience to play with the reality of the past"
(179). How would you answer that question now?

OvdH: I think that the case Janet describes really demanded an extraordinary
intervention. She was a psychiatric inpatient who was in constant despair and
suffered gastrointestinal cramps and vomiting. She was in mortal danger from
these extreme and ongoing symptoms. But, apart from this case, I think that
there is a major risk that a countertransference feeling may turn a loss that actually demands grieving together, and perhaps crying together, into a frightening
experience for the therapist, who might feel scared of it and may be confronted
with his or her own unresolved issues. So with regard to the horrendous abuse
histories that my patients have, I am very reluctant to suggest these kinds of sub-
stitutions that we see in the case of Janet that you just described.

However, the beautiful variation that Milton Erickson presented might still
inspire me. A severely ill woman desperately wanted to have a child, and she and
her husband were very happy when eventually a baby girl, Cynthia, was born.
Cynthia died when she was six months old, a crib death. A few months later,
the woman was mentally and physically in a terrible state. Erickson talked to
her seriously about her wish to end her life: he pointed out that by doing so she
would also destroy the memories of the happiest time of her life. He instructed
the husband to find a eucalyptus sapling for her and plant it according to her
instructions. "I want you to name that eucalyptus sapling 'Cynthia.' I want you
to watch Cynthia grow. I want you to look forward to the day when you can sit
in the shade of Cynthia." Erickson visited her a year later. The tree had grown
very rapidly. The woman was much better, both physically and mentally. She
had many flower beds and showed all of them to him. Erickson later remarked,
"Every flower she grew reminded her of Cynthia, as did the eucalyptus tree that
I named 'Cynthia.'"[44]

CC: So, in that case the reality of the past doesn't exactly get replaced but is rather accompanied by a reality of grieving, which also involves you. So when you say that as a therapist you may bring your own grief into it, that means for the patient that there is a relation to an other, now, which is new in the grieving process. And that's the address. And the response.

OvdH: I should first say that the therapy is about the patient's grief, and the therapist should facilitate it and bear witness to it. But I would like to add something. When we are fully integrated, to the degree that that's possible as human beings, we go back and forth between the past and the present. That's automatic and happens in terms of microseconds, as the neuroscientists have established. When you are integrative and adaptive you are able to play with the past and the present. You are able to differentiate. But when you are traumatized, any trigger makes a part of you think that it will all happen again. There is no mental space to make a differentiation between the present and the past.

CC: It sounds like when you bring together your notion of grieving with this issue of temporality that you've just raised, what you're saying essentially is that the experience of temporality is, in the end, an experience of grieving. Or that grieving is the experience of temporality. And that's partly what you are bringing into therapy. That is one of the things that you're helping to have happen.

OvdH: Yes, absolutely. I would say that grieving is coming to terms with the fact that what was will never be again, in the way that something that is carried along the stream of a river does not return—except, perhaps, on a cosmological level. So life always has two sides: one is the joy of new experiences, the other the grief of what is lost. One cannot exist without the other.

NOTES

1. Milton H. Erickson (1901–1980) was an American psychiatrist who specialized in hypnosis and family therapy. I recall that during the 1990s his work was being discussed at the International Society for Traumatic Stress Studies for clinicians interested in trauma. Jay D. Haley (1923–2007) was a psychotherapist who helped found family therapy, as well as brief therapy and strategic psychotherapy. Paul Watzlawick (1921–2007) was an Austrian-American family therapist.

2. Fritz Perls (1893–1970) was a German Jewish psychiatrist who eventually moved to the Esalen Institute in California. With his wife, Laura Perls, he developed Gestalt therapy, a form of psychotherapy that focuses on bodily sensations. (Bessel van der Kolk, whose interview in this volume notes his own therapeutic focus on bodily awareness, has done some work at the Esalen Institute more recently.) John G. Watkins (1913–2012) was an American psychologist (and husband of Helen H. Watkins) known for his work with divided personalities (including those of the Hillside Strangler, whose confession he elicited). Ego-state therapy, which he founded, focuses on

the analysis of various personalities in a single person, treating them through a modification of family therapy. Henri F. Ellenberger wrote *The Discovery of the Unconscious:
The History and Evolution of Dynamic Psychiatry* (New York: Basic, 1981).

Pierre Janet (1859–1947) was a major French philosopher, psychologist, and psychiatrist who initially specialized in the theory and treatment of dissociation and trauma;
later, he considerably widened his scope of interest. He was also known for his creative
use of hypnosis in treating traumatic memories. Janet was one of the major influences
on Freud, and in the field of traumatic stress studies some researchers consider Janet's
work to be of at least equal importance in the development of notions and psychotherapeutic methods regarding trauma. (In this volume, both Onno van der Hart and
Bessel van der Kolk emphasize Janet's foundational work in the study of trauma.)

3. Helen H. Watkins (1921–2002) was an American psychologist (and wife of John G.
   Watkins) who worked on ego state therapy and hypnosis. She helped develop the hypnotic technique of the "affect bridge," which helps patients access memories by connecting them through shared affects rather than other meaning-related factors.

4. DDNOS is a subcategory under "Dissociative Disorders" in the *Diagnostic and Statistical Manual of Mental Disorders*, 4th ed. (Arlington, VA: APA, 1994) (*DSM-IV*). In
   DSM-V (2013), the subcategory has changed to "Unspecified Dissociative." DID (dissociative identity disorder) and PTSD are in both *DSM-IV* and *DSM-V*. (DID was previously known as "multiple personality disorder.")

5. Details of circumstances and names have been altered to disguise the patients discussed in this response.

6. Dori Laub and Nanette C. Auerhahn, "Knowing and Not Knowing Massive Psychic
   Trauma: Forms of Traumatic Memory," *International Journal of Psychoanalysis* 74.2
   (1993): 287–302.

7. See Onno van der Hart, Ellert Nijenhuis, and Kathy Steele, *The Haunted Self: Structural Dissociation and the Treatment of Chronic Traumatization* (New York: Norton,
   2006), hereafter cited as *HS*.

8. The International Society for the Study of Dissociation was originally founded in 1993
   as the International Society for the Study of Multiple Personality and Dissociation.

9. Bennett Braun is an American psychiatrist known for his work on dissociative disorders, repressed memory, and DID. Richard Kluft is an American psychiatrist and
   previous colleague of Bennett Braun, also known for research and treatment in the
   area of dissociative disorders.

10. See n8, above.

11. Ellert Nijenhuis is a Dutch psychiatrist who is highly respected for his work in dissocia-
    tive disorders and works in Assen, the Netherlands. Suzette Boon is a respected Dutch
    psychologist specializing in dissociative disorders; she works in Zeist, the Netherlands.

12. There has been an ongoing debate concerning the relation between the diagnostic
    categories of PTSD and the dissociative disorders. Previously, PTSD was categorized
    in the *DSM* as an "Anxiety Disorder" (based on a stress model and associated with
    extreme fear reactions) and separated from the dissociative disorders. *DSM-V* intro-
    duced the category of "Trauma- and Stressor-Related Disorders," which is followed
    immediately by "Dissociative Disorders." As this interview demonstrates, many ex-

perts still feel that PTSD is fundamentally a dissociative disorder and remains inappropriately categorized in the *DSM*.

13. Thomas A. Ross, *Lectures on War Neuroses* (Baltimore: Williams, 1941).

14. Bernard Hart, "The Concept of Dissociation" *British Journal of Medical Psychology* 6.4 (1926): 241–63.

15. The terms "night child" and "day child" come from Marilyn van Derbur, a former Miss America, who described her own dissociative experience as a result of long-term sexual abuse by her father. See Marylin van Derbur, *Miss America Today: Lessons Learned from Ultimate Betrayals and Unconditional Love* (Denver: Oak Hill Ridge, 2004).

16. See G. Liotti, "A Model of Dissociation Based on Attachment Therapy and Research," *Journal of Trauma and Dissociation* 7.4, pp. 55–74. [Comment by Dr. van der Hart.]

17. A. A. T. S. Reinders et al., "One Brain, Two Selves," *Neuroimage* 20.4 (2003): 2119–25.

18. Y. R. Schlumpf et al., "Dissociative Part-dependent Biopsychosocial Reactions to Backward Masked Angry and Neutral Faces: An fMRI Study of Dissociative Identity Disorder," *Neuroimage: Clinical* 3 (2013): 54–64.

19. Dr. van der Hart uses the phrases "as ANP" and "as EP" to charactize people with complex trauma-related disorders and with DID as having one personality that is nonetheless acting as a number of different selves.

20. Pierre Janet, "Réalisation et interprétation," *Annales médico-psychologiques* 93 (1935): 329–66.

21. The original text by Janet reads, "Il y a des malades qui arrivent pour ainsi dire à la perfection dans la non-réalisation, car ils ne font plus aucune référence ni à la formule verbale qui exprime l'événement supprimé ni à l'angoisse qui les arrête: pour eux, l'événement ou même la function semble n'avoir jamais existé" (352). This is especially the case in patients with trauma-related dissociative disorders, in which the ANP has amnesia for the traumatizing events and does not know the EPs. [Comment by Dr. van der Hart.]

22. See *HS*, 63–64, and Pierre Janet, *L'évolution de la mémorie et de la notion du temps* (1928; reprint, Paris: L'Harmattan, 2006).

23. See O. van der Hart, E. R. S. Nijenhuis, and R. Solomon, "Dissociation of the Personality in Complex Trauma-Related Disorders and EMDR: Theoretical Considerations," *Journal of EMDR Practice and Research* 4.2 (2010): 76–92.

24. In this context we might think of Janet's hierarchy of degrees of reality; see *HS*, 161ff. [Comment by Dr. van der Hart.]

25. See A. Berthoz, *Emotion and Reason: The Cognitive Neurosciece of Decision Making* (Oxford: Oxford UP, 2006). [Comment by Dr. van der Hart.]

26. Charles Samuel Myers (1873–1976) was a British physician and psychologist who wrote about shell shock during World War I and helped institute its recognition in the British army.

27. On incest and its effects, see Judith Herman, *Father-Daughter Incest* (1981; reprint, Cambridge, MA: Harvard UP, 2000), as well as her interview in chap. 6.

28. For other examples, see *HS*, 75. In some cases a boy part may be developed for school in a girl who is sexually abused by her father at home. [Comment by Dr. van der Hart.]

29. This may help us understand Freud's model of temporality in its early "two-scene"

version in *Studies on Hyesteria*, as well as in its late version in *Moses and Monotheism*, where Freud notes that the Jews were created through a trauma that "one section" of the Jews had experienced and another had not. See Freud, *Moses and Monotheism* (New York: Vintage, 1955), 64–65, and Cathy Caruth, *Unclaimed Experience: Trauma, Narrative, and History* (Baltimore: Johns Hopkins UP, 1996), chap. 1. Another interesting way of thinking about this discontinuous temporality might be in terms of Freud's *Project for a Scientific Psychology*, in particular through Derrida's reading of the neuronal structural of memory in that text as a structure of deferral and repetition. See Jacques Derrida, "Freud and the Scene of Writing," in *Writing and Difference* (Chicago: U of Chicago P, 1978).

30. On Janet's "degrees of reality," see n24, above.

31. Pierre Janet, *Les médications psychologiques* (1919; reprint, Paris: Société Pierre Janet, 1984), 2:272. See also Bessel A. van der Kolk and Onno van der Hart, "The Intrusive Past: The Flexibility of Memory and the Engraving of Trauma," in *Trauma: Explorations in Memory*, ed. Cathy Caruth (Baltimore: Johns Hopkins UP, 1995), 158–82, hereinafter cited as IP. Judith Herman also cites this passage from Janet in her interview in chap. 6 of this volume.

32. Pierre Janet, *Psychological Healing* (1925; reprint, New York: Arno, 1976), 1:663.

33. On Janet's notions of realization, personification, and presentification as it is interpreted by Dr. van der Hart, see *HS*, 151ff. See also, among others, Janet, "Réalisation et interprétation."

34. This is bound up with Janet's hierarchy of degrees of reality. See n24, above. [Comment by Dr. van der Hart.]

35. *HS*, 39–40. The quotations are adapted from L. L. Langer, *Holocaust Testimonies: The Ruines of Memory* (New Haven, CT: Yale UP, 1991) and originally appeared in Charlotte Delbo, *La mémoire et les jours* (Paris: Berg, 1985).

36. See n31, above.

37. The Salpêtrière was, during the period that Janet and Charcot worked there, a noted psychiatric hospital in Paris.

38. IP, 161, citing Janet, *L'évolution de la mémoire*. Dr. van der Hart notes that this is an ANP speaking, thus illustrating Janet's notion of a *syndrome de nonréalisation*.

39. This is my translation of additional material from the case in Pierre Janet, "L'amnésie et la dissociation des souvenirs par l'émotion" *Journal de psychologie normale et pathologique* (Sept. 1904); the extra lines were not discussed in van der Kolk and van der Hart's article. As Dr. van der Kolk emphasizes in the interview, these particular lines reveal a mixture of a traumatic memory in the form of a reenactment—including addressing the dying or dead mother—and a beginning of a narrative possibility. The traumatic memory, as such, appears most clearly—as Dr. van der Hart says—in her behavior that involves actions that repeat her actions from the night of the death (see IP, 162).

40. See Shoshana Felman and Dori Laub, *Testimony: Crises of Witnessing in Literature, Psychoanalysis and History* (New York: Routledge, 1991).

41. See Jennifer Freyd, *Betrayal Trauma: The Logic of Forgetting Childhood Abuse* (Cambridge, MA: Harvard UP, 1998).

42. J. M. Goodwin, *Sexual Abuse: Incest Victims and Their Families* (1982; reprint, Chicago: Yearbook Medical Publishers, 1989), 46.

43. J. M. Goodwin, "Credibility Problems in Multiple Personality Disorder Patients and Abused Children," in *Childhood Antecedents of Multiple Personality*, ed. R. P. Kluft (Washington, DC: American Psychiatric Press, 1985), 1–19.

44. Jeffrey K. Zeig, ed., *A Teaching Seminar with Milton H. Erickson, M.D.* (New York: Brunner/Mazel, 1980), 287; see also Onno van der Hart, ed., *Coping with Loss: The Therapeutic Use of Leave-Taking Rituals* (New York: Irvington, 1988), 6.

Geoffrey Hartman at his home in New Haven, Connecticut, Fall
1994.

Chapter Nine

Words and Wounds

An Interview with Geoffrey Hartman

Geoffrey Hartman's career extends from his pioneering early work on Wordsworth to his more recent writing on video testimony. His essays in the early 1990s emphasized a possible continuity in this career: an exploration of the intricate relation between what he calls "literary knowledge" and the various forms of traumatic loss. I interviewed him in the fall of 1994 on his early and ongoing engagement with Wordsworth, the implications of this work for understanding literary ways of knowing, and the relation these inquiries might have to the kind of knowing and testifying provided by video testimony.

I. TRAUMATIC IMPASSE AND POETIC KNOWLEDGE

CC: I am interested in the implications, for an understanding of poetry, or literature in general, of your comment that your literary critical work has always had a "concern for absences or intermittences of consciousness, for the ambiguous status of accidents in mental life, for the ghosting of the subject."[1] The most obvious place to illustrate this early and ongoing interest in absences and intermittences would be your repeated readings of *The Prelude*, and particularly the paradigmatic episode of the Boy of Winander. You note that in *The Prelude*, which you call the first account of developmental psychology in our era, this particular episode surprisingly describes an impasse in development, and you go on to ask, in regard to it, "What is the relation of memory to loss, to loss of control perhaps, even to trauma? What kind of knowledge is poetry?"[2] You seem to be speaking almost paradoxically, linking impasse and knowledge, trauma and poetry. I'd like you to comment on the kind of impasse we find in Wordsworth, and how it is related specifically to poetic knowledge.

GH: Trauma is generally defined as an experience that is not experienced, that resists or escapes consciousness. In *The Unmediated Vision* I already mentioned a more mystical notion, that of Meister Eckhart's *Unerkennendes Erkennen*, an unknowing knowing. The context there was a necessary, whether deliberate or natural, anti-self-consciousness. And certainly from the beginning I've been interested in how to define a specifically *literary* knowledge, which can reveal without full consciousness, or systematic analysis. Again, thinking back to *The Unmediated Vision*, its last chapter, called "The New Perseus," focused on the figure of the Medusa. It speculated that as we move from the romantics into the modern period, there is an attempt to see things unaided, to catch a reality on the quick. I noticed in modern authors a certain inner distancing or coldness, or an attempt to achieve a coldness despite the nearness to, the apparent nearness to, reality. I associated this coldness, leaning on the Greek myth, with Perseus's shield, which guarded him from the petrifying glance of the Medusa, and speculated that tradition functioned as this shield. It managed to provide obliquity, or representational modes that had an inbuilt obliquity. But absent these traditional decorums, the poet had to go against the real with the unshielded eye or the unshielded senses. This seemed to increase the risk and potential of trauma.

Then, in the Wordsworth book, I posited certain fixations, in particular what I called the spot syndrome, or the obsession with particular places, an obsession which came to the poet often unexpectedly and in ordinary circumstances: "And there's a tree, of many one." I understood the emphasis on oneness, on singularity rather than unity, as being part of the same complex, and which played a role in the drama of individuation.

CC: So the spot syndrome was linked with that perceptual confrontation, or that unmediated vision.

GH: Yes, and I was interested in how Wordsworth drew his stories and fictions out of his fascination with particular places. These highly charged images, I tried to show how the poet unblocked them, how he developed them. Many of them were ocular. Visuality was dominant within his sensory organization; and something—call it nature, call it an economic principle within sensory organization— pitted the other senses against the eye. Symbolic process, I said, was related to this undoing of images.

CC: Are you saying that the image was at first a block that had to be unblocked?
GH: Yes. Or a fixation.
CC: And that Wordsworth's poetry had to do with unblocking the eye?
GH: Yes. It wasn't necessarily that they were always the same images, let's say primal images, or primal scene images. But whatever the psychic etiology, that structure was there, and Wordsworth talked quite openly about the dominance of the eye. He confessed he had passed through a period of "picturesque" composition and later felt that this was related to a stage of obsessive visuality. But there are many other important statements in Wordsworth on the development of visuality and nature's counterpointing of visuality, and how his development as a poet has to do with that.
CC: So visuality here is not something that immediately produces some kind of development but presents itself as an impasse to development, or potentially so.
GH: Yes. But as I also said, there is something powerfully abstract about visuality, in distinction from individual images. So you can fall in love with the visual, whereas you can't fall in love with obsessive images, which overpower you or which you can't get rid of.
CC: The distinction then is between perception as a whole mode and the shock of an individual perception.
GH: That's right. In Wordsworth, the movement from charged individual image to visuality is parallel to the movement from specific and haunting places to Nature. Nature is his most generous concept. I try to connect this evolution with a tension in the history of religion centering on epiphanic places. Bethel, for instance, the place where Jacob lies down and has the dream of angels ascending and descending, is nothing but a stone. Yet here are the gates of Heaven! It is what Mircea Eliade calls an *omphalos*: the umbilical and nether point of the earth. But there is another issue that you and I have talked about in relation to trauma: how almost any place—and that's part of the accidentality of revelation—can be revelatory or charged or have something of a traumatic effect through deferred action. So, on the one hand, you have the omphalos, the umbilicus of the world. On the other hand, it's merely tree or stone; the seminal episode of *The Ruined Cottage* is the poet seeing four bare walls that remain and a broken pane of glass glittering in the moonlight.
CC: So, as with visuality, the place can have, on the one hand, a traumatic, blocking effect, yet on the other hand this traumatic effect is intimately tied up with the possibility of poetic writing, or poetic development. In the Boy of Winander episode, for example, as you point out, there is at once impasse and promise of

development: the first paragraph describing a boy who creates an instrument with his two hands to blow "mimic hootings to the silent owls," and who is suddenly confronted with the nonresponse of the owls, a "lengthened pause," and a "gentle shock of mild surprise." In the second verse paragraph, the boy is said to have died in youth, and the poet stands "Mute, looking at the grave in which he lies." How are "pause" and "shock" linked to development here?

GH: This is one of the most intriguing episodes in Wordsworth. It is in part autobiographical, as we know from the manuscripts. The impassse, to describe it very briefly, is that the first verse paragraph leads one to expect that the boy should grow into maturity, and perhaps become a poet. The imagination of the boy is being prepared through a dissonance: the owls do not respond, or respond as they will. Within the context or experience of responsiveness, something is not symmetrical, and this prepares for the future, develops the boy's consciousness of a world that is independent of him. Remember the lengthened pause, which meets the boy's best skill: it is part of the dissonance because it makes him reflective, and it anticipates a further lengthening, until the final pause is mortality or death—more precisely the philosophical mind that looks at death. So that while horizontally death is foreshadowed, you expect from the first verse paragraph that in the second the poet would say, "I was that boy." Instead the boy dies, and you have the poet as survivor looking at the boy's grave.

CC: So you're saying that normally one would understand the moment of absence in the first verse paragraph as preparing the boy for some kind of self-consciousness, and ultimately, though at a greater temporal distance, his death. But in this case the death comes before self-consciousness emerges. Could one say, then, that the impasse for the poet, the traumatic moment in the developmental scheme, is not the death as such but the fact that the death comes at the wrong time?

GH: Yes, the death is untimely, but not only the death. Wordsworth adds an argumentative frame to the Boy of Winander episode when he inserts it into Book 5 of *The Prelude*. He argues that we cannot totally prepare the developing psyche, the young person, for what befalls. That would be, he claims, engineering the psyche. Natural development is much freer and depends on accident. And accident is always defined as something you cannot prepare for. In that sense development is always both propaedeutic and exceeds formal training. So that trauma is related to development by excess as well as lack. Yet Wordsworth's great myth in *The Prelude* remains: that there could be development—a "growth

There was a Boy: ye knew him well, ye cliffs
And islands of Winander!—many a time
At evening, when the stars began
To move along the edges of the hills,
Rising or setting, would he stand alone
Beneath the trees or by the glimmering lake,
And there, with fingers interwoven, both hands
Pressed closely palm to palm, and to his mouth
Uplifted, he, as through an instrument,
Blew mimic Hootings to the silent owls,
That they might answer him; and they would shout
Across the watery vale, and shout again,
Responsive to his call, with quivering peals,
And long halloos and screams, and echoes loud,
Redoubled and redoubled, concourse wild
Of jocund din; and, when a lengthened pause
Of silence came and baffled his best skill,
Then sometimes, in that silence while he hung
Listening, a gentle shock of mild surprise
Has carried far into his heart the voice
Of mountain torrents; or the visible scene
Would enter unawares into his mind,
With all its solemn imagery, its rocks,
Its woods, and that uncertain heaven, received
Into the bosom of the steady lake.

This Boy was taken from his mates, and died
In childhood, ere he was full twelve years old.
Fair is the spot, most beautiful the vale
Where he was born; the grassy churchyard hangs
Upon a slope above the village school,
And through that churchyard when my way has led
On summer evenings, I believe that there
A long half hour together I have stood
Mute, looking at the grave in which he lies!
—WORDSWORTH, *THE PRELUDE* (1850) 5.364–97

of the poet's mind"—without psychic wounds, that the psyche could be "from all internal injury exempt."

CC: But what is the relation between lack and excess in this accident?

GH: Keeping strictly to the passage, the failure of response may have linked itself, in the mind of the poet, to a thought of death. This intuition is then literalized, by prophetic extension, as in the Lucy poems. A failure of response anticipates —by the extremest reach of Wordsworth's imagination—that there would be no more nature. That if the human mind does not live fully, responsively, within nature, or nature does not respond to us, then the end result, projected forward, is apocalyptic. The death is like a hyperbole of this moment, a hyperbolic act of an imagination that leaps down, not up, taking off from a simple failure of response. Should this failure of response accelerate, then we will have no habitat, no mutuality of nature and the human mind. At this point you transcend the development of the individual; you get a more cosmic model, you speed up time, and that's apocalypse.

So that the moment of excess is not only in the wild hooting of the owls when it comes but in the imagination itself, which reacts to both failure of response and an "ecstatic" correlative of death, that piercing of the skin of the psyche when the natural scene "enter[s] unawares into [the boy's] mind."

CC: Yet the impasse is, in a sense, passed through: at the end of the episode you do not simply have a death but a poet who is looking at, reflecting upon, this death (and writing the poem). The problem that arises, then, is the way that poetic and exemplary moment is characterized: even though it is a poetic moment, it is also a moment of muteness (which peculiarly does not seem to be completely opposed to poetic writing). And this brings back the problem of how development, here, is not simply dialectical, taking the negative and making it positive. You say specifically about that mute moment, "We sense that [the poet] is looking at, as well into, himself—that he is a *posthumous* figure. He stands toward a prior stage of life, as a reader, even an epitaphic reader."[3] The poet's stance, you suggest, emerges as a haunting issue. If the poem is in some sense about poetic knowing, how can it be mute, how is the muteness poetic, or what is the link between muteness and poetry?

GH: Let me bring in the reader at this point. The theme of time—of its flow— brings us to the reader, just as in Milton's *Lycidas*. Milton foresees what he calls "lucky words": "I should utter something in honor of Lycidas, and so in the future, I hope someone will write my epitaph, and make the passerby [who could be the reader] turn and be struck by what has been said about me." This fast-forwarding of imagination is what I mean by a posthumous stance in Wordsworth, and it includes an adumbration of the reader. Wordsworth allows you to move from the poet looking at the grave of the boy to the reader reading the poet, an image of speechless and perhaps epitaphic reading. The problem is then: how do mute speech and (self-) reading relate?

We go from muteness to muteness, even if it is a muteness described in words. That is, the Boy of Winander—and this is one reason why we feel that the episode was meant to be paradigmatic of human development and that the death came too soon—is shown at the point where speech is still mimicry. He is not shown speaking; he makes a pastoral pipe with his hands, but this is not speech. He doesn't mimic speech; he mimics the owls, nature's sounds. And so you expect the question to be: how do you go from that stage to mature poetic speech? Yet *The Prelude* records the growth of the poet's mind, not of speech itself. You are given the pre-mature moment, then the mature moment, but the mature moment is like the pre-mature moment because the pause is lengthened, and you are shown a silent poet. Now what does it mean to be a silent poet? Speech is not theorized, in Wordsworth, as an agency in the growth of the (poetic) mind.

CC: It's almost as if the poem moved from what is called the "preverbal" or the "preverbal trauma"—trauma before it can even enter as a verbal construct—to muteness, and the paradoxical poetic development, at least in this episode, is the link between this preverbal or "shocking" perception and muteness. And the difficulty that you're trying to get at is to say that *that* somehow is linked to poetic insight.

GH: The impasse is not dialectized, as you correctly say. We go from one form of muteness to another form of muteness, yet Wordsworth *speaks* again and again about muteness. About mute insensate things. He doesn't simply want to speak *for* them. It's not an orphic perspective. There is, perhaps, something potentially orphic in the first verse paragraph, but even if it is orphic, nature won't cooperate. It's not really orphic, then, not a myth that animates nature, not a Rilkean myth of internalizing nature or making it invisible, not a Blakean transformation either, not a metamorphosis or anthropomorphizing of any kind. The mute insensate things remain mute and insensate. *But they're brought live into human perception and they play a part, like the mother does.* Mute dialogues with nature exist, as between child and mother. The muteness is not always negative: it can be, at times, the shadow cast by ecstasy.

CC: Maybe one way to restate the question would be to look at something else you say about silence. You say that the entire episode, even if it is based in part on failure of response, is framed, I would say paradoxically, as an address. Your words are specifically, "[Wordsworth] uses a 'turn-tale' (in [George] Puttenham's English) to invoke a preternatural though mute witness (the exemplary, classical case being the noble dead, fallen for their country, whom Demosthenes turned to in a famous speech)."[4] So in the classical case there is a witness, a mute witness, the fields of Winander, the cliffs of Winander. I want to ask: Is there a link between the failure of response that the boy experiences, then the muteness of the poet, and the poem's frame of address, an address that implies a response?

GH: Yes, but I would phrase it differently. The address to the cliffs and islands of Winander evokes a lasting or apparently lasting presence, and this presence recurs at the end of the Boy of Winander episode with the Lady, the Church, also a kind of monitory shape. You really have three figures: the cliffs and islands, the poet himself at the grave, and finally the Church, watching over the children among whom the Boy of Winander lies.

CC: They're all witnesses.

GH: Monitory shapes. One is tempted to say "witness," and "witness" is certainly appropriate to the forms of nature evoked at the beginning of the episode because of the formal force of the apostrophe. I am always reminded of Coleridge's marvelous phrase in his lines after hearing Wordsworth recite the poem on his own life, "The dread watchtower of man's absolute self." It's close to that, almost an eternity figure, a figure for conscience, a superego. The beginning of the episode, the apostrophe to the cliffs and islands of Winander, puts human development within a quasi-eternal frame.

CC: Because the cliffs are eternal?

GH: Yes. The danger of apocalypse, of Nature (familiar nature) disappearing, is distanced here. There is lastingness, the sense of not only watchful but enduring presences. Which sense is instilled in the Boy from Nature. Instilled in Wordsworth also, from nature, and it becomes an instinctive article of faith, that something endures, that something is immortal or universal. It is not in the case of the Boy of Winander quite what Coleridge felt: Coleridge's special emphasis is on anxiety, the dread watchtower. That's not in Wordsworth, but it goes along the same lines, along the same emotional spectrum, though it has more of a consolation, an assurance that nature will *not* be no more. And it has the effect of affirming, in that sense witnessing, the boy's experience. It does not deny the Boy; it does not say, hey little titch, you think you're important. So the entire tonality of the experience is different from Coleridge's watchtower at this moment; it's more like the other presences, the stars rising and setting. That has always intrigued me, "rising or setting." You remember those are the lines that follow the apostrophe. You get a sense of vast cyclical movement: it doesn't matter whether they're rising or setting—they're always rising or setting, or setting and rising. They're always going to be there. The setting is not a death: rising or setting, they will be there. It is a perpetual background which does not negate or threaten but affirms the individual life: if you wish, bears witness to it in fact. And the reason why it can do this, other than some kind of grand sentimental projection, has to do with Wordsworth's peculiar, non-Coleridgean *Angst*, always kept in check by that sense of permanent presences. Wordsworth's fear is that if the human mind separates, divorces itself from nature, and we invest our imagination elsewhere, then and only then is there danger of the fading of nature. In other words, precisely the ego, the psyche, is not ghosted in Wordsworth by nature, as it must be ghosted by the supernatural. Yet Wordsworth sees that if, because of industrialization and a turning away from a Nature ethos, nature is neglected, then the situation will drastically change. But here he remains within the faith that human life is not ghosted but affirmed by nature.

CC: Yet you speak elsewhere, as I said, of the poet's stance as a "haunting" issue. Wouldn't your emphasis now on the "affirmation" by nature be interpreted as overlooking that haunting aspect?

GH: One cannot forget that the child is haunted by Nature, and the death of the Boy of Winander could express this ghosting in the form of a "return to nature." The balance here between affirmative and negative is a "natural" one, and the reader recognizes that and does not wish to intervene concerning what in the poet's brooding is, at once, mortality *and* an intimation of immortality: the promise, cut short, of a communion with Nature which approaches ecstasy.

The poet looking at the grave, and framed by these other witness figures, does not stress the ghosting of human life, does not stress mortification. Mortality is there, but not mortification. So it works against trauma, I would say. Look, everything works against trauma in Wordsworth, yet the basis of trauma is there. "A gentle shock of mild surprise." Now really!

The muteness of the poet in the episode also raises more generally the question of the muteness in poetic speech. For his standing there "mute" is a kind of fading—counterpointed by his "full half-hour" steadfastness. I explore parallels in "Words and Wounds" and the essay on Christopher Smart in *The Fate of Reading*.[5] We avoid, evade muteness, but it's always there. We speak, but under certain conditions, as if we were allowed to speak only when fulfilling these conditions, and so euphemic modes are produced. The muteness indicates that there's something which is too difficult to utter. The way to get past that difficulty, however you conceive of the monitors—the dread you have to get past, however you conceive of it, or whatever Freudian understanding you may give to it—involves euphemism in the strong sense. Even irony may be euphemistic. Irony, the boast of the modern poet, remains within the euphemic mode (though the modern poet would say I'm "destroying euphemism").[6] It's not satire's mad laughter; satire breaks through the euphemic. It is not cursing. In other words, there is a mode of breaking through, and I'm assuming that there was trauma, shock, something dreadful or ecstatic. You know that there exists a pathology of speech in which the person speaks only by cursing. And I say there is also a mode of speech in which the person talks only in terms of blessings. We arrange ourselves between these two extremes.

II. Pausal Style

CC: That brings me to the second point I wanted to raise. The general argument you're making here, and in a number of different places, concerns poetic style, which you refer to as "pausal style," and again it appears to suggest a paradoxical link between something that interrupts and something that continues. You mention specifically that at the very moment of the turn to an ordinary style or conversational language, there's a pressure on conversation, something that remains missed and impossible.

GH: I do say that I feel there is a tension, which I'm not sure how it is resolvable, between the development—almost the genesis, in terms of the history of poetry —of the conversational style and the pressure of imagination, which is more traumatic, interruptive, transcendental. And I think it is part of Wordsworth's gift to contain each within each. There are points, however, where you feel that the suturing will give way.

CC: My impression was nonetheless that it's still the conversational style that's saving poetry. You say that poetry is mortal, and that Wordsworth assured the continuity of great poetry by a revolution of style. And it seems that you were saying that the conversation, or ordinary language, the conversational style, saves poetry, but only in relation to this interruptive or pausal awareness.

GH: Yes. It's *Wordsworth's* conversational style that saves it. Not conversation, because conversational style, insofar as it comes out of the epistolary mode, or middle style, is an achievement of the late seventeenth and eighteenth century and falls into habits of what Wordsworth called "poetic diction." That is, it elevates itself despite itself and isn't really genuinely conversational. It's familiar in the sense that the author tries to speak to the audience as equal to equal, but in fact when we read the epistles, any of the epistles, whether Pope's poetic epistles or Chesterfield's letters, we face an artificial tone and diction. But Wordsworth, as certain notorious lyrics show—think of "The Idiot Boy"—would rather have bathos than an artificially elevated diction.

CC: Does this conversational style found something that would be linked to modern poetry?

GH: I would think yes. The main line of modern poetry develops that link. And in [John] Ashbery, the casualness can become excessive. The more excessive it becomes, the more you feel an internal pressure that is being evaded.

CC: So this so-called ordinary style in Wordsworth is shadowed by that pausal sensitivity.

GH: Always.

CC: Could that be a modern sensibility: that the ordinary is inextricably bound to the pausal or interruptive?

GH: I wonder. Possibly. But trauma is not modern. You don't need a theory of trauma to "experience" trauma. And in terms of a historical schematism, I have only one firm idea, namely that what I call the Eastern epiphanic style, visible in the Great Odes and neoclassicism, has trauma directly inscribed into it. By epiphanic style I mean a style with sharp turns, of which the apostrophe at the beginning of the Boy of Winander is a faint echo. And by Eastern I mean the moment in the Ancient Mariner (written in the older style) when "at one stride comes the dark." That abruptness is inscribed in the older style. But it's not in Wordsworth: "A *gentle* shock of *mild* surprise." Instead we have a sense of continuity or achievement of something much, much milder, not that you ever lose the sense of the pressure of what that mildness is in function of, but the Wordsworthian poetic turn—let's not talk about revolution for a moment—creates a conversational poetic style that subsumes the epiphanic style. So that he does not go from, he doesn't jump from, nature into the supernatural. There is no dream vision, almost none in him. Eastern is not just a geographical category, although it has something to do with the "at one stride comes the dark." Imaginatively, if there's no twilight, then you are already in the zone of trauma.

CC: I wonder if your interest in, on the one hand, the relation between imaginative pressure and this interruptive mode, which you're also trying to see in the relation to style, and, on the other hand, ordinary conversational style has something to do with a more general notion of modern writing. When trauma theory emerges as a modern theoretical mode of writing, after all, it emerges as something within ordinary life.

GH: That is true. Theory as a mode of discourse is anti-conversational and links up with the pressure of trauma. I would prefer to focus here on literary knowledge: how literature is a mode of experience. In the nonpathological course of events, the "unclaimed experience," as you call it, can only be reclaimed by literary knowledge.[7]

CC: When you speak about this literary knowledge in your essay on trauma studies and literature, you suggest that trauma studies allows us to read the relationship of words and wounds without medical or political reductionism, and you say specifically that figurative or poetic language is linked to trauma.[8] Could you expand on that a bit, because there seems to be a kind of a paradox: normally one would think of trauma as the absencing of the possibility of speech, but you link it inherently to figurative language.

GH: I've always been intrigued by certain basic literary forms, and the riddle is one of them. I suggest that all poetic language partakes of the riddle form, with its surplus of signifiers. An answer is evoked, but can you get to the answer? If you could get there, the signifiers would become redundant and fall away. But in poetry you can't get to the answer. So the signifiers keep pointing to what is missing. Or mute. There's too little that is referred to, if you want to use that scheme, and too much that is suggested. But I've not been able to develop fully the poetry-riddle relation. I'm not a systematic thinker. I began this line of speculation in "The Voice of the Shuttle,"[9] where muteness and trauma are at the center, Philomela's tongue having been cut out. "The voice of the shuttle" is, you remember, a phrase cited in Aristotle's *Poetics*. It refers to, we think, the Philomela story: how her shuttle weaves a garment that restores her voice. But the compactness itself of the phrase is riddling, and I try to describe that structure as, basically, overspecified ends ("voice" and "shuttle") and something in the middle that is muted or left out. And I suggest that all figurative language has these overspecified ends, as if the middle were cut out. It is the cutting out that's important.

CC: Yes, and cutting, rather than erasing, which is relevant.

GH: Yes, we glimpse figuration as a counterforce. My essay, however, stops short at one point, and I've never been able to extend it. I speculate that the very structure of figurative language, if it has these overspecified ends and an absent middle —which interpretation can fill in—also holds for narration. But I don't show it by a narratological analysis. I simply suggest that in the Oedipus story you can glimpse an extension from figurative language to narrative structure. Insofar as the Oedipus story converges on incest, persons do not have enough space for development. Incest violates developmental space. It collapses the plot of life. I try to bring that structure together with the overspecified ends and the middle that is lost.

CC: Are you saying that figurative or poetic language is linked in some way to "trauma," or the kind of muteness you've been interested in all along? If we think of muteness through the Boy of Winander, then language wouldn't be so much trying to get at some kind of experience which is ever-receding as at a failure of experience. Because the muteness, the muteness of the Boy, is a failure of response, you said. So is that a way of saying that figurativeness is referential because the referent itself has to do with failure? In other words, you suggest that the figuration uncannily intensifies the referent, and I am asking if that is because the referent for you has always been, insofar as you are Wordsworthian, a failure of response in some way, or linked to untimely speech?

GH: That is a far-reaching thought, and I touch on a "mimetic" strengthening of the referent in "I. A. Richards and the Dream of Communication."[10] Yet I'm not sure I want to give the referent that specific a content. Because in poetry it is not entirely empirical or historical. The fact that figuration, moreover, uncannily intensifies the (deferred) referent, indicates a desire (however frustrated) for "timely utterance"—even for prophetic or ecstatic speech. But I accept everything you say about untimeliness. Trauma is certainly linked to the untimely. In the basic theory of trauma, derived from Freud, you weren't prepared (hence also a certain anxiety). And it is doubtful that you could be prepared, for either shell shock or experience shock. Wordsworth's argument is, Nature does everything to prepare you, to make you immune, or to gentle the shock. He doesn't say there is no shock, or surprise, but that nature aims at a growth of the mind which can absorb or overcome shock.

III. Video Testimony and the Place of Modern Memory

CC: We have been talking about Wordsworth's revolution in style and its way of communicating (without succumbing to) shock. Do you think that there is another, similar revolution of style, after the momentous events in this century that we have passed through? In your recent work, you have begun to focus on the video testimony project in the Fortunoff Video Archive for Holocaust Testimonies at Yale, which you helped found, and in which individuals are filmed telling their stories, in relatively undirected fashion, to trained interviewers. In recent years, you have talked about these videos as providing a means of communicating or witnessing an event that is difficult to represent adequately by other means—

for example, in the seemingly realistic medium of mainstream movies, which, as you suggest, become less realistic, or more surrealistic, the more realistically they attempt to portray visual detail.[11] Would you say, then, that the video testimonies also represent a revolution in style for communicating this kind of event?

GH: Yes, but see for yourself! They are effective as an antidote, within technology, within the era of mechanical reproduction, to the glossy superrealism of the media. They are audiovisual and yet do not privilege the ocular or assault the eye. I have suggested that they avoid the contagion of "secondary trauma," that they allow the sensitive mind space for reflection, even if there is shock.

CC: You have talked about the effacement of an earlier type of recollection marked by memory places. I'm curious if that reflective moment in Wordsworth, which you look at in the Boy of Winander as paradigmatic, is linked in any way, through the problems of muteness and speaking that it raises, to later questions you come up against, in regard to contemporary attempts to remember.

GH: They are linked. The reflective moment must be at the center of this. By "must be," I mean for me, when I compare what interested me in Wordsworth and what I'm interested in now: the role that video testimony can play in remembrance. My focus, on the one hand, on the individual as individual and his memory processes and, on the other hand, on what can be called public memory,[12] how a public knows or could know about events, is linked to an increasingly besieged and competitive condition which many have talked about. A condition in which our mind is actually blocked, rather than encouraged, prevented from developing mentally, experientially, by our very virtuosity in reconstructing technically what occurred. Max Frisch said that technology was the knack of so arranging the world that we didn't have to experience it. You have a surplus of simulacra, technically transmitted, but subtler mediations are elided. So that one is never quite released from this surround of simulacra. The question therefore arises, What happens to reflection in this increasingly ocular situation?

There is a relation between that and my understanding of Wordsworth, or Wordsworth's self-understanding, since he talks prophetically, toward the beginning of the industrial revolution, about the increasing pressure of external stimuli, which act on the mind like a drug that causes dependence. He mentions specifically journalism, urbanization, and (still a part of journalism) "wretched and frantic novels," where the word "novel" contains the word "news." These things converge to besiege the mind and deprive it of the moment of reflection. There is no mind without a pastoral space, and this is disappearing. The pastoral and the utopian may be close, but the pastoral is not quite the utopian because, in Wordsworth at least, it is within time. It may be an imagined place, but it occurs within time. One does have space within time, for reflection; one must have. Where else is mind?

And here of course the psychological dimension comes in, and this fascinated me because it pointed also to what I had observed in the history of religion: that revelation is always linked to specific place. These places can be given a national or nationalistic interpretation. It may be that the revelation, in order to fire up the community beyond the individual who has it, needs to be substantiated by evidential detail, such as the idea of specific place. And it has to be an earth place; it doesn't work as well if it's a place in the air. To have a revelation it has to be associated with specific place, even if you don't know anymore where that place is. And of course, as in modern Israel or Islam, people still claim Moriah is here . . . no, Moriah is over there, and so on. To locate Moriah, you actually need two things, name and place. You need those specifics; you need place names, if you wish. And a certain storied detail.

Now I was made conscious of the arbitrariness of this, why this place and not another. Time is also in question, but the time is always needy—a time of urgency, a time of crisis, and hence the pressure of apocalyptic thoughts. Yet why should it be this place rather than another, since the revealing force—call it God—could manifest itself anywhere?

There is, then, a fertile tension between the potential universality of the message of revelation and the accidentality and individuality of place and person, of the bearer and the location. In Wordsworth's case, and this is part of his originality, place becomes memory-place: spots of time, spots in and creative of a temporal consciousness. That is, the reflective moment is introduced in all its dimensions. And there is recovery. For the recovery to be effective, salutary, it has to be associated with place. It cannot be simply a feeling. There are feelings without place in Wordsworth, but he is not satisfied with those; he wants to follow them to a surreptitious source. "Where shall I seek the origin?" Where the fountain from which this feeling or this specific thought came? But clearly it is impossible to envisage an origin without thinking of emplacement. So the recovery, the retrieval process, insofar as it can be called healing or therapeutic, involves the notion of place, the image of a power place.

I do not know how much of this, in Wordsworth or in my own thinking, is related to a need for thought to be situated, and safely situated. For the power place keeps working the memory, as if it were the pulse which allows that stream, the stream of consciousness, to continue, so it's not that there is only—in Wordsworth—a desire to rest. The reflective moment is not just a moment of pastoral safety and rest but *one where you can be equal to your experience.*

Implicit in much I have done is a meditation on place and its relation to memory and identity (individual rather than collective). It wasn't the study of Wordsworth that led me to study the Holocaust. There is a clear separation between these two subjects. But once I had engaged with questions the Holocaust raised for me—How do I take this into consciousness? What can I do about it? Is this in any way thinkable? Is it representable?—once I had gone along that path, my interest in Wordsworth's understanding of the memory process did come in. I sensed a loss of memory place, of the Wordsworthian memory place, after the Holocaust and after entering an era of mechanical reproduction. While the places of Jewish existence destroyed in the Holocaust are remembered, they cannot be as dynamic in the individual consciousness as the Wordsworthian memory places. Alas, they are severed or fixed or nostalgic. And in relation to the Wordsworthian perspective of a memory not hindered by shock, I think there is always a question in my mind how future generations can be brought to remember the Holocaust without secondary trauma. I don't underestimate defenses, of course, and don't claim that everybody is all that sensitive. My move is not a protectionist move. It's more a question of how trauma can work creatively rather than destructively in one's life.

CC: It's the opposite of protectionism because in your argument, a violent imposition often ends up numbing the psyche so that in fact by making it less violent, one paradoxically allows for more of a shock.

GH: It is, as you say, precisely the question of how sensitivity can be maintained, and how sensory overload, leading to numbing, leading to feelings of impotence, can be avoided. Or, as in some Holocaust studies, to feelings of mystery and enigma, which I do not value. I do not reject all feelings of mystery, but I don't want them to become protectionist, only protective. I want to see as clearly as possible and yet preserve the reflective moment sufficiently so that something creative comes about. In terms of future generations especially, the dialectic there may be very complex, because for them what must be overcome is not only numbness but also indifference.

CC: So the question of representation that we're looking at now concerns not only the nature of the different events that are represented, that is, the Holocaust, as opposed to whatever it was that was traumatic before (or after), but specifically the possibility for modes of representation to prevent, rather than create, indifference.

GH: Yes, I agree with that wholeheartedly. There really is something at once terrible and hypnotic in contemporary representations of violence, in their direct-ness and detail.

CC: Curiously, then, the less direct mode of the video testimony would seem, in your view, to permit more of a sense of events to enter, without the hypnotic or numbing quality of direct visual representation. I am wondering if this would help us understand what you meant when you said, in one essay, that your con-cern with video testimony has to do with the ethical aspect of representation.[13] What would be ethical in this mode of representation would be, paradoxically, how it gives less directly to sight, or raises questions about what it means to see, and what the relation is between seeing and knowing.

GH: That is correct. If it is sufficient to describe the ethical as something that leads to questions, rather than to decisive action. Moreover, the "hypnosis" in literature and art *tests* us ethically. I would have to add that, being an intellectual, it's hard for me to conceive of the ethical as possible without reflection.

CC: I'm not sure that bringing questioning into it, or reflection, actually opposes itself to action.

GH: In Wordsworth this is quite clear in the Boy of Winander episode. He saw the activity within contemplation. He breaks down the dichotomy between ac-tion and reflection, action and contemplation. Not succumbing to the hypnosis replays this issue of reflective answering, of pushing back against what comes from outside. I come back to the Wordsworthian insistence on a creative re-sponse to what is given. Again, to qualify, the Holocaust is not only the type or general instance of a violent historical event, but there are very specific features of it which make video testimony an important agent, an instrument, I would have to say, of memory.

CC: In this light, what are the continuities and differences between the romantic texts that you've worked on and the speech-texts of video testimony?

GH: What one finds occasionally in Wordsworth is something like natural meta-phor. I think of a fragment from the time of writing his first great poem, *The Ruined Cottage*. Margaret is abandoned, her husband having sold himself into the army because he couldn't bear seeing his children and wife starve. In the fragment Margaret says about the baker's wagon, which used to stop but now goes by because the baker knows there's no business there, "[T]hat wagon does not care for us." She doesn't want to say, "The baker doesn't care"; she therefore says the wagon doesn't. That's what Anna Deavere Smith calls "naturally figu-rative speech." A vernacular vigor in the speech of ordinary people.[14] And this you also have in the speech of the [Holocaust] witnesses, many of whom, in the

United States, are not especially literate. Because coming to America, the survivors became displaced persons, separated from their culture, whose education was interrupted and who after the war did not always have the means to take up their education again. They had to live in a strange land; they had to learn a new language. So in America many of the survivors are not people who could write it down. But their speech nevertheless has a certain eloquence. It has the pathos and vigor of the ordinary people Wordsworth tries to evoke in *Lyrical Ballads*.

CC: You have also talked about the "mute eloquence" of the survivors' gestures. The muteness in the gestures suggests that there is a resistance to the telling of these stories beyond the question of skill in writing or speaking, a difficulty linked to the problem of memory and memory places that you mentioned above. I wonder if some of your thinking about the video archive in terms of what it makes possible in the relation between sight and the sound of the words—or the natural eloquence of the speech and the mute eloquence of the gestures—suggests a way of creating a place of memory.[15]

GH: I'd have to repeat first of all that something has happened to memory places, because it's difficult to think of the camps as being such memory places, although obviously they are fixed in the imagination of the survivors. The older *lieux de mémoire*, the memory places the survivor has left behind, were the traditional ones of home or native region. Yet we find it very difficult to get specific information when we try to question survivors about the time before the camps. It is so far in the past, and it may be too painful to recall. But the camps, they are not like a Wordsworthian memory place, although there is something sinister or dark about Wordsworth's spot of time.

I like your formulation that the Archive itself creates a place of memory. But let me talk of what is in the Archive: the stories. And let me also separate these stories from memory place for the moment, although I think the traditional story is often focused by a memory place. I have to say two things. We call the survivor testimonies "stories," but I'm uneasy with that word. I say "story" because it's the most common word. I don't want to say "tale," which is too close to fiction, and "narrative" I find cold. The testimony is not a story with narrative desire. On the few occasions when I have found a story told with suspense or picaresque gusto, for instance, the Schlomo Perl story filmed as *Europa, Europa*, I begin to doubt. It is, in any case, very untypical. The testimonies are not stories about overcoming obstacles by cunning or other qualities so that you could survive. Accident played a much greater role in survival, as did physical strength or having a trade needed in the camps, than powers of intellect, discernment, intuition, and so on.

Secondly, you don't have suspense, and for a very simple reason. The *univers concentrationnaire* in which the inmates lived blinded them to the future. There was no future. "Tomorrow" became, for most, a horizon beyond which mind could not stretch. Everything had to be concentrated on the sheer attempt, this moment, and the next, and the next, to keep alive. So that an element which is essential to storytelling—foreshadowing, keeping things in suspense until you know how to resolve them—that dimension, in the consciousness of the survivor, was rarely there. Yet allowing the survivor *now* to tell something like a story, even though it doesn't have strong properties of suspense or narrative desire, restores what had been taken away. It restores a power of communicating with the future or toward the future, a future most clearly indicated by interviewers themselves and this mode of communication (the video testimony) which can speak to the generation after, including their own sons and daughters. It is retrieval in that sense; it is recuperated in that sense. In other words, the capacity of telling a story, even though it doesn't have the characteristic of a fictional story, restores to the survivor who tells it this capacity to imagine a future, a transgenerational effect coming from his own act of telling.

CC: But how then is what isn't narratively experienced communicated? And does this have something specific to do with the visual mode of the video?

GH: What you call the mute element is to some extent in the broken language, in its poetry. But always in what might be called the reembodiment of the survivors. I mean by that their gestures, the ensemble of their gestures. Allowing them to be represented by the medium is a very important effect of the medium. It makes more sense against the background of deprivation. Because another thing survivors were deprived of, deliberately of course, was their body. Its ordinary, human fullness. That is not speech. Given the historical background of the deprivation, this is an important dimension, quite apart from the semiotics of gestures, which fall into the area of speech.

CC: What about the way in which the survivor faces the camera and seems in that sense to create a kind of address? You have spoken about video testimony as activating a willingness to listen, of a person being made into an addressee of a conversation. You say in speaking about the video testimonies:

> While survivor testimony elicits its own kind of dialogue, it is only partly a
> dialogue with us. Survivors face not only a living audience, or now accept
> that audience rather than insisting on the intransitive character of their
> experience. They also face family members and friends who perished. It is the

witnesses who undertake that descent to the dead. They address the living frontally. Often using warnings and admonishments they also speak for the dead, or in their name. This has its dangers. To go down may be easy, but to come up again, that is the hard task. "I am not among the living, but no one notices it," Charlotte Delbo wrote. So they remember the dead, that they too were in the house of the dead, yet they are not back here, but truly instructing us. ("Learning from Survivors")

This takes us back to the question of response, lack of response, and address. One of the things that you're bringing forward from your earlier work, and for me specifically from the Boy of Winander episode, is the relation between a moment of reflection and an address, an address that is not simply aimed at the living. Here, in the testimonies, you also have an address that is directed not only to the living but to the dead. That is something that you remarked on in talking about the Wordsworth poem: you said the apostrophe as a figure of speech comes from an apostrophe to the dead.

GH: Yes, to define that mode of address is essential. We're talking about a structure. In the classical apostrophe, you turn to the dead in order to summon their help. You swear by them. But it is not that you're asking for their help, necessarily; it is that you have to represent them. At least that's true of the camp survivor. I would put it this way, perhaps: you, the survivor, are alive, they are dead, but you have to speak in some way with the voice of the dead. Obversely, while in the camp, you were in a universe of death, but still there was something alive in you. In both cases there is a chiasmic relation between the survivor and his past self as camp inmate. The survivor, part of him is still with the dead, whether he uses the figure of address or not. For the camp inmate—and that's part of the obligation of the witness, to face it—even though he was dead, or as if dead, there were still moments of extraordinary life.

IV. Interrupted Pastoral

CC: I want to close with a question about your own life. In describing your passage out of Europe, when you were a boy, you talk about the love that you had for the English countryside, how distant you felt from everything, and the love of nature you had then: "I felt at home in the gentle countryside of Buckinghamshire."[16] You didn't experience your experience as a constant shock at that time. And I was struck by something that you say at the end of your introduction to *Ho-*

locaust Remembrance, about your more present situation as an academic, where you are on the way to a lecture during the fall:

> It is mid-October. In New England the leaves have turned. One or two begin to float in the crisp air. Further north many maples have already shed half their gold, a hectic treasure for the children. I see them in the large front-yard of an old house, running and shouting, five of them, all sizes. A woman is raking the leaves, or trying to. The children, romping around, undo her work; she cuffs them with the rake, as tolerantly as a kitten a perplexing ball or comatose object. The pile of raked leaves grows, and the children invent a new game. They collapse into the pile, spreading out deliciously, while the woman—mother, housekeeper—abets their game, and covers them with the still fragrant, light leaves. At first giggles and squeaks, then, as the tumulus rises to a respectable height, total silence. But only for a minute. For, as if on signal, all emerge simultaneously from the leafy tomb, jumping out, laughing, resurrected to the mock surprise of the one who is raking and who patiently begins again.
>
> I am on my way to give a lecture on the Holocaust, when I come across the pastoral scene. What am I doing, I ask myself. How can I talk about such matters, here? I cannot reconcile scenes like this with others I know about.
>
> In a fleeting montage I see or dream I see the green, cursed fields at Auschwitz. A cold calm has settled on them. The blood does not cry from the ground. Yet no place, no wood, meadow, sylvan scene will now be the same.[17]

For me this scene resonated, the moment I read it, with the Boy of Winander, the silence of the children linking up somehow with your own going off to a Holocaust lecture. The pastoral scene has a pause in it here, too. There's something about the movement from that earlier pastoral scene of you in England to this moment of you as a lecturer on the Holocaust, coming across a pastoral scene that strikes me, since it is mediated via a scene from Wordsworth, which has been a focus of your own reading. I'm wondering if there's any comment you'd like to make on this peculiar itinerary for you in your career and in your life. Have you reflected on it at all?

GH: You're right in crossing from that autobiographical sketch to my interest in the interrupted pastoral. I suppose it shows how drawn I am to resilience. Think of the children. And also to the resilience of the pastoral moment itself. And the idea, which is literal, or close to literal in Wordsworth, of rural nature as a shield, as giving some relief, a new chance, or a renewed chance of recovery. But the Holocaust was so traumatic, so interruptive an event, that, as you know well because you've written about such experiences, it exists unintegrated alongside normal memories. So that not only is the pastoral interrupted but you have a juxtaposition that probably can't be resolved. I'm reminded of Charlotte Delbo, who says (I paraphrase), "It's not right to ask how do I live *with* Auschwitz: I live *alongside* of Auschwitz." There it is still, a complete memory. It's not that I have a problem because I want to integrate that memory. There is no chance of that: my Auschwitz place is here, and my ordinary place, or post-Auschwitz self, is here. And the survivor has to live on like that.

CC: Do you think that "alongside," or a reading of that alongside, could have been found already in Wordsworth, or is it precisely something alongside the Wordsworth for you? In other words, do you think your Wordsworth reading has prepared you for thinking about that, or is it rather that now you have to put something alongside your other reading?

GH: That would return us to a discussion of how trauma shows itself in Wordsworth or literature generally—and whether trauma can ever be "integrated." As to my personal case, please remember that since I did not myself pass through the full extent of collective trauma (I was not deported and in a camp), the sense, or recovery of the sense, of trauma comes late. I suspect that my English countryside experience and Wordsworth's poetry converged, or helped me to think about, to articulate, whatever personal trauma there was. And that the much more severe issue of collective trauma, which after all was not my case, did not become an issue till much later still.

CC: When you were commenting on Wordsworth, and specifically on the pause, you said that there could have been something traumatic earlier, and in your pastoral there was something earlier (your leaving Germany alone without your parents), and maybe partly that is what is emerging now. The pastoral scene wasn't your first experience; it came later.

GH: It is hard to say what came first, what came later. And knowledge always seems to be acquired knowledge. But to whatever my consciousness of the Holocaust speaks, its shock has grown on me. Yes, that happens too. It's not just that you start with shock and then try to move away from the shock, or to absorb or integrate it. There are times when the shock grows on you and becomes more severe.

NOTES

1. Geoffrey Hartman, "On Traumatic Knowledge and Literary Studies," *New Literary History* 26.3 (Summer 1995): 537–73, 552.

2. See Geoffrey Hartman, "Reading and Representation: Wordsworth's 'Boy of Winander,'" *European Romantic Review* 5.1 (1994) and "Reading: The Wordsworthian Enlightenment," in *The Wordsworthian Enlightenment: Romantic Poetry and the Ecology of Reading*, ed. Helen Regueiro Elam and Frances Ferguson (Baltimore: Johns Hopkins UP, 2005), 40.

3. Ibid., 39.

4. Ibid., 323n25. Hartman cites J. Douglas Kneale's *Romantic Aversions: Aftermaths of Classicism in Wordsworth and Coleridge* (Toronto: McGill-Queens UP, 1999), writing that Kneale shows how "the poet converts the conventional *exclamatio* into an *aversio*." The "turn-tale" is a term used for apostrophe; George Puttenham describes it in *The Arte of Poesie* (1589).

5. Geoffrey Hartman, "Christopher Smart's Magnificat: Toward a Theory of Representation," in *The Fate of Reading and Other Essays* (Chicago: U of Chicago P, 1975).

6. See also Geoffrey Hartman, "The Interpreter's Freud," in *Easy Pieces* (New York: Columbia UP, 1985). For an excellent elaboration of the idea of euphemism in another Wordsworthian context, see Kevis Goodman, "Making Time for History: Wordsworth, the New Historicism, and the Apocalyptic Fallacy," in Elam and Ferguson, *The Wordsworthian Enlightenment*.

7. See Cathy Caruth, "Unclaimed Experience: Trauma and the Possibility of History" (1991), reprinted in *Unclaimed Experience: Trauma, Narrative, and History* (Baltimore: Johns Hopkins UP, 1996).

8. Hartman, "Literary Studies and Traumatic Knowledge."

9. Geoffrey Hartman, "The Voice of the Shuttle: Language from the Point of View of Literature," in *Beyond Formalism: Literary Essays, 1958–1970* (New Haven, CT: Yale UP, 1970).

10. Included in Hartman, *The Fate of Reading*.

11. See Geoffrey Hartman, "Reading the Wound: Testimony, Art and Trauma," in *The Longest Shadow: In the Aftermath of the Holocaust* (Bloomington: Indiana UP, 1996).

12. See "Public Memory and Its Discontents" in Hartman, *The Longest Shadow*.

13. Ibid.

14. See Anna Deavere Smith, *Twilight—Los Angeles, 1992, On the Road: A Search for American Character* (New York: Anchor, 1994).

15. See "Learning from Survivors: The Yale Testimony Project," *Holocaust and Genocide Studies* 9.2 (Fall 1995), reprinted in Hartman, *The Longest Shadow*.

16. Geoffrey Hartman, "The Longest Shadow," in *Testimony: Contemporary Writers Make the Holocaust Personal*, ed. David Rosenberg (New York: Random House, 1989).

17. Geoffrey Hartman, "Introduction: Darkness Visible," in *Holocaust Remembrance: The Shapes of Memory*, ed. Geoffrey Hartman (Cambridge, MA: Blackwell, 1994), 21–22.

Members of the Nia Project Team at Grady Hospital, Atlanta, May 14, 2013. *Front row (left to right)*: Nadine Kaslow, Kafi Bethea; *second row*: Sara Klco, Hyaiyu Zhang, Nicole Fischer, Rachel Bryant, Dierdre Rudat, Susan Browne, Sarah Dunn; *third row*: Marissa Petersen-Coleman, Claire Lisco, Natasha Mehta, LaTasha Porter, Naomi Gebrelul, Debbie Browen, Sanjay Shah; *fourth row*: Asher Siegleman, Christina Wilson.

Chapter Ten

A Revolutionary Act—The Video Testimonies of the Nia Project

An Interview with Members of the Grady Nia Team

The Nia Project is an innovative intervention project at Grady Health System in Atlanta, Georgia, run by Dr. Nadine Kaslow, chief psychologist at Grady and a professor in psychiatry at Emory University. Dr. Kaslow works with a team of clinicians and researchers who lead intervention groups, and an associated research study, with at-risk women in Atlanta. Some years ago, Dr. Kaslow asked me to join her and the team in undertaking a video testimony project with the women of the suicide intervention group. I met with members of the current Nia team on October 2, 2012, at Grady Hospital to discuss with them the impact of the video testimony project, and of Nia as a whole, for working with and studying trauma, and in particular for adding qualitative measures to the quantitative measures previously used for research related to the groups. I provided additional questions for a follow-up meeting on October 9, at which the questions were read by Dr. Kaslow and Larisa Niles-Carnes. (Descriptions of the individual participants in the discussions may be found at the end of the interview.)

I. Trauma in Quantitative Research and in Clinical Care

CC: I am interested in discussing with all of you today the innovative manner in which the Nia project has combined a research study with a practical intervention for women at risk, and why you felt it important to include video testimonies (which are strictly speaking neither quantitative nor clinical) as a response to the women's experience of trauma. Nadine, since you instituted the Nia Project, could you explain what it is and how its research and clinical dimensions are related?

Nadine Kaslow: *Nia* is a Kwanzaa term that means "purpose." This project has been going on close to twenty years here at Grady Hospital, which serves an inner-city, historically underserved, and underprivileged population, most of whom are people of color. It has been funded by both the Centers for Disease Control and the National Institute of Mental Health, as well as a grant from the Laney Graduate School at Emory, which supports the video testimony project.

Nia first started out as a study in which we were interested in the links between intimate partner violence (or domestic violence) and suicidal behavior in African American women. In the first study we found that, indeed, women who had been abused were more likely to attempt suicide. And so the second project focused on the factors that accounted for that. What were the risk factors and what were the protective factors that might have prevented women from attempting suicide? What we found for risk factors were things like feeling hopeless, not feeling very efficacious, engaging in substance abuse, and displaying psychological symptoms. One of the biggest protective factors was social support. And it was that research finding that led me to feel like I didn't want to just do research but that we knew a little something that could maybe help people.

And it was at that point that we started the support groups. They were built on the finding that social support made a difference. And that's why Nia started as a group therapy program, because I felt the women could get the most social support from being in a group. We started small, with one group, and that one group had somewhere between zero and one members each week, and then that group got to two members. And now we have a suicide support group every week, a domestic violence group, the Nia intervention group, a group for women who have been traumatized and who abuse substances, a dialectical behavior therapy group—two of them now—[and] a spirituality support group; we're starting an ACT [acceptance and commitment therapy] group, and we're starting a parenting group. So Nia has just grown and grown and grown.

I really struggled, as I was in graduate school, with feeling like I was either a researcher or a clinician. And that those were different hats and that those were almost different parts of my personality. And one of the things that Nia has allowed me to do, and I hope my students to do, is to integrate their researcher hats and their clinician hats so that we can do meaningful research while simultaneously providing effective care.

CC: So the research and the clinical dimensions of the Nia project, as I understand it, are divided between, on the one hand, the quantitative evidence gathered by a series of tests given to the women at regular intervals and, on the other hand, the group meetings with the women, which involve, among other things, their sharing of their experiences with others. Could someone explain, first of all, what kind of quantitative testing you do and how trauma, or PTSD, is defined in the quantitative field?

Dorian Lamis: We employ empirically validated measures that are widely used, which assess several risk factors like childhood abuse and depression, hopelessness, and substance abuse, as well as protective factors like social support.

NK: The measures were chosen in accordance with the theory of triadic influence, which considers three streams: the inter/trapersonal, the social situational, and the cultural environmental. Within each stream we look at the risk and protective factors and come up with scores and diagnoses. So, for example, somebody may be high on depressive symptoms or someone meets criterion for having a history of childhood maltreatment; someone does or doesn't have PTSD based on these factors; there is a continuum in determining that diagnosis. We also measure the women's improvement from their participation in the groups.

CC: So trauma is diagnosed on the basis of the scoring of self-reported answers to the questions on the tests. Are these measures used at all in the group intervention process, and how does trauma emerge there?

Kafi Bethea: These measures don't matter in the room. They only matter for how we see that they have gotten better or have fewer symptoms. But what a woman's score is doesn't impact how were we are going to treat her.

In the intervention group, we have a topic for the day, such as the cycle of violence. But what is also very important is that people feel free to talk about what has been happening to them. This has allowed them to feel like they're not completely alone, and they can begin to formulate their experiences, which is one way in which we learn about their trauma and also a way in which they help each other to deal with it.

CC: It sounds like one way that trauma emerges in the group is in relation to storytelling: how more or less capable or enabled women feel to speak to others about their experiences. So the storytelling has a clinical function, both revealing the disengagement produced by trauma and helping to overcome its isolating effects. The group involves an educational dimension as well as this testimonial-clinical dimension.

Shane Davis: Yes. Once the women understand that there are others in their situation, and people who are willing to listen to them, they are eager to talk—with a few exceptions. The process of telling stories is important to them, though it is not always easy. Over time, as people come to feel more connected with the group, they share bits and pieces of their stories.

Jalika Street: I was really struck by the difference between seeing a person the first time she got to group and then seeing her in the eighth session—the empowerment that took place based just on having a voice, or feeling understood. Not feeling empowered to speak and learning to speak out are definitely ways of understanding how trauma emerges in the group and how the group may have positive clinical consequences.

II. Video Testimony and the Struggle to Create a Story

CC: It seems to me that the complexity and importance of this relation between trauma and speech may be something that the video testimonies come to show in a particularly striking way. It is interesting, Nadine, that you decided to add the video testimony dimension to the project, which emphasizes the women's process of coming to tell stories, but not precisely in the meetings' educational/clinical context. What was it, Nadine, that led you to think about having the women speak, separately, before the video camera? Could it be said that these testimonies supplement both the clinical side of the project and the research side, through their testimonial function? What did you feel could be added to both the clinical and research work by undertaking these testimonies?

NK: As you recall, Cathy, you originally came to Nia, at my invitation, to present to the Nia team on your perspective on trauma. We had both been at Yale before and were familiar with the Fortunoff Video Archive for Holocaust Testimony at Yale and the opportunity those video testimonies offered for Holocaust survivors to tell their stories. And two of the Holocaust survivors who told their stories in that project ended up being patients of mine because their daughter developed a serious mental illness. So I was aware of the impact, the value of that storytelling for these people.

It seemed to me that there was tremendous power, healing power, in the storytelling. And that in mental health and psychology and psychiatry, when we do research, we spend a lot of time with the quantitative focus, but clinically so much of what we're interested in is people's stories. I really became interested in what it would mean to listen to people's stories and think about them using a more qualitative approach. And it needed a kind of collaboration. I remember listening to Holocaust testimony tapes early on with you, and you would hear or

Nadine Kaslow at Grady
Hospital, May 14, 2013.

see something, and I would hear and see something very different. And I realized
that the lens one brings really influences what one hears, what one sees, what
one notices. And the interdisciplinary nature of this fascinated me.

I thought that it was really important to hear these women's stories in particular.
CC: So it sounds like it was particularly significant to hear the women speak for
themselves, rather than through the medium of the standard research questionnaire. Shane, you too have emphasized the importance, in these interviews—as
opposed to the quantitative tests—of allowing the women to speak in their own
terms. While this may be part of a healing process, as in the group story-sharing,
the speaking in the video testimonies also seems to supplement the research side
of the project by providing a new form of "evidence" that the quantitative tests
don't provide, which has to do with the relation the women have to their own
stories. Could you say more about how the interviews were structured in order
to allow this to happen?
SD: When we decided to do the video project, one of the things that we wanted
to do was to make sure that the women really had ample time and opportunity to
talk about whatever they wanted to talk about without much interference from

us, although we also had the goal of having them speak about their experiences with suicidality and intimate partner violence. We wanted to give them a form, and an opportunity, to speak freely about whatever came to mind. So we decided to have two interviews. The first would involve a script in which Kafi [Bethea] and I would introduce them to the video project and have them talk about whatever came to mind. When you see these first interviews you hear very little from me or Kafi. And a lot of times there were these pregnant pauses or these long pauses or silences throughout the video, which sometimes felt like an eternity to me, but at that time all we did was kind of nod and encourage them to continue and to talk about whatever it was they wanted to talk about, for up to an hour. The second interview would happen about a week later, and we had a list of about twenty-five questions concerning things they did not address in the first session, to fill in the gaps.

So I felt that it was different interviewing in this format from interviewing in a therapeutic format because in the latter you're trying to get at the processes that underlie the traumatic experience, getting more into depth about things, and here it really was an opportunity for the women to speak about whatever it was they wanted to. I think for many of them it was the first time they spoke about experiences that we would not have heard about otherwise. As an interviewer I just wanted to give them that space to do that. I didn't want to interject much, even though there might have been times where that would have been a fascinating point to continue on with or to lead them down. It's their opportunity to craft their own stories, to tell their own stories in the manner in which they see fit for themselves.

CC: When you suggest that they have the opportunity to craft their own stories, you begin to point to something that interested me, as well, in the interviews. Which is how the women don't always appear to have ready-made stories to tell, and the videos sometimes appear to show us the struggle to produce stories that don't yet exist. I'm interested in how the videos bring out this aspect of trauma, which does not emerge in the quantitative tests and does not seem to be the focus in the clinical setting. One video that is striking in this regard is the testimony of Mary, who begins her testimony in the following manner:

Kafi Bethea: So today we're going to be talking about your personal story. In most of your prior interactions with the Nia Program, that we had a little while ago, we focused on very specific experiences and had specific information we wanted you to provide us, and there was a limited amount of time to focus on your specific experiences. This interview is different in that I'll be doing a lot of listening and very little talking. I'm going to ask you some very general questions, and then you'll just speak about whatever comes to your mind. Do you have any questions before we begin?

Mary: No.

KB: All right, let's begin. The first question is, tell me about yourself and your life.

Mary: [Sighs] Well, I don't even know where to start. When I was little, I remember my father beating my mother regularly through the house. I've been molested, and at about six years old my father killed the man in front of me. Basically I have been raped a lot, molested, and abused a lot since childhood, so there's really not much more I can tell about it. [Pause] And I made it here. Let me tell you, when I came to Nia that was my first time in a domestic violence group where I could talk about the way I feel because I didn't know there was a place I could go, and it really helped me a great deal to be able to open up and share what happened to me with some of the people that had experienced some of the same things I had, and it made me feel a little better.

KB: Anything else?

Mary: Can you repeat the question again? I want to make sure I gave you all of it.

KB: Tell me about yourself and your life, and you may want to start by telling me who you are.

Mary: Oh, my name is Mary. I have three kids and a daughter that's being abused right now. Oh man, there's so much going on I don't know how to start it, but I'll tell you a little bit about me. Once again, I was molested, abused, and watched my father abuse my mother when I was growing up. God, so much it just hurts to even think about my life. I'm 46 years old. [Pause] I just hate to talk about the past. There ain't much I can tell you about me, no more than I was an abused woman most of my life from my childhood up until now.

KB: I'm interested in hearing more about your life experiences during childhood. It can be all experiences, not just negative. Can you talk some about your life growing up?

Mary: No more than, um . . . [Pause] Those were some bad memories. When I was a little girl, Kafi, growing up as a little girl in my house with my mother and father and watching him beat her and drag her around the house, it was nothing nice. I wasn't so much afraid, it's just the next day I would see her with black eyes and bruises and it used to kinda affect me a little bit. But I loved my father so much and I was his favorite out of all the kids. He used to take me everywhere he'd go, do everything he'd do, he'd take me with him, and the rest of his kids would stay at home.

But as time passed on he started drinking or whatever, and started hanging with his friends, he spent less time with me, and it comes where we'd be in the house sleeping and the house was on fire, nobody's there but us, me and my sisters and brothers, and somebody's always saving us, pulling us out, and then when they came to help us with the ambulance or whatever, mom come home, dad gets there and he just takes us out on Amnesty and take us and let us go to the hospital and all of this stuff right here. The last time that the house caught on fire, my father's house was just like a shotgun house, next door in the house was my dad and his friend and they girls, the women, while my mom was at work, and they was partying, and one of the women put something on in the kitchen and it caught on fire. She had forgot she had it on, and the fire came over into the back, into our kitchen, then into the bedroom where me and my sisters and brothers were, and the house was so black, and my daddy's friend El saved us, and all the time they partying but they don't know the house is on fire and we're about to get burned. So that was a bad experience.

And the next thing I remember is we were sitting on the porch while my father and his friends were gambling. It was snowing outside and me and my sisters and brothers are sitting on the front porch, crowded up together trying to stay warm because my mom was at work and my dad and his friends were sitting playing cards and gambling. So, um, my mom finally came home, he got rid of everybody before she got there and got us in the house. And then she found out how [something] seeing as how cold we was, so they got in an argument, and he beat her through the house again.

And then one day he was fixing this man's car. We called him the Candyman, he kept candy in the back of his trunk, a whole bunch of candy, so we called him the Candyman. And my daddy was fixing his car, changing the oil, and he asked me to hand him the half-inch wrench and I did, and he was so proud of me because I knew all the wrenches and I was about six years old.

And I was very hungry and I asked my father to fix me something to eat, and he said you're a big girl, you can fix your own plate. I don't like to talk about this, but, uh, I will. And so he said, go in the kitchen, push this chair up to the sink, and get your plate and fix your plate from the stove. And I said okay. And he said, you're a big girl, you can do it. I went in the kitchen and got me a plate out of the dish rack. I seen the Candyman come in the house and go toward the bathroom. And I was standing there taking the lid off the pot and, um [sighs, looks down], I just started trying to work through this about last year. It came out cuz I had kept it in all these years, so bear with me with this.

I was trying to fix my plate and I got the lid off the pot, and then I see him come out toward the bathroom, from the bathroom coming in the kitchen, and he had his pants down and his thing was sticking out, and at that time I was six years old so I didn't know what a penis was and I seen it. And he kept saying come here and let me hold you, and I said no, no, I can fix my own plate, my daddy said I'm a big girl. [Pause] And he grabbed me, and he kept saying let me hold you, let me hold you, and I said no, no, no. And [pause, crying] and I said no, you can't hold me, I'm a big girl, and he said I'll fix it for you, and I said my daddy said I can fix my own plate, and he grabbed me and he tried to pull my dress off, and my dad came in the door and he seen him messing with me, and I seen him pull a shotgun and he hollered what the hell you think you're doing?

And the next thing I know I dropped to the chair and he shot him, and he just came right and hit the back door, and when the back door hit the porch blood was just everywhere, and he never took me to get me no help, and all that time I needed help so I could talk about it. I hid it all these years. I just held it in, never talked about it. And, um [pause, crying], it had took my father to pass away and I grieved for about five to ten years. And I just started talking about it last year, and I still didn't get no help with it. I kept going to get counseling, but they didn't give me no counseling; they said I need to let it go. But how can you let something go when you don't know how to work through it? Jesus.

Okay, um, that's all of that. My dad left, they got him and took him to the mortuary where they take a dead person, and life went back to normal like nothing else happened. They don't talk about it, didn't say nothing to me about it. It was like nothing happened. But I know what happened, and right today my mom won't even admit, won't say anything about it; she won't admit it even happened. God. (Interview 22a)

It seems to me that Mary is struggling to begin her story here. What factors do you see emerging in this video that help us understand this struggle, and that we might not observe in purely quantitative analysis?

Sara Klco: I was really struck with the way that the trauma had impacted this woman's identity. You wouldn't see that on a questionnaire measure. For example, when she was asked, "just tell me a little bit about yourself and who you are," she didn't even say her name, she just said, "I had all these terrible experiences, I was molested, I watched my father beat my mother," and that just impacted me and made me really sad that she had identified so strongly with the trauma in those negative memories.

CC: So you heard partly what she *didn't* say, which is, "This is my name, I have this many children," etcetera.

SD: In structuring these interviews, we really wanted the first of the two interviews to be as organic as possible. Although the women knew that we wanted them to talk about their experiences, we wanted to provide very little coaxing or structure from us in terms of what they were to talk about. So if you noticed at the very beginning of this interview, Kafi opened with a question, she didn't say much, and there was a kind of pause. And Kafi probably did the same thing I did when I was interviewing for the testimonies, which was to sit there and not ask much else. Just to see what the women would come up with on their own.

I saw this woman on the video we just watched organizing her thoughts, trying to figure out where to start and then saying things that would anchor her, such as, "I'm 46 years old." Then she would anchor herself at some other point, "I have three kids, and I'm married." Then at one point she did say, "My name is Mary." And so it seems like in some way she was trying to figure out how to structure her experience, her memories. Which we don't really have an opportunity to do in the groups, to provide the space to share a story that was so powerful and so meaningful to a woman, and to do so without giving her instructions. It gave her the space to feel trusting and open enough to talk about experiences she never spoke about before.

CC: So what you're saying is that you saw the women figuring out how to structure their memories, that is, learning, precisely, *how* to have a memory of their lives and where to put what?

SD: If you think about how you construct your own memories about your life, there are certain things that you do to anchor yourself and decide where that story begins and what story to tell. There were some women—I think Kafi had more of these women than I did—for whom their story was not as gelled or cohesive as others; it was disjointed, maybe also because of some concurrent psychiatric issues that might be present and that impeded their ability to tell their stories. In this interview, that disjointedness is one of the things that I noticed, and I remember some of the other interviews as well, in which at that first moment we're not saying much at all and just sitting back and allowing the silence to be. Hopefully, many women will just begin, at some point, telling their stories.

CC: So you learn partly just from where they begin?

SD: Yes, and I think that was something we really wanted to do at least in that first session: to see where it takes them. Let's see what they talk about and what sort of things bubble up for them, as opposed to having it externally driven by some interviewer asking for specifics.

Marissa Petersen-Coleman: One thing that I kept thinking about when I was watching this video was that it was such a great illustration of how important early childhood experiences are. And that even when working with adults, there's early childhood trauma, and you can't ignore it. Because it always comes back. It was like a traumatized child was still in the room with that adult.

CC: It is striking, indeed, because she says later in the interview that by the time she left high school she'd "only" been raped twice, and then there were ten more times. But this one is the one where she cries.

MPC: She kept saying, "I didn't get help; nobody got me help; things kept going on like nothing had happened." And it was almost as if she was wondering out loud, "What would my life had been like if I had gotten help at that point?" And then even as she's telling it—looking at her body language—her eyes started to flutter, and she was kind of looking back, and to me it felt as if she was literally looking back at that time in her life.

CC: So one reason she is struggling to tell the story is that her story hasn't really progressed past that event—or series of events. Or that she keeps returning to and reenacting the past when she speaks, rather than telling the story in retrospect. Her speech, which you see specifically on the video, unlike in a questionnaire or even a written narrative, isn't so much storytelling as reenacting.

Rachel Jeanne Ammirati: What struck me was also the complexity of the situation she describes. I found myself thinking a lot about her father's decision in that moment. She says that she goes into the kitchen, she's a big girl, she's feeling good, she's going to fix herself some food, this guy comes in and tries to molest her. And then her father comes in. He protects her and he saves her, which is a positive thing, but he shoots the guy right in front of her. And so it's this incredibly complicated experience, where her father is protecting her, but she's witness to this terrible violence: she's seen this man bleeding to death. And I thought, how does anyone make sense of that, let alone a six-year-old? It's the good and bad all tangled into one.

CC: Yes: there's a moment where she's very proud, giving the half-inch wrench to her father, and she said she was only six, "and I knew what the wrench was." There's a sudden shift from being the father's favorite to that moment where she's nearly being raped. They seem so close together, like the best memory and the worst memory, right next to each other. And then there is the fact that there are several bad memories juxtaposed: the man attempting to rape her and the father killing the man.

It seems, then, if one were to use the language of trauma, that another reason it is difficult for her to tell the story is that it is difficult to locate the trauma in the scene. Is it the rape? Is it the father killing someone who's more or less on her? Or is it that, as she says, no one talked about it afterward?

SK: Is it all of the above?

III. Being Silenced

CC: Would you say, then, that part of the problem of storytelling, here, is trying to figure out where the event is, or how to locate the trauma?

NK: Last week we watched a different video, and the woman was much more fluent, at the beginning, in telling her story. Shane asked her the open-ended question, and she was off and running. In this video, on the other hand, the woman really struggled at the beginning to give much of an answer at all. And she would give a few sentences and then stop. And Kafi would prod her again, and she would give a few more sentences and stop. And so I was really struck by the difference in the two interviews. It is painful to me to listen to this woman's story. And I've heard countless stories; I've watched the videos; I read the transcripts this week again, but even with all of that, it's still painful because it horrifies me that people have such experiences. It horrifies me, it upsets me, it angers me, it scares me, that people live with such horrific trauma. And that they are so silenced, so absolutely silenced. So absolutely silenced in their traumas. And so you were asking, where's the trauma? There are multiple traumas. But one of the worst traumas is being silenced.

CC: Yes, she talks about it in terms of her mother, and that no one treated her, which also means no one listened to her. And then she says, at the end of the clip we watched, that no one ever talked about it: "It was like it didn't happen." So she is also speaking out, in the video testimony, so that people will hear, people in general. My sense is that the silencing isn't simply the mother or father not responding or listening to the little girl but a whole non-recognition, in a larger cultural or societal context, of what's going on. Is that also what you mean by being silenced?

NK: Yes, I think there is family silence, I think there is cultural silence, and I think our professions often don't share these stories. And I think it's hard no matter how well trained we are as therapists, it's hard to listen to these stories. And I think inadvertently in conducting therapy we won't move to certain kinds of intervention protocols. We spend less time really hearing people's stories, we control more the way they tell their stories, and I sometimes worry that we contribute to that silencing.

CC: In your profession.

NK: In our profession. And when people come to us to tell their stories, it's painful for us. And we have countertransference reactions to that. And it's hard for us to listen to that pain.

SD: There are a couple of videos in which, at the end of the tape, you could tell it was a cathartic moment for the women. Where it was like, "Wow, I feel better." I think I even had one woman who actually said that it feels better to say this, to be able to have the opportunity, in a closed environment, to tell the story uninterrupted. That it is not in a clinical setting—where we're using our manualized treatments or we're focused on a particular goal or we have insurance to bill and similar structures that surround clinical work. There was, rather, an opportunity, in one hour, to allow this to happen. And there were a few women for whom their tears weren't just a reliving of the trauma but also tears of relief and of just being able to share their stories with the camera and with us in the room.

CC: Both of you are saying, then, that what the testimonies give us, on the one hand, is being able to hear the silencing, to recognize or to have contact with not just the women's having been silenced but also our own desire to turn away, even while we're watching them. On the other hand, we also witness the relief of speech. So this relation between silence and speech, or perhaps silencing and speech, comes out through the testimonies in a variety of ways that we might not otherwise get through the questionnaires.

NK: I think that there is being silenced and there is also using silence as a way to communicate.

CC: How do you understand that difference?

NK: I think that others may silence us, and that's silencing, but I think that we may silence ourselves. That sometimes for people the trauma is so painful or there's so much pain associated with the trauma or so much fear of how other people are going to respond that we don't have words to talk about the trauma experience. I think about trauma as what affects us in a way for which we don't have words. That it's so emotionally overwhelming we don't have words. So I think we're both silenced and we engage in silent behavior.

CC: She indeed says in the video, "I don't want to talk about this." Although then she says, "But I will." Do you have any response to having watched this again, Kafi?

KB: Well, I do. I really feel like if we didn't have this interview we would not know. So even though she came to groups all the time, and we had a very good relationship with her, and she knew multiple people in the group, we wouldn't have known this specific thing about her. So we may have known her forever and have never known this.

CC: So you wouldn't have known how silenced she was? Or about the event in her childhood?

KB: Both. Because she knew that she had the freedom to say whatever she wished, but it just wouldn't have come up.

Deirdre Rudat: I want to speak about how invalidated most of these women feel. I deal with a lot of trauma interviews, and one of the things I hear about so often is that it wasn't necessarily the event itself that was so traumatizing, it was really that feeling of being so invalidated. And it's so difficult to quantify in a way that you find in all of the measures that we have in our batteries. It's very difficult to do so, so having these opportunities in a testimonial fashion really gets at that piece of what's so important to so many of these women.

CC: When you say "invalidated," can you say in relation to what we just saw in the video, where that moment is, or where those moments are, where you sense what it means to be invalidated?

DR: Well, she talks about her mom dismissing her experience. And that's to me a very invalidating experience; she says she never talks about it again. It's what we're speaking about in terms of her being silenced. I think of that as seeming like the experience didn't exist, that their feelings about the experience are not relevant and not important; they're nothing. And for many women I think it's not only confusing but also part of what makes it traumatizing for people.

CC: So, again it's a different way of not being able to say exactly what the trauma is. It's not just the event . . .

DR: It's not just the event . . .

CC: . . . but also that it's not heard, or not listened to, or not validated in some way. She actually says that throughout the interview. So storytelling is also a struggle because the traumatic event is constituted, in part, by its very silencing.

DR: I think it's a huge contextual factor in a lot of the lives of the people who have been so repeatedly traumatized.

IV. A Collective Phenomenon

CC: That brings me to another question. If we think of the women in this group as traumatized—that is, as having experiences that repeatedly come back to them, that have affected their entire lives, that haven't been listened to or validated, that have been silenced, and about which they sometimes silence themselves—do we consider this as a set of individual traumas or as a larger collective traumatic experience? That is, something societal, something larger than the individual. Sometimes scholars or clinicians will refer to these experiences as individual, and will link them to a particularly bad family or parent, for example. Whereas what we see in these testimonies seems like such a large experience. I'm wondering about your thoughts on that. How would you want to talk about this? Is this individual trauma? Is it collective trauma? For example, regarding the Holocaust, we say it's collective trauma, in part because the violence, the annihilation, was aimed at a group. So you could think here of a group of women as targets, for example? The women, themselves, talk about what it means to be a woman among other women having these experiences.

KB: I think it helps them to feel "I'm not alone." So, looking at it from their standpoint, I think for them to feel "I'm not by myself experiencing this, but other people are experiencing this"—feeling like a collective unit—is important.

CC: That's interesting. So the women themselves might prefer to say it's a collective experience.

KB: At least to know that this is not an experience that I had, just me; there were other people that experienced this.

NK: A number of you, when we were all introducing ourselves, used the words "social justice" [see personal descriptions at end of the interview], which is one of the reasons you wanted to be involved in Nia. I would wonder if the social justice perspective doesn't in part imply collectivity in relation to the women's experiences.

Jalika Street: The problem for me is that it seems like sometimes there is a separation between the individual and collective, and I can't really think how that's possible. We're members of the planet, members of the community, and I think that to say that the trauma is either collective or individual would not really be helpful, or could even be further traumatizing. To call it purely individual, for example, would be not to acknowledge what happened to a woman, that it wasn't anybody else's experience. But I think women are silenced around the world, around violence against women.

CC: That's what I was thinking too. If you say it's just this or that person or family, you deny that there is actually a societal element or a political element that is, for example, about silencing women.

JS: When I think of larger systems, I think of a global phenomenon of women being silenced and of violence against women. We had a speaker who talked about intergenerational trauma and post-traumatic slave syndrome and how violence in the African American community can be passed down in different ways, and in families and through collective trauma from this past.

CC: You said, "post-traumatic slave syndrome"?

JS: Yes. That would be more on a national level of trauma, which has been passed down through the generations, and then there is the family level as well.

CC: And in one of the other interviews the woman says there's a "generational curse." She says, "I wanted to stop that generational curse" (Interview 5b). She is referring specifically to the transmission of abusive behavior from parent to child. But you seem to be saying that we could also see it possibly in terms of the return of something that goes way back and is collective in the strictest sense, like slavery in the United States.

MPC: When you used the word "Holocaust," I was thinking "Ma'afa," which is the word for the African Holocaust, the historical trauma that has affected continental and diasporic Africans. And you said it exactly, there is a collective sense of trauma, which is why I think that Nia is so wonderful, because there's collective healing going on. When there's a group trauma, it's really helpful for there to be group healing. And we've seen that in research with the Rwandan genocide and many other large-scale traumatic events that have affected millions of people throughout the world.

CC: So you're suggesting, then—and this may bear upon the testimonies as well —that if there is collective trauma (and I wonder about this in relation to domestic violence in general), the idea of treating it individually may not be an adequate response to the collective dimension. There are so many traumatizing events that we think of as individual—battering and so on—that do have a collective or political dimension, and maybe the treatment needs to engage with that as well and not just say, for example, "you had a bad childhood."

MPC: Absolutely.

RJA: I have been thinking about the intergenerational piece as well. Watching these videos, I feel like they beg for what in psychology we would call a "family systems" approach. If you have an individual who comes to you, who's had traumas, the likelihood is that these traumas involve other family members. And you may work with someone one on one, but they still are going back to that environment, and there's a good chance that they could be retraumatized. And what makes me so sad is that you see traumatized individuals having children, and those children getting traumatized, and then the trauma comes back, and then you've got children looking for support from people who are traumatized and don't know how to support them.

CC: So it's collective also because you have parents and children involved together. In one video, a woman is upset with her daughter for having slept with her boyfriend.

RJA: I was thinking of that woman.

CC: Here is some of what she says, early on in the first interview:

> It's some bad history behind me and my daughter. Back in 1995 I tried to kill her. The man I had been with for ten years started sleeping with her, she was sixteen years old. I been in the house for almost ten years and they did this to me, I tried to burn it down with them in it. Only by the grace of God I didn't . . . So I ended up moving with my daddy. I hadn't talked to my daughter, I hadn't seen her. She had a baby, I didn't want to see her or the baby. I was like, you did this to me after all I had did for you. (Interview 5a)

And what was your response? You were talking about potential intergenerational trauma as well.

RJA: I actually had a really hard time with that. And I had to keep reminding myself that she had been traumatized too. My knee-jerk reaction was actually to get very angry with her. That she could say she tried to kill both the man and her daughter, but also specifically that she tried to kill her daughter twice, I think it was. And I found myself feeling frustrated, thinking, "Your daughter was sixteen. This man was much older. Your daughter was being traumatized in this situation, and yet you wanted to kill her." And I got really angry, and I could feel my empathy and my sympathy pulling away. And the only way I could start to get back to it was to remind myself, "OK, this woman didn't really have a chance either." And so while I still hang on to some of that anger, thinking about trauma going through generations was what brought me back to being able to care for her again. But it's hard. I am still having a hard time with it.

MPC: Especially because *she* [the daughter] was being sexually abused as a teenager.

RJA: Exactly.

MPC: But the mother never quite labeled the trauma that happened to her daughter as trauma, or as abuse. It was described more maliciously.

V. Redefining Trauma and Testimony

CC: It seems, then, that the stories that are produced in the videos reveal the difficulty not only of creating stories but also of listening to and grasping them. This is because they challenge how we think about the very nature of what they are reporting—that is, about the status of the concept of trauma itself. Have the group experiences in the Nia Project, or the videos specifically, added to or changed what people thought about trauma, or taught them for the first time about trauma? Does the Nia Project in general, or the video testimonies in particular, suggest that we need to change or widen our definitions of trauma? For example, should we think of these women's experiences—to continue with the question we've been discussing—in terms of collective political social trauma, or something more specific to these women's experiences? And how does this affect the way we understand what is happening in the videos?

Larisa Niles-Carnes: One thing that surprises me about trauma, or that I find interesting about it, is how people interpret trauma. Some people will automatically hear something and think about how traumatic that experience is, and about how it is still being silenced, on some level, in the speaker. But it's also interesting how sometimes somebody talking about trauma can tell you every single thing about that experience. Either they can tell you every single thing about it or they've suppressed it, one or the other. And also, how they may not remember what happened before that trauma, even if they remember the event itself. One of the examples in the videos was a woman saying that at the age of six this started happening. Six is a very early memory; other people who had something happen to them at sixteen cannot remember anything from the ages of fifteen and younger. For them, a new life, so to speak, started at the age of fifteen. And so I noticed how the trauma can erase other, and maybe better, memories. Maybe they only have bad memories left.

NK: In terms of my thinking about trauma, I think that it is important in these interviews, and I think Carla said it, to appreciate both the women's individual traumas and the collective traumas. And I think we need to be careful, I think Carla said articulately, not to go to an extreme in either direction. So we need to understand these individual women's traumas, which then occur in the light of intergenerational trauma, which then occur in the light of cultural trauma. It's multilayered, and trauma that occurs in the context of racism and oppression, I think, involves another trauma layer. And in the context of a family environment in which everyone or most people have experienced horrible traumas, everybody is bound together, in a way, by their trauma stories. And so I do think we really need to look at the multiple layers of trauma.

Nicole Fischer: In many instances, the women who participate in the Nia Project are sharing their stories for the very first time. This process can be both empowering and overwhelming. It is our responsibility, as clinicians and thoughtful researchers, to create a safe space for the women to share as much, or as little, about their circumstances as they wish. Eventually, after sufficient time and a good pace to establish meaningful relationships with group and individual therapists, the women learn to articulate traumatic experiences in a more concise manner. They also learn to process their emotions, and express their emotions in a productive way. Trauma is complicated and multifaceted. There is no need to rush the process or pigeonhole the experience of any one person. In addition, our task as culturally competent psychologists is to hear and conceptualize the finite details of our patients and to adapt our worldview accordingly.

SK: One of the things that surprises me is just how prevalent it is. I know I shouldn't be surprised because I've read the statistics, I've done some of this work. But I am continually surprised with how prevalent these kinds of things are. And that is extremely distressing to me. But on the other hand, it does help me to realize that these are collective traumas, these are social traumas, and that is empowering in a sense because we can intervene at so many different levels now. We can intervene at the individual level, but we can also intervene at the systems level and on a greater societal level. And I think that this is also very empowering for our clients to realize, that women are targets of violence and African Americans, low-income people, are targets of violence. And that this is empowering because a lot of these women have so much shame around the abuse, and when a lot of their abusers have been sitting here telling them this is your fault, I think that some of them internalize that. And seeing that it's not just that, that it is a bigger systems issue, helps them to realize that it's not just them, there's something else going on. And the most beautiful thing that I think this realization brings is that it draws a lot of the women together when they start saying, "You know, I told this woman about Nia and this woman about Nia" . . . they start to draw together and form a collective solidarity against violence in general.

MPC: It's a really good question, actually, how we think about trauma in terms of these women's experiences. This was the backbone of my dissertation. Part of why I think Nia is so valuable is because it really is psychology in action. It's allowing the women to receive liberation, but through their own doing. The idea of non-Western trauma interventions, bridging the gap between the current evidence-based practice movement and a lot of the non-Western trauma experiences of people around the world, is something that Nia does really well. It's really taking the strengths and the resiliencies and the power within the community and empowering the women to utilize that power to heal themselves. And the idea of the groups and of the storytelling, in my opinion, breaks a lot of the historical trauma—the disenfranchisement that a lot of the women experience already in day-to-day society—by speaking, and thus taking some of the power back that was taken from them.

Susan Brown: I was struck, as I videotaped the women, by how important it seemed for them to have a chance to talk, and how after speaking to the video camera they insisted on continuing to have their voices heard. They often continued to speak after the video camera was turned off.

CC: You both seem to be saying, then, that the act of storytelling—as testimony to trauma—is not simply about giving information but about acting, actually producing a situation of power, or the conditions for taking some kind of power. This reminds me of an interview I did with Thomas Keenan many years ago, in which we spoke to several AIDS activists about the difficulty of finding an audience as an HIV-positive speaker: such an audience, they said, actually had to be created since most mainstream media was constructed to address only the HIV-negative viewer [see chapter 5]. So I wonder if this issue of struggling to narrate a story and of taking power in doing so also has to do with the problem of address. To whom, would you say, are these videos addressed?

SD: When the women were talking in the videos, when they weren't talking about their own experiences, I think many of the women were talking not only to other women who would be coming through the Nia project but also other women who have gone through experiences such as their own. I won't presume to say that they were only speaking to other African American women, but I think other women who have been battered, other women who have faced suicidal problems. One interview that sticks in my mind is with a woman by the name of Donna. She was pretty opinionated and vocal and very forthright about what she wanted her story to be and how her story ought to be heard. And wanting other women such as herself to hear her story who have had similar experiences as she had, so that either they would not make the same mistake or they would learn from her experiences and see that she still is a survivor, she still is here.

So I think it's interesting that you say that you did an interview in which the difficulty of finding an address in TV interviews became an important topic, because it seems to me that although it wasn't explicitly stated, in some ways the women attempted to speak directly to other women, perhaps for the first time, who have faced the sorts of struggles as they have.

VI. Deathstruck

CC: With regard to the problem of listening to these women's attempts to speak out, I would like to raise another question about how, as an audience to the videos, we listen to the women's language. If we look at the way people give their testimonies, it differs quite dramatically from woman to woman. For example, after being asked to talk about her life, another woman begins with the following:

> Well, let's begin with, my name is Sonia and I'm twenty-eight years old. I have two children. I have a two-year-old son and a ten-year-old daughter. I will say that I'm a lot more fortunate than a lot of other people have been. However, I do feel like I've had a very hectic and tough life. Pretty much stemming from domestic violence and I would say being grown before my time. I moved out of my parent's house when I was around age fifteen to never return. I felt I could take better care of myself then; I felt I could do more for myself. I have seven sisters and brothers, and I just felt I could do a lot better for myself so I moved out. I am currently four and a half months pregnant. I will say my hope and dream is to overcome depression, to overcome domestic violence and abuse, to be a better parent, and entrepreneur, and just to overcome all these obstacles. (Interview 15a)

I'm wondering if you had a sense about whether the level of language capacity makes a difference in the ability to deal with the traumatic experience or not?
NK: I've thought about that issue a lot, both in terms of my own life and in terms of the life of my patients. I do believe that language capacity helps, as well as the capacity for formal operational thinking, which comes not just with the capacity for language but also higher-order cognitive processing. But I also think that

when we have horrible traumas, our capacity for language is diminished. And our capacity for formal operational thinking, even if we possess it about non-traumatic events, is also diminished.

I spent the first six weeks of my life in an ICU. And I know that was traumatic. But I had no words back then. So even though I may have a gift in terms of language capacity, I had no words and no language for that trauma. And one of my good friends just delivered a baby ten days ago who also can't breathe and is in the ICU. And visiting the baby I know that that's what my life was like back then. But I can't remember that. I have no words for it. But I have affective experiences of it. And I think even when we're older, and even if we have wonderful gifts for words, sometimes we lose that in the face of trauma. And so to your question about articulateness, on the one hand my answer is yes, and on the other hand my answer is no. Sometimes it depends on where you are in the healing process. And I think part of good treatment, whatever method of treatment it is, is to help people find words and put words to those experiences so that the affect isn't as overwhelming and that there's a greater balance between the words and the feelings.

CC: So first of all, you're saying that even if you seem to be naturally articulate, or educated and have learned to be formally articulate, trauma will break through. And also that we can't make a judgment about who is naturally more or less articulate because they're very traumatized women whose capacity to speak may well have been affected from the beginning by severe trauma. The capacity to tell the trauma may be effected by the trauma itself, a point you made before, Nadine, concerning silence.

SD: I think sometimes women don't know what the words are to explain certain experiences. I think sometimes women actually come up with their own words, come up with their own expressions, come up with their own phrases that help them describe that experience. And sometimes it resonates, and that language, those words, those phrases, start to be shared by others as a way of discussing an experience for which they haven't been exposed to the words we use, like "validating" or "invalidating."

CC: There is one very evocative word that the woman in the first video clip, Mary, uses later in the interview that struck me. She says, "I was deathstruck." "Deathstruck." Do you have any thoughts on what that means? "Deathstruck." About her life.

SD: I think that that's a good example of a woman trying to describe or trying to put words to an experience or to a feeling that she hasn't had before. Even

Shane Davis at Grady
Hospital, October 2, 2012.

ambivalent feelings. This is something very nuanced. I might have gotten it from
you, Kafi, years ago, or my other girlfriends. Even ambivalent feelings about
something can be expressed as, "I feel some kind of way." And that's something
I hadn't heard. I use that example to point out that maybe some of the language
that's being used . . .

CC: We have to learn to listen.

SD: We have to learn to listen because it could be a way in which they're trying to
describe their experience. What is really unique and interesting in the video testimonies is that every woman speaks about her experience differently and uses
language differently to describe her experiences. And sometimes I think that the
women may know what language to use to describe their experiences. And in an
attempt to do so, maybe some of the women actually come up with their own
phrases, their own terms, their own things for themselves that have meaning for
them. It's very important for us not to assume that we understand the experiences that the women are describing, especially when it's in language that we
have never heard before.

VII. LISTENING ANEW

CC: So how do we listen to these interviews? How do they surprise us, challenge
us, and demand new modes of listening and learning? And how do they break
through our own desire to turn away from them?

LNC: I think it's important that if we don't know what somebody is saying, that we ask them. You know I think that sometimes we either expect people to know what we're talking about when we discuss things or they expect us to understand, but I think when people use certain words, we have to ask them, "What do you mean? Can you please clarify?" Like the phrase discussed before, "feeling some kind of way." Not everybody knows what that means. Or the woman in the first video, who used the word "deathstruck." I can interpret what that word means, but I think it's important that we ask our clients to elaborate a little bit more on what they mean.

Carla Sutton Moore: I think the silencing aspect is important. As they're expressing themselves, and coming up with this language, the words sometimes have a certain level of intensity. I think this may be related to the fact that they weren't able to speak before and are speaking now for the first time. So perhaps asking them about the difference between then and now would be helpful. For example, it seems like it carries a certain weight when someone says "deathstruck." We might ask, "How would you have described that before, when you couldn't speak out? Is that how you're describing it only now, because before you couldn't speak out?" In other words, we could try to learn about the difference between what they might have said had they been able to speak before, and what they are saying now, later, when they speak, belatedly, for the first time. So we might try to understand what it means that their language, emerging from silence, is coming only after the fact.

Christina Wilson: Sometimes when I talk to patients who are giving voice to experiences that have been associated with such intense emotion or that have been so intensely personalized, I speak of their experiences as being kind of like the boogeyman in the closet, or the monster in the closet. In the same way that for a little kid an idea or experience is so terrifying that approaching the closet or even trying to explain to a parent who the monster is can be overwhelming. And it is really important to me as a therapist to listen to the languaging of the trauma and to maintain the space to try to understand what the monster is, both in the experience of the perpetrator and in the terror and emotions of the victim. And to remember that even though we, as therapists, may have backgrounds in research or clinical work, everyone's monster in some ways looks a little different, and it is important to make the space to really understand what it looks like for each individual patient. This is part of the process of validating people in their experiences, as opposed to the trauma, which so often involved being invalidated or being silenced.

Sarah Dunn: It is hard not to make assumptions or to attach certain emotions to other peoples' experiences. Sometimes, when what we are hearing is difficult to hear, the desire to turn away takes hold as a protective mechanism. I have to constantly remind myself that the language that the women use cannot be directly translated but has to be understood in the context in which it is used.

NK: The issue of being silenced, as well as self-silencing, is really critical in trauma. And so often the women had horrible experiences and were told they couldn't talk about it. And because of those messages, as well as the shame associated with the experiences and the extent to which they blame themselves, they feel like it's not safe to speak. And yet speaking about it is critical to the healing process. It's often really difficult to listen to these interviews. The women's pain is often palpable. And many of the stories that we hear, and heard on the videotapes, are just horrific. And to me some of the experiences that they had to deal with are absolutely inconceivable. And so I find myself either being extremely drawn in and hanging on to every word, or finding it just almost too painful to listen.

NF: I often struggle with my own countertransference reactions during individual or group therapy sessions. The unfathomable experiences that are recounted by the women are devastating to hear. I must be mindful of my reactions in the moment and take time to process my emotions afterward. I have tremendous empathy for each woman I encounter, and I commend them for their honesty and earnest desire to heal from the circumstances they have endured. I feel humbled and honored by their trust in me, and their commitment to the Nia Project.

Huaiyu Zhang: I think readiness is very important for us as therapists to really listen to the patients talking to us about their very distressing and very traumatic life experiences. I think we need to deal with our tendency to turn away from painful experiences of patients so that we can create a very safe, warm and accepting, validating space for patients to be willing to share their experiences. And I also think we need to be watchful for patients' readiness to tell us about these traumatic life experiences. Because talking about their life experiences could be potentially traumatizing for them. Therefore, I think as clinicians one of our roles is to create a space so that we can monitor the patients' readiness, to pay attention to their pacing and to find a good pace for patients to be willing to share their life stories. So that they might use appropriate language to tell us what has happened to them in their lives.

CW: In regard to this question about how we stay present and don't necessarily turn away from the stories, I would suggest that one way for therapists to do this is by monitoring for emotion regulation, dissociation, and a person's ability to tolerate the intense affect related to telling a story. And also by creating a space for people to feel like their stories are being validated. I think that, on the one hand, we don't necessarily want to turn away from a story or invalidate or shut down a story for our own reasons. But I also think that sometimes, when someone hasn't spoken her story or doesn't have the ability to manage the intense affect from telling it, the distress may be so intense that it has the potential to be retraumatizing for them. They may dissociate or have a hard time calibrating the affect in an adaptive manner. I think that's when we, as therapists, have to do this tricky dance of trying to provide a positive experience, and be supportive and validating, and of finding ways to calibrate, monitor, and help regulate the patients in a way that doesn't invalidate them as they're telling the stories.

And I find that the process can sometimes be very difficult. Particularly as we're managing our own responses to these experiences. I know, for example, that when intense childhood sexual abuse is revealed as people are doing exposure therapies and telling a lot of those intense stories, I have pretty intense physical reactions so that I have to monitor myself and get support after the process. But sometimes the disclosures are happening in a way that we don't necessarily know they're coming. So I think, for us, finding ways to be aware of certain kinds of trauma, and monitoring certain types of affect or experiences that are more likely to affect us, is part of our development and growth as therapists.

VIII. A Revolutionary Act

CC: This last issue leads to my final question, which is how these interviews, or more largely the work with the women, affected you. How did the team change as a result of viewing the videos and working with the women? Did you get something back from them? Especially since many of the people on the team have had a personal connection with suicide and domestic violence.

RJA: I've always had an interest in community service, volunteering, connecting with people. People that I might not connect with on a day-to-day basis. I always thought that there is something about serving others that is antidepressive. There have been many times when I was ruminating about something and feeling really crappy about it and then talked to somebody about her story, and it put what I was feeling bad about in perspective and actually helped me to pick myself up and problem-solve a little bit better. And so I'd say probably one of the greatest gifts that I get from being involved in this work is putting my own problems into perspective. And it interrupts my rumination, so it's a big gift.

CSM: I remember two years ago, when we were coming up with themes from the video testimony transcripts and we were talking about resiliency and spirituality, we formed a spirituality group and had someone here to provide a religious perspective in the event the women wanted it. So even just hearing their stories from the videos that first time, it gave us feedback and insight about other ways in which they cope that we could help facilitate. Over the couple of years that I've been here, I've seen Nia grow as a result of hearing the women's stories and what their needs are, and how we could assist in their coping. And I remember the resiliency symposium that we did at the American Psychological Association conference, where we talked about the research as it pertained to spirituality and coping and empowerment and protective factors, like being a mother. All of those came out of just hearing the women's stories and creating themes that went along with the stories that were told on the videos.

NK: I believe that I got a great deal back from the women telling their stories. I feel a kind of intimate connection with the women, even if I don't know them personally, because they trusted us to share their stories. There was something healing to me, watching them heal through the process of telling their stories. I do know a lot of people who have killed themselves and who have attempted suicide, and it really helps me to understand why people get to where they feel like their life is untenable and they can't go on. And it's easier to be empathic and compassionate when people share their stories about that.

HZ: Watching the interviews impacted me in two ways. One, as Carla said, was that I really adored the women for how resilient they have been going through their life tribulations. This is very empowering for me, to believe that there is also potential for us to help them to build more resilience.

The second way that watching the interviews impacted me is that it really brings me closer to the women. I feel more connected with them when I feel like they're really opening themselves up by telling their life stories with us. And I also feel like I have a deep sense of compassion for them while watching the levels of suffering vary from person to person. The intensity of the suffering of the women is really disturbing, and the stories are very compelling for us to witness.

For example, I have had an individual patient who initially had a difficult time transitioning to me as a new therapist. She really did not want to connect with me, and she even asked for a different therapist, as she was not really into the therapeutic relationship. And it turned out that the turning point in our relationship was when she started to open herself up by telling me that the most meaningful relationship in her life was with her sister. The story was that both she and her sister suffered a lot from childhood sexual abuse by some family members, and this particular sister, in order to protect this patient, actually took some of the abuse from the other family members for her. And that was really moving when I heard that. And she was in tears, and I was in tears, and upon hearing such a story of her life I felt so much compassion toward her, and that actually kind of changed the dynamic in our relationship, and we started to bond really well.

CW: I think that women speaking their stories is a revolutionary act, on a number of levels. I think that the power around domestic violence and abuse and trauma as well as racism, sexism, and classism are maintained by whose voice you hear and whose voice is silent. And so I think the idea of women, many of whom are African American women, low-income women, women of color who've experienced abuse, to actually speak truth to their experience—and to be heard—is an incredible act. And for me, I find it inspiring, something that takes incredible strength. And I think it gives me hope that, even though much of what we hear during our day can be challenging, it gives me true hope and faith in the possibility for growth and for true leadership. I feel like a lot of the women in these stories are true leaders in their communities and in the Nia Project, and that's something I'm very proud to be a part of.

NIA INTERVIEW PARTICIPANTS

Kafi Bethea is the former Nia Project coordinator. She worked extensively with the women and conducted approximately half of the interviews for the video testimony project.

Susan Brown was the videographer for the video testimony project. She said that she became involved because of her interest in domestic violence, as well as in social justice, women's mental health, and personal storytelling.

Shane Davis, Ph.D., was one of the interviewers for the Nia video project and also worked with the women in the intervention groups while she was an intern and postdoctoral fellow at Emory University in the Department of Psychiatry and Behavioral Sciences. She is currently a licensed psychologist and behavioral scientist at the Centers for Disease Control and Prevention. She says that she was interested in working with an underserved population, and more generally in working within the African American community around violence and other traumatic experiences that have not received adequate attention.

Lida Doret is a medical student at Emory University. She became involved with

Members of the Nia Project Team at Grady Hospital, October 2, 2012 (*clockwise from top left*): Larisa Niles-Carnes, Sy Prior, Christina Wilson, and Huaiyu Zhang.

Nia because of her interest in the particular population of patients referred to Nia and her wish to help them.

Sarah Dunn, Ph.D., is an adjunct faculty member at Emory in the Department of Psychiatry and Behavioral Sciences. She supervises psychology interns that are working with the Nia Project. She wanted to experience working in a large urban hospital with underserved populations, in particular populations with significant trauma histories and serious mental illness, many of whom may have never seen a mental health professional.

Nicole L. Fischer, Ph.D., is a postdoctoral fellow with the Nia Project. She came to Nia out of an interest in working in a clinical capacity with traditionally underserved populations, in particular those who have experienced trauma.

Rachel Jeanne Ammirati is a predoctoral clinical psychology intern with Emory University School of Medicine / Grady Health System in the Department of Psychiatry and Behavioral Sciences. She is interested in social justice and came to the Nia Project also to learn about trauma.

Nadine Kaslow, Ph.D., is chief psychologist at Grady Health System and a professor and vice chair in the Department of Psychiatry and Behavioral Sciences at Emory University and president of the American Psychological Association. She is principal investigator on the Nia Project.

Sara Klco is a doctoral student at Georgia State University working as a practicum Nia therapist. One of the major reasons she is involved with Nia is her interest in social justice and her desire to work with women who have been through so much.

Dorian Lamis is a predoctoral intern in the Department of Psychiatry at Emory University School of Medicine. He is interested in suicidality and why people die by suicide.

Carla Sutton Moore, Ph.D., is a postdoctoral fellow with the Nia Project. She worked previously with Nia as an advanced practicum student. She is interested in trauma and especially working with the African American community in this area, given the stigma associated with suicide, depression, and domestic violence.

Larisa Niles-Carnes is project coordinator of the Nia Project.

Marissa Petersen-Coleman, Ph.D., is a postdoctoral fellow. She became interested in working with Nia because she believes that psychologists should also be involved in advocacy and in giving voice to those that are often forgotten.

Sy Prior is a behavioral health practicum student from Fielding Graduate University. She has had experience working with offenders but wished to have more experience in working with victims. She was present at the October 2 interview.

Dierdre Rudat is the project coordinator for Grady WITT, a PTSD research project for women. She started with Nia as a practicum student and originally joined the team because of her interest in suicide and in diverse populations, especially those that have been underserved in the area of mental health.

Jalika Street is a fifth-year student in the clinical and community psychology program at Georgia State University. She is passionate about helping people heal from experiences of interpersonal trauma, especially within the African American and Latino communities. She has engaged the community around these issues by providing education and research to help raise awareness.

Christina K. Wilson, Ph.D., is a postdoctoral fellow with the Nia Project. Her clinical and research focus is on PTSD, the intergenerational transmission of trauma, and women's mental health. She sees her research and involvement with Nia as an extension of her work in social justice and of her connection with her community, which has been impacted by trauma on many different levels.

Huaiyu Zhang is a psychology intern working in the trauma track. She is interested in working with the Nia population because, as someone coming from a low socioeconomic background herself, she is a believer in change and wishes to help empower this population.

NOTE

I would like to express my gratitude to Larisa Niles-Carnes for her patient and thorough help coordinating the interviews with the team members and assisting me in making identifications in the audiotapes. I am also grateful to the women who participated in the Nia testimony project as interviewees and gave permission for their interviews to be quoted for the purposes of research and general instruction.

PART III / The System Is Weeping

Arthur Blank Jr. at his home in Washington, DC, January 23, 2013.

Chapter Eleven

Apocalypse Terminable and Interminable
An Interview with Arthur S. Blank Jr.

Arthur Blank, M.D., is a psychoanalyst in private practice in Washington, DC. He began his career as a psychiatrist in Vietnam. Upon his return to the United States, he was one of the first psychiatrists to recognize the effects of trauma in returning soldiers and to create a means of treating it within the Veterans Administration. He was an early director of the Vet Centers in the Veterans Administration, which were established by Congress and the president specifically to treat post-traumatic stress disorder. Dr. Blank was also a member of the committees defining the diagnosis of PTSD for *DSM-III-R* and *DSM-IV*. I interviewed him in his home in Washington, DC, on January 23, 2013.

I. A Psychiatrist Goes to War

CC: You are one of the first professionals who recognized post-traumatic stress disorder in Vietnam veterans and who attempted to create an institutional response to their experiences of trauma. But your story is not simply a matter of a professional psychiatrist encountering a psychiatric disorder; it is also the story of a man who experienced the war himself. Could you recount how you came to the recognition of trauma both personally and professionally?

AB: My recognition evolved over time. I was a very naive and ordinary fresh Yale psychiatry graduate in 1965, and I had to go to the army. The doctor's draft was still being enforced. If you didn't want to go into the military as a general physician and you wanted to do specialty training, you enrolled in something called the Berry plan, in which they let you finish your specialty training but then you had to serve two years. So I finished psychiatric residency on June 30, 1965, and on July 2, I was in the army at Fort Sam Houston. I was assigned to Valley Forge Hospital and had just met my now wife, and I thought we were going to have a great two years traveling up and down the Jersey Turnpike. As soon as I got to Valley Forge I was given orders to go to Vietnam as a psychiatrist with the 93rd Evacuation Hospital. It was a new hospital—actually it was still being finished when we got there—on the road northwest of Saigon. I was there for six months. And then the second six months at the Third Field Hospital across the street from Tan Son Nhut airport at the edge of Saigon. I was frightened the entire time because of the amount of terrorism going on there. The front of the Navy psychiatric clinic was blown off by a car full of plastic explosives a couple of months after I got there. I had met the Navy psychiatrist, but he was across town at the time of the explosion, and it was just that kind of thing for a year. I saw 483 people for psychiatric evaluation—kept notes on all of them. We had some extra time at Fort Riley before we left, and I had collected some of the World War II psychoanalytic literature on traumatic neurosis and took it with me.

CC: How did you know to do that?

AB: That's a good question. I don't know. I had started reading Freud in college, so I had already read *Beyond the Pleasure Principle* long before all of this.

CC: And you recognized its relevance.

AB: I was going to a war, and I figured that I would see some war neurosis. What I didn't count on, of course, is how affected I would be myself. So anyway, I was looking for the effects of combat trauma on people, and I perhaps didn't see much. And I'm still trying to figure that out. I don't know if some of it may have had to do with the acuteness of everything. I saw a lot of people who had been in combat, but I saw them the day after their battlefield experiences, so there were a lot of things going on besides visible trauma reactions in that kind of situation. But I did see some people who had acute PTSD and was able to diagnose that. Unfortunately I couldn't treat anybody.

CC: How did you diagnose it in those years? Was the *DSM-I*[1] in place at that point?

AB: Yes. I ignored the *DSM-I* and went according to the symptoms in [Otto] Fenichel's *Psychoanalytic Theory of Neurosis* from 1945, which are the same as the PTSD criteria diagnostic symptoms.[2]

CC: Was anybody else doing this at the time except for you?

AB: No.

CC: So no one told you to go look for this—you just knew.

AB: Yes. I had my copy of Fenichel's textbook with me and had read his chapter 7, on traumatic neurosis, which summarizes the analytic literature on war neurosis up to that point. I made a chart later—many years later—of Fenichel's diagnostic symptoms of traumatic neurosis and *DSM-III*.[3]

CC: And they were similar to the later *DSM* criteria?

AB: They were the same thing. The *DSM-III* criteria symptoms are from the analytic literature, although that was never acknowledged.

CC: Oh that's interesting! Because one hears of the diagnostic criteria deriving from the work with veterans and various other nonanalytic sources.

AB: They're all in Fenichel's 1945 textbook.

CC: So for some reason—because you had not been trained, clearly, to do this— you sensed that you might need this material, and you went to war and you brought it with you. But you really didn't see much trauma at first.

AB: Yes. But I had my own experiences there as well. I had one near miss at the first hospital. The anesthesiologist and I were brushing our teeth in an outdoor sink made of oil drums that we had outside, and a sniper's bullet went by. First we heard—how did it go? We heard the zing and thud. All that, plus the exposure to bodies and casualties in the hospital, set me up to react to something that happened a few months later. I saw a trooper who had performed in an outstanding way in combat and was now on stationary guard duty. However, he was struggling with impulses to shoot U.S. troops while on guard and therefore came to see the psychiatrist. It seemed he would be able to come for psychotherapy because he would be staying in place for a while, unlike most of the people I saw.

In the second hour, after twenty minutes he pulled out a grenade and said that he had come with the intention of killing both of us, but he had decided that I was a nice guy so I could get out if I wanted to, and he pulled the pin, and held the handle. It was a very small room, about half the size of this one, and I went over to the door, with a hand on the knob, yelling at him to put the pin back in, not really being clear whether or not one could do that.

Well, his response was to let go of the handle. I went out the door and around the corner, putting a brick wall between me and the room—this was all very instinctive, maybe because I had seen the wall being built; the little office was carved out of the Red Cross recreation room specifically because there had not been an adequate room at this hospital for a psychiatrist. The room blew up. He was not killed; he survived, at least he survived enough to be medevac'd back to the states. I don't know what happened after that. And I was severely freaked out at the time. I was reminded of this in reading again the first part of your book, where you suggest that what is traumatic is not the brush with death but survival.[4] And I have some thoughts about that.

CC: I'd like to hear them.

AB: I don't think it's the survival per se, which is traumatic; I think it's the future months or years of work that it will take to understand the experiences that are instinctively and unconsciously felt as a burden. I think the gap is between the traumatic event and the non-understanding of what is experienced. At least that has been my personal experience. I also see that with many other people.

CC: So that your survival becomes a struggle to grasp what happened.

AB: To grasp—exactly. To grasp, understand, integrate, process, etcetera.

CC: So it also means your survival will be reshaped around that event. Forever.

AB: Yes. It's like this is a very big deal. As it happened, in my case, I repressed all that. I shut it all off. Not intellectually—I never forgot what had happened—but I shut off all the affect, all the emotion, the terror, so on and so forth, which I think, looking back at it now, was adaptive.

CC: So at first, coming to the war as a professional, you failed to see the traumatic effects of the war on the soldiers. But then, you yourself were made to experience that kind of encounter by a traumatized soldier. Yet this, in its turn, caused you not to see in a different way.

AB: Yes, and that is supported by what I experienced when I came back in October '66. I was at Fort Dix for the rest of the two years, which was a psychiatric evaluation site for soldiers returning from Vietnam. So now I'm seeing at Fort Dix—in a hospital ward—all kinds of evacuees. And it was very interesting, there was an intense campaign in the Army—I can only call it a propaganda campaign. The psychiatric line was, "Yes, combat events are disturbing to people, but it's temporary, it goes away, and we mustn't treat it."

CC: We mustn't treat it?

AB: We mustn't treat it.

CC: Why?

AB: Well, because if we treat it we're going to make it worse.

CC: Because treating it means talking about the things?

AB: That's right.

CC: So making it worse means making it worse for those who don't want to know about the situation.

AB: That's right [chuckling]. But please understand this was official doctrine.

There was a series of lectures at Fort Sam Houston, for a large training cohort of doctors, about combat neurosis, combat exhaustion—"combat fatigue," I think, was the preferred term—given by a neurologist whom I had known at Yale, who simply conveyed the military line. But it was vigorously enforced. There were a number of us draftee psychiatrists in Vietnam, and there was a lieutenant colonel who was a regular Army psychiatrist in charge of everybody, and he was essentially the supervisor of all the psychiatrists in-country. And we had a number of very clear rules. We couldn't evacuate anybody for combat neurosis, traumatic neurosis. The only people that we could evacuate were people who were acutely schizophrenic, and we couldn't keep anybody in the hospital longer than five days. They had to be sent back to duty or evacuated to the states, so all the people with traumatic neurosis whom we saw during the course of the year were sent back to duty.

CC: So what was your function as a psychiatrist exactly? Why did they have psychiatrists there?

AB: That's a good question.

CC: Just to get the schizophrenic people out?

AB: Yes.

CC: And to get everybody else back in?

AB: Yes. That's exactly right.

CC: So your function was to weed out the mad people and return the traumatized people to duty?

AB: Yup. And marijuana made that easier, so to speak, for them. So the use of marijuana, even as early as '65 and '66, was widespread. Everybody had access to it, including in the hospital. And the troops used that as an anti-anxiety, anti-PTSD drug.

When I came back, the atmosphere within the military was the same, including at Fort Dix. Anything that had to do with trauma symptoms was regarded as something temporary, evanescent; it will go away, we don't give it a diagnosis, we don't give it any treatment to speak of—we move people on. This led to a generalized denial within military psychiatry, which I was part of and I believed. I believed that this war was not producing any significant amount of lingering trauma symptoms.

CC: Is that because you had not seen so much acute stress as a psychiatrist when you were there, or was that your own participation in the generalized denial? Because you had read all of the books, right?

AB: I had read all the books, and the military psychiatry authorities said that these things only linger if they are paid attention to. And if they aren't paid attention to, they won't linger. We also thought the twelve-to-thirteen-month limitation on tours would tend to prevent lasting trauma effects.

CC: So the official policy was denial.

AB: Right. I participated in the first Walter Reed conference on Vietnam psychiatry, summoned in 1967. I still have a *New York Times* article from that, in which all of us—several psychiatrists there who had been in Vietnam—said it's really quite remarkable how this very controversial and difficult war is not producing much by way of psychiatric casualties. We actually said that. And keep in mind I had repressed my own traumatic effects.

CC: Do you think that, given your previous uncanny intuitiveness about trauma, your participation in the official doctrine of denial was (paradoxically) linked to what happened to you? That is, that you yourself had had very close contact with war?

AB: Which I needed to deny. And which I had nobody to talk with about, other than my wife.

CC: So at first, going over as a psychiatrist, you didn't see trauma because of the general atmosphere of denial in the military and in psychiatry, and then you continued to deny the presence of trauma precisely because you, yourself, had been through it.

AB: Yes. I was being very consistent on all levels!

II. Fighting on the Home Front

AB: So that is part of the story. The other part of the story was the general atmosphere of our society at that point in time, 1967, 1968. There was the Tet Offensive,[5] and the antiwar movement was just beginning to escalate, and there was an enormous amount of hostility to people who had served in Vietnam.

I returned to the Department of Psychiatry at Yale in the summer of 1967 and went to work in the department with people who had been my teachers, whom I dearly loved and admired. Absolutely no one wanted to hear anything about my experiences in Vietnam. And I mean very actively did not want to hear. People were furious about the war. New Haven, of course, was a center of opposition to the war, which included the president of the university, the chaplain, the mayor, and the chairman of the Democratic town committee, all of whom were speaking publicly against the war. So there was a further impetus to shut it off, and to keep it shut off.

CC: Were you antiwar?

AB: I was antiwar from about the first week I was in Vietnam.

Which is another interesting twist to this whole story. Most of the physicians —of which there were about thirty—in the first hospital that I went over with recognized the war was crazy and wasn't going to get anyplace. It was hopeless. In 1965 the physicians in the hospitals in Vietnam recognized this—including myself. That's a whole complex story, but it has to do with seeing the country and seeing the people, the poverty, and the desperation of the people. So anyway, my wife went to antiwar rallies. I didn't go the rallies. I sent money. But I was one of the many who needed to keep it shut off.

Then a few things happened. Murray Polner came to interview me. He wrote a book, an oral history of the Vietnam War.[6] He was the only person that I can remember in the first few years who wanted to hear anything about my Vietnam experiences. We were having a party one night and a friend of ours was there, a lovely person who is still a friend and now lives here, and I started to tell her, kind of casually, standing in the kitchen. I started to tell her a fairly mild version of the events at the hospital. After not too long, she said, "You know, I'm sorry to interrupt, but I have to tell you I'm getting sick to my stomach, and I don't think I can listen anymore." I understood enough not to press the point at Yale. I did five years at a residential treatment center, which was marvelous work, which had nothing to do with trauma directly.

And then I started teaching and supervising at the VA hospital in West Haven in 1972. What happened was that the residents started bringing me Vietnam returnee patients and also asked for supervision. And I recognized right away two things: a certain percentage of the patients had traumatic neurosis, and they were misdiagnosed as schizophrenic, alcoholic, having panic disorder, whatever. I observed that, and I talked to the residents about it. Many of these patients had been in for the third or fourth admission. These were all in-patients. So I would look at the psychiatric record, and it would say such and such a year of service in Vietnam and nothing else at all about the Vietnam experience. There was even one person in particular who was a severe alcoholic and came in from time to time with DTs [delirium tremens]. And there was nothing about the war or Vietnam except that the content of his hallucinations was of little Asian people in military vehicles.

CC: And nobody made the link.

AB: Nobody said anything about that. But it was typed out in the record that that was the content of his hallucinations.

CC: So what was happening institutionally was a little like what you describe, in your essay "Trauma Disorders and a Psychology of External Experience," as the structure of trauma itself. You describe it as a kind of record that enters people's minds without awareness and remains isolated there.[7] In this case, the information got recorded, without institutional awareness, on the intake forms.

AB: Yes. We had a card file that showed everybody who had come in for the last ten years or so and what area of service they were in. There were maybe sixty or seventy people who had been in Vietnam, and it said so on their cards. And I pulled their charts and read them all. In about thirty of those it was clear that they had a traumatic neurosis. The same things were all in the charts, diagnosed as something else.

CC: And no one had noticed this before.

AB: No. The diagnosis didn't exist. I mean, it wasn't a concept. But in the chart would be the flashbacks and intrusive memories, you know, going off at a war movie, numbness, etcetera. The symptoms meeting traumatic neurosis criteria would be in the chart. So I separated those out who were diagnosable from the chart, and I called them on the telephone, and I had a pitch. I said, "You know, we've discovered that some people have some reactions to their time in Vietnam, and I'm wondering if you have any interest in coming in to talk that over," and so on. And quite a few did. I saw about twenty-five guys. Some of them were actually doing pretty well. But others weren't doing so well. And I started a treatment group with the ones who wanted to come. And that's how it all began. I started the treatment group with about eight or nine guys, and I had a psychology post-doc who was very interested. We ran that group together for a couple of years, and by this time the number of patients coming in with PTSD steadily increased, from 1973 to 1980.

CC: And what happened to you psychologically, intellectually, or personally when you began to realize that you had participated in the denial of what was happening? Did you recognize this at that point?

AB: I did. I recognized it, and I told myself, "We really screwed up." And I called Sarah Haley, Jack Smith, Chaim Shatan, and Bob Lifton.[8] As you know, at that time the Vietnam Veterans against the War were talking about their war experiences with each other. And then two of them, Arthur Egendorf and Jack Smith, decided they needed a little consultation. So they called Robert Jay Lifton and Chaim Shatan to come in and start sitting in their groups as consultants. And they brought a couple of other people in, psychologists named Florence Volkman Pincus and Robert Shapiro.[9] Lifton had me come and talk to one of his Yale seminars. But it wasn't until I started seeing more and more veterans' cases in supervision that I got in contact with these people. And in 1973 I read Sarah Haley's paper "When the Patient Reports Atrocities,"[10] and of course I was supervising residents at Yale treating patients who were reporting atrocities, so that was very helpful. I basically started consulting with all of these people on the telephone.

III. The Personal Is the Political

AB: Then I had an experience that turned me around another corner. In 1978 I was in the middle of the process I had been describing, and my father died. And several months after he died I was back in Vietnam. There was something about—and I think this happens with a lot of people—there was something about the death of a parent who in one way or another has served as a bulwark in support of the denial. The death releases the experience, if you will. That happened to me, unfortunately. At first it resulted in overwhelming symptoms. I had huge, intense anxiety and various obsessive symptoms—at the time I thought they were obsessive symptoms, but actually they were PTSD symptoms.

I had done five years of analysis, which was very successful and helpful in many ways, and never touched the war experiences. Which was extremely common in those days. Sarah Haley told a wonderful story—she had been seeing vets with PTSD in the Boston VA clinic from 1969 on—about a guy who called her up and came to see her for a consultation. He was a very successful businessman, had been an army officer in Vietnam, and was in analysis with a highly respected training analyst in Boston when the ex-officer's Vietnam experience erupted. And the response of his analyst was to say, "There's a woman who knows about these things, and I'd like you to see her for a consultation. And when you have worked it out, you can come back." There was a lot of that going on in the '60s and '70s.

CC: When your father died, were you in analysis?

AB: No, it was over.

CC: So the event in which you were almost killed by the soldier in your office had never come up?

AB: That's a very interesting thing, and I think this also happened to a lot of people. It came up. I went over it in detail—with no emotion, with no affect. And the analyst, bless his heart, who was a wonderful person, didn't know any better.

CC: So you let it go.

AB: And he let it go. And I let it go. And we went on by.

CC: In my interview with Françoise Davoine and Jean-Max Gaudilliere, she says that when the trauma first comes up in a therapeutic situation it is often mentioned casually and is treated as such by both patient and analyst, which is a form of denial. It sounds like the way you told the story was slightly dissociated, and your analyst allowed that denial to continue.

AB: Actually my emotion, at that time, was focused on my antiwar views and activities. And I brought that up a lot in the analysis. I was also very angry about the isolation—not being able to talk to anyone about Vietnam, so on and so forth. And I recall very vividly that partway through the analysis I was describing my observations about the social status of Vietnam returnees (this would have been between '67 and '72, before the war ended), and I was complaining over and over about it. "Nobody wants to hear, nobody really wants to know about what's going on over there." I finally said, very angrily, "I feel like a Holocaust survivor!" He got angry and said, "You can't make that kind of comparison. That's not a fair comparison." It was very interesting because I think I was trying to get to it.

CC: As some Holocaust survivors say, it's the silence upon coming home that is part of what's traumatizing.

Do you think that his breaking of the analytic stance was because you had actually touched on a reality, both the reality of what was happening in Vietnam and the reality of the silencing that was going on as well? Because it seems that his outburst shut down any further exploration.

AB: Yes. And because this was several years before the death of my father, neither of us was prepared to deal with it at that time.

So I thought, "Well, that's kind of an overreaction," and went on to other things. But then, after I had this huge upsurge of angst following the death of my father, I didn't know at first what it was. I knew I wasn't going crazy. I was probably lucky to have been trained and have all the psychiatric experience and worked with veterans and group therapy. But it wasn't clear what had happened. I saw—and this is not an exaggeration—eleven therapists and analysts for consultation at that point. It was 1979 now, still no *DSM*, still no huge opening up to treating PTSD and Vietnam veterans.

The reactions from the various people I saw were remarkable. I saw a very well-known, now deceased, Holocaust survivor analyst in New York City and told her what I had been going through. And by this time, by seeing all these consultants, I recognized that this had something to do with my Vietnam experience. So I told her all that, and oh, part of the angst that I had was crying. I would have these episodes of weeping. I don't know where they were coming from. And so I told her all of this. She pulls up her sleeve, showing her concentration camp tattoo, and says, "Do you really know what grief is? I'm not sure you do. Let me tell you what happened to me." And she's this wonderful, well-respected woman. She got very angry, and it was a larger version of what had happened with my first analyst.

CC: Yes.

AB: Anyway, I kept going. I finally said to myself, "OK, who do you think is the best analyst in the country?" And at that time the person I thought was the best analyst in America was Peter Giovacchini, who actually a lot of people thought was very good. So I called him on the telephone, and I said this is going on, I'd like to come and see you for a consultation. And what a remarkable response; he said, "OK, we'll work it out. Why don't you come and we'll do a double hour every day." And I went out to Chicago, I stayed in a hotel, and I did two hours a day. In the first session we went through all of this crap, and he said, "You have a traumatic neurosis." Thank you very much!

CC: It sounds like you had to rediscover PTSD. Because you went into the war knowing about it intellectually but didn't know how to see it, and then you experienced it but participated in the denial both personally and institutionally. Then after the death of your father, when it started to come back, you rediscovered it, but not as something you just knew about from books.

AB: I had to deal with it on my own inside.

CC: So you rediscovered it. You found it a second time.

AB: Yes. I hadn't thought of it that way, but it's very true. It was quite an experience. I was back in Vietnam. All the affect, all the memories. That's where I got fascinated with the idea of "freeze-dried memories."[11] One does not have amnesia for what happened. But there is no affect. And the image—if you add tears to the freeze-dried memories—they become alive. And I had that experience. It was quite startling. I would sit there and have dinner and play a movie in my mind of what had happened in Vietnam. Various scenes with various patients. Various scenes, this time with feeling.

CC: Did you think, at the time, that the grief response was to your father, or did you know that it was Vietnam coming back?

AB: I figured out it had to do with the notion of the "fatherland" and the war and the nature of the war. My father was a very patriotic, warmhearted, generous, conservative who never imagined that America could do anything wrong like that. And I was still identified enough with him that I couldn't face how truly an atrocity the war was. Intellectually I knew that. I was very clear about that. But emotionally I couldn't. When he was gone, I no longer had to worry about his reaction; I could face what I really thought and felt—if that makes sense.

CC: Yes, it does.

AB: And I think this happened with many people in relation to Vietnam, but it also figures in other experiences. When the society has gone bad, and in some very important ways is the cause of the trauma—which would be true for people who grew up in Germany, for example, or some other part of Europe in which the society came to participate in the destruction and the killing—if you're going to deeply recognize what happened, you've got to change your relationship to the society of which you're a native. And I think most people who were in Vietnam, for example, have experienced this.

CC: So it was the death of your father that allowed you to bring together the knowledge *about* trauma that you had as a psychiatrist (which nonetheless didn't allow you to see it when you arrived in-country) with the experience *of* trauma you yourself had in Vietnam (which led to your denying what you yourself had gone through), and that connection allowed you to begin, truly, to bear witness to the nature of the war.

AB: Yes. It was only after the death of my father that I rediscovered trauma, and in that rediscovery the notion of trauma began to attain some real meaning for me.

IV. The Beginnings of an Institution

AB: And then there was a remarkable coincidence. I gave a clinical conference at the VA hospital in the early summer of 1979 about some PTSD cases on the ward, and after the conference someone comes up to me and says, "Can you come down to my office? I'd like to talk to you." And he's a psychologist who has worked there for the past few years, although we had never met, partly because there was an ongoing feud between the chief of psychiatry and the chief of psychology. The two disciplines tended to stay apart.

So I go into his office, and he says, "I've just been hired to come down to Washington and head up a new system of counseling centers for Vietnam veterans nationwide. Max Cleland and Senator [Alan] Cranston and Jimmy Carter have gotten it though the Congress. And I was thinking you might be interested in helping with that."

I said I was interested. Within a few weeks I was at a meeting in VA headquarters here with that psychologist, Don Crawford, plus Charles Figley and John Wilson and other people who had been working already for a few years with Vietnam vets.[12] I ended up being the lead psychiatrist consultant to setting up the Vet Centers. There were going to be eighty-one of them around the U.S. All small, staff of four, mostly veterans, veteran mental health professionals. It was going to run for three years and then shut down. And that was going to take care of all this psychological disturbance of Vietnam veterans.

CC: So it was set up a little bit the way that Vietnam vets were originally treated—as if their trauma would go away very quickly.

AB: Right. So that was 1979. And I spent the next year helping to get the program going. And then I got a telephone call one day in Connecticut from one of the officials in the headquarters who said, "We need a new director of the program. Would you be interested?" My reaction (to myself) was "Oh, shit."

CC: Why?

AB: Because I knew I was interested, and I knew it was going to change my life.

CC: How?

AB: I didn't know for sure until I started the whole process. I came down to Washington and had thirty-two interviews with eighteen different people, including Charles Hagel, who was then the deputy head of the VA.[13] By the way, I think the number of vet centers now [2013] approaches three hundred, and they're open to combat veterans of all wars. They're doing a lot of good work with people coming back from Iraq and Afghanistan.[14]

CC: Listening to your personal history, which is also an institutional history, I recall your 1994 article, "Trauma Disorders and a Psychology of External Experience," which I referred to earlier, in which you write:

> Currently, there is an enormous flowering of research into and treatment of the trauma disorders. The thesis of this lecture, however, is that this thing is vulnerable and subject to repression because of lack of study of the traumatic events themselves, and that a psychology of *external* experiences is needed to provide permanence to the current revolution in psychiatric understanding of trauma . . . The critique offered here is that just as traumatic events often go directly from the environment into an internal dissociated sphere of the individual, bypassing cognitive processing systems, so, in the written scientific record of the psychological trauma field, the events themselves and their objective characteristics remain hidden, largely unstudied and not reported. This [is a] dissociation, so to speak, of the traumatic events themselves, in our field of study. (A12)

You seem to be suggesting that the experience of trauma, as a recording of an event that is not experienced as it occurs, replicated itself in the research on trauma, to the extent that this research repeated, rather than recognized, the deferral of the very event this research responded to and purported to study. So in the scientific record we got the medical definition of PTSD, even while the events themselves disappeared from the research.

You and your work, then, were like the unconscious record of the institution, which maintained a record of trauma between the *DSM-I* and the *DSM-III*, when PTSD had been removed from the *DSM* and was not officially recognized, and also after 1980, when the return of the definition in the *DSM* was accompanied by this deferral of the reality that lay behind the symptoms. What the recognition of trauma faced, consistently, was the returning force of denial.

AB: I can tell you an anecdote about that force of denial. I once was at a meeting here in Washington, after I came down here. We were working on the Vietnam Veterans Readjustment Study, so it would have been on the order of '85 or '86. I was at a meeting downtown, and one of the participants was the editor of *DSM-II*. He sat there for a better part of the meeting saying nothing. The whole meeting was about the intricacies of the diagnosis of PTSD in a large scale, nationwide epidemiological study. And he said nothing. And finally he erupted and said, in essence, "I don't know why we're doing this anyway. This is not a real disorder. It doesn't have a beginning, middle, and end."

CC: Oh, what an interesting comment! But there's some truth to that, right? That's precisely why it is what it is! Although we might say it has a beginning, it doesn't have a beginning, middle, and end.

AB: The way a panic disorder is supposed to. I am quoting him very closely. And then he kind of mumbled something or other, and there were like thirty or forty people there, most of them mental health professionals, and everyone kind of looked at him. The *DSM-II*[15] came out in '68. And this was '85. And there he was.

CC: So the man's denial continued. Why did they take it out of *DSM-II*, by the way, in '68, just during the war years?

AB: A lot of people think that the denial is specific to war, but this would also be true for rape, and is very much based on aversion to knowing. People just can't stand to know what happened. As a clinician I've seen a lot of denial that's based on an inability to shoulder the burden of treating. And if people are suffering and have pain and have symptoms and are reacting to these events, then as a physician I have a responsibility and an obligation of some kind. And I think that's a major factor in the mental health field still. I've had many, many therapists talk to me about this: "I don't know what to do, how can I treat these people? Should I try to treat them when I don't know how?"

CC: This makes me think back to one of your first comments a little while ago about how the problem isn't just about surviving PTSD but the fact that the rest of your life, or much of your life, will be shaped by the burden of figuring out what you experienced. And it sounds like you're saying that for clinicians, part of the problem in seeing these people is a little bit like experiencing something inexplicable that the clinicians are now going to have to spend their time figuring out. Because *they* now have the burden of understanding not their own trauma but another person's trauma. And their therapeutic lives are going to have to be shaped around figuring out how to change their own therapeutic methods to treat these people. And you're saying that they feel it's better to deny it.

AB: Like Freud and others who said that there couldn't be so many abused women around. There just can't be this many.

So I think it's too painful and horrifying and difficult for so many people and that it requires effort and structures and thought and care for people to be able to look at the external events as part of research. I've always experienced this from a different angle. Because of my immersion in the Vietnam experience and then with vets with PTSD, I found it absolutely impossible to read anything of, about, or from the Holocaust until my second analysis was under way, or maybe a little before that. So that would be, let's say, 1990. I couldn't cope with it. I couldn't bear it. It was too much. It was too painful. It was just overload. Overload of death and dying and torture and gruesomeness and so on and so forth.

And then the first thing that I read about the Holocaust that I could really allow myself to absorb was Terence De Pres's *The Survivor*.[16] And I really locked onto his discussion early on about the kind of language, the search for a language that would help, that would make it possible for anybody to come to terms with or grasp the phenomenon. Now, that's the kind of care that I'm talking about. Whether it has to do with social scientists, psychiatrists, or even to a certain degree psychoanalytic writers, all have a problem about, on the one hand, being clear we have to talk about the events that caused this and, on the other hand, figuring out a way of making it possible for people to read what we write when we do that. And that's the kind of thing that Des Pres is struggling with. And if you recall, in that book, *The Survivor*, he talks very directly about some terrible things. I still have trouble with reading the chapter about excrement. But even there he exercises care. One has to work not to traumatize the reader.

V. TRAUMA AS WITNESS TO BLINDNESS

CC: In many ways your story, then, and the story of how PTSD became a recognized diagnosis within various clinical and research institutions, involved a struggle with denial: not only with the learning of new facts, that is—such as the horrors of war—but learning the ways in which these things are systematically denied by individuals, cultures, and social and political institutions. This seems to illustrate the way in which the war was, in Daniel Ellsberg's terms, an "invisible war,"[17] even within the psychiatric field.

I am wondering if we might approach the symptoms of trauma from this perspective. I think you point in this direction, indirectly, when you append a particular story as an epigraph to your 1985 essay, "Irrational Reactions to Post-Traumatic Stress Disorder and Vietnam Veterans."[18] This is a story from Seymour Hersh's *My Lai 4*:

> When . . . correspondent Jonathan Schell was touring Quang Ngai Province in late summer of 1967 . . . a GI who was driving him around in a jeep suddenly turned and said, "You wouldn't believe the things that go on in this war."
>
> "What things?" Schell asked.
>
> "You wouldn't believe it."
>
> "What kind of things, then?"
>
> "You wouldn't believe it, so I'm not going to tell you," the GI said, shaking his head no. "No one's ever going to find out about some things, and after this war is over, and we've all gone home, no one is ever going to know."[19]

When you cite this story in your 1985 essay (and tell it in two other essays as well),[20] you seem to suggest that what veterans experience is not only various kinds of atrocity but also the refusal or inability of others to believe in this experience. I am wondering if traumatic symptoms such as the flashback—a form of seeing that is closely bound up with not knowing—could themselves be linked, in some way, to the lack of responsiveness, to the denial by others, that the soldier is talking about here.

AB: I would think about this in terms of Dori Laub's notion of the shutdown of the empathic other. He writes that if I am to understand what has happened, there has to be an other who can understand. We live in relationship with others from the beginning. And now that you bring it up, I think we could apply Dori's insight to the man who speaks to Jonathan Schell. What the guy is saying is "I can't imagine someone who would want to know and be able to know." So the symptoms, then, to expand on what you're saying, would in a sense have to do with a kind of expectation of the refusal of recognition by others.

CC: So the combination of seeing and not knowing in the traumatic experience, and in its repetitions such as the flashback, already anticipates, in a way, that there is no one who will be able to see or hear. Perhaps, then, the flashback doesn't only see the war but also the blindness of others, which then condemns this traumatic sight, itself, to its own blindness.

AB: Right. So part of what's traumatic about traumatic events is something about aloneness—being cut off, being alone—which could also include a conscious awareness that "my mother and father aren't going to understand and aren't going to be able to help me with this." It actually reminds me of a very interesting study that was published in 1982.[21] The author was a combat infantryman, a lieutenant in Vietnam, who after the war became a clinical psychologist. And he was inspired at a certain point to do a survey of his own officers' candidate's school graduating class from Fort Benning, which I believe was also the class of 1965. He sent them a fairly good PTSD questionnaire, and he found that the degree to which they said they could talk to their wives about their experiences in Vietnam after the war correlated more closely with the amount of PTSD than did the degree of combat exposure.

CC: This also seems to suggest that the traumatic symptom has, from the beginning, a kind of social or political implication to it, to the extent that it is bound up with modes of collective denial of reality. This seems to be the case, as well, with other traumatic events such as the Holocaust, which is why Dori Laub and Shoshana Felman refer to it as an "event without a witness."[22]

AB: And rape.

CC: And incest.

AB: They all violate the order of things, and they are all surrounded by denial. I'll tell you another anecdote that pertains to this. When the Research Triangle Institute (RTI) set out to do the Vietnam Veterans Readjustment Study, which was a definitive epidemiological study about PTSD and Vietnam, all of the questionnaires had to be submitted to OMB [the Office of Budget and Management] to be approved. That's what happens with a federally funded study. The original set of questionnaires developed by RTI included a set of questions concerning attitudes about the war—was it worth it, did we accomplish anything, etcetera, etcetera. And we had detailed discussions of how important the questions were because we wanted some data about whether or not that mattered in relation to the presence of PTSD symptoms. OMB wouldn't allow the questions. It took them out. They didn't want anybody to be asked about their attitudes on the war.

So that's one side of it. The other side of it is from my personal experience with the many vets with PTSD whose treatment I've supervised, consulted on, or treated myself, heard presented in case conferences, which is well over a thousand: I have never encountered anyone who had significant PTSD symptoms who did not have some significant questions and reservations about the nature of the war. I have never met a veteran who had genuine clinical PTSD who thought the war was just a great thing.

CC: And which would you say is the cause of which?

AB: Well I think that the sense of lack of purpose is very important. I think it's a major contributing factor.

CC: It does seem to me that PTSD is always a protest, whether it's PTSD now or back when Freud was studying it under other names; it's always a protest against something unacceptable, and that's why it's not just a pathology. It is a protest against what you describe as being "against the order of things," and it is a protest against denial.

AB: Right. I'm very interested in your idea also that the disorder is, has to do with, conveying history, bearing history.

VI. Learning to Listen

CC: If, indeed, we do think of PTSD as having to do with history, then how might this history come to be witnessed? Because it seems that you're saying that part of the truth conveyed by trauma is how this history is constituted, in part, by its denial. What would it mean, in that case, to bear witness?

AB: Well, the positive side, with both individuals and society, is that there may also be growth through trauma.

CC: What do you mean?

AB: I have described PTSD as a processing deficiency disorder, which is just a thumbnail way of saying what both Pierre Janet and Freud said, namely that things happen to people that they don't have the capacity to integrate, digest, narrate, understand, comprehend, fit in with their world views, fit in with their views of themselves. It's a foreign body. It's an experience that is a foreign body in the psyche.[23]

What happens in recovery and treatment is that one grows the capacity for processing. That's a very irregular and complex process. It's not a straight line or simple process. That's why Chaim Shatan, for example, talking about the original rap groups at VVAW [Vietnam Vets Against the War] in NYC, said that the vets would come and not come to the groups. They would go away and come back. The attendance was never very regular. He said he finally figured out that if somebody came once a month, they were slowly integrating it.

I have noticed this over and over again in working therapeutically with people. People are growing in a very deep way and need to develop the capacity for containing the experience. But it's a very complicated, deep, psychological growth process, and you can't see it much of the time. I think that's a reason for the coming and going. You could even look at what's happening in our society now: compared to where we were in the 1950s and 1960s, the openness to the trauma of war is enormous. We've got the American Psychoanalytic Association with a special program to try to get analysts to provide free treatment to vets, which would have been impossible in the 1970's. The VA has also hired a thousand new people to deal with PTSD, so you can look at that as having resulted from growth.

CC: It seems that the growth, as you describe it, is something that involves a fundamental change of frameworks, new ways of seeing that weren't there before. Like when your father died, and you said it allowed you to realize that we did do these atrocities.

AB: Yes.

CC: And that knowledge is not just factual knowledge. It's ethical knowledge, which changes you. And also political knowledge. So you had not only to take in a fact that was hard to assimilate but actually to shift your entire concept of what it means to be an American, or even . . .

AB: . . . a psychiatrist. I had to forgive myself for not being able to help any of the patients I saw in Vietnam.

CC: What do you mean?

AB: Well, I never was able to help anybody. We weren't allowed to.

CC: So part of what you were going through after your father died wasn't only that you had nearly been killed and had also been witness to other people being killed or facing death but also that you had not been able to help them?

AB: Yes. And I was the national director of the Vet Centers from 1982 to 1994, during which time the staffs of the Vet Centers saw about 500,000 people— Vietnam veterans—with PTSD. Saw another million people for employment and other problems. I think among other things, I was making up for what I was unable to do as a military psychiatrist.

CC: I see. So the people you saw were your witness to the people you didn't help. In a way, then, two things were going on. Because it seems like you were bearing witness personally, but you were also bearing witness institutionally for previous institutional failures.

AB: That's a very interesting point, and it's probably still going on to some extent in the Department of Veterans Affairs. But I had planned to remain in that position for two years and then go back to New Haven. I ended up staying twelve years. One of the reasons for that is that the program was under fierce attack within the bureaucracy at the point when I got there. And we actually spent about five years defending it against attacks, both from parts of the Congress and from the VA establishment. It was forced down the VA's throat in the first place. Senator Cranston spent ten years trying to get the Vet Centers legislated. He got them passed three times by the Senate and three times they were voted down by the House, or not brought to a vote. Jimmy Carter was the first president of the United States to get involved directly. He had two ceremonies at the White House in support of Vet Centers. And then it was enacted only for three years.

In order for me to do my job as director of the Vet Centers, which involved helping myself and a great number of other people work out their Vietnam experience, I had to become a street fighter in the bureaucracy. I was fortunate enough to have a deputy who had grown up in the barrio and who was much more comfortable with all of that than I originally was as a Yale psychiatrist. Because we were fiercely attacked and ambushed—attacked in broad daylight and under the cover of darkness. I mean people really wanted to destroy it as soon as possible. But anyway, I had to change. I really had to develop my skills as a bureaucratic in-fighter, which I did do. And I had to be prepared to learn about that from other people, not just the deputy.

CC: It sounds like in that process of fighting, you converted your emerging personal witness into a means of helping the country through its governmental institutions. Because the fact that it took so long points to the government's (and the country's) own need to process the war.

AB: Yes. The Vet Centers were first introduced by the Senate in 1969 but not legislated until 1979. This unusually lengthy period of time signals that the government and the nation were having to overcome the history of the government's betrayal of its citizens, which it had consigned to a senseless war.

CC: So the collective and political nature of the trauma demanded a political form of response: not only in terms of ending the war but in terms of bearing witness to the trauma created as a result of the government's own blindness. And this political response was in part constituted by the creation of the Vet Centers, which had to go through a political process, the approval within the government, in order to be established.

AB: The creation of the Vet Centers by the Congress and the president was a political act of facing the history of the Vietnam War as experienced by veterans, family members, journalists, and at least indirectly the Vietnamese people, via the establishing of hundreds of thousands of dialogues in the framework of coun-seling or psychotherapy. So there was an emergence of collective witnessing in books, papers, poetry, the national Vietnam Veterans Memorial with a recently added learning center, all of which continues to this day. The individual witness-ing or therapy and the collective or political witnessing are interactive; once ei-ther starts, they facilitate each other. This interaction has been present from the beginning, with the rap groups in New York in 1969, in which telling the story of what was experienced was associated with public education and activities to enlighten the public about the war. Thus, individual and collective witnessing were interacting with each other from the beginning.

VII. Psychoanalysis and Trauma

CC: You pointed out early in the interview that you took psychoanalysts' cat-egories into the war with you. What does psychoanalysis add to the thinking of trauma, or what does Freud add, that perhaps isn't recognized adequately through general psychiatric uses of the *DSM*, or why do you think that being a psychoanalyst can help either in treatment or as a theoretician of trauma?

AB: I love the question, and I'm working on that. But right off, I would say that the first line of contribution is in treatment. If I'm right in my basic concept, then PTSD is a processing deficiency disorder. That is to say that people lack the wherewithal with which to understand what has happened in their world and life. The kind of therapy that helps people grow is psychoanalytic therapy. But people have barriers to the kind of growth that they need to do in order to com-prehend the experience. A simple example is the "just world hypothesis." Some of us have the concept that life is fair and life is just and the world is just, and depending on what we've learned from our families, we more or less believe that. In order to deal with having been raped, if you have had a just world hypothesis entrenched in your psyche, you're going to have to get over that. You're going to have to agree with John Kennedy—life is unfair.

But you can't just change overnight. The psychology of developing new per-sonality structures with which to contain the experience is very complicated. And that kind of complexity, taking a lot of time, and involving, maybe, deep emotional contact with the other person, those are all the stock-in-trade of psy-choanalytic therapy. And this is one reason why Laub and Auerhahn's writings are so relevant. Jacob Lindy has also written very relevant things about this.[24]

CC: Doesn't psychoanalysis also have to be changed, then, by rediscovering its own past?

AB: Yes. It's very interesting that the relational movement and the self-psychology movement in psychoanalysis are very much oriented toward the treatment of severe trauma. So working effectively with trauma survivors and the development of the relational and self-psychology movements have gone hand in hand. That's one of the most rewarding areas of psychoanalysis.

CC: Do you think psychoanalysis can become a place where those realities that are not socially acceptable can begin to be entered into the record?

AB: That's a very interesting question. Maybe. I think that's possible. Certainly the Warrior Project that's going on in the American Psychoanalytic Association right now suggests that possibility. The literature of the relational and self-psychology movements and also contemporized classical psychoanalysis is directly addressing sexual trauma like never before.

CC: So psychoanalysis is beginning to become a site of memory, an archive of war. Because it seems like the memory is handed over to your profession, which can do something with it or not. It seems like what you're saying is that it's beginning to be a place where trauma can be archived, if not in the culture.

AB: I would say that psychoanalysis is building the conceptual structures with which to better contain and understand the effects of severe trauma, in a fashion analogous to how the individual survivor must grow in order to recover from post-traumatic shock. This effort can be seen to begin to emerge in the analytic literature in the 1940s but has been accelerating since the 1970s, with the Vietnam veterans movement, the women's movement of the 1980s, the appearance of the analytic understanding of traumatic neurosis in the PTSD diagnostic criteria in the *DSM* in 1980 and since, and the flowering of the treatment of severe trauma effects in self-psychology and relational psychoanalysis, and thus psychoanalysis generally, ever since.

Coda: The System Is Weeping

CC: In the dedication to the book you coedited, *The Trauma of War: Stress and Recovery in Vietnam Veterans*,[25] you and your co-editors tell the story of a man, Eric M., who was not diagnosed properly after coming back from Vietnam. In spite of frequent attempts to get help, his PTSD went unrecognized. Eventually, Eric M. killed himself. For years his wife fought unsuccessfully for compensation, which she was denied repeatedly because her husband's suicide had not been officially linked to the war. But finally, in 1980, the year the *DSM* recognized PTSD, she received a positive decision for compensation for her husband's death:

Upon hearing the news of this decision by the Board in 1980, a Vietnam veteran psychologist observed, "The system is weeping." Since 1980, there has been no river of tears, save perhaps among veterans and their families at the Viet Nam Veterans Memorial in Washington, D.C. The "system"—our institutions and the professions—appears however to be attempting to fully confront the challenge of healing the psychological wounds of the war. This attempt, yet tense and painful, is still uncertain of outcome. (xi)

This is a very moving statement. What does that mean to you, "the system is weeping"?

AB: What happened there was he was awarded service recognition for PTSD several years after his death. As far as any of us knew, that had never happened before. And it came about because of an unusual combination of things. Specifically, all of his letters from Vietnam described his mind falling apart under the impact of certain events. Another thing was that I got involved in writing up the case. And his wife was very dedicated to her husband's cause. And the person who made that statement was thinking that maybe the system was changing to some extent.

CC: So the weeping is like the weeping that loosens up those freeze-dried memories, which you mentioned before.

AB: The system is showing some feeling.

CC: And yet we hear just recently that the suicide rate in active-duty (and returned) veterans was at a new high in 2012.[26] So it seems like there is more weeping to be done.

AB: There's a lot more weeping to be done.

NOTES

1. *Diagnostic and Statistical Manual of Mental Disorders*, 1st ed. (Washington, DC: APA, 1952). Hereafter all editions of this work will be referred to as the *DSM*.
2. Otto Fenichel, *The Psychoanalytic Theory of Neurosis* (New York: Norton, 1945).
3. *Diagnostic and Statistical Manual of Mental Disorders*, 3rd ed. (Washington, DC: APA, 1980). This is the first edition of the *DSM* that contained the specific term "post-traumatic stress disorder."
4. See Cathy Caruth, "Traumatic Departures: Survival and History in Freud," in *Unclaimed Experience: Trauma, Narrative, and History* (Baltimore: Johns Hopkins UP, 1996).
5. The Tet Offensive was a military campaign during the Vietnam War that was launched in January 1968 by the Viet Cong and North Vietnam against South Vietnam and the United States forces. It took place during the Tet holiday, when no attacks were

expected. The Tet Offensive is generally credited with turning the tide of American opinion against the war.

6. See Murray Polner, *No Victory Parades: The Return of the Vietnam Veteran* (New York: Holt, 1971).

7. Arthur S. Blank Jr., "Trauma Disorders and a Psychology of External Experience," William C. Porter Award Lecture, *Military Medicine* 159 (Apr. 1994): A11–A16.

8. Sarah Haley was a clinician who wrote an important article entitled "When the Patient Reports Atrocities: Specific Treatment Considerations of the Vietnam Vet," *Archives of General Psychiatry* 30 (1974): 191–96; Chaim Shatan was a psychiatrist who, with the psychiatrist Robert Jay Lifton, participated in the "rap groups" with Vietnam Vets against the War (VVAW); Jack Smith was a member of VVAW who became involved with the process of creating the PTSD diagnosis in *DSM-III*.

9. Arthur Egendorf is a Vietnam veteran and psychologist who has written on healing after the war. See Egendorf, *Healing from the War: Trauma and Transformation after Vietnam* (Berkeley: Shambhala, 1986). Florence Volkman Pincus and Robert Shapiro were psychologists in practice in New York.

10. Haley, "When the Patient Reports Atrocities."

11. The origin of the phrase "freeze-dried memories" is unclear, but Dr. Blank and Raymond Scurfield in "Post-Katrina Aftermath and Helpful Interventions to the Mississippi Gulf Coast," *Traumatology* 12.104 (2006), attribute it to Chaim Shatan, author of the "The Grief of Soldiers: Vietnam Combat Veterans' Self-Help Movement," *American Journal of Orthopsychiatry* 43.4 (1973).

12. Don Crawford is a psychologist; Dr. Charles Figley edited early important books on trauma and continues to write in this field; John Wilson is a psychologist at Cleveland State University who has written extensively on PTSD. See, for example Wilson, *Treating Psychological Trauma and PTSD* (New York: Guilford, 2001) and *The Posttraumatic Self: Restoring Meaning and Wholeness to Personality* (New York: Routledge, 2005).

13. Charles Hagel is a veteran of Vietnam who has served as the U.S. Secretary of Defense since 2013.

14. For more on the Vet Centers, see Arthur S. Blank Jr., "Vet Centers: A New Paradigm in Delivery of Services for Victims and Survivors of Traumatic Stress," in *International Handbook of Traumatic Stress Syndromes*, ed. John P. Wilson and Beverley Raphael (New York: Plenum, 1993).

15. *Diagnostic and Statistical Manual of Mental Disorders*, 2nd ed. (Washington, DC: APA, 1974).

16. Terence des Pres, *The Survivor: An Anatomy of Life in the Death Camps* (New York: Pocket, 1977).

17. Daniel Ellsberg, "Introduction," *Papers on the War* (New York: Simon & Schuster, 1972). On Ellsberg's notion of the "invisible war" in relation to PTSD, see Cathy Caruth, "Confronting Political Trauma (On the 25th Anniversary of the U.S. Withdrawal from Viet Nam)," originally published in Japanese in *Tokyo shinbun*, July 2000, and reprinted in English in *Connecticut Review* 28.1 (2006).

18. Arthur S. Blank Jr., "Irrational Reactions to Post-Traumatic Stress Disorder and Vietnam Veterans," in *The Trauma of War: Stress and Recovery in Vietnam Veterans*, ed.

Stephen M. Sonnenberg, Arthur S. Blank Jr., and John A. Talbott (Washington, DC: American Psychiatric Press, 1985).

19. Seymour M. Hersh, *My Lai 4: A Report on the Massacre and Its Aftermath* (New York: Random House, 1970).

20. See also Arthur S. Blank Jr., "Apocalypse Terminable and Interminable: Operation Outreach for Vietnam Veterans," *Hospital and Community Psychiatry* 33.11 (1982) and "Operation Outreach: The Therapeutic Model," Vet Centers Working Paper, Apr. 7, 1980.

21. S. Frye and R. A. Stockton, "Discriminant Analysis of Posttraumatic Stress Disorder among a Group of Vietnam Veterans," *American Journal of Psychiatry* 139.1 (1982).

22. Shoshana Felman and Dori Laub, *Testimony: Crises of Witnessing in Literature, Psychoanalysis, and History* (New York: Routledge, 1992).

23. On the "foreign body," see Josef Breuer and Sigmund Freud, *Studies on Hysteria* (New York: Basic, 2000).

24. See, for example Dori Laub and Nanette Auerhan, "Annihilation and Restoration: Post-traumatic Memory as Pathway and Obstacle to Recovery," *International Review of Psychoanalysis* 11 (1984), and Jacob D. Lindy, *Vietnam: A Casebook* (New York: Brunner/Mazel, 1988).

25. Dedication, in Sonnenberg, Blank, and Talbott, *The Trauma of War*.

26. See Timothy Williams, "Suicides Outpacing War Deaths for Troops," *New York Times*, June 8, 2012, and Bill Briggs, "Military Suicide Rate Hit Record High in 2012," nbc news.com, Jan. 2013.

Mieke Bal and Françoise Davoine in Vevey, Switzerland, November 26, 2011.

Chapter Twelve

Filming Madness

A Conversation with Mieke Bal and Françoise Davoine

Mieke Bal is a leading cultural and art critic and a video artist whose theoretical and artistic endeavors have crossed the boundaries between literary, theoretical, and visual art. It was her idea to create a film version of Françoise Davoine's *Mère folle* (*Crazy Mother*, 1998), working in conjunction with filmmaker Michele Williams Gamaker.[1] Françoise Davoine is a psychoanalyst in a public hospital and private practice, as well as professor at the École des Hautes Études en Science Sociales, whose clinical and theoretical work on madness has reshaped this notion in relation to traumatic history. (See the interview with Dr. Davoine and Jean-Max Gaudillière in chapter 4.) The book *Mère folle* takes as its point of departure the death of one of Davoine's patients at the psychiatric hospital in Paris where she worked for more than thirty years. Through the framework of her experience and reflections on this event—and in the form of a fictional narrative interspersed with case histories and theoretical reflections, invented dialogues and turbulent, carnivalesque events—she attempts to provide a new way of thinking about madness and history, which emerges in the literary and theatrical traditions of fools. These traditions of folly, she shows us, have much to tell us about political and historical truths we would prefer not to see. I interviewed Bal and Davoine on November 26, 2011, in Vevey, Switzerland, the morning after the film had its Swiss pre-premiere at the Fondation de Nant, and asked them about varying modes of witnessing in the book and the film.

The film's creators describe *Mère folle* as follows:

> Tomorrow is All Saints Day. In the present, Françoise the narrator just
> learned of the death by overdose of one of her psychotic patients [Ariste].
> Discouraged, she blames herself and blames psychoanalysis for this failure.
> She is tempted to abandon her job at the psychiatric hospital. While ponder-
> ing this decision in the courtyard of the hospital, she is suddenly accosted by
> medieval fools who challenge psychoanalysis as fraudulent. Their primary
> grievance is the privileging of the word over gesture. But a crisis is harder
> to actually live than she had thought, and reluctantly she returns to work
> anyway. There she talks with patients, and slowly the distinction between the
> fools and the mad fades away. Françoise is struck by the unexpected wisdom
> both groups bring forth.
>
> Exhausted and dejected, she goes back home, parks her car. In her own ga-
> rage, she is abducted and begins a strange voyage. She is taken to the Middle
> Ages—or else, the Middles Ages surface in the present, in a small Parisian
> theatre. She is brought before a court where she is blamed not for the death
> of her patient but for lack of insight. The episodes of that court case confront
> her, and us, with the sanity of reasoning hiding behind the fool's mask. The
> "fools" come from the tradition of *sotties*, a political theatre from the late
> Middle Ages that puts on stage a trial of the abuses of the present time. The
> main character is Mère Folle, Crazy Mother, calling her fools to the scene of
> a judgment that is a kind of carnival of fools. These fools merge with the pa-
> tients at the hospital. But as opposed to the patients, the fools have apparent
> impunity.
>
> The narrator's own literary and philosophical sources, in turn, also mix
> in during the trial, in the form of imaginary or dreamed dialogues with
> great thinkers such as Antonin Artaud, Ludwig Wittgenstein, T. S. Eliot, and
> Friedrich Nietzsche. The film also tells the story of another mad patient with
> whom Françoise struggled, a woman named Sissi, who was abused by her
> father when she was a child, and whose analysis is told in juxtaposition with
> the story of Françoise's attempt to deal with the death of Ariste by overdose.
> As Françoise attempts to think through the memory of Sissi's analysis from
> the point of view of Ariste's death, she is transported back to her early years
> as a psychoanalyst. She also comes to realize, at the end, that Ariste's refer-
> ences to a concentration camp in World War I called Holzminden, where his
> relatives had been—a claim she had taken as delusional—was in fact a true

story.[2] Ariste's madness was linked to this traumatic past. (The film is set in Paris, in a psychiatric hospital in Finland, in Spain, and in Basel, Switzerland.)[3]

Madness as Witness to History

I. FACING DISAPPEARANCE

CC: I would like to begin with a comment about *Mère folle* as a book and as a film. Both of them are in many ways about madness. They tell the story of a psychoanalyst, Françoise, who works with mad people, who loses a mad patient, Ariste, and who is then confronted by fools from the Middle Ages (apparently played by patients from the asylum). The book and the film are also, themselves, full of seemingly delusional shifts: between the present and the past, between true madness and staged madness, and between living patients and dead ones.

Yet if the book and film are about madness, they also seem to make a very strong claim for being about history, and indeed for bringing into appearance certain historical events that have hardly been known before. Madness seems to have a privileged relation to history, and in particular to a history that has disappeared: that has been denied or has been left out of the history books and cultural memory. There are references to events in World War I, World War II, wars in Spain, torture in Iran, and more, and the film includes photographs of a hardly known World War I concentration camp referred to by Ariste as "Holzminden." Several scenes, in addition, are performed on the site of a real psychiatric clinic with a dark past.[4] The film thus seems to suggest that these events are occurrences that have disappeared from the history books and that are now reappearing in the context of the mad patients and their treatment.

So on the one hand, we have the representation and enactment of the delusions and distortions of the mad. On the other hand, we have precise historical references that claim to make new historical realities emerge.

My first question, then, is what is the relation between madness and history in the book, and how is this relation restaged in the film? Or, put somewhat differently, what is the relation in the book and the film between the disappearance of history and the appearance of madness? What kind of witness might we be said to have in the book, on the one hand, and in the film, on the other?

FD: You speak about a paradox. And when you are confronted with madness, of course, you are pushed away from any understanding, and all your rational interpretations fail. At the same time, the patient drives you into a realm where you have to be a witness, as you say, but this is only incrementally reached. It is not that right away, for each new patient, you say, "Oh, you look haggard, you are a witness, and there is history there!" [Laughter] It doesn't work like that. So the paradox you are describing is at work for each person who comes to see you. Each time you are baffled. And each time you are facing disappearance. You are made to experience this disappearance, which is, first of all, the disappearance of your categories, the fading away of common rationality. You try to understand, each time, and you fail, and only then can you start to be at that place of a witness.

CC: So each time you don't know what will happen. You cannot say, "I know there is a history here." You are actually faced with a complete lack of understanding.

FD: Yes, that is why what you say speaks very eloquently. Because the historical disappearing and reappearing are staged inside the relationship between the analyst and the patient. You face the disappearance, you know, because your categories disappear.

CC: What happens first, then, is that instead of observing a disappearance of an event, you enact it through the disappearance of your own understanding.

FD: Exactly.

MB: We took as our basis what Françoise wrote in the book. We do not theorize it, we do it. But how do we do it in a medium that is both audiovisual and public-oriented? We are not facing the patient, we are facing a public, which is a different level altogether. So with regard to the idea of facing disappearance and fading away, what we try to do in the film is to make the disappearance itself visual, or rather audiovisual. And the way we try to do that is by staging it. Take the character of Ariste, who is, on the one hand, already gone from the beginning, and on the other hand he is the main character. Throughout, he remains a ghost, a specter. He is there, and he is not there. And his disappearance has to be kept alive, somehow, so that the disappearance can be a new ground for an appearance. To do that, we had to have him fade in and out of the image and to be an object of talk by others who miss him, who grieve for him, who grieve at the way he was treated, who gossip about the psychoanalyst.

And in the end his truth comes out because at that point, Françoise, the psychoanalyst, has gone back to her own past enough to be able to face the past of the other. And the image of the World War I concentration camp Holzminden can come only at the end, after Françoise has failed to see, has failed to believe Ariste, failed to read the book about the World War I camps, failed to do the research, and now he is dead. But it was true—Holzminden was a real place, a real concentration camp—and the image comes, and it comes fading through her image at the end. So now you can see her enacting the fading-away. We work with a public that we want to entice to go along on that quest and become those witnesses, too.

CC: So just as Françoise enacts the disappearing history through the disappearing of her understanding, our categories of understanding—as an audience—are visually disrupted because we see the film but cannot completely make sense of it. We have alternating times, and we have this phantom of Ariste—what you referred to now, and in your short piece on the film, as a "specter"[5]—that keeps reappearing. And we begin to put into question Ariste's reality. And through that process we are put in a parallel position to Françoise.

MB: We are not asking the audience to identify completely with Françoise's position; we are asking the audience to be witness to the process between Françoise and Ariste and the memory of Ariste. So it is another level of witnessing. Because we cannot work with identification in a simple way.

FD: I was thinking—concerning what you said, Mieke, about the fading away and the specter returning—that it is as if when you start with a patient, you are confronting an invisible wall of denial. And you bump into that. Even if something of the history is said right away, you forget it. It has to be erased. So you contribute to the denial because this history that is mentioned is so light and so bypassing. The trauma is introduced as, "Oh, I've been raped and that's normal" —the tone of voice, the information is like on TV, when you look at the news, and it's "Oh yes, many died."

CC: One can tell a story many times, but the telling of the story is, indeed, not necessarily the witnessing of it.

You said right now that you contribute your own forgetting, and I recall that in the film you had two books, one you kept forgetting to read and one you kept forgetting to bring to Ariste. You have the book about Holzminden, but you forget to read it. Is that the forgetting by the analyst that you are talking about? And the other book is a textbook of literature on the Middle Ages and Renaissance that Ariste had asked you for, which you kept forgetting to bring him. When you bring it after his death, too late, you stop to read it in the courtyard of the hospital, where the medieval fools appear, so to speak, out of this book. Later on, another book will be given to you by Don Luis, an old friend, showing the photo of the camp of Holzminden mentioned by Ariste.

So the truth, which you said can only appear at the end, is not only about the camps at Holzminden. The truth of Holzminden, would you say then, is also the truth of the forgetting of Holzminden?

MB: Yes, that is wonderful. I think it is really important that it is not the truth that you see. In Holzminden it is not Holzminden as such, it is the image of Holzminden superimposed over Françoise's face. It is her being able to see Holzminden that becomes visible, so we see her seeing.

CC: So first of all it seems like a truth of denial that is coming out in the psychoanalysis. The truth in the story of Ariste involves the truth of Holzminden and the truth of the denial of Holzminden. You seem to be saying that in the film we see the truth of the denial as well as the emergence of the witness to it.

MB: Françoise's access to witnessing is what we get to witness.

II. Seeing without Seeing

CC: This brings me to a remark made by a doctor who saw the showing of *Mère folle* last night and participated in the ensuing discussion, Dag Söderström. He commented on what was being brought out by the book and the film in different ways. Normally, he said, psychotic patients are considered not to have insight: they don't reflect on themselves so they don't adequately see what is going on inside of them. But the film, he says, shows that what they see is on the outside, and they see too much of the outside. As I understood him, he was suggesting that the psychotics' delusions are not exactly distortions. They rather make something appear, from outside, that had not been adequately seen before.

FD: In the film, the patient Herlat says that there is "no boundary between me and the others." So "inside" is not a relevant category; the boundary of the ego is not there. There is, rather, a scanning, what Aby Warburg would call "the seismograph of my soul": there is a seismograph, and it is on the alert.[6] Madness tapes what is banalized; it tapes it as denied; it is a tool to record the denial. I always give this example: a baby is at the breast and his or her mother receives a telegram about some catastrophe, someone's death. That baby stops sucking; it is a baby's knowledge because he hears the pounding of the heart or he catches glimpses of body language, which is a language game.

CC: That helps explain why the film would be so important as a film, something that also records. The psychotics, you seem to be saying—it's an impossible figure —they record denials. They record what cannot be recorded.

FD: Let us say, rather than "psychotics record denial," that "psychosis records denial," for one is not crazy twenty-four hours a day.

CC: And the film is actually recording visually and aurally. Is there something that the film does that shows, differently, individuals' or society's lack of recording certain events?

MB: That was the challenge for the whole project. Which was why we were taken in by it, because we thought, "This is something that I have to learn to do; we cannot do it, nobody has done it." And so we tried all sorts of tools of cinema, of cinematography, where you have sound, you have music, you have voice, you have lights, you have body language. I think this is basically why theater is so important in this film, as the other of the cinema and as the predecessor of cinema. It is the past of cinema but also cinema's possible partnership with the outside. The theater shows an outside; it is not about the inside, it is the outside, and it is another form of seismography of what is going on out there. So it was very important, in that respect, that the actors had the freedom to bring their own interpretations. Because if we had been directors who do what they usually do, saying "do it this way," we would have missed a lot of what the actors brought in, with their own, unreflected, unconscious body language. And there are certain moments of improvisation in the film that would only happen in performance on the stage and not in the cinema studio.

CC: So you are saying that the theater also has a way of recording something from the outside. But in this case the theater is a mad theater. It is the fools' theater, so it does not seem to be recording something that is simply available; it is not recording something you could see in any simple way.

MB: It is extreme theater.

FD: In a sense, you did something, Mieke, to those recordings by putting the previous patient, Sissi, in the present with the analyst. I will give just one example. In my book *Mère folle*, I read the notes that this patient, Sissi, obliged me to take while she was speaking. I read them once she was discharged, and I understood, then, that everything I had written of what she was telling me as a patient in fact described her scanning my reactions to her. But Sissi wasn't there when I recognized that.

What did Mieke and Michelle do? They replaced me with another Finnish analyst—Marjo Vuorela, who is actually a psychoanalyst in Finland—and you can see in her face the interaction between her and Sissi.[7] She makes subtle facial movements when she enters the room and you see on her face an "Oh!" Then Sissi says, "Why do doctors blush when they look at us?" It sounds like a very general statement, and you cannot understand immediately that Sissi is talking about the analyst. Because in psychiatric hospitals, patients often speak without directly addressing you. They speak and they look elsewhere. So you say, "Oh! Good! It's not me." But in fact it is addressed right to you. So you collude in the denial. And then Sissi says, "But why do they blush?" And she continues,

"Because they are ashamed of us." So the issue of shame, both for the patient and for the analyst, has been brought out. That is a wonderful staging, by the film, of something in the book that you make present.

MB: Yes, it was very important that Sissi be present, although in the book her analysis with Françoise is in the past, it is retrospective. But we had to bring it into the present, and, in a sense, stage her analysis as if it were after—rather than before—the moment of Françoise's writing. In one scene, Françoise is reflecting on Sissi after the treatment, and then in the next scene you see Sissi in the treatment with the Finnish woman. That is how we change the book, by bringing Sissi into a second analysis.

CC: So the second analysis is also telling us about the first analysis. It sounds like, in this second analysis, we see the effects of this patient-analyst interaction on the body, on the face, on the image of the body, on the clothing. And we see Sissi's response to the blush. We actually see the body as the recording device. So it is not only the acting but the body, too, that registers and transmits. The theater is also a bodily theater that records what is happening.

MB: The fancy clothing was our way of realizing and visualizing Sissi's dreams of grandeur. They became the theatrical costume of her delusion, and at the same time a tool to recuperate some dignity in the face of her abjection. I have a colleague in theater studies who wrote this fantastic phrase, "theatricality is a critical vision machine."[8] And I think that is very deeply true. A critical visual machine: which means, first of all, that it is showing critical happenings, but also that it is showing them critically. And that is why theater is so important. It does this is in the present of the viewing experience. So we want to bring theater back into cinema in that way.

CC: So there, too, you have a temporal reversal. Instead of saying, "We have progressed from the past of theater to the present of film," film is, rather, being inflected by this disappearing past of theater. And it seems like that is another line of witness in the film. To the extent that film would presumably surpass, and perhaps erase, the history of theater, it was going to erase a specific theatrical history, in this case the sottie, which is a particular kind of theater, and one that is linked to madness and folly.[9] You made it present again, within a cinema in dialogue with theater. For example, the character Artaud appears as a thinker of the theater of madness in the trial scene of the film, which is staged as a medieval theatrical mock trial. So in a way the film is also bearing witness to the disappearance of a specific theatrical tradition, which is the theater of madness that is inscribed within the history of film.

MB: And its return is staged as well. We tried to make the film integrate the temporality—or rather the non-temporality—of madness, and of this cultural history of the theater. We bring into the film the erasure and return of the theater. We tried to make a film that is theatrical in its temporality while restaging the erased political street theater. So that the witnessing can happen, also, for a certain "low" cultural history that we need to re-vitalize in our struggle against social madness.

CC: So perhaps we could say that if psychosis is providing, through its delusions, a kind of archive of a history that can't simply appear, the film is doing something similar by archiving its own history: one that disappears through its very showing. And the temporality of that is never going to be straightforward.

FD: What we are speaking about is not inscribed. We have to constitute the archive. The moment there is a witness, there is an archive, but before that, there is no archive. The witness is the event, waiting to be addressed.

CC: So here is that temporality that you are talking about. Because something is being archived that has no history until the moment that its archive is created. At this moment, a memory is created in order to allow for this history to come into being. So it would seem that this history you are talking about is what we call a traumatic history, a history that disappears . . .

FD: That history has been negated, forced to disappear. Now I would emphasize that there are forces that make it disappear. There is a violence of erasing.

MB: This is violently erasing; it is a totalitarian process.

CC: So the forgetting has a political dimension as well because it is something that does not have to happen and it does not naturally happen, but there is a kind of force to it. Would you say, then, that some of the violence of the delusions is, itself, a recording of the violence of that suppression? And in what way would the film add specifically to the witness of this suppression, by performing or staging the book, which performs, or stages this history through madness? Does the film also stage the violent suppression?

MB: I think that one instance where you can see that happen is with Sissi's mother, who holds on to her denial about the previous abuse of her now-mad daughter and who says, "I never said, I never did, anything wrong." Why didn't Sissi's mother tell the truth about what was being done to Sissi by her father? The mother's answer is, "They would not have believed me. They would have thought I was bad-mouthing their father." And she thus rationalizes her turning away from what was being done to her daughter by her own husband. So Sissi has been denied the possibility of acknowledging what happened to her, by her mother among others. In that sense we had to stage the mother in this denial.

In the film Sissi never says anything about the abuse literally, but we have her come in with an Issey Miyake dress that has an Ingres painting on it, which is a painting of an antique sculpture, *La source*, which has bare breasts—to show, essentially, what she is now able to say: "My father was fondling my breasts."[10] Thus she enacts it. She is not touching her breasts, but you see that she has some difficulty breathing; you see it is almost there, it is a volcano, it is going to erupt, but it stays somehow on the edge, on that boundary of the body. And the dress is the boundary.

CC: In choosing a dress with a painting with that name, were you thinking of the phrase that Ariste uses, when he says that he is looking for the "land of sources"? In that sense Sissi would also allow us to witness, or to bring back, the source that Ariste is looking for but cannot find.

MB: Yes, the topic of the source runs through the film: finding the source, divining, being sensitive to the other. I think this searching for the source—rather than finding it—is a metaphor for the seismography that psychoanalysis itself is.

FD: What I find very interesting is what you revealed, Mieke, that I had not really seen. The mother in the book, for example, says explicitly that the father wanted to poison her. Of course everybody, in the hospital, said she was paranoid—"Look at this schizogenic (meaning inducing schizophrenia in her children) mother, she is toxic. . . . " When Sissi asked me to see her mother for a consultation, I just trusted her. For the mother, too, there was no witness.

There is death all around her. She lost her older daughter. Sissi says, "There is someone dead. I have to wear a black dress. I have a cardboard illness in myself." It is her sister's tuberculosis. The only girl who tried to escape and left the family at seventeen years old to become a seamstress, died in her twenties. The dead are all around. When I reread the files afterward, I understood what she meant by firing me that I had not understood. But what I did not quite grasp, and you revealed in the film, was the rape by her father. I had registered it. You rightly placed emphasis on showing how the mother did not let her daughter leave the house because the mother would say . . .

MB: "I need you." And thus, implicitly, "I need you to be right by your father every night because I did not see that."

FD: At that time, I focused on the so-called insensitivity of Sissi's mother. As I saw her regularly in the dispensary, she disclosed little by little the hell she endured. I was astonished how her daughter in the hospital, so to speak, could build on that opening a space to think, without knowing what her mother had said.

CC: So Mieke and Michelle registered what you did not see.

FD: What I knew without knowing.

MB: Seeing without seeing.

III. Trauma Speaks to Trauma

CC: This problem of seeing raises another question about how these untold histories emerge in the book and in the film. You, Françoise, come to understand the story of your patient Sissi—and, belatedly, of Ariste—through your emerging relation, in the analyses with your patients, to your own partly unconscious history, which includes your parents' histories. And you, Mieke, tell Françoise's story, and thus those of the mad, in part through the film's relation to its own cut-out theatrical history. So it seems that, in both cases, one history speaks through another.

FD: Jean-Max [Gaudillière] always says, "Trauma speaks to trauma." It is just as in London during World War II, when de Gaulle spoke from London to the resistance fighters in France: the French spoke to the French.[11] Thus, trauma speaks to trauma. It's foreign stories that resonate with each other because they travel a common path on which they pursue their research. Both use the other in order to make appear that which disappears.

CC: I think what is also coming out here is both a possibility—that my trauma speaks through your trauma—and a betrayal, because your trauma and mine are absolutely incomparable.

FD: Yes, but remember, as I said to the medieval fools in the film during the trial, "In your time, plagiarism did not exist." They could use whatever they wished as they wrote. They would use a version of Percival or Lancelot or Arthur and would transform it with their own ideas. The other would never protest.

MB: On the contrary, it was an honor.

FD: Mieke and I had an argument. She said, "Am I betraying you when I make such changes?" And I said, "No, you are enriching me." Not me exactly, but the book, because it emerges from authorship—which is something that comes from the very root, *augere*, which in Latin means to augment, to author. Of course there could be vampirism, there could be a perverse use of a story or text, and they did not like it either at that time. But that is not what we are doing; we dialogue together.

CC: So that is why we have the fools together as a group. There's also humor; it is a film that is very funny. And you are also working together.

FD: I will give you an example. When *Don Quixote* was written, Shakespeare immediately made a play of it, which is lost. He didn't say to Cervantes, "Please give me your copyright." It happened in the same period that a plagiarist published a sequel to *Don Quixote* in order to ruin the novel. Cervantes was furious and wrote the second part of *Don Quixote*. Shakespeare augmented the story; the other just distorted it.[12]

MB: I'd like to return, in this context, to the question of cinema reflecting on itself in relation to its past, and the relation between different histories. One of the themes that runs through the film is how Françoise needed to get to her own past in order to be able to understand and to see what happened to Ariste. So right after he dies, in the beginning, and you see his specter, the movie shifts to the young Françoise, who says to the younger Don Luis (a figure we modified, a friend of Françoise's father), "I was just reading a story about an Iranian woman in prison." Don Luis responds, "Does it make you think of your own history?" And she says, "Exactly," although up to that moment she hadn't realized it. That self-implication is very difficult because it cannot be a direct identification, which would be an appropriation. One cannot say, "Your trauma is mine." But putting yourself in that space in-between—to have the guts to do that and to come out of your protective shell—that was necessary. We had to do that for cinema, too. Cinema had to come out of its shell and put itself at risk by acknowledging theater and actually making theater.

FD: That's fantastic.

CC: So we have something that is not quite film and something that is not quite theater, and there is a risk, a danger and a risk as in a psychoanalysis, where you (as analyst) come out of yourself—you are no longer just you—in order to be in the space between you and the patient. So to speak from trauma to trauma is not to speak from two places of presence because both are, in a sense, not present to themselves. And you are saying what happens occurs in between.

MB: Yes.

Psychoanalysis as Witness to Madness

I. Fools of the Future

CC: We have been talking about psychosis as attempting to bear witness to history, and we have already started to see how in order to tell that story, psychoanalysis has to become witness to madness. So we seem to have a second testimonial story line in the book and film: we are not just talking about madness and history but also about psychoanalysis and madness. How does psychoanalysis, then, bear witness to the history of the mad, or of madness? It seems that bringing in the fools from the Middle Ages and merging them with the patients in the asylum is telling us that we have forgotten a way of relating to madness that existed before. That is, in order for the mad patients Ariste and Sissi to tell us something about history, psychoanalysis has to tell us something about the history of madness itself, and how the notion of it has already disappeared for us.

FD: I address you, Cathy, as coming from literature. This literature is very important; madness was never, as historians tell us, so well received and was not listened to. People were given a bang on the head, like electroshock today. And the theory of madness as brain damage was always there.

MB: From the beginning.

FD: Since the Greeks. So madness took refuge in literature. We have the Greek tragedies . . . It was often only literature that enacted a psychoanalytical cathartic process by which madness might tell us something and be witness. And the fools say that if we were not in the novels and in the romances, you wouldn't know that we existed. It is not all literature, of course, but literature coming out of trauma. A special kind of literature, which is a kind of ritual, which is also something that enacts a process of catharsis, of making a language out of images. A transmission. So, over the centuries, in every culture, you have either oral transmission or oral myth. Myths are stories of madness, all the time, and they record what has happened and has been transformed into a myth after this transposition. Otherwise, madness looks for an inscription along generations.

CC: So it's not just that once we were more aware of madness and now we've lost our presence to madness. Madness is something that was always disappearing from history. And literature was always having to bring it back.

FD: Yes. There were no "good old times"! I believe it was around 500 years BC, for example, that Greek tragedies were put on the stage in Athens in order to create the catharsis of traumas. The rule was not to mention the actuality, in order to avoid traumatic reviviscences and to transpose crimes, incest, rapes, murders, and other abuses into the realm of mythological time. Another rule was that every citizen had to attend it. This theater was a healing ceremony.

CC: So at the heart of the suppression of madness is the suppression of the trauma, of the traumatic history.

MB: The danger, what society fears, is that the trauma will come out in the madness. The societal space is always political and public. That's where the danger is. The mad can go into the woods. That's fine; they have their clutches, and they kill animals. The wild man is fine. But the madness cannot be in the public space, which is appropriated by the political.

CC: So it seems that the literary, as the site of this madness—as what tells us both about madness and about its disappearance—is going to be a political site as well, and not just outside the political, as one often thinks of it. Thus the truly forceful political response to a history that is denied, a traumatic history, may emerge at the site of literature, rather than more directly through some other form.

MB: Yes, but I want to qualify that a bit. Literature is the record we have of it because it is written. But the performances—the live performances, of course—got lost. There are other modes of recording madness, like the gargoyle—hence the actor who's playing a Fool in the film who's enacting the gargoyle, which is a mad monster. They're on the cathedrals. They're there. We have them, as we have literature. But we forget that they are a record of madness.

CC: When you say "literature," here, you seem to mean "art," not as the beautiful or the Hegelian "sensuous expression of the Idea" but rather as an expression of what cannot be expressed elsewhere. An allegory in that sense.

MB: Right.

FD: At that time, they were most likely capable of telling stories around those monsters. The monster recalls, to people, the whole story that they have lost. So it's a language game, in the end.[13]

CC: But it's a story that has to be lost. In this case, you say it's a story, a storytelling, but it's a storytelling of a story that can't be told in the public realm. So it's really not "stories" in the ordinary sense. Nor is it "expression" in the ordinary sense, because what is told—or what is expressed—is not available in any ordinary form. It's not available as a simple story.

FD: Yes, but there are various forms that can trigger a story, stemming from intense impressions registered by the body.

MB: Think of the moment in the film when the man is playing the gargoyle. He is the monster, the madman. He starts to lick his foot. And, at the same time, the other mad guy, the Tall Fool, is invoking the carnival in Basel and talks about "the noble parts indeed," as when psychoanalysis put the psyche away from the head into the lower body. The one man is licking his foot, but licking your foot is also licking your wounds. And then you see the carnival in Basel. So that's a moment where these two different times, performed by the mad "gargoyle" in the asylum and by the people in the carnival, come together to enact something that's not a story: the wounding and the licking of the wound, on the one hand, and the attempt to overcome the wound, on the other. That is a moment in the film where you have a potential story, and you can fantasize a potential, but it's only a potential story.

FD: Like children, who tell us stories all the time. I do that too! So you see that gargoyle and you start a story.

CC: So is the way in which psychoanalysis stages something and then the film stages it the starting of the story rather than the actual story? In that case it would not be exactly storytelling. It's the possibility of storytelling throughout, rather than the actual story itself.

MB: And that's why it doesn't bother me when people say, "I didn't understand the whole film." I want it to stay in their heads because they couldn't work it out. So they can make further stories.

CC: And so they have to tell another story later. The witness in this case is still to come. So in regard to this film, if we talk about witness, it means making possible a story. The witness is not simply present, although it's not simply absent. Something is happening. Something is being shown, but the showing is about something to come in the future.

MB: Exactly. That's very good, yes.

FD: In the case of something written, you have some traces. But with the oral it's a potential, it's a hope, it's an expectancy, it's the dimension of expectancy. The witness is not always there. But there is the expectancy of a witness.

CC: So you're not only witnessing the past. You're witnessing a future witness.

MB: That is creating the condition of witnessing: the compossible.[14]

CC: So the witness witnesses a past history that hasn't been told, by witnessing the future witness. That would be us, potentially, who are yet to come.

FD: And that's exactly what happens in the analysis of psychosis, of trauma. As an analyst you know that you're not the witness right away, but you stand in for one. And you know the expectation is that "some day, perhaps, I will be at that place."[15] So it's a potential. Which changes everything because the psychosis as it is experienced and theorized does not meet the conventional opinion that your mind is impaired forever.

CC: So, in a way, what we call the past that isn't there, the erased past, is also the future.

II. Landscapes of Trauma

CC: I want to talk now about the relation between the film, which is in a sense belatedly born from what is not yet available in the book, and the book itself. As you say, Mieke, we have in the film an image that "re-images" what is in the book.[16] But in the case of trauma, the original image was never simply available as an image. It was an uninscribed history. So if we have an afterimage in the film, it's an afterimage of something that was not present. What does "afterimaging" mean in the case of a traumatic history?

FD: *Landscapes of Madness* is the title of a book written by a Mexican psychoanalyst, Alberto Montoya, who plays the character of the young Don Luis in the film.[17] Here I have a specific example of what you did, Mieke. In the book, I go to the cemetery of my grandparents in the Franche-Comté, which was Spanish from 1556 until the eighteenth century. In the film, Mieke and Michelle create from scratch another landscape of craziness, bringing me to Bullas, Spain, near Murcia. When they were first doing the filming, she showed me the shots she took of that landscape. And she said, "I am betraying you, because instead of being in France, which would be too local a scene, I am putting these scenes in the civil war in Spain." But I said, "Oh, that's a landscape of the Franche-Comté!" Because that area was Spanish at one time. So, by chance, we had, here, a disappeared history coming back. Because she could have chosen Italy or America or wherever. But it was Spain. The disappeared Spain of the Franche-Comté appeared in this image. That was amazing. So we could relate then, through the landscapes.

CC: I see—the afterimage, then, is also about the relation between traumatic histories. That is, the afterimage we have—an image from Spain, which is the image from France—is both a repetition of a trauma and an invention, to a certain extent, because it is creating something new.

MB: Of course you never create something from scratch. By listening to the social resonances of the world it becomes possible to stumble on a territory, which in this case is both Spain and the past of the Franche-Comté. It's not pure coincidence. It's not pure creation. Nor is it simply repetition. It's all those things together. But I really strongly believe that it's our seismographic "feelers" that try to get at what really is, rather than the anecdotal tools, for example, of Françoise's autobiography. We wanted to get away from that.

FD: And these tiny details can make bridges to other tiny details that resonate. Wittgenstein said, with regard to Frazer's *The Golden Bough*, that the dangers in life, be it for the natives or the white people, are represented in limited figures.[18] Although you can represent the threat with a lot of little details. Still, the threat is the same.

MB: And to come back to what you said, Françoise, about choosing this landscape in Spain as a landscape of madness, instead of the Franche-Comté. The great thing about cinema—and here we come to cinema as a medium—is that it's out of our hands. We can choose the filming site, but what appears in the image we cannot entirely control. The scenography of the image is one thing that we as directors can set up, but the actors do what they feel is right at the moment we film, and the set itself may have elements we cannot remove or prevent from appearing. In our conception of the collective endeavor that is cinema, we appreciate these two unforeseeable elements.

Art as Witness to Psychoanalysis

I. Psychoanalysis on Trial

CC: This leads us, finally, to a third issue that I would like to address. The narratives of the book and the film involve a trial, which is at the center of the story about Françoise and Ariste. It is the trial of a psychoanalyst in relation to the death of her patient, or perhaps more importantly, the trial of psychoanalysis in relation to the madness of the patient and to the history he has tried to tell through it. In the end, Françoise, the psychoanalyst, is sentenced to go to the carnival at Basel. But this is not simply a condemnation; it also seems to be a way of rethinking psychoanalysis in terms of the madness it must encounter, and perhaps was always bound up with from the beginning.

What did it mean to you, then, to approach the problem of psychoanalysis and madness through the story of a trial of psychoanalysis? Do these questions always arise when working with mad patients? Or is psychoanalysis, in the context of madness, always put on trial?

FD: Historically, those trials were the canonical shape that the theater of the fools took. It was a little like the International Court in the Hague, nowadays, a way to judge the abuses of the time. This was also in the law schools' mock trials, which would try matters that escape the law. Ultimately the question was, how can we judge people that are above the law and who just make fun of the law as they rule the country?

In this sense, the trial addressed a problem that is, we would say from the perspective of analysis, how to judge things that are erased from existence. How could we make a judgment—a judgment is also a thought—about something that is expelled from language? How can we think about it? So it's judgment in both senses.

So it's an issue of the law when there is no law. When there are no ancestors' laws anymore, what happens? And when there is no thought. It's unthinkable. The Real, the unthinkable, the unimaginable. The trial is all about that.

CC: So it's something of an impossible trial, though also necessary.

FD: And they have a solution; that's what is amazing at that time. But the issue of the trial is not to say, "This is good, this is bad." It's not a dualistic issue because we know that even if you say, "that man is bad," he will continue to rape, if he can. Or the tyrant will do what he does. It's an addiction. That will never stop.

So the issue in the sottie is that at the end, all the fools jump on the abuser— the king, the Pope, the whatever—and strip him of his clothes. Under his garments, he's dressed like a fool. Because the perverse use of power is to hide behind double-talk. Like Tartuffe! Tartuffe is an addict of power, but he hides that under his pretense. Thus when you talk about the character of the analyst going to Basel, you are touching on the fact that she must go confront the masks of the carnival. And what are the masks? They are the monsters that inhabit the place that they refer to in the Middle Ages as "the space of the marvel": the forest, the wild space, the mountains . . .

MB: The space in between.

FD: . . . the space in between, this space of the marvel, where fairies, spirits, etc., come. In order to confront my foolishness or my own roots that come from this wild space, I have to be in touch with these agencies. As if they could teach me about my belonging to that space too.

CC: The discussion of the king dressed as a fool made me think of some of our contemporary political satire, our late-night political TV shows that do satirical news skits, which make us laugh in order to make political points.

FD: Oh yes, we have to speak about laughter.

MB: There is a Dutch feminist film I saw from the '70s or '80s, *A Question of Silence*, where four women arbitrarily kill a shopkeeper.[19] They are put on trial. And at some point, there is a psychoanalyst who is asked to give expert testimony concerning whether they are sane or mad, and he can't decide. And then the women say, "No, we are sane." And the judge says, "But my dear madam," in that condescending tone. And at that point, one of the women, then another and another, start to laugh. And they laugh for ten minutes, and that's the end of the film. And at the end of the film, the whole audience was bursting in laughter. We went home on our bicycles and we had no light on the bicycles. A policeman stopped us and we laughed—and he had to let us go. He could not give us a fine because we couldn't speak our names, really. Just kept laughing.

CC: I think of "The Laugh of the Medusa" and of various anecdotes of laughter before the king.[20]

MB: Laughter makes the simple upholding of power impossible.

CC: In the case of the book *Mère folle* and the film, the political gesture is very specific: if there is something political in your art here, Françoise and Mieke, it would have to be in relation to something that, as we have discussed earlier, is not simply or readily available to us. The art makes a kind of social-political gesture in a space where we do not have straightforward knowledge to work from. So what kind of a gesture is it?

MB: First, to clarify: As I use the terms, "politics" and "the political" are opposed to each other. Politics is the institutional power based on consensus; this always excludes and silences those who don't consent. But this institutional politics is not what we are talking about. We're talking about the political as a social domain where people can disagree, be empowered by the possibility of disagreeing, of speaking up, and of bonding and interacting socially around that. That domain is constantly depleted by the politics that regulates it. So laughter in the feminist film is a subversion of that. The judge cannot judge.

But in general, I think art is also a domain where people are invited, enticed to respond to something that cannot be said, that cannot be revealed, in a way that allows it maybe to surface a little better. I have published a book about the Colombian artist Doris Salcedo, whose whole life work is about grieving, about allowing the mourning of the death of those who have been disappeared in her country, Colombia, as well as other places.[21] About all that anonymous violence, that bureaucratic violence. All the violence that really kills people or makes their lives impossible. And she protests not the violence per se but the erasure of it. And that protest is through art. That is the political.

Coda: The Land of Sources

CC: I want to close with something more personal. Françoise, in *Mère folle*, as we said at the beginning of this interview, you write about a book that you had kept forgetting to bring to Ariste, a book he had asked for which tells about the theater of the fools. You remember, too late, after he has died, to give it to him. And there is another book you have forgotten to read, the book that includes a reference to Holzminden. But then you write a book yourself, which is *Mère folle*. So in a way, we have *Mère folle* instead of the forgotten books. To me, that's very moving. It is also a gift. I wanted to ask you, first of all, if you experienced this as a gift, both to him and to us.

FD: Yes, a sort of give away and a return. I received the film as a gift.

CC: So your gift to him, and his gift to us, is the book you write. Would you say, Mieke, that the film also, perhaps, gives us a gift from Françoise, who cannot simply master this situation, cannot simply give directly what she wants? What may you have been giving?

MB: Yes, I think the film is, in a sense, another version of her gift, but also another way of demonstrating that the book is performative. It made us want to make the film, to visualize the erasure and the need for witnesses. By showing a film, you bring it to life in a different way and that makes it possible for people to participate in that possibility of witnessing.

CC: So if you "bring it to life," as you say, maybe there is something in Françoise that died with Ariste but that now survives in your film.

FD: I want to tell you personally something that is very precise on this point. My mother wanted to erase all of this past that I brought to the film in coming to understand Ariste. The war she went through, her imprisonment by the Germans during World War II, but also her roots. I wrote that book to make it appear again. And so that's what Mieke showed when they chose those landscapes that were meant to be erased.

CC: So what died with Ariste, you're saying, also has to do with your mother.

FD: Not died exactly, but meant to disappear. There are countries that have no value, that are considered archaically restrictive and regressive.

MB: The great thing about the medium of cinema is that you need a setting. You need to do it somewhere. And so we have to choose a good setting. And so we chose Finland for the scenes in the asylum, for example. And the landscape that came with it. We could not have done it without landscape.

CC: So the landscape is the site of the survival. What you cannot give us in the writing but comes through the landscape in the film.

FD: Exactly. I remember one of my first patients, whom I didn't understand very well. He was completely delusional. But he said, "I have a little landscape I go to every time. I have a little landscape." From this landscape where I managed to join him, he stepped out of madness through our common work and research, but that's another story.

CC: The land of sources.

FD: Indeed.

MB: The desire for the landscape. And that is what the film gives us, as Françoise's patient also does. A way to enter that world.

NOTES

1. Françoise Davoine, *Mère folle: récit* (Strasbourg: Éditions Arcanes, 1998), trans. by Judith Miller as *Mother Folly* (Stanford, CA: Stanford UP, 2014). *Mère folle*, a film by Mieke Bal and Michelle Williams Gamaker (Cinema Suitcase, 2012), is part of a larger project, *A Long History of Madness*. See www.miekebal.org/artworks/installations/the-mere-folle-project/. The film has also been included in an installation project, *Saying*

It, at the Freud Museum in London (2012). See Mieke Bal, Michelle Williams Gamaker, and Renate Ferro, *Saying It* (London: Occasional Papers, 2012).

2. Holzminden is a town in Lower Saxony, Germany. During World War I, the town had a "concentration" camp that held up to ten thousand Polish, Russian, Belgian, and French nationals, as well as a prisoner-of-war camp for British officers.

3. This description is adapted with permission from the synopsis on the film's website, http://crazymothermovie.com.

4. The scenes with Sissi and her Finnish therapist were filmed in the old Hospital of the Holy Ghost on the island of Seili, off Finland. Apparently the women entering this mental hospital were asked to bring their caskets with them, as no one ever left.

5. This is from an unpublished presentation on the film.

6. Aby Warburg (1866–1929) was a German art historian and founder of a renowned private library for cultural studies, who was also hospitalized in Binsanger's clinic in Switzerland and, while in the psychiatric institution, gave a famous talk on the ritual of the snake among the Hopis, which led to his release.

7. In the book, Françoise remembers the therapy she conducted with her former patient Sissi. In the film, Françoise is replaced by a fictional Finnish therapist, who reads notes that, in reality, Françoise had written.

8. See Maaike Bleeker, "Limited Visibility," in *Art and Visibility in Migratory Culture: Conflict, Resistance, and Agency*, ed. Mieke Bal and Miguel A. Hernandez-Navarro (Amsterdam: Rodopi, 2011).

9. A *sottie* is a short satirical play common in fifteenth- and sixteenth-century France. The word comes from the *sots* (fools) who appeared as characters in the play. In the plays, the fools—jesters—through the virtuosity of their gestures and verbal games, would convey their criticism of contemporary abusive deeds and individuals. The *sotties* originated in the Feast of Fools and other carnival-related festivities. The *sottie* and other related events attempted to present the world turned on its head, with the fools providing their own insights.

10. Jean Auguste Dominique Ingres's *La source* (completed 1856) shows a naked woman in the cleft of a rock holding a pitcher of flowing water. She is presumably meant to represent a water source or spring (and more broadly, a source of inspiration).

11. Charles de Gaulle gave a famous radio address from Britain, to which he had escaped during World War II, broadcast by the BBC on June 18, 1940. In this address he exhorted the French people to resist the Nazis. This formula, "the French speak to the French," spoken after the first notes of Beethoven's Fifth Symphony, would continue to open the Radio Londres broadcast to occupied France from that date until the end of the war.

12. Françoise Davoine, *Don Quichotte, pour combattre la mélancolie* (Paris: Stock, 2008), trans. by Horacio Pons as *Don Quijote, para combatir la melancolía* (Buenos Aires: Fondo de Cultura Económica, 2012), and *À bon entendeur salut! Face à la perversion, le retour de Don Quichotte*, with clinical essays by Jean-Max Gaudillière (Paris: Stock, 2013).

13. The term "language game" comes from Ludwig Wittgenstein's *Philosophical Investigations* (1953). See Françoise Davoine, *La folie Wittgenstein* (1992; rev. ed., Bellecommbe-

en-Bauges: Editions du Croquant, 2012), trans. by William J. Hurst as *Wittgenstein's Folly* (New York: YBK, 2012).

14. "Compossibility" is a philosophical term used by Gottfried Wilhelm Leibniz and refers to incompatible things that can coexist with each other. On Mieke Bal's use of this term, see her *Quoting Caravaggio: Contemporary Art, Preposterous History* (Chicago: U of Chicago P, 1999).

15. See Françoise Davoine and Jean-Max Gaudillière on the "Thomas Salmon principles" in *History beyond Trauma*, trans. Susan Fairfield (New York: Other Press, 2004), reprinted as *Histoire et trauma: la folie des guerres* (Paris: Stock, 2006).

16. Mieke Bal refers to "re-imaging" in her presentation on the film.

17. See Alberto Montoya Hernández, *Paisajes de la locura* (Mexico City: Paradigma, 2006).

18. Dr. Davoine is referring to the following passage from Wittgenstein's remarks on Sir James George Frazer's *The Golden Bough*:

Eating and drinking have their dangers, not only for savages but also for us; nothing more natural than wanting to protect oneself against these; and we could think out protective measures ourselves.—But what principle do we follow in imagining them? Clearly that of reducing the various forms of danger to a few very simple ones that anyone can see. In other words, the same principle that leads uneducated people in our society to say that the illness is moving from the head into the chest &c., &c. In these simple images personification will of course play a large part, for men (spirits) can become dangerous to a man and everyone knows this.

Ludwig Wittgenstein, *Remarks on Frazer's Golden Bough*, ed. Rush Rhees, trans. A.C. Miles (Nottinghamshire, UK: Brynmill, 1979), 6e.

19. *A Question of Silence* (*De stilte rond Christine M.*), dir. Marleen Gorris (Quartet Films, 1982).

20. Hélène Cixous, "The Laugh of the Medusa," trans. Keith Cohen and Paula Cohen, *Signs* 1.4 (1976): 874–93, originally published as "Le rire de la méduse" (*L'arc* 45, 1975).

21. Mieke Bal, *Of What One Cannot Speak: Doris Salcedo's Political Art* (Chicago: U of Chicago P, 2011).

Shoshana Felman at her home in Tel Aviv, Israel, July 24, 2013.

Chapter Thirteen

A Ghost in the House of Justice

A Conversation with Shoshana Felman

Shoshana Felman is one of the world's leading literary critics and theorists and a founder of the contemporary notion of "testimony" in the context of traumatic histories. On August 7, 2013, I met with her in her home in Tel Aviv to discuss her ideas about testimony, language, and history, with particular focus on her essays on the trial of Adolf Eichmann[1] and on the testimonial dimensions of her own intellectual itinerary.

I. THE SURPRISE OF TESTIMONY

CC: Your book *Testimony: Crises of Witnessing in Literature, Psychoanalysis and History,*[2] co-authored with Dori Laub in 1992 is now, twenty years later, a classic. It established for the first time the theoretical notion of testimony in the context of the humanities—a notion that has spread to many disciplines outside of the humanities as well. The term "testimony" has broad resonance today, in large part as a result of your work, but it also means something very unique and specific in your own writing. Could you tell me what you mean by the notion of testimony?

SF: To bear witness or to testify is what is called a performative utterance; it acts in very specific ways.[3] The best way to illustrate this might be by giving an example of a literary writer who, as such, considers himself a witness. Elie Wiesel says, in one of his essays, "If someone else could have written my stories, I would not have written them. I have written them in order to testify. My role is the role of the witness. Not to tell or to tell another story is to commit perjury."[4]

Elie Wiesel is a Holocaust survivor, and his literary writing is trying to testify to a new, contemporary function of literature. There are more and more writers nowadays who see their role as one of testifying, either to a historical event or to an injustice or to a catastrophe, or to something they feel needs to be addressed to others and made sense of or healed. So I have elaborated my thinking from the sense in which Elie Wiesel says that it is only he who can write his own stories and nobody else can. And in general, to bear witness in this enlarged sense is to take responsibility for truth. And that means to speak—implicitly—from within the legal pledge of the witness oath, whether one is actually on the witness stand or not, whether one is in a trial or one is in the court of history. One can testify before a court of law in the most restricted sense, but writers also testify before the court of history, and the court of history usually means the court of the future, of posterity. We too, as readers and spectators, are also witnesses in the second degree to what we are reading.

To bear witness is thus always more than simply to narrate or to report a fact or an event, or even to relate an experience (narrate what is relived or what is remembered); it is always a use of memory or of one's experience *in order to address another*. This capacity to address is very important—it is an appeal to another, to other human beings, and more generally, an appeal to a community. To testify is, in this sense, always metaphorically to take the witness stand, and the narrative account of the witness is always implicitly engaged both in an appeal and in an oath. In other words, to testify is not merely to narrate but to make a commitment, to commit oneself and to commit one's narrative to others. This also means to take responsibility, in speech, for history and for the truth of an occurrence. And this commitment goes beyond the personal. There is a paradox here, because while testimony goes beyond the personal toward the public or the general or the universal, there is only one specific person, one specific subject who can bear witness to what he/she has experienced, and no one else can report what this particular subject has lived and narrated.

So the question that I ask myself in the book *Testimony* is, what is it in the witness's speech, which is so uniquely and literally irreplaceable, what is its uniqueness and what constitutes its irreplaceability? And here I return to the sentence of Elie Wiesel, "If someone else could have written my stories, I would not have written them." What does it mean that the testimony cannot simply be reported or narrated by another in its role as testimony? What does it mean that a story cannot be told by someone else? And that is in my view the defining feature that is specific to testimony.

CC: You started out by saying that testimony is performative, and I hear two different ways in which language is acting here. First of all, you say that in all testimony, whether or not it is in a courtroom, the one who testifies is taking an oath, as one takes an oath, in a trial, to tell the truth. In the courtroom this particular performative utterance seems to be bound up with the performative dimension of the legal language of the trial as a whole, its power not just to describe things but to effect things. But you also say, with regard to your notion of testimony, that there is an address, which is not a performative utterance in the strict sense but does involve some form of action. Can you say more about what it means to say that testimony is an appeal or an address?

SF: It means that it is an appeal to a community. In a trial, testimony is addressed to the judges, it is addressed to the audience of the trial. It's always a communication. It's an utterance that only the witness can narrate, and it is addressed to a specific audience that should be affected by this testimony.

CC: There is some pathos for me in hearing that, and thinking about the paradoxical dimension of testimony, as you described it. On the one hand, there is the singularity of the testimony, the fact that no one can replace me in my testimony, perhaps similarly to the way in which no one can replace me in my death. And on the other hand, the testimony is an appeal to a community. So while the testimony is an attempt to make a bridge of some kind, it comes from a place of loneliness. There is a gap between the loneliness of the testifier and the community he or she is trying to reach.

SF: This reminds me of a lovely quotation that I put as an epigraph to my book, *Testimony*. It is a short poetic text by Borges called "The Witness." "Great deeds," Borges writes, "may cause us wonderment, but one thing, or an infinite number of things, dies in every final agony, unless there is a universal memory."[5] In an elliptical way, Borges suggests that in every testimony is included a wonder, a wonderment, a surprise, but also an agony that is the death, or the capacity to die, of the witness. So that temporally the capacity for a human subject to testify is limited, "unless there is a universal memory." For this reason the testimony is usually directed toward something universal, or some record of memory that will survive the witness and would become a collective memory. It is always shared. In the legal context it is shared with the court but also implicitly with the community.

Borges ends the paragraph by asking (from the witness position), "What will die with me when I die?" This explains why, for instance, people have established video archives of Holocaust survivors' testimonies, like the one at Yale that I encountered while I was teaching there (which was perhaps the first).[6] Because the thinking is that the survivors who witnessed the event will not be living indefinitely, and thus they are called upon to narrate their stories.

CC: The notion of being called upon to tell a story brings me to a question about the singular trajectory of your own writing and teaching career. Prior to writing *Testimony*, you were known for your work in literature and literary theory, and also in psychoanalysis.[7] *Testimony* seems to involve more directly referential and historical issues, specifically the Holocaust, which is potentially closer to your own history. What was it that led to your interest in doing this work, and specifically in theorizing the notion of testimony?

SF: I'm not sure how close it is to my own history, because no immediate members of my family, at least to my knowledge, were Holocaust survivors—they were already in Israel. In any case, at home my parents never mentioned members of the family who had died in the Holocaust. So the Holocaust did not constitute a real force in my emotional life until I was a professor teaching at Yale and I unexpectedly encountered the testimony of somebody I knew from childhood. I had been aware of the Video Archive for Holocaust Testimonies at Yale and had watched some of those testimonies. One day my childhood friend from Israel, Menachem, who had in the meantime become a physician, visited Yale in his professional capacity and told me he had also given a testimony for the video archive. I watched the videotape and was totally flabbergasted. This was someone I had been very close with in high school; his life story—which I discovered on the videotape—was extraordinary, and I had had no clue about it. When we were at school together, we used to go to movies together. In our shared adolescence, he was my very close friend for a while. I had always thought that he was a born Israeli like the rest of us. He had never said that he had gone through any horrifying, atrocious, or tragic experience. He had never said a thing about his past.

And then I learnt from the videotape that he was a child survivor of a concentration camp from which, at the age of four, his parents, in order to save him, told him to run away.[8] He survived for a few years with gangs of children on the street. His mother had given him a picture of herself, and every time that he despaired he looked at the picture of his mother; she had promised him that after the war she and his father would come and find him. He survived through the street wisdom that he developed and also through the trust and the belief that he would eventually be found by his parents and would reunite with them. He did ultimately manage, miraculously, after the war, to find his parents, but they came back from a concentration camp; they returned like ghostly shadows of themselves, and he didn't recognize them and couldn't accept them as his parents. So he called them "Mr." and "Mrs." They were strangers, and at first he refused to address them as "mother" and "father," could not call them "Mom" and "Dad."

Menachem had apparently never talked about this even to his wife or his family. He just kept it under silence, until he came into contact with the video archive at Yale and they managed to convince him to give his testimony. So on the videotape I saw somebody who was very close to me from childhood, whom I did not realize had a past that was so tragic and traumatic, and so heroic as well—to have survived that way as a child. I realized that around me were children who had a completely different fate in history and that they could keep it under silence as Menachem did in such a way that I, who was his very close friend, did not know anything about it until we were both in our forties and I saw the video testimony, at Yale University of all places.

This drove me to become more interested in the video testimony work of my colleague Dr. Dori Laub, a psychoanalyst who was among the founders of the video archive at Yale, and who had himself been a child survivor. I saw how important his work was, because Menachem told me that the giving of this testimony was a turning point in his life—he felt a great sense of relief and his nightmares ended. I realized that giving testimony produced a sort of revolution in people, in their lives, in their destinies. And I thought, what made it so important? There was something in the very essence of testimony that needed to be theorized. It's not only the empirical fact that survivors were going to die, after which there will be no more first-hand witnesses. It was a kind of instinctive response to record and to archive, to create an archive of history or of the memory of trauma, to try both to preserve—to share, and to understand—those traumatic destinies. So I decided that I wanted to reflect on the meaning of this whole endeavor, working henceforth in collaboration with Dori Laub, to see if a theory of testimony could be conceptualized out of this existential practice. Later I decided to give a course on these emerging reflections, a course that I entitled "Testimony," in which I included a number of literary writers, along with two video testimonies of Holocaust survivors from the Yale archive. That was the beginning of this direction in my research.

CC: It sounds like what drove you, first of all, was this enigmatic silence that was broken by the testimony. And second, when it was broken, you discovered that your own community was more than one, that there were, as you said, different histories in it, and different fates.

SF: There was a foreignness. To the native Israelis of my youth, survivor experience was very, very foreign, and it was a completely different formative, historical, political, and cultural makeup. It was both heroic and terrible. And I was profoundly impressed by the fact that a child could keep all of that anguished memory in total silence, so that none of us suspected that such was his past. And probably there were more like him, many more silences that surrounded us.

CC: So that was, for you, a very concrete experience of testimony, as being bound up with something that was muted and reduced to silence.

SF: Yes. From the beginning I conceived of testimony as the counterpart of a silence that was also bound up with an oath to silence. The survivors who returned from the secret gas chambers (and especially the *Sonderkommandos* who were sworn to silence by the Nazis) continued to consider themselves as "the bearers of the silence." They referred to themselves that way.[9] And the strength of the continuation—of the surviving loyalty to that oath—was very awesome.

CC: In your notion of testimony, then, the oath to truth is struggling with an oath to secrecy. So in that sense when you said there was something revolutionized in Menachem, and in what you saw on the videos, part of that revolution was being able to replace that imposed oath to secrecy with discourse. To break the silence was a real act, the breaking of an oath and replacing it with another oath—to truth.

SF: Yes. Replacing it with an oath to speech. With a commitment to truth and to communication.

II. A New Language

CC: It is interesting that your work on testimony began in a sense with a return, the return at Yale of someone from your childhood, someone from your early life in Israel. I would like to discuss your next book, *The Juridical Unconscious: Trials and Traumas in the Twentieth Century* (2002), from the perspective of another return, your own (symbolic) return to Israel (your native country) in the later development of your thinking about testimony. In *The Juridical Unconscious*, you consider the problem of historical, collective testimony as it emerges on the stage of the legal trial. You show how the courtroom becomes a site of memory, a site that both reenacts, and through this reenactment may bear witness to, collective historical trauma. You conceptualize a constitutive relationship between trial and trauma. But the two chapters on the trial of Adolf Eichmann in Jerusalem[10] carry an extra weight, beyond the theoretical analysis, because they involve what for me is a highly significant, a highly revealing critical encounter between you and (the work of) Hannah Arendt, both Jewish intellectuals who literally (in her case) and intellectually (in your case) travel to Jerusalem to think about issues of justice and testimony in relation to the Holocaust. I am curious about your personal relation to these issues. Do you remember the trial and also what happened to lead you to work on it after your book on testimony?

SF: When the trial took place I was very young, and as far as I can tell, it had no real-time emotional impact on me. I remember that it was occurring; we didn't have television, but it was reported on the radio all the time. But sometimes I would turn off the radio; I didn't really relate to it. It was in the background. And as I said, I always lived my own biography as not having to do with the Holocaust. It was only through teaching Hannah Arendt's *Eichmann in Jerusalem* that I got to look more closely at the Eichmann trial. I felt that I wanted to respond to her because my emotional experience—in watching the actual videotapes of the trial—was so different from hers. So my "return" was indirect; I did not go back to Jerusalem—I went back with Hannah Arendt, and joined her own (literal and philosophical) travel to Jerusalem, and that's how I found myself (so to speak) "back in Jerusalem."

CC: It seems that this indirect return, like the return of the Holocaust that emerged for you through your encounter with Menachem's videotape and was developed in *Testimony*, was bound up with a new understanding of speech and communication in the context of historical trauma. In the first of your two chapters on the Eichmann trial—"Theaters of Justice: Arendt in Jerusalem, the Eichmann Trial, and the Redefinition of Legal Meaning in the Wake of the Holocaust," you suggest that Arendt's definition of Eichmann's "banality of evil" is both legal, regarding evil as criminal action devoid of human motivation, and linguistic, regarding evil through clichés that screen human reality and actuality. The trial, as you read Arendt, is thus centrally about restoring a certain capacity of language: the key to Arendt's view of the law, in your interpretation, is to "keep meaning to the word humanity." In her book, as you describe it, Arendt reveals how for her the trial can provide human meaning through its own legal language and is thus the place where "the significance of legal meaning in the wake of the Holocaust" is revealed (108). Yet while you seem to agree with Arendt on the centrality of language in the trial—indeed, your own reading of the trial would appear to arise from that central insight you see in her own response to the trial—you disagree with her argument that the trial fails, in the task of restoring meaning, to the extent that it focuses on the stories, or on the language, of the survivors, of the victims rather than the criminal. How do you understand Arendt's notion of this legal failure, and how did this generate your own original understanding of the trial's testimonial achievement?

SF: This idea that there was a dimension of failure in the trial—in its use of survivor testimony—was not Arendt's first, spontaneous feeling about the trial nor was it her whole attitude about it; in her correspondence with [Karl] Jaspers she says that Israel has the right to judge Eichmann and that it was right to kill him. It had the right to judge him because Israel is the country where the victims have gone, and the country where the victims live has the right to try him. So her spontaneous reaction is not to erase the victims. But then when she comes to the trial she proceeds from a traditional legal point of view, which says that this is a criminal trial and what we are interested in is not the victims or the suffering of the Jews, or history, but the deeds of the perpetrator, the criminal. And here she brings in her theory of totalitarianism—the way in which totalitarian governments attempt to produce *thoughtless* people, people who cannot "act" in the true political sense—a theory which was already made, ready-made, when she comes to the trial. Her theory precedes the trial. She does not really learn it from the trial. She kind of illustrates it from the trial. And she says it's false and legally not right to concentrate on the victims.

But what the prosecution and what the state of Israel wanted to do is to tell a story that had never been told, and that had been completely eclipsed in the Nuremberg trials, because the Nuremberg trials presented the story of Nazism from the point of view of the Allies: a story of the Nazi regime as judged by the Western democracies. This was *their* story of the Second World War; it was not the story of the Holocaust. The story of the Holocaust—of the magnitude of the catastrophe inflicted by the Nazis on their victims—did not exist as a collective story. It did not exist in the world's consciousness and could not be recognized, I claim, nor grasped in its totality even in the Jewish consciousness, prior to the Eichmann trial. And so the prosecution had this vision that the trial should narrate the story of the Jews as the Nazis have inflicted it through the so-called final solution. And that was the never-yet told story of the extermination of the Jews.

Now Arendt was always self-critical with respect to the notion of the self. Psychologically and sociologically, she always wants to take distance from the self. She is consistent on that point when she speaks of other things as well and, in general, she mercilessly satirizes and rejects any shade of self-complacency. Moreover, when Arendt narrates how her own mother educated her, she says that she herself only learnt she was Jewish from anti-Semitic remarks from children in the street, but it was prohibited to talk about it at home if the anti-Semitic remarks came only from children. The mother thus instructed Arendt that she had to learn to defend herself: anti-Semitism from children did not count and should not be talked about at home. If the insults about Jewishness came from adults, from teachers, then the mother would write registered letters to the school. But if they came from children, then Arendt had to deal with it and could not complain about them or mention them to her mother.

So the family environment was very prohibitive with regard to certain kinds of discourse. And thus for Arendt anti-Semitism is something that you should not talk about. I'm exaggerating a bit now in emphasizing what I see as a technique (at least partly) of denial through discursive censorship, but I want to make a point. Arendt's home education was that you deal with certain things by excluding them from speech, as if they didn't exist. And I think that Arendt had some built-in blind spots in her makeup, inherited from these discursive rules of her assimilated past. She came to the trial and she knew that the prime minister of Israel was saying publicly that the state of Israel had this plan to teach the world a lesson, and she angrily responded that she was "in no mood to learn any lessons" because, as an immigrant and a survivor like the rest of them, she "knew all there was to know." So she came to the trial as though knowing in advance all there was to know. I think, on the other hand, that the trial created something new in bringing forth a narrative that was not available before, and that nobody—neither the audience nor the judges nor the prosecutors—could predict it, no one knew all there was to know: not even the witnesses, the real concentration camps survivors, knew all there was to know.

CC: Presumably you don't simply mean that there were lots of facts that people didn't know.

SF: Well, historical research about the Holocaust was not developed at that point; Hilberg's book was published in the same year as the trial, 1961,[11] though not a lot of people knew about it. But I mean something beyond a mere knowledge of facts. Elie Wiesel, for instance, wrote to Arendt, "I was there in the camps, and I do not know, and you were elsewhere, so how can you say you know all there is to know?" And she answered him, as he reports in his memoirs, "You are a writer, you have the right to ask questions; I am a political theorist. I have to come up with answers."[12]

CC: Elie Wiesel's comment is interesting; even if you had the most direct access to some of the facts, you didn't know. So your own notion of what the trial told and taught us, at least in part, was how we don't know, or rather, when we think we do know we may not really know, and that seems to be bound up with what you are also trying to theorize with your notion of testimony, which isn't just teaching a fact but also showing how, even if one has the facts of a trauma, one may not truly know it, authentically and emotionally.

You also say that the trial was a "groundbreaking narrative event" that created a story that had not previously existed. What do you mean by that?

SF: The survivors had many fragmented stories; each witness told a small detail of his or her own experience. They were private traumas. Only after the trial did the story of the Holocaust become a communal history, giving a previously unavailable view of a cataclysmic collective trauma.

CC: This is also, as you suggest, specifically a problem of language. You write, "A victim is by definition not only one who is oppressed but also one who has no language of his own"—so not even a fragmented language, no language of his own—"one who, quite precisely, is robbed of a language with which to articulate his or her victimization . . . Since history by definition silences the victim, the reality of degradation and of suffering are intrinsically inaccessible to history" (*JU*, 125). What does it mean to say that victims have no language of their own?

SF: In the film *Shoah*, for instance, we see that people have testified that the Nazis prohibited the *Sonderkommandos*[13]—the people who worked with the corpses—from using the word "corpse."[14] They had to call the corpses *Figuren* [figures] or *schmattes* [ragged garments] or "pieces of shit." So the language of the oppressor is repressing reality and repressing reference. Those people were not only sworn to secrets and to silence, but they were given different ways to talk about it that deprived corpses of their humanity; they became disgusting objects.

CC: So even when they spoke, they were being silenced again in a certain manner.

SF: Yes. The language of the oppressor is imposed on them so as to limit their perceptions. And that is a philosophical problem. This definition of a victim is by Thomas Szasz,[15] a political psychiatrist who said that language always bears the imprint of the ideology of the oppressor, an ideology that dominates the language, and the victim cannot talk about his/her victimization except in the language of the oppressor. And so the injury cannot be articulated or redeemed. I suggested that the Eichmann trial created new language by converting the victims into witnesses; this is a different position of the subject. They became subjects and not objects, and not *Figuren*.

CC: It seems to me that when you only have the perpetrator's language, then there is no crime, because the perpetrator, at least in the case of the Nazis, is saying, "I didn't commit a crime. There is no crime there." So in this case, even when you speak of the crime, somehow you are eliminating the fact that it was a crime. Is that correct?

SF: Yes. This changes only when you create a new language, and the trial is struggling to articulate a language that is not at hand. Such a phenomenon can occur, as the American philosopher Richard Rorty suggests,[16] only when someone has a dream which invents something new. "Injustices," writes Rorty, "may not be perceived as injustices, until somebody invents a previously unplayed role. Only if somebody has a dream, and a voice to describe that dream, does what looked like nature begin to look like culture, what looked like fate begin to look like a moral abomination."[17] It is my interpretation that the trial gives this transformative "new role" to the victims by making them take the witness stand. It makes it possible for them to restore their subjecthood, to say "I" for the first time from within this history of their (failed) extermination: they can now say "I accuse," in echoing Emile Zola's *J'accuse*.[18]

CC: Given that most, if not all, Holocaust video testimonies—at least as archival collections—came after the Eichmann trial and after Justice [Moshe] Landau created the archive of testimonies from the trial,[19] it would seem that, quite literally, the video testimonies have a historical bond to an actual trial. So the word "testimony," even as you use it in your extended sense, does have a sort of legal history; it's not just metaphorical. What is it, then, about a trial per se, that allows a collective history to be told?

SF: There is a chorus of testimonies; everybody tells a fragment, but then a total picture emerges. The law is a discipline of totalization. The judges totalize all the facts, although they say that the judgment relied on documents more than on the witnesses. But the witnesses narrated a story that had never been a communal story. It had been a number of private traumas that could not even articulate themselves—most witnesses did not even talk about it to their families—and all of a sudden there was this beginning, this possibility, of an articulation—an awareness—of a national destiny.

CC: Do you think one can make an analogy to the stories of incest that, during the late '70s and early '90s, various activists and scholars in the US, such as Judith Herman, helped us to see as a collective story rather than as individual narratives?

SF: Yes. The feminists made incest and domestic violence public because it used to be that raping one's daughter or raping or beating one's wife was a private family story. And the feminists that brought that into the open and talked about domestic violence and made a crime of it made it a public matter. That conversion of what was supposed to be private into something public was also done in the Eichmann trial.

CC: So that is partly what you mean by speaking of the revolution in the victim, who goes from using the perpetrator's language in which, at least in the cases of women, it's always private and therefore not of interest to anybody outside. Although the Holocaust was, of course, a very different matter from the issues concerning sexual and domestic abuse, it seems that we can understand from looking at both in this way the importance of creating a collective public story that can be told and heard.

SF: Exactly. That's what the architects of the trial wanted to bring to the attention of the world, and they did.

CC: And the language also changes, then, in the sense that it is no longer personal.

SF: And in addition, as I have suggested in my book, the Eichmann trial universalized the victim through the testimony. For the first time the victim became universal and not private. Zola anticipated that when he said *J'accuse* about Dreyfus, who was just a private person.[20] As Zola said, it is in the name of humanity that I am accusing the French government.

CC: If we think of more recent events, we might compare Zola's gesture to the movement that has said, in response to the murder of an African American child in Florida and to the way it has been handled under Florida's "Stand Your Ground" law, "We are all Trayvon Martin."[21] Here a community—quite a large one—has collectively protested a crime, as well as the authorities' legal response to that crime; we have protested in the name of the collective a situation that seems to be private or individual, and thus seems like it will disappear of its own accord. The private death of one black kid, we assume it's going to disappear. Saying "We are all Trayvon Martin" strikes me as similar to the gestures you describe, which make an injustice that has previously seemed to occur on the individual level (even when it has involved millions of individuals) clearly recognizable as collective, public, or universal. Maybe that is also a legacy of some of these events we have discussed, in a different context.

SF: Yes, this is also part of the universalization of the victim.

III. Fragile Evidence

CC: It is striking that in spite of your focus on the narrative achievements of the trial in your first Eichmann chapter ("Theaters of Justice: Arendt in Jerusalem and the Redefinition of Legal Meaning in the Wake of the Holocaust," in *JU*, chap.

3), the problem of silence—so important in your earlier work on testimony—returns in your second Eichmann chapter ("A Ghost in the House of Justice: Death and the Language of the Law," in *JU*, chap. 4). This chapter begins abruptly with the following words:

> A witness faints on the stand during the Eichmann trial. This chapter will
> explore the meaning of this unexpected legal moment and will ask: Is the wit-
> ness's collapse relevant—and if so, in what sense—to the legal framework of
> the trial? How does this courtroom event affect the trial's definition of legal
> meaning in the wake of the Holocaust? Under what circumstances and in
> what ways can the legal default of a witness constitute a legal testimony in its
> own right? (*JU*, 131)

The scene you analyze in this chapter is specifically the collapse of the witness K-Zetnik, a literary writer who had been at Auschwitz and who had seen Eichmann there.[22] K-Zetnik collapses while he is trying to give his testimony. How was K-Zetnik's fall into silence bound up, for you, with the achievement of the other witnesses' speech?

SF: This structural shift from speech to silence that you have perceived in my book was completely unconscious on my part. My own perception was that the first chapter is about the Eichmann trial in general, and the second is about a detail, a moment that was a dramatic moment, and about one particular witness who didn't even manage to give testimony.

CC: It is a detail perhaps in the sense that, as you say in *Testimony*, Lanzmann's film *Shoah* is made up of a lot of details, but they don't make a single whole.[23] And the scene of K-Zetnik, as a detail, can't be assimilated in some way. So maybe the fall of K-Zetnik is exemplary—even though the survivors at the trial do create a collective story—of something unassimilable in all of the testimonies, even when they succeed in taking place.

SF: Absolutely. That is part of what I'm trying to say, that there is something that exceeds and breaks up the legal frame, because when K-Zetnik collapses, he is no longer a witness, he unintentionally brings about a momentary breakdown of the legal frame.

CC: So on the one hand, he is completely different from the others because he is the one who cannot give his testimony. On the other hand, he is one of the collective, and so he is also inside.

SF: He is inside the trial. For traditional jurists or legal scholars this would be completely extraneous to the legal framework. But I am arguing that this breakdown is a moment inside the trial, that it is also part of what gives meaning to the trial. And even the judgment of the judges acknowledges that. The presiding judge, [Moshe] Landau, writes that the transmission of the meaning of the Holocaust is a task for the great writers and poets, but then he says, "Perhaps it is symbolic that even the author who himself went through the hell named Auschwitz could not stand the ordeal in the witness box and collapsed" (*JU*, 155). This is from the text of the judgment. So the judge is saying that there was something that was uncontained, and the judgment recognizes and encompasses what was uncontainable within it. And it is also the role of literature, to narrate this uncontainable. Because he says it is the task of the great writers and poets.

CC: So this is one reason, maybe, that you could see K-Zetnik's collapse not so much as an aberration that shouldn't have been in the trial but rather, perhaps—in the words of Mallarmé[24]—as an accident that you have to pursue.

SF: Right, exactly.

CC: It is very surprising to place K-Zetnik at the center of the meaning of what he seems to fail at (in this case, giving testimony). I wonder if we might understand this further by what you say about the role of "fragile evidence" in the trial, when you suggest that unlike the Nuremberg trials, which deliberately excluded "the fragile testimony of the persecuted," the Eichmann trial "consciously embraces the vulnerability, the legal fallibility, and the fragility of the human witness" (*JU*, 134). Here you come into direct conflict with Hannah Arendt, for whom K-Zetnik's fall is the example of why the fallibility of witnesses should not be included: K-Zetnik embodies fallibility par excellence; he is far more feeble and far more fallible than all of the other fallible witnesses, as he literally fails to testify. You said that it is her response to K-Zetnik that got you really interested in writing on this trial. Can you speak more about Arendt's reading, how you understand it, and what you felt was wrong with it?

SF: I watched the ABC documentary of the trial, *The Trial of Adolf Eichmann*, and later I also showed it to my class. You see in the videotape of the actual trial the testimony of K-Zetnik and his collapse; that is extremely moving. I felt there is an emotional pathos both to the testimony that he starts to give, and then to the sudden collapse, which no one can predict. And that is literally the most breathtaking moment, the most dramatic moment of the trial. Everybody was taken by surprise—in the world as well, because it was screened as TV news in real time. Arendt completely denies this pathos. That was a moment in which my emotional response to the tragic significance embodied by the trial was very powerful, and she was only laughing at it, talking about it in a mocking and condescending way, and also with a kind of superficial, psychologizing explanation—describing this unpredictable physical response as his being "deeply wounded" by the judge (who admonishes him), and thus, collapsing so as to "answer no more questions."[25]

Arendt did not see the trauma: she saw K-Zetnik as very narcissistic, and she thought that he was very eager to appear and that he volunteered to go witness. This happens to be untrue because he was known only under a pseudonym—he never made public appearances—he never wanted anybody to identify him. And he was more or less forced to testify by the prosecution. So he was imposed on, and he came reluctantly and his testimony quickly becomes literary. He starts by saying "Auschwitz was another planet," which means there is no way to go from that planet to this one, it's inexpressible, it's not easy to cross the border between this other world and the world of the courtroom, or the world of the present. He says the "people there had no names, they had no parents, and they had no children." Now obviously they had parents, but this is a poetic way of saying why it was a different world, in which all people thrown there were like abandoned children with no recourse, no protection, no connection, no defense. And then Arendt says mockingly that even the prosecutor saw that something needed to be done about this "testimony," so he interrupted very gently, "May I perhaps put a few questions to you, if you will agree?" And at this point K-Zetnik seems to be in a trance; he's not hearing the prosecutor's intervention. He starts to tell about how at the moment of selection, the people who went to the crematorium were chosen. And he describes how he was looking into their eyes, and he says, "I see them, I see them; they always left me and left me behind." Which means that for two years he managed to be lucky enough not to be selected to go to a crematorium. He's trying to talk about this moment of exchange of looks that is ungraspable, where life divides itself from that death. And he relives this looking, and it's a silent look, he's looking into the eyes of those who know that they are going to their deaths. And they are looking at him. It's a moment of human communication in that silence. He's trying to say all that, and he relives it as though it were again taking place right now, and then the prosecutor says, "Maybe I can ask you a few questions." And K-Zetnik keeps on saying and repeating, "I see them, I see them," and he's in a trance. The judge intervenes very authoritatively, "Maybe you should listen to the prosecutor, and to me." And then all of a sudden K-Zetnik faints. This is a moment that needs interpretation and has a lot of emotional power.

CC: You pointed out that before he collapsed he had started to use literary language. He uses it at the moment that he can't cross from that planet to this, when there's no language to do that—this is when he begins to speak literarily. So maybe what he's doing is saying, I can't translate this trauma into the legal language. And that is a failure for Arendt. The literary language emerges at a moment when he can't cross borders. That has something to do with his failure.

SF: He also moves from the past to the present. He says, "The people there had no names," so he begins with the past tense, and then he says, "I see them. I see them. They left me, they always left me, they left me behind. I see them." When he falls is when he passes from the past tense into the present tense, and that's when, in my interpretation, he hears the judge's intervention as the command of an SS officer.

CC: So not only the boundary of the law, but the boundary of history as time, as temporal progression, changes in the trauma.

SF: You cannot cross, but at the same time the two worlds mix.

CC: Whereas for Arendt, as you suggest, the trial should, with its legal language, restore human meaning; it should to be a bridge over the abyss.

SF: And definitely not repeat the trauma or reenact it.

CC: So for her the legal translatability is actually, as you suggest, a form of distance from the trauma, whereas for him, the untranslatability is a confusion of the two times.

SF: He can't make it into a past story. As Christa Wolf says in a different context, from a different position, about this history: "What is past is not dead; it is not even past. We cut ourselves from it. We pretend to be strangers."[26]

CC: And this traumatic reenactment occurs specifically in terms of the impossibility of simply translating between the literary idiom and the legal idiom. In this context it is interesting to think of your suggestion that when he falls, he falls between his two names.

SF: He has a private name, which was a secret name, because he used a pseudonym in his writing, "K-Zetnik"—which means concentration camp inmate. This, he says, is his literary name, which testifies to the dead, to the anonymous, to the people that are called by numbers. And he is addressed, at that moment by the judge and by the prosecutor, by his real name because the witness has to have a signature of his real name.

CC: A legal performative.

SF: A legal performative. So they call him Mr. Dinoor, and he's K-Zetnik, and there is a clash: on the one hand, he hears the admonishment of the judge as a

Nazi officer; on the other hand, he has to be loyal to the name K-Zetnik, and that's his loyalty to the dead. He cannot cross back from the dead to the living, so he falls as if he were himself a corpse. But he's not acting it—that's what happens to him.

CC: So he fails from the legal perspective, and in relation to the legal performative of his official name, but you also claim that this failure has another kind of power in the trial:

> The fainting that cuts through the witness's speech and petrifies his body
> interrupts the legal process and creates a moment that is legally traumatic
> not just for the witness but also chiefly for the court and for the trial. But it
> is through this breakdown of the legal framework that history emerges in the
> courtroom and in the legal body of the witness. (JU, 404–5)

In *The Scandal of the Speaking Body*, you say that language and the body are bound up in the failure of the promise (in Molière's *Don Juan*), a failure that produces desire.[27] Here, the failure to keep the oath is a falling, a fainting body. How are these bodies linked?

SF: Every witness is a speaking body. And it's kind of interesting also that when Lanzmann convokes witnesses and makes a work of art of it in *Shoah*, he also says that his film is an incarnation and resuscitation, or something along those lines. And at the same time he says it's a philosophical process. So it's philosophical, but it's through the body.

But to go back to the trial: the witnesses take the witness stand. It has a physical dimension; they are there. They are speaking bodies. And they also promise to tell the truth. It's performative in that sense. But they are not supposed to fall and faint outside of the witness stand. So the falling body is a testimony in its own way: K-Zetnik testifies to the trauma. And he brings in the other planet.

CC: So the failure of the promise, here, has a performative dimension of its own, but not, in this case, through a speaking body but rather through the dead body of the Holocaust.

SF: Right. K-Zetnik testifies to the dead; that is, those who left him. Or rather, to the dying. He sees them at the moment they are going to die, at the most human moment. Not when they are corpses but when they know that they are going to die and he and they are going two directions: he is going to live and they are going to die, and they exchange looks. And that is the look that he is obsessed with. He made an oath to the dead. He says in his books, in his novels, that he made an oath to the dead to be their mouthpiece. And his name testifies. So he is loyal to that oath. But there is also a conflict between the two oaths: the oath to the dead and the oath to the living.

CC: And what you said in your very first definition of testimony is that I am the only one who can testify to my story. But he's actually trying to testify . . .

SF: . . . for them.

CC: And that's the impossibility.

SF: Because he's the voice. He says he promised them to give them voice, and he feels that it is a moral obligation.

CC: If he is exemplary in some way of the trial, then perhaps there is a way in which we can say that testimony, in becoming collective, isn't personal. Because behind it is something impossible: I testify for the one who cannot testify.

SF: Yes. And that is also what Arendt misreads in him because she thinks that he is complacent and self-staging. But he is not, precisely, himself.

IV. MUTE WITNESS

CC: K-Zetnik might also be said to bear witness for another within Arendt's text, too, as you suggest, when you hear in her description of him a mute and unconscious testimony of her own.

SF: I hear an echo of Walter Benjamin's essay "The Storyteller"[28] in Arendt's emphasis, at various places in *Eichmann in Jerusalem*, on narrative and storytelling, and in her claim that this is where K-Zetnik fails. Of K-Zetnik, she says that he "did not prove the ability to tell a story" (224). She often speaks about "the difficulty" of telling a story (229), and she takes K-Zetnik's collapse as an extreme example of this difficulty. For her, this aborted testimony embodies the trial's failure, and my interpretation is—in contrast—that this unintended moment turns out to be an expression, an embodiment of the very essence of the trial: to articulate the difficulty of narrating this trauma.

CC: But also, importantly in your reading, Arendt's own language, precisely at this point of criticism of K-Zetnik, emerges as a kind of testimony about Arendt herself. You write:

> Has Arendt in her turn borrowed her authority as a storyteller of the trial
> from a legacy of death of which she does not speak and cannot speak? I
> would suggest indeed that . . . *Eichmann in Jerusalem* is also Arendt's book of
> mourning. It is, in other words, a book—an unarticulated statement—on the
> relation between grief and justice, as well as on the counterparts of grief and
> justice in narrative and storytelling . . . Both the Eichmann trial and Arendt's

critical rehearsal of it are preoccupied—albeit in different styles—with the translation of grief into justice. Both are therefore mirror images of the translation of grief into grievance . . . There is, in other words, a crucial story Arendt does not tell and cannot tell that underlies the story of the trial she does tell. (*JU*, 158)

How and why does this seemingly very personal testimony of Arendt enter *Eichmann in Jerusalem?*

SF: I think that, in Arendt's language, there is a memory of Benjamin, and she experienced a great grief over his death. Because their destinies were linked. First of all, they befriended each other in Paris, where both of them lived after they had fled from Germany. And both of them were speaking fluent French, even while being both German-Jewish refugees. They read each other's works. They finally met in Marseilles; he gave her his manuscript, which she later would publish, after his death, in 1968, in the volume *Illuminations*.[29] And they were supposed to have the same destiny, because both of them were going to try to leave France illegally, to cross the border to Spain and then to emigrate to the United States. But Benjamin was stopped on the border between France and Spain and, in captivity during the night, committed suicide, thinking that he would be handed over to the Gestapo, although his group was freed the next day, and they could cross the border. Arendt went to the graveyard on the Spanish border to find his grave, but she did not find his name.

What is important is not only that they communicated and that they were friends and cultural and intellectual mutual supporters, but that they had a common German-Jewish refugee fate—and thus his fate could have been hers, and her fate should have been his. But it didn't happen like that. So I think her grief means that (like K-Zetnik?) she is also carrying the dead in her. Maybe not altogether like K-Zetnik, but a little bit. She has her own dead, and I think that she also had a traumatic, traumatizing history, which is obvious when you read her autobiographical interview with Günter Gaus[30] later on. I think that *Eichmann in Jerusalem* is a very passionate book, and it's passionate in self-criticism and in criticism of Israel and in anger (she gets angry about a lot of things), and she only admires the three German-born judges and their beautiful German, compared to Eichmann's pedestrian German, which makes her laugh. She is very emotional on the whole, and I think that there is much more in that book than the purely theoretical criticism she articulates à propos the totalitarian banality of evil. I think that a lot of this "more" is the grief of her own participation in this Jewish history, and part of it is her personal, perhaps partly unconscious, grief about her loss of Germany.

CC: So when you encounter the collapse of K-Zetnik through Arendt, you are, in a sense, hearing a subtextual story and a silence, a silent story that comes out through your reading of K-Zetnik's story and his collapse. Her silence, in that sense, is not unlike K-Zetnik's silence in his collapse.

SF: The story that she is unable to tell—the impossibility of telling a story—is also hers.

CC: And that is also linked, in a way, to the manner in which K-Zetnik talked about seeing his fellow concentration camp inhabitants "leaving" for the crematorium. "They always left me, and left me behind." It is about leaving, about one surviving and one dying (like Arendt and Benjamin). But it is also about problems of crossing over borders. Because in the case of Benjamin, her friend, who is also a theorist of language and of translation and untranslatability,[31] he literally did not manage to cross the border. And it seems like your reading of a moment of nontranslation in the trial—that is, the moment the literary interrupts the legal instead of going over into it—is also a reading of her own (perhaps unconscious) personal struggle to bring back Benjamin, or the story of his death, into language, where it has stopped at the border.

SF: It's her own story; it's not only his story. She will bring his texts to publication, and then she will mourn him in the introduction that she writes to this volume of his texts (*Illuminations*), but she would see his fate through her sense of irony, as a bitterly ironic fate. In all her observations, she always emphasizes the ironic aspects. So in her introduction to his works she speaks of her grief and her frustration realizing that he had committed suicide, and then ironically enough the group was let go the next day. She talks about him as having been (above all) unlucky. But I feel that his death means more than an unlucky accident. Taking his own life so as not to be captive of the Nazis was his gesture—a meaningful, heroic gesture of resistance, expressing his absolute refusal of collaboration even with his own entrapment in the Fascist framework.

But it's not simply that she mourns Benjamin in *Eichmann in Jerusalem*; she mourns herself, she mourns what she lost. He was part of the Germany that she lost also.

CC: So the untold story of Benjamin, as you read it, is also Arendt's untold story of herself.

SF: Part of it. She wrote to [Mary] McCarthy that she wrote the book in a state of euphoria, a euphoria which is still an enigma for me, and that it was a cure for her. And I think it may have been a cure with respect to other aspects of her life, like her relationship with Heidegger or other aspects of her past. But there was this dimension of the grief of Jewishness and the fact that Benjamin was not able to do as she did, to cross over.

CC: And with regard to her grief, it, too, is bound up with the loss, not only of a homeland or of a state but also of a native language. You mentioned earlier Arendt's 1964 interview with the German journalist Günter Gaus for German television, an interview later published in English translation under the title, "What Remains? The Language Remains." You told me, years ago, that for you the most moving words of Arendt you had read occurred in what she says, in this interview, about her relation to language. Arendt's dialogue with Gaus on this topic reads as follows:

> **Gaus:** I should like to ask you whether you miss the Europe of the pre-Hitler period, which will never exist again. When you come to Europe, what, in your impression, remains and what is irretrievably lost?
>
> **Arendt:** The Europe of the pre-Hitler period? I do not long for that, I can tell you. What remains? The language remains.
>
> **Gaus:** And that means a great deal to you?
>
> **Arendt:** A great deal. I have always consciously refused to lose my mother tongue. I have always maintained a certain distance from French, which I then spoke very well, as well as from English, which I write today.
>
> **Gaus:** I wanted to ask you about that. You write in English now?
>
> **Arendt:** I write in English, but I have never lost a feeling of distance from it. There is a tremendous difference between your mother tongue and another language. For myself I can put it extremely simply: In German I know a rather large part of German poetry by heart; the poems are always somehow in the back of my mind. I can never do that again. I do things in German that I would not permit myself to do in English . . . The German language is the essential thing that has remained and that I have always consciously preserved. (12–13)

SF: And he asks, almost incredulously, "Even in the most bitter time?" And she says, "Always." I was very impressed by this "always." For it is the loyalty to whatever she loved there, the people that she loved also.

CC: How, then, is this related, in your interpretation, to Arendt's writing on the Eichmann trial?

SF: In the trial, there is one witness that she really puts on a pedestal, and that is Zindel Grynszpan (*EiJ*, 228–29), a man who was deported, who in 1938 was expelled from Germany (like other Polish Jews residing in Germany, by a sudden German decree). She says that he had come to Germany in 1911, became a grocer and had lived there twenty-seven years, and one day they came and brutally took him over the border to Poland. He writes to his son, "You must no longer write to me in Germany." And Arendt says that Grynszpan (the only witness whom she likes) uses a minimum of words, and in ten minutes he has told how twenty-seven years of his life were destroyed in twenty-four hours. And that's where she uses Benjamin's vocabulary, saying that he was a "righteous man," and that no other witness lived up to his shining honesty. She's extremely moved by this. This is the only moment in which she allows herself to feel and to express some pathos; after having criticized all of the other witnesses, she says à propos Grynszpan, "one thought foolishly, everyone should have his day in court" (229). And so all of a sudden she is justifying the fact that there is meaning in the very act of taking the witness stand.

I asked myself, why is she so moved precisely by this witness? Maybe he had shining honesty, but what was it in his story that was so moving? His story was about the loss of Germany, and my interpretation is that she identifies with that particular loss. Because he doesn't testify about the terrible things in the concentration camps; he only testifies to how he lost twenty-seven years of living in Germany by having been suddenly expelled to another country—Poland. And she in turn was expelled—she wasn't expelled exactly—she crossed, she fled to France. She had been arrested, and then she was freed thanks to the friendly relationship she managed to establish with her decent German captor, but her name was not cleared and she had to cross illegally. So in this sense her fate is similar to Grynszpan's: because of the Nazis both of them had to lose this country. I think that she is very moved because his destiny has something in common with her own destiny. She doesn't acknowledge that; probably it's unconscious.

CC: Well, she is writing *Eichmann in Jerusalem* in English. You say in your book that she loves the German of presiding Justice Moshe Landau and of the other judges who could speak German so elegantly, but she herself is writing in a tongue that is not her mother tongue. So there is a way in which she suffers from . . .

SF: . . . the loss. In the 1964 interview with Gaus she says that in 1949, when she returned to Germany again for the first time after the war, she had an indescribable joy in hearing German spoken in the streets. She says she had a violent emotion, and that it was the same violent emotion that she would have in renewing her acquaintances as well. But she adds, "Today I have more distance." I think that her emotion in hearing German is revealing—this emotion is not triggered in hearing the German of Eichmann, because he keeps talking Nazi bureaucratic language, and he says cliché after cliché; she cannot forgive him this linguistic mediocrity which replicates the Nazi discourse verbatim. The banality of evil is in the banality of language also. But I think that this emotion on hearing German when she returns, this violent emotion is about the loss of Germany. Her recognition of good German is linked to the German culture she had absorbed and within which she was raised. I think that she never consciously came to terms with the loss of Germany. She also married (in her second marriage) a non-Jewish German with whom she kept talking about Germany. And she often writes to him in their correspondence that he was her portable homeland, her stable anchor within her four walls. She maintained the German language connection with her significant others, with [Karl] Jaspers in Germany, and later with [Martin] Heidegger, as well as with her husband [Heinrich Blücher], whom she had also met in Paris as another—communist—German refugee who, like her, had to flee from Germany. She kept speaking the German language at home. And it is only in this language that she can be at home. She is at home in the world because, in that conversation in German with her husband, and with her German mentors, there is a world for her.

V. A GRANDFATHER'S OATH

CC: Of course, you, like Arendt, are also writing about Arendt's *Eichmann in Jerusalem* in English, and one is tempted to hear in your reading of Arendt a source of pathos, not simply in Arendt's relation to the trial but in your own relation to Arendt. It is, after all, your writing—and not Arendt's—that one would associate with pathos. If we were to trace this question back through your own relation to language, we would have to go back to your own comments on the question of languages in *Writing and Madness: Literature/Philosophy/Psychoanalysis*.

SF: I reflected on this question for the first time in my introduction to the original French edition of *La folie et la chose littéraire*,[32] part of which was translated in the English edition of *Writing and Madness*. When I had to define my own position as a writer, for the first time in Paris, I quoted Henry James, who was moving back and forth (geographically and culturally) between America and England. (This involved the same language, of course, although [Oscar] Wilde said that the one thing that the British and the Americans don't have in common is the language. . . .) Henry James said, "I aspire to write in such a way that it would be impossible for an outsider to say whether I am at a given moment an American writing about England, or an Englishman writing about America, dealing as I do with both countries."[33] I said that I, too, aspired to write in such a way that it would be impossible for an outsider to say whether I was a French person writing about America or an American writing about France. I was talking about the necessity to commute between languages. And then I noted in parentheses that, as it happens, I am neither French nor American.[34]

CC: It's interesting that you managed not to name your nationality or your mother tongue. Have you ever written in your mother tongue?

SF: I have written a preface to the Hebrew edition of *Testimony* (2008), but nothing else. But really, I don't write in my mother tongue. That's the language in which I am silent in my publications.

CC: Unlike Arendt, though, you have a home in Israel, as well as a home in the United States.

SF: Yes. But I'm not sure that I can say that "like Arendt" I am "at home in the world"—a Heideggerian expression which she liked to use—because I tend to feel homeless. Once you leave, as a proverb in English says, you can't go home again. Of course I do have a homeland, and Arendt lost her homeland; I was born in the homeland of the Jews, you know, but Arendt had a sadness and ambivalence in relation to her distance not just from the state of Israel but also from her lost Jewish community, as a result of the controversy over her publication of *Eichmann in Jerusalem*.

CC: So in your writing on *Eichmann in Jerusalem* you encountered a woman who was a real refugee from the Holocaust, who lived for many years during the war and after it as a real stateless person, but who has nonetheless made her home, even though she lost her homeland; whereas you have a homeland but do not feel at home in the world. And although you were born in the Jewish homeland, you do not maintain your written work in Hebrew, your mother tongue. Could you speak about when you first left your native language? How did that come about?

SF: To speak about my relation to languages, I would have to begin with my grandfather. My maternal grandfather was a Zionist revolutionary in Russia, one of the few who knew Hebrew when it was still a dead language. The early Zionists strived to build a homeland here and to establish the Hebrew language as a living language, which is one of the miracles, I find, in Zionism's accomplishments. He was an educated member of the Haskalah, the secular Jewish enlightenment movement, in Russia, and he brought his wife and his five children to Palestine, including my mother, who was at that time two and a half years old.

He came here both to create a homeland and to create a national language that would be spoken by all the Jews in this country.

He also made a vow—this actually brings us back to the topic of the oath. He made an oath in Russia that he was going to revive the Hebrew language that no one knew. The revolution of this project was translated into a concrete vow. The moment that his foot would tread the land of Palestine, he swore, he would stop speaking any other language than Hebrew. This was despite the fact that his wife did not know Hebrew. There were a few crazy people like that, and they managed, with their fanaticism, to make Hebrew into a language that eventually everybody spoke in Israel. I know that he made this oath because my mother told me this, with great pride and admiration for the radical idealism of her father. I think today that my mother must have been traumatized by this whole mutation of the family. I think that the Zionist revolution was traumatic, as every revolution is, but especially because it was a displacement from one culture and one language to another that was not yet formed. My grandfather actually strictly maintained the oath even though his wife, I was told, at first did not speak a word of Hebrew, but apparently she learned the language very quickly. From the moment that they were in Israel—my mother was two and a half years old, and had heard only Russian for two and a half years—but suddenly, abruptly, she started to hear around her only Hebrew. I think (retrospectively, today, by presumption) that for my mother the trauma of this displacement occurred when the Russian language was blocked to her at two and a half, when she couldn't yet speak Russian but she could already understand it. And Hebrew must have been at first a foreign language, in which she was suddenly imbued without being able to make sense of the sudden language change. So there was this split between languages. I was raised on the purity of Hebrew. By that time my grandmother had learned Hebrew and I knew that it was an ideal, and I knew that it was an iron law and that all other languages were (implicitly) prohibited.

So how did I learn other languages? We learned English as a second language, but I was very bad in it in high school. And one day I wanted to read a novel that was called *We the Living*, and I knew that it existed only in English. So I took a dictionary, because I absolutely wanted to read it, and in the first two or three pages I translated, I looked up in the dictionary and wrote beside every word its meaning. And after several pages I stopped looking in the dictionary and I continued reading through it. And I could read English because I wanted so much to get through this novel. It was like a breakthrough.

French I didn't study in high school—that was a second language we had in high school, but we had to choose between French and Latin, and as my father told me Latin was the entry into all other languages, I chose Latin. When I went to the university I registered to study Hebrew literature and English literature. Because I was already attracted by foreign cultures. I went to audit a course of literature in French, and I saw that it was a whole world that was completely different from the world in English, and I was very attracted by the literary content that I heard. So I immediately made a decision that was kind of crazy, that I wanted to study not Hebrew literature but French. To be able to enroll in the French department we had to pass an examination entry in the language, and I didn't pass the examination. They said that they saw that I was pretty intelligent, but my French was not good enough, so they accepted me for three trial months, to see if at the end of three months I would catch up with the class. And I did, after three months, catch up with the class. So I had a drive to study foreign languages and to read foreign literatures. I was drawn to the foreignness.

CC: I find it interesting that you began your venture into English with a book entitled *We the Living*, which on the surface sounds like a book about survival, given that your mother tongue involved, as you suggested, the history of some sort of trauma.

SF: I think (or more correctly I suppose) that a displacement like my mother had endured, in the middle of one's language learning process, must be traumatic. When my mother was in her forties or fifties I remember she would sometimes sing Russian songs in Russian, and she would say, "I sing instead of crying." And I never understood this sentence, but I registered it. And even today it's an enigma to me. And when many decades later my mother lost part of her lucidity and memory in old age, she was beginning to sing a lot more in Russian, which she couldn't speak, but she could understand.

CC: So even though Russian wasn't your language, you could hear, through what she said, the pathos of the Russian, and the pathos in a song.

SF: I didn't understand it. Even today I don't understand it. But today I can re-project, imagine what it must have meant for the whole family, to live through such a radical displacement, decreed exclusively, uncompromisingly by a decision of the patriarch, without any female input into the decision that has become a life rule. My mother idealized her father, whom I never met because he died young, before my birth, and I do believe my mother's sense that he was indeed an extraordinary person, an exceptionally dignified, uncommon man and a noble, founding educator, one who lived for his vocation. But I think that in my mother all these factors—the abrupt geographical and cultural displacement, the uncompromising iron law of Hebrew as the one exclusive language, the idealization of her father, and the Zionist ideology—were all mixed. So the trauma is obscurely mixed in with this pathos.

CC: It seems to me that you heard the song as a kind of testimony, even if not a conscious one, and even if not consciously received. And that is what you are now hearing: the testimony to her trauma.

SF: A testimony which was in a foreign language.

CC: What's interesting, as well, in this story is what she was testifying to: the home language, the mother tongue, which also meant (for you) that your mother tongue was silencing something: another language. So perhaps it was testimony, among other things, to an oath of silencing.

SF: And of speaking in one language only.

VI. Languages of Departure

CC: There would seem to be in this story of your family's language a relation to your own reading of the Eichmann trial. For your grandfather was the revolutionary whose oath was to create a new people and a new country. So it was the ideal of creating a homeland for the Jews. And it was revolutionary in the positive sense, and echoes what you say, in your chapter on the trial, about the Holocaust survivors creating a new language as a collective. On the other hand, inside of that revolutionary oath was another oath that was sworn in the family, which was not to speak Russian. You said it was a law, so there is another oath you had to promise to keep as well.

SF: I think sometimes that I had to escape this iron law. And in my movements to other languages—teaching in other languages, writing in other languages—I think that (unconsciously) I did something parallel to what my grandfather did, but in the opposite direction. He came to Israel and started to speak only Hebrew; I left and led my intellectual life in French and English.

CC: So in a way your itinerary repeated and changed his. Your path, in a sense, testified to that history of your family, including its linguistic history. Because you said just now that your grandfather came over to Israel to create a new language and (so as to enable that creation) to forbid others in the household to speak anything but Hebrew. He was somebody who left, but he arrives somewhere. You also left your homeland and your language, first going to France to do your Ph.D., which you did in French, and then to Switzerland.

SF: Yes. I also published in French. French became a second native tongue to me. And I completely identified with that—I had the period that I identified with French, even after I moved to Yale.

CC: Indeed, when I arrived at Yale in 1979, I thought you were French. And your first book in English, *Lacan and the Adventure of Insight*, was of course about a French author.

SF: *Writing and Madness* was also a kind of conflation between European culture and American culture, somewhat as Arendt's work was. We were both at the crossroads between two continents, though in different ways. One thing that makes her so relevant, I believe, is that she was at a crossroads.

CC: What is striking to me, however, is that you hear in her story, and in her political theory—as it emerges, for example, particularly in the Eichmann trial—the story of a traumatic loss of her homeland. And as I listen to you, what I hear is that your grandfather was a political founder, and that political moment was also a trauma. So your linguistic journey was linked to a political past in its own traumatic way (though we could not simply equate that past with Arendt's forced leaving of her homeland).

And yet Arendt was able to make a home outside of Germany. She's a theorist of the stateless, but she ultimately did get a state, even though it is not her original homeland. You still have your original homeland, the Jewish homeland, but you have not written in Hebrew. What is your relation to Hebrew now? And do you feel that you have also made yourself a home?

SF: I do not feel the distance that Arendt says she feels when she writes in languages that are not those of her homeland. When I write in French I feel at home in French, and when I write in English I feel at home in the writing. The writing is perhaps my homeland, but I still have to remain silent in Hebrew. I speak it with my friends, but it is not like Arendt, who establishes a way of being at home in the world. I am not at home in the world, and I am not at home today in Israel, either.

CC: You are in fact still passing back and forth between Israel and the United States.

SF: I am in between, in this separation of two countries and three cultures. And it is probably not by coincidence that I am not writing in Hebrew. I think that in some way it is for me perhaps the language of the trauma. It is the language of the iron law. I am very proud of what my grandfather did, and I was proud of the establishment of the the state of Israel, especially in its beginning; but a trauma is inscribed in this native tongue, and that is why, I think, it was liberating to write in foreign languages.

Shoshana Felman at her home in Tel Aviv, Israel, December 28, 2010.

CC: It sounds like what is liberating for you about language, and in particular, literary language, is tied up with that silencing in your linguistic past, and also with what you call testimony. Your theory of testimony is actually your own relation to language, which is a struggle between an oath to silence and a vow to make an address. And for you, that happens in part through writing about literature.

SF: Literature enables a liberating speech. A liberating speech that is a creation of a new subjectivity as well. The original Zionists wanted to found Israel to get out of the persecuted victimhood of the Jew, and I think that they created free Jews. But my native tongue was also marked with the repression of other languages. And maybe I needed to get to the other languages. In a way I also needed the world as Arendt talks about a world. There is a world for her, because her world is constituted by the correspondence with Jaspers and with Heidegger (as well as with her husband), and by the German language—by the continuity of the German language.

CC: I would say, using Heideggerian language, that she seems to dwell, whereas you don't.[35] You said that you make a home in different languages, but you say maybe you don't dwell in any single one.

SF: Or in any single country that I could really call my home.

CC: So she crosses boundaries, but you seem to testify to a problem with crossing boundaries, even though you do it.

SF: Arendt says that she feels that her creativity is tied up with the German language, and it was true for [Paul] Celan also, who was fluent in many languages but said he could not write poetry in any language other than his mother tongue (German). And I don't feel that my creativity is limited in foreign languages. I think, on the contrary, that my creativity was liberated by them.

CC: It seems to me, if we go back to the book *We the Living*, that these languages are also your survival in some way, that moving into the otherness of the other language is also your survival, whereas for Arendt there is always an attempt to return to the German to be at home.

SF: Arendt and Jaspers keep communicating about the political problems of the world. At first they are hoping that Europe would be reorganized, and she even wants the Jewish homeland to be in Europe. In their correspondence they keep discussing the politics of the world. And they hope that there will be a new world, and for her the new world becomes really her absorption of the American ideals. So she lives in the politics of the world together with him. I also need the world, but it's not a world in which I am at home.

CC: Isn't literature a place for people who are not at home? Wouldn't literature be the place in which you have a literary home?

SF: Yes. I could say I dwell in literature. And also, as Lanzmann said, "my film is my country." And I could say that my writing is my country.

NOTES

1. See Shoshana Felman, *The Juridical Unconscious: Trials and Traumas in the Twentieth Century* (Cambridge, MA: Harvard UP, 2002). The two chapters of this book that constitute the focus of this interview are chap. 3, "Theaters of Justice: Arendt in Jerusalem, the Eichmann Trial, and the Redefinition of Legal Meaning in the Wake of the Holocaust" (106–30), and chap. 4, "A Ghost in the House of Justice: Death and the Language of the Law" (131–66). Subsequent citations abbreviated *JU*.

2. Shoshana Felman and Dori Laub, *Testimony: Crises of Witnessing in Literature, Psychoanalysis and History* (New York: Routledge, 1992).

3. The notion of the "performative utterance" comes from the British ordinary language philosopher J. L. Austin. For the implications of this term and for Austin's philosophy related to it, see J. L. Austin, *How to Do Things with Words* (Oxford: Oxford UP, 1962). For a further reading of the implications of the concept, see Shoshana Felman, *The Scandal of the Speaking Body: Don Juan with J. L. Austin, or Seduction in Two Languages* (Stanford: Stanford UP, 2002), 6–11. Felman's book was originally published in French

as *Le scandale du corps parlant: Don Juan avec Austin, ou la séduction en deux langues* (Paris: Seuil, 1980).

4. Elie Wiesel, "The Loneliness of God," published in *Dvar Hashavu'a* (a weekly magazine of the Tel-Aviv newspaper *Davar*),1984, cited in *Testimony*, 204 (in Felman's translation from the Hebrew).

5. Jorge Luis Borges, "The Witness," in *A Personal Anthology* (New York: Grove, 1967), 178.

6. First established as the Video Archive for Holocaust Testimonies at Yale, the archive was later renamed the Fortunoff Video Archive for Holocaust Testimony at Yale. See the interviews with Dori Laub (chap. 3) and Geoffrey Hartman (chap. 9) for more on this archive.

7. See, among others, Felman, *Writing and Madness: Literature/Philosophy/Psychoanalysis* (Stanford: Stanford UP, 2003); *Jacques Lacan and the Adventure of Insight: Psychoanalysis in Contemporary Thought* (Cambridge, MA: Harvard UP, 1987); *What Does a Woman Want?: Reading and Sexual Difference* (Baltimore: Johns Hopkins UP, 1993); *The Scandal of the Speaking Body* (2002, mentioned above); and the pathbreaking anthology edited by Felman, *Literature and Psychoanalysis: The Question of Reading—Otherwise* (Baltimore: Johns Hopkins UP, 1982).

8. For more on this story, see Shoshana Felman, "Education and Crisis, or The Vicissitudes of Teaching," esp. 44–47, and Dori Laub, "An Event without a Witness: Truth, Testimony, and Survival," 75–92, both in Felman and Laub, *Testimony*.

9. See, for example, Louis Micheels, "Bearer of the Secret," *Psychoanalytic Inquiry* 5.1 (1985): 21–30.

10. See n1, above. The trial of Adolf Eichmann, the Nazi coordinator for deporting the Jews to extermination camps during the Holocaust, took place in Jerusalem in 1961 after the Israelis kidnapped Eichmann in Argentina and took him to Israel. He was convicted and executed for, among other charges, crimes against humanity, war crimes, and crimes against the Jewish people.

11. Raul Hilberg, *The Destruction of the European Jews* (1961; rev. ed., Teaneck, NY: Holmes & Meier, 1985).

12. Cited in Elie Wiesel's autobiography, *All Rivers Run to the Sea: Memoirs, vol. 1 (1928–1969)* (New York: Harper Collins, 1995), 348.

13. The *Sonderkommandos* were work details in the Nazi extermination camps made up of Jewish prisoners who were forced under threat of death to dispose of the bodies of gassed prisoners.

14. On the forced use of words like *Figuren*, see Claude Lanzmann's 1985 film *Shoah*, and the transcription of the film's text in *Shoah: The Complete Text of the Acclaimed Holocaust Film by Claude Lanzmann* (New York: De Capo, 1995), for example, p. 9 (Testimony of Motke Zaidl and Izhak Dugin).

15. See Thomas Szasz, *Ideology and Insanity: Essays on the Psychiatric Dehumanization of Man* (New York: Doubleday/Anchor, 1970), cited in *JU*, 224 n53.

16. See Richard Rorty, "Feminism and Pragmatism," *Michigan Quarterly Review* 30 (1991), in particular p. 251: "Especially when you are part of a subordinated group," writes Rorty, "your definition of your injuries is powerfully shaped by your assessment of whether you could get anyone to do anything about it, including anything official." Cited in *JU*, 225n54.

17. Rorty, "Feminism and Pragmatism," 232–33, cited in *JU*, 127.
18. *"J'accuse"* refers to Émile Zola's open letter in the newspaper *L'Aurore* on January 1, 1898, denouncing the injustice done to Alfred Dreyfus, a French Jewish officer who had been unfairly convicted for treason, setting off the turmoil of the so-called Dreyfus Affair. Felman writes about the Dreyfus Affair, and the Israeli prosecutor's quotation of Zola's words in his opening speech, in *JU*, 114–20.
19. See Michal Shaked, "The Eichmann Trial," in *Moshe Landau, Shofet* [Moshe Landau, A Judge] (Tel Aviv: Aliat Haggag, Yediot Achronot, 2012).
20. See n18, above.
21. Trayvon Martin was an African American teenager who while walking home in his apartment complex was shot to death in 2012 by George Zimmerman, a member of a neighborhood patrol. Zimmerman was acquitted under Florida's "Stand Your Ground" law, which makes it legal to shoot anybody who one feels is threatening serious bodily harm. The incident provoked a nationwide protest.
22. K-Zetnik is the name under which the Jewish writer Yehiel Dinoor wrote works on the Holocaust. He had survived Auschwitz and, as an eyewitness to Eichmann at the camp, was brought to the trial to bear witness to this fact, but he could not complete his testimony because of his physical collapse on the witness stand.
23. See Felman and Laub, *Testimony*, 218–19: "As an interviewer, Lanzmann asks not for great explations of the Holocaust, but for concrete descriptions of minute particular details . . . It is not the big generalizations but the concrete particulars which translate into a vision."
24. In chap. 1 of Felman and Laub, *Testimony*—"Education and Crisis, or the Vicissitudes of Teaching"—Felman quotes Mallarmé, a French poet she taught in her first class on testimony. In his invited lecture at Oxford on the present news or innovations of French poetry, Mallarmé says: "In effect I am bringing news, and the most surprising. Such a case has never been seen. / They have done violence to verse . . . / It is appropriate to relieve myself of that news right away—to talk about it now already—much like an invited traveler who, without delay, in breathless gasps, discharges himself of the testimony of an accident known, and pursuing him" (cited in *Testimony*, 18). The quotation is translated by Felman from Stéphane Mallarmé, "La musique et les lettres," in *Oeuvres complètes* (Paris: Gallimard, 1945), 643–44. Compare Barbara Johnson's translation of the same lines in a newer American edition of Mallarmé's prose, *Divagations*, trans. Barbara Johnson (Cambridge, MA: Belknap P of Harvard UP, 2007), 183: "I do indeed bring news. The most surprising kind. Such a thing has not been seen before. Verse has been tampered with . . . It is fitting to speak about it already, just as an invited traveler immediately unburdens himself of gasping words that testify to an accident he witnessed and is pursued by." Felman derived her interpretative emphasis on Mallarmé's description of the "accident"—and on the relation between accident and testimony—from Barbara Johnson's reading of Mallarmé in *Défigurations du language poétique: La seconde révolution baudelairenne* (Paris: Flammarion, 1979), 169–71.
25. Hannah Arendt, *Eichmann in Jerusalem: A Report on the Banality of Evil* (New York: Penguin, 2006), 224. Herienafter abbreviated *EiJ*.

26. Christa Wolf, *Patterns of Childhood*, trans. Ursule Molinaro and Hedwig Rappolt (New York: Farrar, Straus & Giroux, 1984), 3.

27. See Felman, *The Scandal of the Speaking Body*, 12–40, 48–111.

28. Walter Benjamin, "The Storyteller: Reflections on the Works of Nikolai Leskov," in *Illuminations: Essays and Reflections*, ed. and intro. Hannah Arendt (1969; reprint, New York: Schocken, 2007), 83–107. See also Felman's essay "The Storyteller's Silence: Walter Benjamin's Dilemma of Justice," in *JU*, 10–53, in particular the focused reading of "The Storyteller," 25–28.

29. See n28, above.

30. See " 'What Remains? The Language Remains': A Conversation with Günter Gaus," in *The Portable Hannah Arendt*, ed. Peter Baehr (New York: Penguin, 2000).

31. See Benjamin, "The Task of the Translator: An Introduction to the Translation of Baudelaire's *Tableaux parisienes*," in *Illuminations*, 69–82.

32. Felman, introduction to *La folie et la chose littératire* (Paris: Seuil, 1978), 11–31, translated in *Writing and Madness*, 11–32.

33. Felman, *Writing and Madness*, 17.

34. Ibid., 18.

35. See Martin Heidegger, "Building Dwelling Thinking," in *Basic Writings*, ed. David Farrell Krell (New York: HarperCollins, 1993).

Index